HOW THE DESTINATION CONTENT WORKS

Each destination includes a short introduction, an A–Z of practical information and recommended points of interest, split into 4 different categories:

- Highlights
- Accommodation
- Eating out
- What to do

You can view the location of every point of interest and save it by adding it to your Favourites. In the 'Around Me' section you can view all the points of interest within 5km.

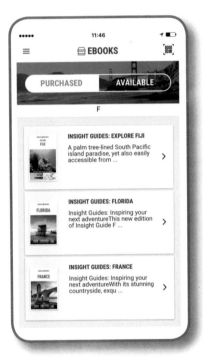

HOW THE EBOOKS WORK

The eBooks are provided in EPUB file format. Please note that you will need an eBook reader installed on your device to open the file. Many devices come with this as standard, but you may still need to install one manually from Google Play.

The eBook content is identical to the content in the printed guide.

HOW TO DOWNLOAD THE WALKING EYE APP

1. Download the Walking Eye App from the App Store or Google Play.
2. Open the app and select the scanning function from the main menu.
3. Scan the QR code on this page – you will then be asked a security question to verify ownership of the book.
4. Once this has been verified, you will see your eBook and destination content in the purchased ebook and destination sections, where you will be able to download them.

Other destination apps and eBooks are available for purchase separately or are free with the purchase of the Insight Guide book.

CONTENTS

Travel tips

TRANSPORT

A – Z

LANGUAGE

FURTHER READING

Maps

LEGEND
ρ Insight on
📷 Photo story

THE BEST OF MADAGASCAR: TOP ATTRACTIONS

△ **Antananarivo and the Hills of Imerina.** Scattered across a dozen sacred hilltops, the historic highlights of the Imerina Kingdom include the grand palaces and museums of Antananarivo's Haute-Ville district, and the outlying Rova Ambohimanga, Rova Ilafy and Rova Ambohidrabiby. See page 137.

▽ **Parc National de l'Isalo.** Renowned for its evocative formations of water- and wind-eroded sandstone, Isalo also supports an otherworldly succulent flora and wooded canyons where Verreaux's sifaka, red-fronted brown lemur and ring-tailed lemur are all common. See page 160.

△ **Parc National de Ranomafana.** Ranked among Madagascar's most biodiverse protected areas, this readily accessible and well-equipped tract of rainforest is home to 12 lemur and 115 bird species. Activities include guided hikes and river kayaking trips. See page 153.

△ **Allée des Baobabs.** One of the most photographed landmarks in Madagascar, this alley of towering 800-year-old Grandidier's baobabs outside Morondava is best visited in the golden light of sunset. See page 167.

△ **Mandrare River Valley**. Flanked by spiny forest dominated by the bizarre multi-tendrilled Didierea octopus tree, the Mandrare River basin offers fabulous dry-country lemur-viewing and birdwatching at the Mandrare River and Bérenty Lodges. See page 193.

◁ **Parc National Andasibe-Mantadia**. The most accessible and arguably the best one-stop wildlife destination in Madagascar is the place to see – and hear – the indri (the largest lemur) as well as a fine range of forest birds, frogs and orchids. See page 197.

△ **Manambolo and Tsiribihina Rivers**. The multi-day pirogue or motorboat descent of one of these beautiful rivers is the most thrilling way to travel between Antananarivo and the Morondava region. The Manambolo is the less heavily touristed and more scenic option. See page 167.

△ **Parc National des Tsingy de Bemaraha**. This magnificent Unesco World Heritage Site comprises the world's largest 'stone forest', a labyrinthine karstic formation whose jagged pinnacles supports a rich xerophile flora and fauna including the magnificent Von der Decken's sifaka. See page 266.

△ **Nosy Be**. Madagascar's most popular attraction, this gorgeous Indian Ocean island is dotted with idyllic beaches and pretty crater lakes, and it also offers great opportunities for snorkelling, whale-watching and lemur-viewing. See page 243.

▽ **Parc National de la Montagne d'Ambre**. Madagascar's oldest national park protects a tangled rainforest whose biodiversity embraces more than 1,000 plant species, nine unique varieties of chameleon, the world's greatest diversity of leaf-tailed geckos, and 75 bird and five lemur species. See page 264.

THE BEST OF MADAGASCAR: EDITOR'S CHOICE

Ring-tailed lemur feeding on berries in the Réserve d'Anja.

BEST LANDSCAPES

La Fenêtre de l'Isalo. This spectacular window-like rock arch is a scenic highlight of the Parc National de l'Isalo, and is especially photogenic at sunset. See page 161.

Réserve Spéciale du Cap Sainte-Marie. The island's most southerly point is a desolate, windswept headland swathed in a stunted variation of the region's spiny forest. See page 185.

Grande Tsingy. The main block of the Tsingy de Bemaraha is a magnificently stark rockscape traversed by suspension bridges and offering opportunities for abseiling and harnessed climbs. See page 170.

Tsingy Rouges. This unique and highly photogenic community-protected site comprises an otherworldly landscape of curvaceous laterite chimneys set in the base of a riverine gorge. See page 265.

La Fenêtre de l'Isalo at sunset.

BEST LEMUR-VIEWING

Lemurs' Park. Though somewhat contrived, this educational facility within day tripping distance of Antananarivo is home to introduced but free-ranging populations of seven diurnal species. See page 142.

Réserve d'Anja. Set below an imposing domed mountain, this small but popular community-managed reserve is home to around 400 delightful ring-tailed lemurs. See page 158.

Réserve Spéciale d'Analamazaotra. This sector of the Parc National Andasibe-Mantadia is the place to see the panda-like indri, renowned both as Madagascar's largest lemur and for its eerie far-reaching call. See page 201.

Île au Coq. This private reserve in the Pangalanes is the most reliable site anywhere in Madagascar for the uniquely bizarre nocturnal aye-aye. See page 209.

BEST BIRDWATCHING

Parc National Zombitse-Vohibasia. The best place to see the super-localised Appert's tetraka, this small forested park hosts almost 100 other species including giant coua, Coquerel's coua and white-browed owl. See page 161.

Mangily. This southwestern seaside village is the best place to tick subdesert mesite, long-tailed ground-roller, running green-capped coua, thamnornis-warbler, Archbold's newtonia and Lefresnaye's vanga. See page 180.

Parc National de Tsimanampetsotsa. Centred on the eponymous shallow lake, this is a great place both for waterbirds (including flamingos and the Madagascan plover) and for dry-country specials. See page 185.

Parc National de Mantadia. The guided Circuit de Tsakoka through Mantadia offers a chance of seeing all four of scaly, pitta-like, rufous-headed and short-legged ground-rollers. See page 203.

Parc National de Masoala. This rather inaccessible park is a stronghold for Madagascar serpent eagle, Madagascar red owl, running coua, pitta-like ground-roller, Bernier's vanga and helmet vanga. See page 221.

The Rova, or palace, tops sacred Ambohimanga Hill.

A nesting helmet vanga, Parc National de Masoala.

BEST HISTORIC SITES

Haute-Ville. The historic heart of Antananarivo, ridge-top Haute-Ville is studded with significant buildings, most notably the Rova Antananarivo founded by King Andrianjaka circa 1610. See page 129.

Rova Ambohimanga. Madagascar's only cultural Unesco World Heritage Site, Ambo-himanga Hill is topped by a wooden palace built in 1788 by King Andrianampoinimerina, the summer residence of Queen Ranavalona II, and several royal tombs. See page 138.

Rova Tsinjoarivo. Built in the 1830s as a summer residence for Queen Ranavalona I, this restored five-building palace served as a seasonal retreat for two other queens and offers great views over a pair of powerful waterfalls. See page 147.

Fianarantsoa. Incorporating hundreds of churches and houses built in the late 19th century, the sloping cobbled alleys of Fianarantsoa's Haute-Ville is smaller but more architecturally cohesive than its namesake in Antananarivo. See page 156.

Fort Tranovato. This mysterious stone ruin near Fort Dauphin was built by unknown Swahili or Portuguese settlers during or before the 16th century. See page 192.

Fort Manda. The circular fort at Foulpointe was built by King Radama I following the annexation of the east coast to Imerina in the early 19th century. See page 212.

Postcard-perfect beach on Nosy Be.

BEST CULTURAL ACTIVITIES

Marché Artisanal de la Digue. Situated on the outskirts of Antananarivo, Madagascar's largest handicrafts market incorporates 100-plus stalls selling a mind-boggling selection of local handicrafts. See page 137.

Artisan Antsirabe. Visit Maminirina Corne de Zébu to watch how zebu horns are manufactured into an array of richly-textured and multihued souvenirs. See page 149.

Pays Zafimaniry. The only Madagascan inclusion on Unesco's Intangible Cultural Heritage List, the woodworking tradition of the Zafimaniry is encapsulated by their elaborately engraved timber houses. See page 150.

Soatanana. This picturesque village of traditional Merina houses is a renowned centre of handcrafted silk scarves. Local guides can demonstrate silk production from start to finish. See page 152.

BEST BEACHES

Baie de Sainte Luce. This staggeringly beautiful stretch of isolated coastline is home to Manafiafy Lodge, an idyllic boutique resort where activities range from swimming and snorkelling to forest walks and whale-watching. See page 191.

Île Sainte-Marie. Though not as scenic as Nosy Be, its east coast counterpart is less heavily touristed and also offers good swimming, snorkelling, diving and whale-watching opportunities. See page 216.

Ambondrona. Hemmed in by tall craggy headlands, Nosy Be's loveliest beach is lined with low-key owner-managed lodges whose grounds literally spill out onto the sand. See page 248.

Plage de Ramena. Set on the Baie des Français opposite Diego Suarez, this fine swimming beach is ideal for budget-conscious travellers, and the springboard for day trips to the stunning Mer d'Emeraude. See page 261.

Chameleon souvenirs for sale on a roadside stall.

BEST ADVENTURE AND OUTDOOR ACTIVITIES

Fianarantsoa-Côte Est Railway. Navigating more than 100 tunnels and bridges, the narrow-gauge rail descent from Fianarantsoa and Manakara is as scenic as it is unsuited to timetable-focussed travellers. See page 157.

Parc National d'Andringitra. Not only does this hiker's paradise boast Madagascar's highest mammalian diversity, it also incorporates the country's tallest walkable summit in the form of 2,658m (8,720ft) Pic Boby. See page 159.

Manambolo Gorge. Boat trips down the Manambolo River pass through this stunning gorge flanked by the surreal landscapes of the Tsingy de Bemaraha. See page 167.

Parc National de Marojejy. This top-notch hiking destination protects a rugged forested massif renowned for its diversity of birds, ferns and lemurs, and is best explored on a multiple-night trek taking in Mantella, Marojejia and Simpona Camps. See page 271.

Baie de Ranobe. This shallow bay overlooked by Ifaty-Mangily offers the opportunity for snorkelling or scuba diving on coral formations dense with colourful reef dwellers and larger marine creatures. See page 181.

Enjoy a scenic ride on a Fianarantsoa–Côte Est train.

Limestone cliffs along the Manambolo River.

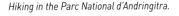

Hiking in the Parc National d'Andringitra.

Washing the day's catch in Ambolomailaka, on the west coast of Madagascar.

Common flat-tail gecko camouflaged in the Parc National de Marojejy.

Getting around by zebu-drawn cart in Miary, in the southwestern region of Atsimo-Andrefana.

Palm-fringed beach at Ifaty.

THE WONDER ISLAND

Idyllic tropical beaches are what first draw many visitors to Madagascar, but this immense island also hosts a fascinating assemblage of wildlife and unique fusion of African and Asiatic cultures.

Panther chameleon with catch.

Madagascar makes for a scintillating beach destination. Indeed, for many visitors, the primary attraction of this Indian Ocean island is the postcard-perfect beaches, turquoise lagoons, whispering palm plantations, craggy islets and snorkel-friendly coral reefs that adorn its 10,000km (6,000-mile) coastline, from well-developed seaside resorts such as Nosy Be and Ifaty-Mangily to the more uncrowded likes of Île Sainte-Marie and the magnificent Baie de Sainte Luce.

For adventurous travellers, however, Madagascar really comes into its own away from the beaches. This immense tropical island is sometimes referred to as the Eighth Continent on account of its unique biodiversity, which incorporates an estimated 10,000 animal and plant species found nowhere else in the world. Now protected in a network of roughly 50 official national parks and reserves, this diversity includes 100 species of loveable lemur, and a similar tally of chameleons and endemic birds.

There is a through-the-looking-glass quality to Madagascar's natural landscapes. From the preposterous octopus trees that dominate the 'spiny forest' of the semi-arid south to the cuddly panda-meets-koala indris that wail with ear-shattering abandon from the eastern rainforest canopy; from the surrealist serrated limestone formations known as tsingy to the magnificently photogenic Allée des Baobabs, Madagascar often seems to exist in an evolutionary universe parallel to the rest of the planet.

Ring-tailed lemur next to an aloalo (Mahafaly tomb carving).

An engaging cultural destination, Madagascar was one of the last habitable places on earth to be settled by humans. By the 18th century, its Asiatic and African settlers had merged to form a unique cultural entity dominated by kingdoms such as Imerina, which was ruled from a set of a dozen sacred hills including the present-day capital Antananarivo and the palace-studded Rova Ambohimanga, now a Unesco World Heritage Site.

Madagascar is, in a word, different. And the idyllic beaches are more than enough to justify a visit. But why stop there when it is easy enough to put together a best-of-both-worlds itinerary that combines an extended beach stay with forays to the fascinating national parks and cultural sites that stud the interior?

The famous Allée des Baobabs
looks its best just before sunset.

A UNIQUE PLACE

Madagascar's remote location, moist tropical climate and varied topography have led to it becoming a uniquely rich and rewarding biodiversity hotspot.

Madagascar is like nowhere else on earth. Set adrift in the middle of the Indian Ocean about 500km (300 miles) from Africa and almost 10 times as distant from Asia, it is the world's fourth-largest island, extending over some 587,041 sq km (226,658 sq miles), and the most isolated landmass of comparable proportions anywhere in the tropics. Ecologically, the island shares the bulk of its DNA with mainland Africa and/or the Indian subcontinent, but it also incorporates wild-card elements from as far afield as South America and Australasia to create a whole that is strikingly unique. Culturally and ethnically, the Malagasy people have equally diverse origins, essentially being a fusion of Indonesian and African stock, but once liberally spiced with influences from Arabia, India, China, France and elsewhere.

A LAND APART

Madagascar today is in many respects a product of its singular geological history. Protruding from its own tectonic plate, the island formed part of Gondwanaland until around 160 million years ago, when rifting and associated oceanic flooding finally caused this supercontinent to fragment into three separate components: one comprising modern-day Africa, South America and Arabia; another Antarctica, New Zealand and Australia; and the third India and Madagascar. The last of these split into two around 90 million years ago, when India started its northward drift towards Asia, leaving the Madagacar Plate stranded in isolation off the east coast of Africa.

So, while Madagascar formed an ecological continuum with Africa and India for much of the Cretaceous Period, the island's indigenous flora and fauna has since been allowed to evolve in virtual isolation. True, many Gondwanaland-era

Hybrid lemur, Palmarium Reserve.

⊘ NEW PARKS AND RESERVES

At the 2003 IUCN World Parks Congress, President Ravalomanana announced a five-year plan to expand Madagascar's protected area network from 17,000 sq km (6,564 sq miles, or 3 percent of the island's surface area) to 60,000 sq km (23,166 sq miles, or 10 percent of its area). Two years later, he took the first step in making good on this promise with the creation of 15 new conservation areas encompassing a total of 10,000 sq km (3,861 sq miles). Several new conservation areas have been created since Ravalomanana was ousted in 2009, among them Montagne des Français and a marine park at Nosy Ve-Androka.

lineages, including those of the dinosaurs, were curtailed by a mass extinction that took place some 66 million years ago. But the island's fauna has also been supplemented by occasional chance vagrants that flapped their way across the Indian Ocean, or set sail from the African mainland on an island of floating vegetation, often with evolutionarily explosive results. Indeed, many of Madagascar's most distinctive and diverse lineages – not only lemurs, tenrecs and other mammals, but also endemic avian families such as the Vangidae, and even its 100-odd species of chame-

southwest typically receives less than 500mm (20in) of rainfall annually, most of it over December to March. All around the island, the coastal belt has a hot and humid climate, whereas much of the interior comprises temperate midlands (around 1,000m/3,280ft) dotted with chillier highland pockets rising to a maximum altitude of 2,876 metres (9,436ft) in the remote Tsaratanana Massif.

The island's vegetation falls into four broad geographic zones. The natural cover across most of eastern and northern Madagascar is dense rainforest, which is uniformly rich in bio-

Forest path deep in the Parc National de la Montagne d'Ambre.

leon – are assumed to be the product of one or another such pioneering colonising event.

GEOGRAPHIC ZONES AND BIOLOGICAL NICHES

Regional variations in altitude, rainfall and temperature have played no small part in shaping the island's ecological landscape. Broadly speaking, the wettest part of the island is the east and north, where many areas are doused with 3,000mm (118in) of precipitation annually, and rain falls more days than not in even the driest of months. The northwest is also wet, with an annual precipitation of 2,000mm (79in), but far more seasonal, with almost no rain falling between May and September. By contrast, the semi-arid

diversity, though its exact species composition is strongly influenced by altitude and climate. The northwest typically supports deciduous forest, which is slightly less biodiverse than the rainforest, but still rich in endemics. The central highlands naturally support a mosaic of high-altitude heath and grassland, and mid-altitude forest and savannah. But the most unique and memorable of Malagasy ecosystems lies in the southwest, which supports a distinctive cover of tall, spiky, bulbous-based succulent referred to collectively both as the spiny forest and spiny desert. In addition to these broad geographic zones, the island also supports a wealth of speciation-friendly niche habitats, ranging from coastal mangroves and saltflats to all manner of upcountry wetlands

The list of species endemic to Madagascar keeps growing. Since the turn of the millennium, scientists working on the island have identified more than 600 previously undescribed species, a list that includes 40 mammals and 60 reptiles.

and forest pockets – not to mention isolated rock outcrops such as the surrealist karstic 'tsingy' formations of Bemaraha and Ankarana.

endemics). As for invertebrates and plants, you'd lose count somewhere in the tens of thousands – but to give some idea, 4,000 moth, 1,000 flowering orchid and 170 palm species are known from Madagascar, almost all of them endemic.

Statistics, as we all know, are malleable. But in the case of Madagascar, the cold facts fail to convey the sheer weirdness of an evolutionary laboratory larger and even more fecund than the Darwin-inspiring Galápagos Islands. For anthropomorphic visitors, it tends to be all about lemurs: impossibly cute bug-eyed noc-

Vezo fishing village in the south of the island.

A RIOT OF BIODIVERSITY

Madagascar's inherent geographic variety, tropical location, and long isolation from other large landmasses has moulded an incomparable wealth of unique species substantiating its claim to be the world's single most important biodiversity hotspot. The statistics are truly extraordinary. Around 1,000 vertebrate species, 16 families and 170 genera are endemic to Madagascar (that is, found nowhere else), far more than any other global biodiversity hotspot. The island also stakes a claim to being the world's most significant centre of primate speciation, supporting at least 100 unique lemur species (Brazil, by comparison, harbours slightly more than 100 primate species but far fewer

turnal sportive and mouse lemurs, mischievous bands of monkey-like ring-tailed lemurs, and the glamorous silken-haired indri and sifakas. For bird enthusiasts, a checklist of almost 290 species includes 105 endemics along with another 20 species shared only with the Comoros or Seychelles. And for aficionados of the outlandish, Madagascar's cast of whacky endemics also includes hissing cockroaches, branch-length stick insects, ripe-looking tomato frogs, ponderous horn-nosed chameleons and their fingernail-sized dwarfish kin, masterfully camouflaged leaf-tailed geckos, orgiastic parrots, flamenco-dancing lemurs, bulbous baobabs and spiky-tendrilled octopus trees. It's a fascinating and invigorating natural cocktail.

A HUMAN FACE

People arrived late on Madagascar. The oldest unambiguous evidence of permanent human habitation dates back 1,500 years, and while it is quite possible that the odd passing Indonesian, Chinese or Arab sailor made earlier landfalls, most historians agree that the island is unlikely to have been settled any earlier than 500 BC, and that the deep interior remained largely uninhabited until around AD 1000. These earliest settlers almost certainly sailed across from Indonesia on outriggers, an astonishing 6,000km (3,728 miles) journey replicated by the British sailor Philip Beale in a similar boat over 2003–4. These early settlements may well have been founded to service an already existing trade route between southeast Asia and the Middle East via Madagascar and the East African coast, and genetic and linguistic evidence suggests they were soon joined by Bantu-speaking African migrants, as well as smaller numbers of Arabs and Somali, who integrated with them to become the modern Malagasy people. Today, the island supports around 20 different ethno-cultural groups, all of whom speak the Malagasy language

Peeling cocoons in the Soalandy wild silk workshop.

Posing in Toliara.

☉ SPORT IN MADAGASCAR

Madagascar is unusual among African countries in that rugby union outranks football in popularity. In international terms, the national rugby team, nicknamed the Makis (the local name for a ring-tailed lemur) only just scrapes into the world top 50 rankings, and it has yet to qualify for a rugby world cup. It did, however, enjoy limited success in the Africa Cup, having finished runner-up – to Morocco and Uganda respectively – in the 2005 and 2007 events of this annual tournament.

The national football team, nicknamed the Bareas (after a type of zebu), falls outside the top 100 rankings, and has yet to qualify for the biennial Africa Nations Cup or FIFA World Cup, but it has enjoyed some success in the Indian Ocean Island Games, emerging as champion in 1990 and 1993 and as runner-up in 1998 and 2007.

The one admittedly rather obscure sport where Madagascar truly shines is pétanque, a form of boules played with metal balls in parks and open areas throughout the country. Madagascar won the men's triples (the main event) at the Pétanque World Championships – a tournament normally dominated by France and Belgium – in both 1999 and 2016, as well as finishing runner-up on numerous occasions.

Aerial photography comparisons suggest that 50 percent of the 75,000 sq km (28,957 sq miles) of indigenous forest present in 1950 is gone. Unmonitored slash-and-burn farming is the main cause, but logging and fuelwood also take a large toll.

– which forms part of the Austronesian linguistic group, but is liberally laced with Bantu and other borrowed words – but who vary greatly in their

forests and installed monotypic eucalyptus and pine plantations in their place, and claimed as their own whatever wealth was generated by these enterprises. And deforestation has continued apace since independence, thanks to a succession of corrupt and inept governments, and a quite staggering population growth (from around 5.18 million in 1960 to more than 25 million today).

Despite this, Madagascar still retains a high proportion of natural cover, a breathtaking level of biodiversity, and an enviable network of official conservation areas that collectively protect

Antandroy dance at the Mandrare River Camp, Ifotaka Community Forest.

traditional cultural practices and customs.

In ecological terms, the arrival of people on Madagascar had disastrous consequences. Within a few centuries of that first landfall, almost all the island's megafauna – among them, flightless birds taller than an ostrich, semi-terrestrial hippos and gorilla-sized sloth-lemurs – had become extinct. Forests were chopped down to make way for cultivation, swamps were cleared to become rice paddies or lakes, while introduced cattle and waterfowl were able to gatecrash ecological niches occupied by certain indigenous species. This environmental destruction was exacerbated under the French colonists, who chopped down vast tracts of spiny forest and replaced them with sisal crops and invasive cacti, logged indigenous

practically all the country's major habitats, from craggy mountaintops to coral reefs. This growing network incorporates almost 50 strict nature reserves, national parks and special reserves managed by Madagascar National Parks (MNP), most of which are accessible to tourists but only on foot, and numerous other government-run, community-managed or private conservation areas. Visitors to Madagascar are fortunate indeed to have access to this superb array of protected areas, and can also explore them in the knowledge that theirs is an important financial contribution not only to conservation per se, but also to the local communities and private operators who depend on tourism as one of this poor country's few viable and sustainable industries.

Map of East Africa and Madagascar, 1596.

DECISIVE DATES

EARLY SETTLERS

c.140–160 million years ago
A landmass comprising Madagascar, India, Australia and Antarctica splits from Africa.

c.90 million years ago
Madagascar breaks away from India to take roughly its present shape.

c.45 million years ago
The prosimian ancestors of lemurs arrive in Madagascar.

1,500–2,500 years ago
Madagascar settled by Indonesians and soon after by African and Arab seafarers.

c.1200 AD
The central highlands are settled by Vazimba farmers and hunter-gatherers.

THE EUROPEANS ARRIVE

1500
The Portuguese navigator Diogo Dias becomes the first European to sight Madagascar.

1643
Jacques Pronis establishes a French colony at Fort Dauphin (one abandoned in 1673 after an attack by locals).

1685
Adam Baldridge is the first of many pirates to settle near Île Sainte-Marie, which is soon after dubbed the 'Island of Pirates'.

FIRST KINGDOMS

Early 18th century
The Betsimisaraka Kingdom is founded on the east coast by King Ratsimilaho, while the Sakalava kingdom of Boina emerges as dominant on the west coast. Both grow rich on the slave trade.

1793
King Andrianampoinimerina of Imerina captures Antananarivo on a drive to extend his realm across the whole island.

1817
Andrianampoinimerina's son Radama I signs a treaty with

England recognising him as King of Madagascar, and boosting his military power, in exchange for abolishing the export of slaves.

1825
Radama I secures control of almost the whole island for Imerina.

1828
Radama I is succeeded by his widow, Ranavalona I, a traditionalist tyrant whose 33-year reign is characterised by parochialism and religious oppression.

1833
The Frenchman Jean Laborde brings the industrial revolution to Madagascar in the form of a diverse manufacturing complex at Mantasoa.

1861–3
Ranavalona I is succeeded by her more progressive son, Radama II, who is assassinated 18 months later to be succeeded by his wife Rasoherina.

1883–5
A naval attack persuades Ranavalona III (the third successive queen to marry string-pulling Prime Minister Rainilaiarivony) to sign a treaty ceding Diego Suarez to France.

FRENCH COLONIALISM

1895
France captures Mahajanga and dispatches a column of 15,000 soldiers to the capital. Ranavalona III surrenders, placing the island under French rule.

A kabar (party) in Antananarivo in presence of Queen Ranavalona III, 1885.

Édité par la CHOCOLATERIE D'AIGUEBELLE, Monastère de la Trappe (Drôme)

Expédition de Madagascar : ASSAUT D'UN FORT HOVA.

Battle in the Franco-Hova War, 1893–6.

1896
Madagascar is formally made a French Colony. Oppressive and unpopular policies such as the head tax and corvée labour are introduced.

1939–45
Following the outbreak of war, Madagascar is placed under the German-allied Vichy. It is captured by British Allied Forces in 1942 and handed to the Free French government-in-exile in 1943.

1946
Madagascar is recast as an overseas territory in the Union Française. Its inhabitants are accorded full French citizenship.

INDEPENDENCE

1947–8
The Malagasy Uprising, led by nationalists demanding full independence from France, leads to an estimated 89,000 Malagasy civilians being killed by the French army.

1960
Madagascar gains independence under Philibert Tsiranana on 26 June.

1972
Tsiranana resigns in the face of riots that claimed more than 2,000 civilian lives since April of the previous year.

1975
Under President Didier Ratsiraka, Madagascar severs historic ties with France and adopts socialist policies that lead to an economic collapse in the late 1980s, and the re-adoption of free market policies following the fall of the Berlin Wall.

1993
Ratsiraka is ousted and replaced by Albert Zafy, who is impeached for corruption in 1997, paving the way for Ratsiraka to regain power and serve a fourth presidential term.

2001
Marc Ravalomanana is elected president with 52 percent of the vote in December. Ratsiraka refuses to accept the result and initiates a short but bloody civil war before fleeing to exile in July 2002.

2009
Having won a second presidential term, Ravalomanana is ousted in a military coup led by Andry Rajoelina, who serves as temporary President of the High Transitional Authority until a proper election is held under a new constitution.

2013
Hery Rajaonarimampianina wins the presidential election with 53.5 percent of the vote.

2015
The intervention of the constitutional court prevents Rajaonarimampianina from being removed from office following a two-thirds majority parliamentary vote citing constitutional violations and general incompetence.

2018
Madagascar is due another second presidential election with Rajaonarimampianina, Ravalomanana and Rajoelina all likely to stand as candidates.

Hery Rajaonarimampianina.

An early engraving of fishermen in Tamatave.

EARLY HISTORY

Untouched by humankind as recently as 2,000 years ago,
Madagascar was subsequently settled by Indonesians,
African and Arabs, along with a motley selection of
European shipwreck victims, adventurers and pirates.

Its isolation from Africa and Asia ensured that Madagascar was one of the last major land-masses to be settled by humans. Exactly how and when this happened is a matter of con-jecture. The earliest unambiguous evidence of long-term human habitation, comprising shards of locally-made pottery and animal bones found in a rock shelter at Andavakoera on the east coast a short distance south of Diego Suarez, have been carbon-dated to AD 500. Cut-marked bones and stone tools discovered elsewhere have been dated, rather controversially, to 2000 BC. Even if these relicts are indeed that old, however, the absence of supporting evidence suggests that they were left behind by transient foragers who set anchor whilst sailing between Asia and Africa, or shipwrecked sailors who never established a permanent settlement on the island.

EARLY MIGRANTS

A substantial body of linguistic, genetic and archaeological evidence indicates that the first settlers on Madagascar hailed not from Africa, as might be expected, nor even from Arabia or India, but from the significantly more distant Sunda Islands in the Malay Archipelago. These Austronesian settlers are thought to have crossed the 6,000km (4,738 miles) of Indian Ocean that separated their original homeland from Madagascar in the large outrigger canoes known as waka, and they most likely landed on the island's west coast some time between 200 BC and 500 AD. The latest genetic studies indicate that these pioneers almost certainly originated from the Banjar Region of Indonesian Borneo. Whether they crossed the Indian Ocean with the intent to settle on Madagascar, or were

Austronesian outrigger canoe, known as waka.

⊘ SAILING FROM INDONESIA

A linguistic clue to the origin of Madagascar's ear-liest settlers, and to their mode of transport, lies in the Malagasy word vahoaka, meaning people. This most likely derives from the Indonesian va waka ('people of the outrigger canoes'), the name by which the fresh arrivals may have referred to themselves. Over 2003–4, the British sailor Philip Beale crossed from Indonesia to Ghana via Mada-gascar on a reconstructed waka outrigger, based on depictions in an 8th-century bas relief at the Javan temple of Borobudur, demonstrating the fea-sibility of an ancient trade route linking the three landmasses.

blown there by happenstance, is an open question. However, it seems probable that a trade route between southeast Asia and the Middle East via Madagascar and the East African coast was already well entrenched at this point, and the fact that the settlers brought along enough women to establish a viable colony would point to an intent to settle.

The Malagasy language, which is spoken throughout the whole island, unambiguously belongs to the Austronesian linguistic family, but it also contains a significant proportion of

Dutch drawing of 1598 showing Maroantsetra, in the northeast of Madagascar.

words of Bantu and Arabic origin. Backed up by recent genetic studies, this suggests that the early Indonesian settlers were joined by a steady trickle of Bantu-speaking Swahili settlers from East Africa, along with traders and sailors from the Arabian Gulf and the Somali Coast. Indeed, some authorities reckon that small numbers of Bantu-speaking Africans had settled on the island before the arrival of the Indonesians. Others claim that the first Bantu-speaking settlers were brought across from the mainland by Arab traders to serve as slaves. Others still cite the high correlation of Malagasy and Swahili words relating to foodstuffs, livestock and household tasks as evidence of a

trend towards intermarriage between Indonesian men and African women. There is ample room for speculation. Furthermore, recent genetic analysis has shown that the coastal denizens of Madagascar have a far higher proportion of African ancestry than their highlander compatriots, most likely because Asian settlement was essentially a one-off event that occurred at least 1,500 years ago, whereas sporadic immigration from Africa to the Malagasy coast was an ongoing process that continued long after the highlanders headed inland.

Early settlement on Madagascar was concentrated along the coastal belt and lower-lying river valleys. So far as can be ascertained, these settlements tended to be politically non-centralised and to thrive mainly on fishing, agriculture and sporadic trade with passing ships from Arabia and Asia. Ecologically, the impact along the coastal belt was quite profound, as forests were cleared for timber and cultivation, and wildlife – unused to people, and thus blithely fearless of the threat they posed – was slaughtered for the pot. Among the earliest victims of this human activity were the half-dozen 'elephant bird' species of the genera Aepyornis and Mullerornis, whose extinction was probably not primarily a result of direct hunting but of the collection of their outsized and highly nutritious eggs, which they habitually laid on open sand. The extinction of the giant sloth-lemurs of the family Palaeopropithecidae and the once-prolific Malagasy hippopotamus is also most likely attributable to human activity, in the form both of direct hunting and of habitat destruction.

URBANISATION AND CENTRALISATION

The establishment of urbanised settlements on Madagascar was most likely influenced by the emergence of the Islamic city-states that dominated medieval trade on the Swahili Coast of East Africa. These larger trade ports were situated mostly on the northwest coast, the closest part of the island to Swahili emporiums such as Mozambique, Kilwa, Zanzibar and Mombasa. Most important among them was Mahilaka, a walled Muslim city that extended across 60 hectares (150 acres) of mangrove-lined coast close to Nosy Be, and that flourished as a centre of rice and timber export from the 11th to the 15th centuries. It is unclear to what extent

the medieval Islamisation of some parts of the Malagasy coast reflects an actual influx of Arab or Swahili immigrants, or whether it was simply that the religion espoused by these foreign traders started to take root on the island.

The turn of the first millennium evidently coincided with several other important developments that led to greater economic and social diversification on Madagascar. This included the emergence of two new clans. The Vazimba, literally 'People of the Forest', was the name adopted by a clan of farmers and hunter-gatherers who

Diogo Dias, the first European to see Madagascar, was the brother of Bartolomeu Dias, the Portuguese captain whose 'discovery' of the Cape of Good Hope, Africa's southernmost tip, in 1488 opened the Indian Ocean to mercantile ships from Europe.

abandoned the coast in favour of the fertile but previously unsettled interior to forage in the forests of the central highlands, or clear them to make way for rice paddies and other cultivation. By contrast, the Vezo, or 'People who fish', emerged as a nomadic people who relocated to the semi-arid and relatively infertile southwest coast, where, as their name suggests, they eked out a living as fishermen. More significant still was the landmark introduction of zebu from mainland Africa c.1000. Not only did this transform Madagascar from a purely agricultural to a mixed pastoral economy, causing large tracts of highland forest to be transformed to grassland for grazing, it also led to the cultification of the zebu as a measure of prosperity and a mystical symbol of royalty.

The 16th century witnessed the emergence of several centralised kingdoms in Madagascar. It is unclear to what extent this transformation is attributable to the arrival of the Portuguese in the Indian Ocean in 1498, and the subsequent opportunity to trade with merchant Arab and European ships, and or whether it was essentially the culmination of an ongoing internal trend towards centralisation and urbanisation. Either way, major coastal kingdoms founded

between the 15th and 17th centuries include Vezo, Antakarana and Sakalava (later divided into Boina and Menabe) in the west, Antesaka, Antambahoka, Antemoro, Antanala and Betsimisaraka in the east, and Mahafaly and Antandroy in the far south. Influenced by events on the coast, the Vazimba of the central highlands also organised themselves into centralised kingdoms, the most important of which were Imerina (centred on present-day Antananarivo) and its more southerly counterpart Betsileo. All these kingdoms were effectively

Diogo Dias's ship.

sublimated to Imerina during the reigns of King Andrianampoinimerina (1787–1810) and Radama I (1810–28), after which Imerina and the Kingdom of Madagascar were practically synonymous to the outside world. Nevertheless, many of these obsolete polities were antecedent to the modern ethnic groups and administrative regions of Madagascar.

CONTACT WITH EUROPE

The first reference to Madagascar by a European writer is a lengthy description of the island (under the name 'Madeigascar') included in the *Travels of Marco Polo*, published c.1300. It would be another 200 years before the first European sighting of Madagascar was recorded.

On 10 August 1500, a Portuguese ship under the command of Diogo Dias, having become separated from the rest of the India-bound Second Armada during a storm, sailed past the island and named it São Lourenço, on account of it being St Lawrence's Day. Madagascar by then was already well-known to Islamic navigators, who knew it as Juzur al-Qamar (Island of the Moon), and had established several trade outposts there over the centuries. Oddly, however, the island seems not to have piqued the conquistadorial interest of the Portuguese, despite

Map of Madagascar from 1662.

its potential as a source of spices and slaves, and as a refreshment point en route between their African and Indian strongholds of Ilha do Moçambique and Goa.

Over the subsequent centuries, dozens of European ships crossing between Africa and India ran aground off the shores of Madagascar, and in several cases the survivors established short-lived settlements prior to being rescued by other ships, or perishing. Despite this, early European attempts to establish a formal foothold along the coast of Madagascar were sporadic and mostly ill fated, largely due to the high incidence of malaria and dysentery, and the hostility of the local Malagasy. In December 1642, Jacques Pronis, the nominal French

governor of Madagascar, established a trading post at Saint Luce Bay, but more than half the settlers were dead within months, forcing him to relocate to Fort Dauphin. In the late 1640s, two English trade settlements were established on Madagascar, one near Toliara and the other on Île Sainte-Marie, but neither survived for more than a couple of years. Pronis's second French colony at Fort Dauphin fared somewhat better, but it was temporarily abandoned in 1673 after a group of local Antanosy tribesmen attacked Fort Flacourt and killed 27 of its occupants: 14 French soldiers who had divorced their Malagasy wives in order to marry orphaned girls shipped to the colony for that purpose, and all but one of the young brides.

In the late 17th century, Madagascar emerged as hotbed of piracy, thanks largely to its remoteness from any European possessions and its convenience as a base for plundering merchant ships sailing between Arabia, East Africa and India along the Mozambique Channel. The bases favoured by the pirates were Île Sainte-Marie, which stands off the northeast shore of the main island, and Antongil Bay a short distance to its north (see page 214). A popular target was the so-called Pilgrim Fleet, which predictably carried a host of wealthy Mecca-bound Muslims, decked out in their finest jewellery, from Gujarat (India) to the Yemeni port of Mocha. But no captain was safe from the pirates, who – having plundered any valuables carried on the ship – often tried to recruit the crew for their own ships. The most famous pirate associated with Madagascar is William 'Captain' Kidd, who was hanged in London before he could return to Île Sainte-Marie to recover the vast treasure he legendarily buried somewhere in the vicinity. The self-serving buccaneers of Île Sainte-Marie were most probably also the rather ignoble model behind the utopian pirate colony of Libertatia, as described in the bestselling General History of the Pyrates written in 1724 by Captain Charles Johnson (possibly a pseudonym used by Daniel Defoe of Robinson Crusoe fame; see page 263).

SLAVES AND FIREARMS

The 18th century witnessed a major escalation in the longstanding but formerly low-key slave trade out of Madagascar. This was prompted to

Otto Hemmy, who visited the Boina royal palace in 1741, found it to be larger than the governor's residence at Cape Town. It was enclosed by five concentric walls, a defensive arrangement that also emphasised the king's cosmic centrality.

some extent by an influx of European firearms associated with the pirates of Sainte-Marie. The main east coast beneficiary of this circumstance was King Ratsimilaho, the son of a local Malagasy princess and an unknown European settler (possibly the pirate Thomas Tew) who was born in 1685 and grew up in Fénérive-Est on the mainland facing Sainte-Marie. The charismatic and long-ruling Ratsimilaho founded the Betsimisaraka Kingdom in the early 18th century, used his superior firepower to expand his domain into the neighbouring territories of Antakarana and Tsimihety, and to conduct regular slave raids both territories, as well as across the ocean to the Comoros.

The west coast counterpart to Betsimisaraka, Sakalava stood as the most powerful polity anywhere in Madagascar for most of the 17th and 18th centuries. Sakalava's origin is shrouded in a tangle of contradictory myth and legend, but it probably started life as a local fiefdom centred on a southwestern coastal village called Bengy in the 16th century, and expanded northwards under the Maroserana dynasty to peak in influence and in extent during the 17th century reign of King Andriandahifotsy. The death of Andriandahifotsy in 1685 led to Sakalava being divided in two by his rival sons Andriamandisoarivo and Andriamanetiarivo, who are respectively credited as the founders of Menabe (a kingdom centred on Belo sur Tsiribihina, which was also his father's capital) and its more northerly counterpart Boina (centred on the ports of Marovoay and later Mahajanga).

Menabe and Boina both grew rich and powerful on the back of the slave trade. The original 17th-century expansion of Sakalava had been facilitated by its superior firepower, which took the form of muskets and other weapons traded with Arab and later European merchants. And every new territorial campaign led to the acquisition of fresh captives, who were almost invariably sold as slaves, gaining the Sakalava yet more firearms. Indeed, as time progressed, it became customary for the Boina monarchy to launch an annual round of slave raids into the highlands prior to the seasonal arrival of merchant ships on the back of the monsoon winds. And it was partly in response to these regular incursions that Madagascar would be unified under the military might of what was ultimately the most enduring of the island's indigenous polities: the Imerina Kingdom of the central highlands.

Madagascan slaves, dressed to be sold, c.1790.

⊘ MARCO POLO & MADAGASCAR

The great Venetian traveller Marco Polo never visited the island he referred to as Madeigascar, and several aspects of his secondhand assertions – among them its governance by four Mohammedan sheiks, the dedicated eating of camel flesh, and the abundance of elephants and traffic in ivory – indicate that the subject of his description is actually the Somali coast of mainland Africa. In which case, Madagascar is probably not, as is often assumed, the medieval name for the island to which it now applied, but simply a mistranscription of Mogadishu, then as now the most important port on the Somali coast.

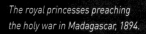

The royal princesses preaching the holy war in Madagascar, 1894.

THE RISE AND FALL OF IMERINA

Founded in the 16th century, the highland kingdom of Imerina, centred on Antananarivo, was the most powerful polity in Madagascar from the 1790s until the French invasion of 1895.

The modern history of Madagascar could be said to start with the creation of Imerina, the highland kingdom under which the island was unified in the late 18th and early 19th centuries. According to tradition, the roots of the Imerina monarchy date back to the early 16th century and the birth of Prince Andriamanelo to a Vazimba queen called Rafohy (or, in some versions of the legend, Rangita) and her husband Manelobe, a Merina commoner of the Hova clan. Andriamanelo ascended to the throne in 1540, and during his 35-year reign he embarked on an ongoing military campaign to subjugate the Vazimba, paving the way for the creation of a stratified social system comprising three endogamous castes, namely the Andriana (nobility), Hova (free commoners) and Andevo (serfs and slaves).

The name Imerina reputedly dates to the reign of Andriamanelo's son and successor, the legendary King Ralambo (r.1575–1612), whose powerful army further expanded the kingdom and also repelled several attacks from neighbouring territories. Imerina took on a recognisable geographic shape under King Andrianjaka, who succeeded his father in 1612 and ruled for 18 years. Andrianjaka is best known for capturing Analamanga Hill, a former Vazimba stronghold where he established the most enduring of Imerina capitals in the form of the present-day rova at Antananarivo. He was also responsible for designating the 12 sacred hills of Imerina, a set of historic sites that retain their important to the present day (though some of the original dozen were replaced with other hills under subsequent rulers).

Imerina experienced its first golden age under a succession of tongue-twistingly named

Queen Ranavalona III.

monarchs – Andriantsitakatrandriana (r.1630–50), Andriantsimitoviaminandriandehibe (r.1650–70), Andrianjaka Razakatsitakatrandriana (r.1670–75) and Andriamasinavalona (r.1675–1710) – who were evidently concerned less with fresh territorial conquest than with maintaining domestic order. The first two kings on this list are best remembered for constructing an ingenious dyke system that transformed the swamps around Antananarivo into a vast network of rice paddies, while the last among them dedicated much of his lengthy rule to the pacification of local rebellions under various minor chiefs. Indeed, it was in the face of these ongoing rebellions that Andriamasinavalona decided to divide Imerina into a

quartet of sub-realms, to be governed by the four most trusted of his 13 sons. This attempt to strengthen the kingdom's defences completely backfired, as the four princes turned on each other, launching a series of military campaigns against each other's subkingdoms that triggered almost eight decades of ongoing internecine conflict during which Imerina became increasingly splintered and vulnerable to slave raids and territorial expansion from more organised and powerful coastal rivals such as Boina, Menabe and Betsimisaraka.

IMERINA REASCENDANT

The reascendance of Imerina was engineered by King Andrianampoinimerina and his son and successor Radama I, both of whom are remembered as national heroes, and rank among the shrewdest politicians and military tacticians the island ever produced.

Born a minor prince called Ramboasalama c.1745, Andrianampoinimerina deposed his unpopular uncle Andrianjafy as king of North Imerina in 1787, and then launched a military campaign reunite the rest of Imerina, capturing

Islanders' clothing and weaponry, as illustrated in 1727.

⊘ THE EXPLOITS OF KING RALAMBO

A great many social innovations and legendary feats are attributed to King Ralambo, who was born, auspiciously, on the first day of the first month of the year, and reigned from around 1575 to 1612, during which time he reputedly coined the name Imerina to describe the kingdom founded by his father. Ralambo was probably the first highland ruler to acquire firearms from the coastal traders, and although he relied on a combination of superior firepower and military cunning to expand his kingdom, he was also a canny diplomat. Ralambo is widely credited with the introduction to Imerina of practices such as head taxes, male circumcision, ancestor worship and polygamy (he personally took four wives and had 15 children). He is also said to have initiated the division of the nobility into four sub-castes, within which the practice of intermarriage between closely related family members was encouraged. Most famously, perhaps, it was Ralambo, legend has it, who – after having tasted the cooked flesh of a sacrificial ox and deemed it fit for human consumption – domesticated the feral zebus that roamed the highlands, an occasion celebrated annually in the regenerative Fandroana ceremony that falls on his birthday. This legendary king's tomb can still be seen today, alongside that of his maternal grandfather Rabiby, at his former capital of Ambohidrabiby.

Antananarivo in 1793, and relocating his capital to its venerable rova a year later. By the turn of the century, Andrianampoinimerina controlled all four sub-realms of Imerina. He then expanded his horizons beyond the traditional bounds of Imerina with the capture of highland territories traditionally associated with the likes of Betsileo, Bezanozano and Bara prior to his death in 1809.

Much of Andrianampoinimerina's success can be attributed to the grassroots support he courted with assurances that all who dwelt in his

> King Andrianampoinimerina's diplomatic coups included strategic marriages into several important noble families. He reputedly took a dozen wives, each of whom was allocated a purpose-built house on one of the 12 sacred hills of Imerina.

once-factional realm were safe from enslavement, and by developing the capital Antananarivo into a peaceful and agriculturally productive city of 25,000 inhabitants. Those living outside his protection were somewhat less safe: indeed, much of the wealth accumulated by Andrianampoinimerina was thanks to his intermediary role selling captives taken in those parts of the highlands that fell outside his control to the slave traders of Betsimisaraka.

Only 18 years old when he ascended the Imerina throne in 1810, the literate, educated and voraciously ambitious King Radama I continued more-or-less where his father had left off. Shortly after taking power, he was obliged to quell rebellions in Betsileo and elsewhere prompted by Andrianampoinimerina's sudden death. Supported by a 40,000-strong army, he then took control of the main slave trade routes between the highlands and the coast, an endeavour that culminated with an arduous march to the east coast port of Toamasina in 1817. It was there, on 23 October, that Radama I made the defining decision of his career, entering into a formal alliance with the abolitionist British crown that recognised him as King of Madagascar and accorded him an annual stipend in gold and silver coins and

a supply of arms, horses and British military uniforms. In return, Radama undertook to prohibit the shipment of slaves (in line with the abolitionist Slave Trade Act passed by British parliament in 1807) and permitted the crown to establish a diplomatic mission on the island.

Over the next 10 years, the officially acknowledged King of Madagascar, now customarily dressed in full British military attire, set about fulfilling his father's deathbed wish that 'the sea be the border of my rice field'. The loss of life entailed by this campaign was devastating.

King Andrianampoinimerina (r. 1787–1810).

Radama's army alighted on countless non-Merina villages, often massacring every last inhabitant, now the ban on the slave trade rendered redundant the taking of captives. Tens of thousands of Imerina soldiers died during the 1820s, mostly not in combat but from starvation or disease. Nevertheless, by 1825, Radama had asserted control over the whole island, installing garrisons at most of its main ports and other economically significant areas. Three years later, the first King of Madagascar died in his palace at the age of 36; exhausted, say some, by the long years of war and his insatiable appetite for alcohol; poisoned, say others, by or on behalf of his wife, cousin and successor Queen Ranavalona I.

RANAVALONA I

There was more to Radama I's legacy than conquest and death. He was in many respects a dedicated reformer who embraced technical innovation, took an active interest in formalising the transcription of Malagasy in the Latin alphabet, supported the provision of education by the London Missionary Society, and attempted to create an accountable European-style administration. He also initiated the translation of the Bible into Malagasy and the import of the first printing press to Antananarivo, projects completed only after his

to Andrianampoinimerina, and who has also helped engineer Ranavalona I's ascension to the throne. In 1833, Rainiharo achieved the triple coup of becoming Ranavalona I's third husband, being promoted to Commander-in-Chief of the army, and being appointed as Prime Minister of Madagascar. When he died in office in 1852, Rainharo was succeeded by his eldest son Rainivoninahitriniony, who was in turn succeeded by a younger brother Rainilaiarivony in 1862.

Having tolerated the growing influence of Christian missionaries during her first two years

The Rova (palace) in Antananarivo in 1859.

death. His successor Ranavalona I – whose ascent to the throne contravened the conventional Imerina laws of succession and the explicit wishes of Radama, but won the support of a coterie of powerful military co-conspirators – was by contrast a dedicated isolationist who revoked the British treaty made by her husband and rebuffed subsequent French diplomatic approaches.

An important political development in the early years of Ranavalona I's reign was the appointment of the first in a succession of prime ministers who often wielded more power than the monarch under whom they served when it came to policy-making. This was Field Marshal Rainiharo, a distinguished Hova military campaigner whose father has served as an adviser

on the throne, Ranavalona came to revile Malagasy converts as sacrilegious, even treasonous, for their 'substitution of the respect of her ancestors, Andrianampoinimerina and Radama, for the respect of the ancestor of the whites: Jesus Christ'. In 1831, the queen banned her subjects from indulging in Christian practices. And although Ranavalona explicitly tolerated Christian practices among foreigners (presumably regarding it as legitimate for them to worship their own ancestors), many Christians and other foreigners fled the country in the wake of her pronouncement, in 1835, that Malagasy converts must either renounce their faith or be put to death. In 1857, Ranavalona I expelled every last foreigner from the island, after uncovering

a plot to remove her from power involving her son and chosen heir Prince Rakoto – the future Radama II – and a group of French residents that included the businessman Joseph-François Lambert and her employee, former ally and possibly lover Jean Laborde.

Ranavalona I's reign was marked by a death toll even higher than that of her predecessor's. This was partly due to ongoing losses among and at the hands of the Imerina military, which was embroiled in an ongoing campaign to maintain and extend the kingdom's boundaries. Even more so,

THE BUILD-UP TO COLONISATION

Radama II's reign, though tragically short, contrasted with that of his mother in almost every respect. Within 18 months of his coronation, the 32-year-old king reopened the country to foreign investment, rescinded the ban on Christianity in favour of freedom of religion, encouraged the settlement of foreign missionaries and investors, freed many of the political prisoners held captured by Ranavalona I, restored diplomatic relations with smaller kingdoms that had been subjugated into Imerina, and abolished the dreaded tangena ordeal

Queen Ranavalo I (r. 1828-61) established a reign of terror.

perhaps, it was a result of the queen's enthusiasm and inventiveness when it came to torturing and executing suspected thieves, witches, Christians and other transgressors (in 1838 alone, an estimated 100,000 Malagasy are thought to have been poisoned to death by the tangena ordeal (see page 132). Claims that the population of Madagascar halved under Ranavalona are almost certainly exaggerated, but they give some idea of the scale of the killing by this unpopular queen. Despite this, her death in August 1861 at the age of 83 was greeted by a nine-month period of official mourning during which 12,000 zebu were sacrificed in her honour, and an elaborate funeral was held at her burial place at the traditional Merina spiritual capital of Ambohimanga.

and several other unpopular fadys. This bouquet of liberal policies wasn't universally popular, however, and was most likely the reason behind his assassination – strangled with a silk sash, in deference to a fady on shedding royal blood – on 12 May 1863, by a group of army officers taking orders from Prime Minister Rainivoninahitriniony.

The assassination marked a shift in the balance of power between the monarchy and the office of prime minister. Rainivoninahitriniony agreed to install Radama II's wife Rasoherina as queen, provided that she consulted with him on all matters of policy, married him to cement their political alliance, and made it illegal to acknowledge or mourn the king's passing. Ironically, evidence has since emerged to suggest that the

king did not actually die in the attack, but may have recovered consciousness some hours later and escaped to the countryside, where he lived to an old age. By contrast, Rainivoninahitriniony proved ultimately to have overplayed his hand, since his unpopularity with the Malagasy public following his role in the assassination of Radama II allowed Queen Rasoherina to strip him of his position in 1864 and exile him to a village in the southern highlands. He was replaced as prime minister by his younger brother Rainilaiarivony, who would effectively rule Madagascar from

and exiled Rainivoninahitriniony. Despite having severe dysentery, the queen responded by organising a parade through the city and asking those of her subjects who still supported her rule to march behind her. The turnout was unequivocally in her favour, but four days later, she died.

With the incestuousness that characterised 19th-century Imerina politics, Rasoherina chose as her successor another of Radama II's widows, one who also happened to be her first cousin and the official custodian of her children, and would go on to marry Prime Minister Rainilaiarivony 10

Prime Minister Rainilaiarivony.

Queen Ranavalona III and her prime minister.

behind the scenes for the next 32 years, marrying not only Queen Rasoherina but also her successors Ranavalona II and III.

Queen Rasoherina pursued the liberal religious and social policies implemented by Radama II. Politically, as had been the case 50 years earlier with Radama I, her allegiances were broadly Anglophile; indeed, a year into her reign she signed a treaty with Britain granting it permission to establish an embassy in her capital, and its citizens the right to rent property in her realm. She also signed a trade agreement with the United States and initiated a peace treaty with France. On 27 March 1868, Rasoherina survived a foiled coup attempt against her and the prime minister, one most likely instigated by the disgruntled

months into her 15-year reign. Taking the throne name Ranavalona II, the new queen was a devout Protestant who made Christianity the official religion of Madagascar (but allowed her subjects freedom of worship) and replaced the traditional royal talismans with the Bible. She was the first monarch to address the issue of deforestation, by placing a ban on traditional slash-and-burn farming and on charcoal-making from indigenous trees, and lifting a longstanding fady forbidding non-royals from building stone or other permanent structures in the cities such as Antananarivo and Fianarantsoa. Influenced by the progressive and Anglophile Rainilaiarivony, she also placed a nominal ban on slave ownership (as opposed to just the trade in slaves), oversaw

intensive legal reforms, implemented the country's first constitution, and courted a British strong economic and religious presence.

FRENCH CONQUEST

In February 1883, somewhat against the historical trend, and partly to suppress the interests of what was then its main European rival in the Indian Ocean region, France launched a naval attack on Madagascar, somewhat disingenuously citing a 30-year-old letter written by Prince Rakoto (the future Radama II) and the equally ancient Lambert Charter as legal pretexts to place the island under its protectorateship. In May, the French navy bombarded and occupied the northwestern port of Mahajanga, from where a column of soldiers was dispatched to carry a proposed treaty of protectorateship to Ranavalona II in Antananarivo. After the queen refused to sign it, the French took occupation of Toamasina, the main port serving the Imerina capital.

Ranavalona II died in July 1883, to be succeeded by a niece (and great-granddaughter of King Andrianampoinimerina) who despite her

French expedition, 1895.

⊘ RADAMA II'S LEGACY

Three of the most enduringly significant acts taken by Radama II, the progressive Europhile son and chosen successor of Ranavalona I, were actually undertaken some years before he took the throne.

In 1854, the crown prince dictated a letter to Napoleon III, inviting the French emperor to invade the island in order to curtail the reign of his tyrannical mother.

A year later, he signed the so-called Lambert Charter, an agreement granting the French businessman Joseph-François Lambert exclusive right to exploit all the island's minerals, forests and uninhabited land provided that he paid a 10 percent levy to the monarchy of Imerina.

Finally, in 1857, the prince conspired with the likes of Lambert and Jean Laborde in a failed plot to oust his mother from the throne (see page 45), one that eventually led to the expulsion of all foreigners from Madagascar and the confiscation of their possessions by the queen.

In the years to come, the letter to Napoleon and Lambert Charter would both be used by France to justify its attempts to colonise Madagascar, as would the Merina monarchy's failure to make reparations for possessions confiscated from the French settlers deported by Ranavalona I.

relatively tender age of 22 was already a widow, and had been earmarked for the role some years in advance. Taking the throne name Ranavalona III, the young woman entered into the by-now-customary marriage with Prime Minister Rainilaiarivony, her senior by 33 years. Far more so than her two predecessors, Ranavalona III was genuinely little more than a figurehead for the machiavellian Rainilaiarivony, though it could be argued, persuasively, that the latter's vast political and military experience was a vital asset at a time when France occupied the kingdom's two largest ports and har-

Lambert Charter, and provided for the establishment of a French resident-general in Antananarivo. France claimed that the treaty granted it protectorateship over northwest Madagascar, but Ranavalona III and Rainilaiarivony denied this. The French navy evacuated Mahajanga and Toamasina, and another stalemate ensued.

The French navy returned to occupy Toamasina in December 1894 and Mahajanga in January 1895. This was backed up by an expeditionary force of 15,000 men, supported by some 6,000 local porters, which landed at Mahajanga in May

A battle during the French conquest of the island.

Only 25 French soldiers died in combat during the conflict of 1896. Dysentery and malaria took a far higher toll, however, claiming the lives of 4,600 of the 15,000 French troops who marched south from Mahajanga, as well as 1,000 porters.

boured unambiguous colonial aspirations towards the rest of the island. In December 1885, two years into Ranavalona III's reign, the stalemate was broken when the queen and her prime minister signed a treaty that ceded Diego Suarez Bay to France, required the Malagasy government to pay 10 million francs in reparations against the discarded

1895. Marching during the rainy season, it took the expedition four arduous months to reach Antananarivo. Despite this, the French met with little in the way of effective military resistance, and it required just one artillery bombardment of the royal palace in late September to persuade Ranavalona III to surrender. Prime Minister Rainilaiarivony was placed under house arrest, then put on a ship bound for Algiers, where he died only a month after docking, on 14 July 1896. Queen Ranavalona III, the last monarch of Imerina, was deposed in January 1897 and exiled to Algiers, where she died of natural causes 20 years later. Her disinterred remains were shipped to Madagascar and entombed at the Antananarivo Rova in the late 1930s.

JEAN LABORDE

From ship-wrecked to consul via queen's lover, Jean Laborde was foremost a skilled engineer who brought modernisation to Madagascar.

The most important individual foreign influence on the modernisation of Madagascar in the mid to late 19th century was Jean-Baptiste Laborde (1805–78), a 26-year-old French adventurer and shipwreck victim who washed ashore on the island's east coast at the mouth of the Matitanana River (near present-day Vohipeno) during the early years of the Ranavalona I's reign. Guided by locals, Laborde hiked north along the coast for around 200km (124 miles) to Mahela, where he found employment on a sugar plantation owned by the Mauritian-born French-creole adventurer Napoléon de Lastelle.

Impressed with Laborde's engineering skills and all-round resourcefulness, de Lastelle introduced him to Ranavalona I, who offered him a royal commission to transform a patch of swampland below her palace into what is now Lac Anosy. Rumour has it that Laborde and Ranavalona I also became lovers at around this time, despite her being old enough to be his mother (an age gap of 27 years). This has never been verified, but it is known that Laborde met and married Emilie Roux, a métisse woman five years his senior, at Mahela circa 1831, and that they had at least one child in prior to him divorcing her for adultery in 1857.

In 1833, Ranavalona I granted Laborde a large tract of land at Mantasoa, some 65km (40 miles) east of the capital, and practically limitless resources in order for him to establish a modern manufacturing complex, comprising, among other things, an arms factory, foundry, brickworks and glassmaking centre. The polymathic Laborde was also active as an architect and builder under Ranavalona I, and is associated with several of the capital's most historic buildings. Indeed, it was he who engineered the original wooden Palais de Manjakamiadana in 1839–40, who designed the elaborate Hindu-influenced tomb where Prime Minister Rainiharo was buried in 1852, and who added the extant tiled roof to Mahandrihono Palace at the Rova Ambohimanga.

In 1857, frustrated by the queen's tyrannical ways and hostility to Christianity and other outside influences, Laborde became involved in a planned coup to oust her in favour of her more tolerant and progressive son and chosen heir, the future Radama II. When this plot was uncovered, he was forced to leave Madagascar, along with all other foreign settlers, and had his possessions confiscated by the irate queen.

Following the death of Ranavalona I in 1861, Laborde returned to Antananarivo at the invitation of Radama II, and was appointed by Napoleon III as

Jean Laborde.

French consul to the Imerina court. In 1863, he constructed a French embassy a short walk downhill from Antananarivo Rova (the beautiful wide-balconied wooden house now known as Maison de Jean Laborde). He stayed on as ambassador after the assassination of Radama II and made a last major contribution to the island's architectural legacy in 1870, when he designed the two-storey Fandriampahalemana Palace on Rova Ambohimanga for Queen Ranavalona II. Jean Laborde died in Antananarivo on 27 December 1878 aged 73, and was accorded a national funeral by Ranavalona II. His remains were then interred in a grand tomb at Mantasoa, which – in true Malagasy style – he designed and built himself some years earlier.

French soldiers at the Antananarivo market, 1895.

THE FRENCH COLONIAL ERA

Over 64 years of French rule, Madagascar was affected by two world wars and experienced regular outbreaks of resistance to harsh colonial policies such as head taxes and forced labour.

Madagascar was formally annexed to France on 1 January 1896. Two weeks later, Resident-General Hippolyte Laroche arrived in Antananarivo to manage the takeover of a tottering administration still nominally presided over by Ranavalona III. The most significant achievement of Laroche's 10-month term, the passing of a law that abolished slavery, had the admirable effect of liberating some 20 percent of the island's population of 2.5 million from a life of unpaid servitude, but it nevertheless added to the post-invasion chaos. Otherwise, the Laroche administration was primarily concerned with quelling resistance to colonisation in the form of the Menalamba Revolt, which targeted foreigners and Christian converts.

COLONISATION AND REVOLT

In August 1896, the French national assembly voted in favour of administering Madagascar as a colony. The ineffectual Laroche was replaced by General Joseph Gallieni, an experienced military campaigner whose nine-year terms as Governor-General of Madagascar did much to mould the country's future. On 16 October, literally days after his arrival in Antananarivo, Gallieni decided to make an example of three prominent Malagasy leaders suspected of involvement in the Menalamba Revolt. These were Ranavalona III's minister of the interior Rainandriamampandry and her uncle Ratsimamanga, both of whom were executed by firing squad in a public square close to the present-day Palais d'Ambohitsorohitra, and the queen's chief female advisor Ramisindrazana, who was placed under house arrest and later exiled to Réunion. The monarchy was abolished in January 1897 and the deposed Ranavalona III and her leading couriers were exiled to Algiers a month later.

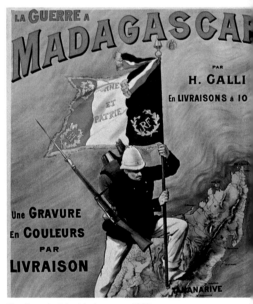

The French claim Madagascar, 1895

The Menalamba Revolt was named after the laterite-smeared red togas (menalamba) donned by the bands of traditionalist peasants who were its main protagonists.

Further afield, Gallieni adopted a scorched earth military policy to crush the Menalamba Revolt, capturing or killing the rebel bands one by one until the movement gradually petered out. With limited financial resources at his disposal, the governor-general recognised that the only way to control this vast and thinly inhabited territory was through a system of indirect rule.

This he implemented with the introduction of a *'politique des races'* tribal policy that made strong ethnic distinctions between highlanders and their coastal counterparts, gave overt preference to the former when it came to administrative work and positions of local authority, and divided the colony into a patchwork of ethnically-defined mini-protectorates ruled by pliant local kings and chiefs. In parallel, large tracts of land earmarked for individual settlers were allocated to a coterie of half-a-dozen companies, many of which wrought wholesale environmental destruction to surrounding areas of forest. Meanwhile, the peasantry was subjected to an oppressive hybrid system of head taxes and *corvée* (unpaid labour in lieu of tax) that helped to fund the colonial administration and to push the country away from a subsistence economy.

VY VATO SAKELIKA AND JEAN RALAIMONGO

The first formal resistance to colonialism came in the form of Vy Vato Sakelika (VVS; literally 'Iron Stone Solidarity') a nationalist cultural society

General Joseph Simon Gallieni, Governor-General of Madagascar from 1896.

⊘ SAINT JACQUES BERTHIEU

The most prominent foreign victim of the Menalamba Revolt, Father Jacques Berthieu was a 57-year-old Malagasy-speaking French Jesuit missionary who had arrived on the island in 1881 and served at missions in Ambohimandroso and Ambositra prior to being posted to Andrainarivo in 1891. When the revolt broke out in 1896, Berthieu decided the he and the converts in his charge should leave Andrainarivo for the relative safety of Antananarivo. On 8 June, whilst en route to the capital, he was taken captive by a menalamba band, which smashed his crucifix, struck him across the head with a machete, then marched him to a church he had built at Ambohitra, and castrated him. As daylight fell,

Berthieu's captors stopped at Ambiatibe, 50km (30 miles) north of Antananarivo, where he was thrown before a firing squad and told he would be spared only if he renounced Christianity and agreed to make no further Malagasy converts. The priest said he would rather die than betray his faith, then bowed his head in silent prayer. Four shots were fired at, and missed, the kneeling priest. A fifth shot wounded Berthieu, but it took a sixth, fired at close range, to kill him. In 1964, Jacques Berthieu became first martyr of Madagascar to be beatified, and he was finally canonised as a saint at a Mass held in the Vatican under Pope Benedict XVI on 21 October 2012.

formed in 1913 by a group of Merina medical students of noble birth. VVA soon attracted a strong following among Merina and other Malagasy professionals in Antananarivo, and as its goals became more public, the French authorities – then also embroiled in World War I – attempted to shut it down. In early 1916, VVA was made illegal, the press used to print a sympathetic newspaper was confiscated, and several of its leaders were arrested and jailed, only to be released after the end of the war. In many respects, the administration's harsh treatment of what was essentially

leaders from other French colonies, among them the future Vietnamese president Ho Chi Minh, who introduced him to broader socialist theories. By the time Ralaimongo returned to Madagascar in late 1924, he was advocating the Madagascar be made an overseas department of France, a move that would bestow automatic citizenship on all his compatriots. Following a march on the governor's office by 3,000 protesters carrying red flags and armed with sticks on 19 May 1929, Ralaimongo and several other nationalist leaders were placed under house arrest until 1936. He

Madagascan soldiers in training, 1942.

an intellectual pacifist organisation proved to be counterproductive, as it spurred a countrywide groundswell of anti-colonial sentiment that cut across most ethnic and religious lines.

The postwar nationalist call was spearheaded by Jean Ralaimongo (1885–1944), a mission-educated teacher who first visited France in 1910 and was one of 40,000 indigenous Malagasy who served on behalf of the colonial power in World War I. Having risked his life demonstrating his allegiance to France, Ralaimongo proposed that he and other returning Malagasy servicemen should be given the opportunity to acquire French citizenship. Convicted of sedition in 1922, he escaped to Paris, where he established a nationalist newspaper and associated with nationalist

faded from public life after this and died in 1944, but his legacy was a strong and increasingly vocal faction of Malagasy leaders committed to amalgamation with France or independence from it.

WORLD WAR II

Madagascar was profoundly affected by World War II. Following the German capture of northern and western France in June 1940, the island was administered by the Vichy Regime, a puppet government that collaborated with the Germans and shared its anti-Semitic views. In May 1942, the British, fearing that Madagascar might be seized by the Japanese, launched a successful naval attack on the port of Diego Suarez, and used it as a base from which to capture the entire island,

a goal it achieved by 6 November, when an armistice was declared. Having secured the island for the Allied forces, administration was handed to the Free French (the British allied government-in-exile led by Charles de Gaulle) under General Paul Legentilhomme in 1943.

As was the case in many African mainland colonies, World War II galvanised calls for Madagascar's independence. Of the 45,000 Malagasy conscripted into the Allied or French army during the war, around 2,000 lost their lives fighting for European democracy, and those

taxes and *corvée*, nor did it address the growing demand for full independence.

THE DRIVE FOR INDEPENDENCE

The dominant political parties of the immediate postwar era were the Mouvement démocratique de la rénovation malgache (MDRM) and Parti des déshérités de Madagascar (PADESM). The former was a pacifist nationalist party led by doctors Joseph Raseta and Joseph Ravoahangy and the writer Jacques Rabemananjara, all of whom came from elite families that had been prominent

Rebels surrender in the area of Tamatave after the Malagasy uprising of Sepember 1947.

who returned alive had high hopes of benefiting from the ideals for which they had been obliged to fight. These hopes were kindled by General de Gaulle's 1944 announcement that all France's colonies were to be redesignated as overseas territories, with representation in the national assembly. In October 1946, barely a year after the war ended, this promise was fulfilled in the form of the new Constitution of the Fourth Republic, which recast Madagascar and other colonies as an overseas territory in a Union Française, and accorded their inhabitants full French citizenship. This progressive development was in keeping with demands made by Jean Ralaimongo two decades earlier, but it did not put an end to the reviled system of head

in the Imerina royal court. PADESM, an organisation concerned mainly with the empowerment and fair treatment of coastal peoples and highlander descendants of slaves, formed in response to the perception that the primary goal of the MDRM was not so much democracy as the restoration of Merina rule elite. Although the French authorities actively supported PADESM, the MDRM was elected to represent Madagascar in the French National Assembly in November 1946, and was represented by the three aforementioned leaders, who duly submitted a bill to grant the island independence, which was rejected.

Tensions exploded on 29 March 1947 in the form of the so-called Malagasy Uprising, which was instigated by a series of coordinated attacks

in the vicinity of Moramanga and Manakara, and at several French-owned plantations. The MDRM maintained it had no involvement in the attacks, but it was held responsible by the authorities, who outlawed the party and arrested dozens of its officials – among them Raseta, Ravoahangy and Rabemananjara, who were given life sentences and held in prison in 1958. The French military responded with a scorched earth policy in which an estimated 89,000 Malagasy had been killed by the end of 1948, most of them innocent civilians who happened to be in the wrong place at the

Tabled by Adolf Eichmann on 15 August 1940 with the direct approval of Adolf Hitler, the so-called Madagascar Plan proposed relocating Europe's entire Jewish population to Madagascar and placing the island under the rule of the SS.

Merina-dominated Antokon'ny Kongresy Fana-fahana an'i Madagasikara (AKFM), formed two years later by the protestant clergyman Richard

General de Gaulle and Philibert Tsiranana, the first president of Madagascar, in Antananarivo, 1958.

wrong time. By contrast, only 550 French nationals died during the conflict, most of them soldiers. The uprising, which subsided in late 1948, also pitted MDRM and PADESM supporters against each other, with lasting ramifications on the country's conflicted post-independence politics.

In 1956, France responded to ongoing pressure from its colonies with a reform act that transferred centralised power from the national assembly in Paris to local parliaments elected under universal suffrage. Two main parties emerged to contest the first election. The Parti social-démocrate (PSD), formed in 1956 by Philibert Tsiranana, was a progressive offshoot of PADESM that favoured self-rule but wanted to maintain close ties with France. The

Andriamanjato, was a more hardline socialist party that favoured severing all tie with France and the Franc Zone, the nationalisation of foreign-owned industries, collectivisation of land, and restoring an emphasis on traditional Malagasy customs.

A referendum held in 1958 came out 75 percent in favour of the PSD's model of Madagascar as a self-governing republic within the newly formed French Community. Tsiranana was elected president on 27 April 1959. Soon after, he entered into negotiations with the French government that resulted in Madagascar being recognised as a fully independent sovereign state, albeit with strong ties to its former coloniser, on 26 June 1960 – a date now celebrated as Independence Day.

Ravalomanana speaks to the crowd during a rally in Antananarivo in 2006.

INDEPENDENT MADAGASCAR

Self-serving leadership and regular political crises, exacerbated by a population growth that routinely outstrips economic growth, have been hallmarks of Madagascar's patchy post-independence progress.

THE FIRST REPUBLIC

Over the period referred to as the First Republic (1960–72), the PSD and the government of Madagascar were practically synonymous. In part, this is because the electoral laws negotiated by Tsiranana and the departing French encouraged something close to a winner-takes-all scenario. A full 27 parties contested the first parliamentary elections in September 1960, with the PSD gaining 63 percent of the vote and the AKFM 15 percent, yet the system ensured that 82 of the available 107 seats went to the former, while the latter was accorded just three, with the other 20 going to minor parties broadly aligned with Tsiranana. The country's first presidential election, held in March 1965, resulted in Tsiranana taking 97.2 percent of the vote. The second such election, held in January 1972, was more like a referendum, with 99.7 percent of the electorate voting for the incumbent.

Away from the manipulable polling stations, however, many ordinary Malagasy were uncomfortable with Tsiranana, due to his close relationship with France, the large number of French settlers in his government, his adherence to a strongly anti-communist agenda, the continued use of French as the official language and presence of several French military bases on the island, and high levels of taxation that felt like a hangover from the colonial era. It did not help that the level of employment and average standard of living dropped significantly under Tsiranana, a circumstance abetted by soaring population growth (from 5.18 million in 1960 to 7.32 million in 1970, an astonishing increase of 40 percent in just 10 years). Furthermore, the president's ongoing ill health – most dramatically, a heart attack and consequent 10-day coma

Philibert Tsiranana, president during the First Republic.

in January 1970 – placed question marks over his fitness to govern and the issue of secession.

REBELLION AND COMMUNISM

In April 1971, brooding dissatisfaction among the southern peasantry over high levels of taxation erupted into an anti-government rebellion during which at least 2,000 civilians were killed by armed forces. On 8 May 1972, police overreaction to a non-violent strike at the University of Antananarivo led to a nationwide outbreak of student protests, and the arrest of 380 prominent student leaders. On 13 May, 5,000 students amassed in Antananarivo to protest against the arrests, and were fired upon by police, who killed 21 civilians and left more than 200 wounded. Five days later, Tsiranana resigned

and effectively gave over the country to military rule by transferring his executive powers to General Gabriel Ramanantsoa, a Merina aristocratic who had served in the French army before becoming Chief of Defence. The handover was completed in October 1972 when Ramanantsoa gained 94.5 percent approval in a constitutional referendum to confirm public support for himself and for his proposal to suspend civilian government for a five-year transition period.

President Ramanantsoa downgraded Madagascar's historical economic ties with France and

Didier Ratsiraka, the island's longest-serving president.

focussed instead on forging a new relationship with the USSR and nationalising foreign-owned business, a transformation that led to lower levels of efficiency, food shortages and a rise in corruption. The fragile economy was also hit hard by outside factors such as the 1973 oil crisis and concurrent introduction of floating exchange rates. Ramanantsoa was pressured to resign in favour of the less aristocratic and thus more popular Colonel Richard Ratsimandrava, whose six-day presidency ended on 11 February 1975, when he was assassinated by persons unknown while driving home from the presidential palace in Antananarivo. In the wake of this assassination, renewed tensions between supporters of the former President Tsiranana and the transitional military

government almost plunged the country into civil war, a fate averted through the efforts of Gilles Andriamahazo, a non-Merina general who served as caretaker president prior to handing over the role to Vice Admiral Didier Ratsiraka in June 1975.

THE SECOND REPUBLIC

In a constitutional referendum held in December 1975, Ratsiraka gained 95.5 percent approval for the newly-drafted Charter of the Malagasy Socialist Revolution, which restored civilian rule under the Second Republic, and automatically made him president for an initial seven-year term. In 1976, he founded a socialist party initially known as FNDR but later rebranded the Association for the Rebirth of Madagascar (AREMA). Initially, Ratsiraka pursued similar policies to his predecessors, leading to an economic decline that reached its nadir in the early 1980s and led to his gradual adoption of less socialistic policies, resumption of ties with France, and implementation of reforms recommended by the International Monetary Fund (IMF).

Economically, the 1980s were characterised by ongoing recession, critical food shortages, rapid devaluation of the Malagasy franc, and a high level of military repression in response to sporadic protests and riots. Indeed, a 1986 UN assessment placed Madagascar among the world's 20 poorest countries, and population growth outstripped economic growth in all but the last year of the decade. Despite this, Ratsiraka ploughed on to become Madagascar's longest-serving president, winning the 1982 presidential election for AREMA fair-and-square, with almost 80 percent of the vote, then being re-elected with 62.7 percent support in a 1989 election condemned as fraudulent by a losing trio of opposition parties.

THE THIRD REPUBLIC

In the wake of the 1989 election, the Comité des Forces Vives (CFV), a coalition of 16 political parties led by former opposition leader Albert Zafy, organised a series of mass demonstrations against the unpopular Ratsiraka. Events came to a head in October 1991 when the presidential guard opened fire on demonstrators amassed outside the presidential palace at Iavoloha, on the outskirts of Antananarivo, killing at least 30 and possibly more than 100 people. This prompted a general strike in which more than 300,000 participated. Ratsiraka

stood down as a result, and the CFV tabled the new and more democratic Constitution of the Third Republic, which was approved by 73 percent of voters in a referendum held in August 1992.

Presidential elections were held in November 1992 with seven starting candidates. A run-off between the top two contenders in February 1993 resulted in Zafy beating Ratsiraka with roughly two-thirds of the vote. Parliamentary elections held four months later saw the CFV claim 46 of 134 seats and more than 20 other parties each taking at least one seat. This fragmented voting

pattern led to the formation of a fractious and ineffective coalition government that underwent 10 cabinet reshuffles and three changes of prime minister in the space of three years, and was so rotten with corruption and wasteful spending that the World Bank, IMF and several other donors suspended all support in 1994.

In July 1996, President Zafy was impeached for corruption and abuse of power by the National Assembly in a motion that won the support of 99 of 134 parliamentarians. Constitutionally, the impeachment of the president necessitated a

This bridge connecting southern Madagascar to the centre was bombed ahead of the 2001 elections.

⊘ THE ELECTION OF 2001

The presidential election of 2001 played out in a rather peculiar manner.

The initial count of first-round votes gave 46.5 percent to Marc Ravalomanana and 40.6 percent to President Ratsiraka, with Albert Zafy coming first among the four runners-up with just 5.34 percent. Constitutionally, if no candidate obtained a clear majority in the first round, the election would go to a second round pitting the two top candidates against each other, as had happened in 1993 and 1996. However, Ravalomanana rejected the initial count, accusing his main rival of engineering an electoral fraud, and demanded a recount. Ratsiraka refused,

leading to violent protests and strikes by Ravalomanana's supporters in and around the capital, and the setting up of roadblocks and blowing up of key bridges by the pro-Ratsiraka faction.

Ravalomanana declared himself president in February 2002, a claim supported by a recount that awarded him an outright majority of 51.46 percent and was ratified by the High Constitutional Court in April and the US government in June.

Nevertheless, hundreds of Malagasy died in clashes associated with the contested election, and a full-blown civil war might well have broken out were it not for the intervention of the international community.

new presidential election but it did not prevent the impeached incumbent from standing again. Ultimately, though, Zafy was narrowly beaten by Ratsiraka in a second round that took place in December 1996 and attracted a million fewer voters than its 1993 counterpart, reflecting the unpopularity of both pole candidates. Ratsiraka's relatively uneventful fourth presidential term was characterised by an increased commitment to free market principles, the privatisation of many government institutions, the reengagement of institutions such as the Word Bank and IMF, and

of his party Tiako I Madagasikara (literally 'I Love Madagascar', TIM).

As the first Malagasy president to come from a business (as opposed to military or political) background, Ravalomanana was able to work closely with the IMF and World Bank and did much to improve the country's transport infrastructure along with public services such as education and healthcare, and to curb government corruption and profligacy. Having survived attempted coups in January 2003 and November 2006, Ravalomanana ran for a second presidential term in

President Marc Ravalomanana casts his vote in Antananarivo, 2006.

the first sustained period of economic growth the island had enjoyed since independence.

THE RISE OF MARC RAVALOMANANA

The late 1990s also saw the emergence of a new face in Malagasy politics in the form of Marc Ravalomanana, a relatively young (born 1949) self-made businessman who was elected mayor of Antananarivo in 1999 and impressed with his commitment to making civil improvements and freedom from the jadedness and taint of corruption that clung to the political status quo. The fast-rising Ravalomanana stood against Ratsiraka, Zafy and three other candidates in the hotly contested 2001 presidential election, and the first round on a recount, taking 51.5 percent of the vote on behalf

Former President Didier Ratsiraka fled to France in 2002, and was tried in absentia for embezzlement of US$8m of public funds. Despite receiving a 10-year sentence, he returned home in 2011 and was welcomed back by the Rajoelina regime.

December 2006, taking 54.8 percent of the vote as compared to 11.6 percent by the closest of 13 other candidates.

In 2007, Ravalomanana disbanded parliament in order to hold to a constitutional referendum that expanded emergency presidential powers, abolished the existing six provinces in favour of

22 smaller regions in order to facilitate regional development, and adopted English as a third official language in addition to French and Malagasy. The vote went 75 percent in his favour.

THE 2009 CRISIS

Over the course of 2008, tensions grew between Ravalomanana and Andry Rajoelina, a self-made media mogul who had been elected mayor of Antananarivo the year before, aged only 33. Rajoelina was highly critical of the Ravalomanana government's conservative social policies the

government troops opened fire on an opposition rally. On 8 March, troops at a military base outside Antananarivo mutinied in protest at being expected to use force against the opposition. On 14 March, Rajoelina gave the president four hours to voluntarily resign. The next day, Ravalomanana responded by offering to hold a referendum on whether or not he should remain president. Rajoelina rejected this proposal.

On 16 March, the Palais d'Ambohitsorohitra was seized in a military coup, Ravalomanana resigned, and the army handed over the presidency on a

President Hery Rajaonarimampianina gives a speech in 2015.

lack of progress it had made in combating individual poverty, and plans to lease large tracts of land to the Korean industrial company Daewoo. In December 2008, Ravalomanana shut down a television channel owned by Rajoelina (under the pretext it had broadcast an illegal interview with the exiled ex-president Ratsiraka). Rajoelina responded by calling for a general strike in Antananarivo over 24 and 25 January 2009.

Things turned violent on 26 January when thousands of protesters ransacked two progovernment television stations and burned down the Ravalomanana-owned Malagasy Broadcasting System, and the bodies of 25 looters were found in a partially razed shop. On 7 February, 28 people were killed and 83 wounded when

transitional basis to Andry Rajoelina, who formed a provisional executive body called the Fitondrana Avon'ny Tetezamita (FAT; literately 'High Transitional Authority') to preside over a political crisis that once again threatened to topple over into outright civil war. Ravalomanana fled to exile in South Africa but in August he was tried in absentia for his role in the protests and ensuing deaths, and given a life sentence. A new constitution establishing the Fourth Republic was passed in 2010 following 75 percent approval in a constitutional referendum.

THE 2013 ELECTION AND BEYOND

Backed by the Southern African Development Community (SADC), a document entitled 'Roadmap for Ending the Crisis in Madagascar' was

signed in September 2011, paving the way for a fresh presidential election. This was delayed, however, when the SADC insisted that Rajoelina and Ravalomanana, the two most prominent protagonists is the 2009 crisis, both withdraw their candidature. The exiled Ravalomanana acceded to this demand in December 2012, and Rajoelina in February 2013. The Rajoelina-endorsed Hery Rajaonarimampianina, of the Hery Vaovao ho an'i Madagasikara (New Forces for Madagascar) Party, emerged as the winner in field of more than 30 starting candidates, taking the second

Now approaching its seventh decade of independence, Madagascar remains one of the world's poorest and most underdeveloped nations, and prone to sporadic political upheaval. As of 2018, the population stood at 25 million, a fivefold increase in fewer than 60 years. Economically, the country remains almost entirely agricultural, the road and transport infrastructure compares unfavourably to all but the very poorest countries on the African mainland, and the per capita GDP of around US$400 is significantly lower than the 1960 figure of US$700.

Active campaigning ahead of the 2015 elections.

Elected president in 2013, Hery Martial Rajaonarimampianina Rakotoarimanana was heralded for holding the world record as Head of State with the longest name (44 characters) and longest family name (19 characters).

round with 53.5 percent of the vote. Marc Ravalomanana returned to Madagascar in October 2014 and was arrested on arrival in keeping with the life sentence imposed on him four years earlier. The sentence was lifted in May 2015, since when he has reactivated the Malagasy Broadcasting System and was reelected as president of TIM.

Politically, Madagascar has maintained stability in the aftermath of the 2009 crisis, but ethnic factionalism and petty politics retain the capacity to provoke periods of costly and infrastructurally destructive internal conflict. The next election is due in 2018 and the incumbent's position is far from secure. He has already survived a parliamentary motion to remove him from office due to 'constitutional violations and general incompetence'. The motion gained the required two-third majority in a parliamentary vote held in May 2015, but he survived due to the intervention of the constitutional court, which ruled that the allegations were unfounded and inadmissible. He will most likely also square up against two former presidents, Marc Ravalomanana and Andry Rajoelina.

The new generation.

Enjoying the sunset over the city from Haute-Ville, Antananarivo.

Sakalava woman with a traditionally painted face, Nosy Be.

THE MALAGASY

Rooted in Indonesia but influenced by waves of settlement from Africa, Arabia and Europe, the Malagasy share a common language and a culture that emphasises community and ancestor worship.

Many facets of traditional Malagasy culture reveal its Indonesian roots. These range from the appearance of the bamboo-tube valiha (a type of zither similar to those found in modern-day Indonesia) and construction of rectangular houses with a central support pillar and sloping roofs (reminiscent of their counterparts in parts of Borneo) to the ubiquity of rice at all meals. Equally, the culture of Malagasy people has had more than 1,500 years to develop in isolation from Indonesia, a period during which it has been infused with a succession of other influences – African, Arabian, Cormoran and more recently Portuguese, English and of course French – to develop a character almost as unique as the island's flora and fauna. Despite this, the modern Malagasy essentially form one uniform entity, with the common cultural and linguistic ground between the island's various ethnic subgroups far outweighing the regional differences.

Friendly smile in Toliara.

HIGHLANDERS AND LOWLANDERS

The Malagasy can be divided into two main subgroups, both of which speak the same language, (also known as Malagasy). The highlanders, a subgroup that includes the Merina of Antananarivo as well as the Betsileo, Sihanaka and Zafimaniry, are essentially the descendants of early Indonesian settlers who moved upcountry soon after the island was first inhabited to take advantage of a relatively cool and disease-free climate conducive to cattle-rearing and rice-growing. By contrast, the coastal peoples have relied more on fishing and maritime trade as their economic mainstays, and also have a more diverse ethnic make-up

thanks to regular injections of fresh African, Arabic, Indian and more recently European stock. This difference is reflected in the more Asian appearance of the highlanders, as well as in recent DNA analysis that revealed the coastal Malagasy to have a far greater proportion of African ancestry.

Less simplistically, the Malagasy are divided into 22 cultural groups. Beyond the aforementioned division between highlanders and coastal people, however, the validity of these groupings is rather contentious, since they appear to have little meaning in ethnic terms, but instead reflect traditional differences in lifestyle (between, for instance, fisher-people and cattle-herders) and/or

geographic location, as well as the boundaries of the island's political kingdoms as they were defined the 19th century. These roots are often reflected in the name used for the various groups: Antanosy, for instance, means 'People of the Island', Antandroy 'People of the Spiny Forest', and Sakalava 'People of the Long Valleys'.

The most populous cultural group in Madagascar, the Merina (approximately 3 million), who live in the highlands around Antananarivo, were the dominant political force island-wide for much of the 19th century, and remain so to a lesser extent today. The Merina used to be devised into three distinct classes: the Andriana (royal family and nobles), Hova (free commoners) and Andevo (slaves). These castes are now illegal, and have no official meaning, but old grudges die hard, and friction between people of Hova and Andevo descent has been a major factor in the country's post-independence politics. Other populous groups are the Betsileo (2 million), Betsimisaraka (1.5 million) and the Tsimihety and Sakalava (each around

Selling zebu kebabs in Ambositra.

Girls in Antsirabe.

⊘ MALAGASY PLACE NAMES

Places names in Madagascar tend to be long, impenetrable and difficult to remember, but in most cases their meaning is quite simple and prosaic. Many names start with one of the prefixes 'an', 'ant', 'am' or 'i', which literally means 'in' or 'on', but are often translated as 'place of'. This prefix is typically followed by one or two geographic descriptors. Place names starting Ambohi-', for instance, derive from 'vohitra', meaning hill, while those starting with Antana- derive from 'tanana', meaning town. Thus the common place names Ambohitra and Ivohitra both simply translate as 'on the hill', Ambohimanga as 'on the blue hill' ('manga' meaning blue) and Antanabao as 'in the new town' ('bao' meaning new). Other common prefix/descriptor compounds include Anala- ('ala' means forest), Andrano- ('rano' means water), Ambato- ('vato' means rock), Ambodi- ('vodi' is the base of a hill or rock) and Ankili ('kili' means tamarind tree). Elsewhere, Ambositra is named after a vositra, a place where animals were sacrificed in times gone by, while Antsirabe derives from sira (salt) and be (big), indicating it was once the site of an important salt market. Look out too for names starting with Andriana, a prefix that usually denotes an important link, whether past or present, with the Imerina royal family, or with the deities Andriamanitra or Andrianerinerina.

1 million). Culturally, the most outlying minority groups are the Vezo and Mikea, both of which still partially adhere to a nomadic lifestyle, the former as fisherfolk, the latter as hunter-gatherers in the southwest.

DAY-TO-DAY LIFE

One of the world's poorest and most undeveloped countries, Madasgacar was ranked 158th among the 188 countries surveyed in the 2017 Human Development Index. This ranking reflects a per capita GDP of little

capital, and is largely hereditary, reinforced by the infinitely superior education available to children from wealthy families.

Traditionally, Malagasy society is highly patriarchal. Gender-based discrimination is now constitutionally forbidden, but still rife on an everyday basis. In 2007, for instance, the legal age of marriage was raised to 18, but it has been estimated that around 10 percent of girls are married in all but legal name by the age of 15, and more than 40 percent by the time they turn 18. This has resulted in far lower levels of

An intense game of table football in Antananarivo.

more than US$400, a birth rate of almost 5 percent (almost half the population is aged 15 or under), an adult literacy rate of around 65 percent, and a transport, power and economic infrastructure that is rudimentary even by African standards. As might be expected, it remains a predominantly rural society, with only 35 percent of the population living in urban areas, and the remainder mostly eking out an existence as subsistence farmers, cattle-herders or fisher-people. A well-established middle class dates back to the 19th century, when the Hova (free commoners) played an important role in the governance of Imerina and associated military, but it is very small in numeric terms, largely confined to the

The most ancient of Malagasy ancestors, the pygmoid Vazimba are said to have been the island's first inhabitants. The Imerina royalty claimed Vazimba ancestry through Queen Rafohy, the mother of the dynasty's founder King Andriamanelo.

education among girls than boys, and very high teenage and child mortality pregnancy rates. In traditional Malagasy society, women still generally divide their time between working on the paddies and fields, cooking, and raising children

– though in many cases, economic pragmatism forces the latter role onto slightly older siblings.

There are bright spots in this economically bleak picture. A strong sense of community and family ensures that Malagasy society remains relatively crime free (at least if you discount cattle rustling in a few rural areas). The fertility of the highlands and east coast ensure that most people are reasonably well fed (though certain more arid areas are prone to periodic local food shortages). And overall, considering the sometimes fractious events of the 18th century, tolerance of tribal and religious differences is high. For visitors, the Malagasy people also come across as genuinely friendly and hospitable, and there's almost none of the hassle you might experience in parts of mainland Africa and Asia. As for the future, many of Madagascar's economic woes are clearly the result of poor governance both in the colonial and post-independence era, and it is to be hoped that the new era of stability ushered by the 2009 crisis will result in a brighter economic outlook.

A popular bridge in Maroantsetra.

⊘ KEEPING THE FADY

A Malagasy cultural concept to which all visitors should be sensitive is *fady*, a set of taboos that are believed to be enforced by the ancestors. Some of these taboos are held more-or-less countrywide, for instance the widespread *fady* on pointing a finger at a tomb and any other venerated object (the acceptable alternative is to point your knuckles with your finger crooked back towards your body), on denying hospitality to a stranger, or on killing or otherwise harming all or certain species of lemur. Many of these prohibitions concern specific foods, for instance eels are forbidden to pregnant women and the consumption of pork is *fady* is many areas.

And whilst some of these taboos are widespread, others – such as the killing of crocodiles in certain places where they are associated with the ancestors, or swimming in a few specific lake and rivers, urinating on a mountain slope or whistling a certain stretch of beach outdoors – are confined to specific locations or clans.

Locals who break a *fady* will be shunned as unclean and for upsetting the ancestors, even if the transgression happens to be accidental – and while it's true that some allowances are made for foreigners, a good local guide will ensure that you avoid any such major infractions.

RELIGION IN MADAGASCAR

It's a game of two halves between traditional beliefs and the Christian faith, with a Muslim minority.

Roughly half of the Malagasy people adhere to traditional beliefs, which are broadly similar throughout the country (with some regional variation) and combine elements of monotheism, ancestor worship and animism. The genderless supreme being is known by a number of names, most commonly Zanahary (the creator) or Andriamanitra (Fragrant Lord). His rebellious son Andrianerinerina, the founder of the Malagasy people, is an important focal point of worship. Another significant element in Malagasy tradition is the animist belief that certain natural features, often rivers or caves, but also sometimes animals or trees, host nature spirits associated with the *vazimba*, legendarily the island's earliest inhabitants.

Crucial to Malagasy religion is the worship of dead ancestors, known collectively as *razana*. It is widely believed that these ancestors are a benevolent influence, but that they will transform into more malevolent disease-bearing sprits known called *angatra* when neglected or offended. Most Malagasy traditions place a strong emphasis on ancestral tombs, which are built according to the local tribal custom on a designated patch of family land known as a *tanindrazana* (place of the ancestors). Tombs are usually tended carefully by the living descendants and many cultures hold exhumation rituals every few years. Among the Merina and Betsileo, for instance, the septennial *famadihana* ceremony, or turning of the bones, entails removing the embalmed body or bones from the tomb, unwrapping the shroud, then embarking on a period of intense and often joyful communication with the dead ancestor, before the remains are wrapped in a fresh silk burial cloth and reinterred.

Traditional diviners are consulted to determine the most auspicious date to hold any important event or to embark on a new enterprise, be it a funeral or a wedding, or laying the foundation stone of a house or tomb. The advice of the diviners is informed by a complex astrology-like system called *vintana*, which is based on the movements of the moon, sun, and stars, but also on geographic relations (north and east are better than south or west), and with qualities attributed to the various days of the week (Thursday, for instance, is an auspicious day for weddings, as is Friday for funerals).

Islam and Christianity both have a strong foothold in Madagascar and tend to be most widely practised in the larger highland towns and longer-serving coastal ports. Of the two, Islam has the more ancient presence, since it was introduced in medieval times by Arab traders, and evidently formed the main religion of Mahilaka, a walled city that flourished on the coast opposite Nosy Be over the 11th–15th centuries. Today, Islam is practised by around 6 percent of the population, mostly people of Comoran or Indo-Pakistani

Church in Fianarantsoa.

descent living in or around Mahajanga. A small minority of the Indian community practices Hinduism.

At least 45 percent of the population is Christian. Protestantism was introduced by the English in the early 19th century and Roman Catholicism arrived with the French towards the end of the same century. The two are equally represented today, with the former enjoying its largest support among the Marina and the latter among the Betsileo. Christianity is often practised syncretically with traditional beliefs, making it difficult for outsiders to determine where one ends and the other begins – Malagasy Christians will, for instance, routinely invite pastors to bless the dead at a traditional burial or wedding, or visit diviners for advice.

Sakalava tomb marker at the Musée Cedratom in Toliara.

ARTS AND CRAFTS

Madagascar is characterised by long and colourful musical, architectural and oral literary traditions, while the visual arts are represented by a Unesco-listed woodcarving tradition and silk textile production.

ORAL AND WRITTEN LITERATURE

Madagascar has a strong oral literary tradition. *Hainteny* (literally 'knowledge of words') is a lyrical metaphor-heavy form of oral literature that resembles the *pantun* poetic tradition of Malaysia sufficiently closely to suggest it travelled to Madagascar together with the island's first settlers. The most famous *hainteny* work is the *Ibonia*, an Odyssean epic whose eponymous hero has to overcome a series of challenges to wrestle away his betrothed Rasoamananoro (usually translated as Joy-Giving Girl) from her abductor Ravatovolovoay (Trouble-Stone Man). First transcribed in the 1870s, the *Ibonia* is unquestionably many centuries older than that, and several different versions with distinct variations in story line have been collected from around the island.

Another important oral literary tradition, often incorporated into *Hainteny*, comprises the pithy proverb-like *ohabolana*, each of which expresses a moral or philosophical point with epigrammatic concision. More than 6,000 *ohabolana* have been transcribed, typical examples being 'don't kick away the canoe that assisted you across the river' and 'blame is like the wind: felt but not seen'. The *ohabolana* are also a key element in the oratorial tradition of *kabary*, which originated as a stylised display of eloquence in the royal court of Imerina and other Malagasy kingdoms, and is now practised by political leaders as well as speechmakers at formal events such as weddings and funerals.

Written literature is a relatively modern concept in Madagascar, assuming one discounts a number of mostly religious treatises transcribed in the Arabic-style script known as *Sorabe* prior to 1823. The earliest forays into secular writing date to the early 20th century, when a number of Malagasy writers associated with the organisation Vy Vato

Silk weaver at work, Soatanana silk village.

Sakelika published poems and journals whose themes were often overtly nationalist. The country's leading literary light between the world wars – and arguably the most influential writer Madagascar has ever produced – was Jean-Joseph Rabearivelo (1903–37), whose poetry and novels, written in both French and Malagasy, blended traditional forms with surrealism and other modern influences with skill and originality. Tragically, Rabearivelo committed suicide by cyanide, partly in frustration at the colonial government's decision to exclude him from the list of Malagasy exhibitors invited to the 1937 Universal Exposition in Paris. Rabearivelo was honoured as the national poet upon independence in 1960, and he is cited as an influence more modern writers such

as the novelist Michèle Rakotoson (born 1948), poet Esther Nirina (born 1932) and political writer Jean-Luc Raharimanana (born 1967). The most important modern literary figure in Madagascar is the poet and artist Elie Rajaonarison (1951–2010). Unfortunately, few of these writers' works have been translated into English.

HIRAGASY

Tononkira, the Malagasy word for poem, literally means word-song, and the islanders' poetic oral tradition is indeed difficult to disentangle from

TRADITIONAL MUSIC

Madagascar's vibrant and diverse music scene embraces the island's own traditions whilst being receptive to outside modern influences. Most traditional music harks back to Indonesia rather than Africa, and is driven mainly by stringed instruments as opposed to percussion. The national instrument is the *valiha*, which strongly resembles an Indonesian tube zither, comprising a large bamboo cylinder surrounded by up to 28 strings (traditionally thin strips of bamboo fibre, now more likely to be bicycle

Vezo villagers singing and playing the kabosy, Toliara province.

its inherent kinship with music. The two forms are melded in a song-based musical tradition called *Hiragasy*, which probably originated during the 18th-century reign of King Andrianampoinimerina, who pioneered the use of musical and dance troupes to help convey his message to his subjects. *Hiragasy* performances later took on a life of their own, offering the opportunity for the audience to ritually applaud or boo the performance as well as the message, and were even used by the French to convey information to rural areas. Today, *Hiragasy* performances – which are broken into five parts and typically last for about two hours in total – are still used to attract crowds to political rallies, and various troupes also hold regular competitions.

brake cables or guitar strings). Its close cousin, the *marovany*, is a rectangular box zither with strings on either side. Tuned in sequences of thirds, the zithers are plucked with the fingernails, and used both for secular music and at ritual gatherings to summon ancestral spirits. The best-known *valiha* maestro is Justin Vali, who has recorded with the likes of Peter Gabriel and Paddy Bush.

Other traditional chordophones include the four- to six-stringed *kabosy*, a guitar lookalike whose soundbox originally comprised a whole tortoiseshell but is now made from wood; the similar-looking *gitara*, which has up to seven movable frets; and the three-stringed fiddle-like *lokanga*. Ancient non-stringed instruments

Live music concerts in Antananarivo and other large towns tend to be prominently advertised. A great introduction to recorded Malagasy music, the World Network CD Music of Madagascar includes tracks by Mahaleo, Rossy and Justin Vali.

with Indonesian roots include the *sodina* flute and the large xylophone-like *atranatrana*, which is played by two women, one seated with the bars resting on her outstretched legs while she keeps a repetitive beat, the other striking the melody. A feature common to most traditional Malagasy music is polyharmonic singing, which is informed by African traditions in some coastal regions, but elsewhere melds ancient Indonesian influences with more recently introduced church music.

The London Missionary Society brought the first piano to Madagascar, inspiring the mutation of traditional *valiha* works into a Malagasy classical style known as Kalonny Fahiny, which peaked in the 1930s under theatrical composers such as Andrianary Ratianarivo and Naka Rabemananatsoa. Post World War II, Kalonny Fahiny was adapted to a finger-picking guitar genre known as *ba-gasy*. Because guitars are so much cheaper than pianos (and easily substituted with homemade replicas), *ba-gasy* evolved islandwide into a variety of distinctive regional styles using different tunings.

MODERN MUSIC

A more contemporary Malagasy sound started to emerge in the 1960s, when it became customary for young guitar groups based in and around Antananarivo to adapt and cover international hits. The most successful homegrown group of all time is Mahaleo which formed in the wake of the student strikes of May 1972, applied a soft rock sheen to traditional Malagasy sounds but spiced with outspoken political commentary, and is still active today despite the death of two founder members. Long-serving artists to emerge in the wake of Mahaleo include the accordion-brandishing singer-songwriter Rossy and the London-based sister duo Tarika. Recent years have seen the emergence of several

distinct local styles: an energetic fusion of traditional southwestern sounds and South African *mbaqanga* called *tsapika*, a funky electrified call-and-response coastal dance style known as *salegy*, and even Malagasy hip-hop (known locally as 'Haintso Haintso').

VISUAL ARTS AND CRAFTS

Despite the presence of a few galleries in Antananarivo, Madagascar seems to lack for a significant contemporary fine arts scene. That said, the visual arts are represented in

Woodcarving workshop, Ambositra.

a number of striking traditional forms, from woodcarving to handwoven textiles. The former reaches its highest expression in the woodworking tradition of the Zafimaniry people, who live in the remote forested highlands east of Ambositra. Inscribed on the Unesco Intangible Cultural Heritage list in 2008, the Zafimaniry woodworking tradition – best seen in situ over the course of a multi-day hike – combines great engineering skill and functionality with decorative geometric patterns that display a combination of Indonesian and Arab influences. Another important woodworking tradition, also with Indonesian antecedents, are the elaborately carved *aloalo* (funerary posts) that mark tombs of important

ancestors. The most significant textile industry, at least from a touristic point of view, comprises the handwoven dyed silk items produced at the likes of Soatanana (near Ambositra) and Soalandy Atelier (Ambalavao).

ARCHITECTURE

A striking feature of the central highlands is the solid traditional houses built by the Marina and Betsileo people. Rectangular, narrow, and usually spanning two storeys, these neat brick houses are characterised by an open

The 2005 movie Mahaleo, directed by Raymond Rajaonarivelo, uses a combination of concert footage and interviews to document the emergence of the eponymous pop group in the wake of the 1972 uprising, and its long subsequent career.

The all-wood Mahandrihono Palace.

ground-floor veranda, several small framed windows, and a tall steep peaked roof supported by a central pillar and crossed gable beams adorned with decorative carvings. Quite unlike any other buildings constructed in Africa, these traditional highland homesteads shared several features in common with their counterparts in the part of Indonesia from where Madagascar's first settlers originated. This continuity is no less surprising when you realise that all such buildings would have been made entirely from wood until prior to 1868, when Queen Ranavalona II lifted an edict forbidding commoners from constructing stone houses. An excellent example of an all-wood Merina house is Mahandrihono Palace, which was built by King Andrianampoinimerina at the Rova Ambohimanga in 1788. In other parts of Madagascar, houses tend to be more simple, organic and African in style, and are often less elaborate and interesting than tombs, which – as homes for the dead ancestors – the Malagasy traditionally regard to be more important constructions.

⊘ SORABE SCRIPT

Prior to the introduction of the Latin alphabet in 1823, Malagasy was transcribed in Sorabe, a 34-letter Arabic-style script whose name literally means 'Big Writing' (from the Arabic *sura* and Malagasy *be*). The use of Sorabe was confined to Antemoro mystics whose command of the written word frequently led Malagasy monarchs to appoint them as oracles. (Andrianampoinimerina of Imerina employed one such scribe to teach literacy to his children, including the future Radama I). Around 200 Sorabe documents survive today, and while some deal with local history, most are primarily concerned with spells and spiritual rituals that show a clear Muslim influence without actually referring to the religion.

As is so often the case in Madagascar, the origin of Sorabe is obscure. The oldest specimen – a leather-bound document preserved in a library in France – has been dated to the 17th century. But whether this dating reflects the earliest usage of the script, or it is simply the case that no older specimens have survived, is anybody's guess. And while the most obvious provenance of Sorabe would be literate settlers or traders from Oman or the Swahili Coast, recent studies noting the strong similarity between certain characters and their counterparts in Pegon (a Javanese variant on Arabic) suggest that, like the first Malagasy settlers, it might actually be Indonesian.

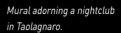
Mural adorning a nightclub in Taolagnaro.

Market seller at the
Beramanja food market
in northern Madagascar.

FOOD AND DRINK

Tasty home-grown stews, grilled zebu kebabs and an abundance of fresh seafood are highlights of a national cuisine informed by an insatiable appetite for rice.

Rice is not merely the main Malagasy staple, but the very foundation of the national cuisine. The most important of several crops thought to have been shipped to the island by its original Indonesian settlers (the others include bananas, ginger and sugarcane), rice is now grown in paddies all over Madagascar, which ranks as the world's largest non-Asian producer, and is claimed to be second only to Vietnam in terms of per capita annual consumption. This is because rice forms the basis of all three main meals in most Malagasy households, a convention that has been little altered by decades of French colonialism or – despite the growing popularity of pizza among the urban middle classes – subsequent exposure to a variety of international cuisines.

LOCAL CUISINE

Known locally as vary, rice is commonly eaten for breakfast in the form of *vary sosoa*, a runny gruel-like porridge eaten plain or with a meaty sauce, or *vary aminanana*, a rice porridge cooked together with rice, meat and chopped greens. For the more sweet of tooth, *mofo gasy* (literally Malagasy bread) is a grilled circular patty of sugary rice-flour dough that rather resembles a donut and goes well with coffee or tea. Breakfast dishes not based on rice include *misao* (noodles stir-fried with chopped vegetables and meat) and *soupe chinoise* (a thin noodle soup), both of which were introduced in the early 20th century by Chinese labourers recruited to construct the railway line between Antananarivo and Toamasina. Fresh baguettes and egg dishes such as omelette are also often eaten at breakfast, but generally only in hotels, smarter cafés and other establishments catering to western palates.

Malagasy twist on a French classic: baguettes filled with shredded vegetables and hot sauce.

Lunch (the main meal in Madagascar) and dinner usually consist of boiled rice served with a meat- or vegetable-based accompaniment (known generically as laoka). Best known among these is the national dish *romazava*, a gingery stew made from beef and vegetables (in particular a spicy leaf called bredy mafana). Other popular traditional accompaniments include *ravitoto* (fried meat stewed with cassava leaves and coconut milk), *voanjobory* (cubed meat and groundnuts in a garlicky tomato sauce), *vorivorinkena* (tripe and pork stew), *varanga* (shredded roast beef) and *Akoho sy Voanio* (chicken in a gingery coconut sauce). In practice, many local eateries in Madagascar just serve a generic

tomato-based chicken, fish and/or beef stew alongside the customary mound of rice, so you generally need to visit a restaurant specialising in local cuisine to try the dishes named above.

COSMOPOLITAN INFLUENCES

Antananarivo offers visitors a good range of international restaurants, with Indian, Chinese, Southeast Asian and Italian cuisines all well represented, along with fast-food chains serving burgers, pizzas, fried chicken and the like. Elsewhere, the choices tend to be more limited,

Vanilla production is extremely labour-intensive.

though you'll find that most hotels and tourist-oriented hotels serve a varied (but after a while rather predictable) menu of French-Malagasy dishes catering to western palates. Accompaniments invariably include rice, but most restaurants also offer the choice of pommes frites, sautéed potatoes or boiled vegetables (often swaddled in butter). Menus in Madagascar tend to focus strongly on red meat, fish and poultry, but vegetarians are unlikely to feel too excluded, as most place have a few suitable choices. That said, salads or other dishes listed in the vegetarian section do often include meaty elements, so it pays to check the small print carefully, and to interrogate the waiter when in doubt. Vegans are seldom catered for actively, and may find it difficult to establish what if any animal products (eggs, milk, fat) were used in the creation of a vegetarian dish.

Seafood is well represented, especially on the coast, where fresh whole line-fish, tuna steak, calamari and prawns are usually served grilled or fried with a simple lemon, ginger or coconut sauce. Inland, the most popular meat is beef, which in Madagascar is practically synonymous with zebu, a form of humped cattle introduced to the island by African settlers circa AD 1000 and later went feral, only to be re-domesticated during the 16th-century reign of King Ralambo. Usually served grilled in the form of kebabs or a steak (often with Malagasy green peppercorn sauce), zebu meat tends to be far healthier than cattle meat elsewhere, because most of the island's meat comes from more-or-less

⊘ VANILLA

Madagascar vies with Indonesia as the world's largest producer of vanilla, a labour-intensive crop that comprises the hand-pollinated and cured seedpods of Vanilla planifolia, a Mexican climbing orchid introduced by plantation owners in the late 19th century.

Within Madagascar, vanilla production is focussed on the northwest, in particular coastal parts of Sava Region, whose climate is ideal for this temperamental plant. Typically, Madagascar produces up to 4,000 tonnes of vanilla annually, twice as much as its nearest rival Indonesia, and around 40 percent of the global yield. However, after the Sava coast was battered by successive cyclones in 2016 and 2017, the Malagasy

crop decreased to such an extent that Indonesia for the first time overtook Madagascar as the world's main producer. The resultant global shortage has also caused the international vanilla price to climb from US$100/kg in 2015 to more than US$600/kg in 2017, making it the world's second most expensive spice, after saffron (though it should be noted that more than 95 percent of 'vanilla' products worldwide are actually flavoured with an artificial substitute called vanillin). The global price hike has yet to trickle down to the beleaguered smallholders who grow most of Madagascar's vanilla and receive as little as US$8/kg for their hard labour.

If a stew is too bland for your taste, it can be spiced up – with caution – by adding a small teaspoon of a local condiment such as sakay (a fiery chilli and ginger paste) or achard (a South Indian-style pickled mango and lemon relish).

free-ranging herds. Pork is also popular outside of Muslim areas (or other coastal areas where pig meat is *fady*) but be alert to the fact that the Malagasy tend to enjoy and serve far fattier cuts than most westerners would ideally opt for. Poultry is also represented on all hotel menus, and many smarter establishments supplement the usual chicken dishes with French specialities such as duck and rabbit.

DRINKS

Tap water is not always safe to drink but still mineral water (and to a lesser extent sparkling) is widely available. Many restaurants sell delicious freshly-squeezed or blended fruit juices, known as jus naturel, though sugar is almost always added unless you specify otherwise. Unusual fruit juices include those made from tamarind and baobab fruits. The usual international fizzy soft drinks are ubiquitous. A refreshing, healthy and inexpensive alternative, especially along the coast, is green coconut milk, which is sold by street vendors who will decapitate the green coconut to create a natural cup from which the juice can be sipped.

Not content with eating rice three times daily, the Malagasy also enjoy drinking it in the form of *ranovola* (also known as *ranonapango*), a tea-like concoction made by hot boiling water to the burnt rice stuck on the inside of a cooking pot. It tastes rather odd, but health-wise it has the advantage over tap water of having been boiled. Ordinary and herbal teas are also widely drunk in Madagascar, often flavoured with spices such as vanilla and ginger. The rather stew-like Malagasy-style coffee served in local eateries is an acquired taste, but larger towns usually have a few proper cafés whose coffee is geared more towards international palates.

Practically synonymous with beer in Madagascar, Three Horses (THB) is an inexpensive medium-strong (5.4 percent alcohol) pale pilsner brewed by Star Breweries at Antsirabe since 1958, and now also produced at a second brewery in Diego Suarez catering mainly to the northern part of the island. Star Breweries also produces the stronger THB Special (6.2 percent) and a very light shandy called THB Fresh. Wine is produced at several small vineyards in the highlands around Fianarantsoa, and can be bought in most supermarkets. In most case, the quality pales by comparison to bottles imported from France and South Africa, which cost about twice as much as local produce.

A selection of rhums arrangés.

⊘ MALAGASY RUM

Appropriately for a former pirate refuge, Madagascar is renowned for its excellent rum. A popular local speciality is *rhum arrangé*, which is basically a bottle of rum wherein a combination of tropical ingredients (most commonly ginger, vanilla, cinnamon and/or various fruits) have been left to soak to make a tasty aperitif or nightcap. Illegal home-brewed palm wine (*trembo*) and sugar cane spirits (*betsabetsa*) are also available but tend to be treacherously strong. It is traditional to throw the first capful of bottle of rum or other spirits into northeast corner of the room as an offering to the ancestral sprits.

Tsingy and deciduous forest tower above the Lac Vert at the Réserve Spéciale d'Ankarana.

LAY OF THE LAND

With its varied terrain and climate patterns, Madagascar is possibly the world's most florally diverse island, supporting at least 10,000 plant species that occur nowhere else.

Lapped by the waters of the Indian Ocean, Madagascar is a large, long and rather narrow island that stretches a full 1,570km (976 miles) from Cap d'Ambre in the north to Cap Sainte Marie in the south, but is nowhere more than 569km (354 miles) wide. Until 160 million years ago, Madagascar was a landlocked component of the supercontinent Gondwanaland, sandwiched between what is now the east coast of Mozambique and west coast of India, but it has been completely isolated from other landmasses for around 90 million years.

Most of the island's bedrock predates the break-up of Gondwanaland. The Precambrian crystalline rocks of the eastern and central regions typically formed between 500 and 1,000 million years ago, while the more recent sedimentary strata of the west were laid down during or after the Carboniferous Era (350–300 million years ago). A scattering of basaltic, rhyolitic and other volcanic intrusions account for Madagascar's immense wealth of sapphires, rubies, emeralds, amethysts and other gemstones.

GEOGRAPHY

In simplistic altitudinal terms, Madagascar can be divided into three longitudinal zones. The wide and gently sloping western coastal belt is separated from Africa by the relatively shallow (up to 3.2km/2 miles) Mozambique Channel. The coastal belt rises gradually towards the central highlands, which run spine-like down the island from north to south, and typically have a tall eastern escarpment. This in turn plunges towards a narrow eastern coastal belt that shelves rather more sharply than its western counterpart.

The terrain tends to be hilly and varied. Major massifs range from the contorted sandstone outcrops of Isalo and weird limestone formations of

Vezo fishing village in the south of Madagascar.

The topography of Madagascar dictates that its longest rivers – the Mangoky (564km/350 miles), Onilahy and Betsiboka (525km/326 miles) – meander towards the west coast, while their east-coast counterparts are shorter and faster flowing.

Tsingy de Bemaraha to the bald granitic protrusions of Andringitra and crater-studded volcanic slopes of Montagne d'Ambre. The most extensive tract of highlands stands in the east-central part of the island, around Antananarivo and Antsirabe. The highest and second highest peaks, however, respectively lie in the far north and south. These

NATIONAL PARKS AND PROTECTED AREAS

An official network of 50-plus national parks, special reserves and other conservation areas collectively protects around 5 percent of Madagascar's surface area.

Administered by Madagascar National Parks (MNP; www.parcs-madagascar.com), Madagascar's extensive network of official protected areas incorporates four strict nature reserves, 23 national parks, 21 special reserves and several lower-status conservancies. It dates back to 1927, when the French set aside half-

A guided visit in the Parc National de l'Isalo.

a-dozen strict nature reserves (most focussed on inaccessible montane or tsingy habitats) for the exclusive purpose of scientific research. During the 1950s, another 17 properties, including Montagne d'Ambre, Ankarana and Marojejy, were accorded official protection. Over the course of the 1990s, several strict nature reserves, then closed to the public, were redesignated as national parks or special reserves in order to develop them for tourism. In 2003, the government identified an additional 92 areas as meriting conservation status. At least 20 have since been set aside as protected areas, a process that ground to a near-halt in the wake of the 2009 political crisis.

With the exception of strict nature reserves, most MNP properties are now open to tourist visits, though some are considerably more accessible and have better amenities than others. In terms of ready accessibility, landscapes and wildlife viewing, the most popular and worthwhile are probably Andasibe-Mantadia, Ranomafana, Ankarana, Isalo and Montagne d'Ambre. At the other end of the scale, the places that hold the most off-the-beaten-track appeal to dedicated hikers and serious wildlife enthusiasts include Andringitra, Marojejy, Masoala and Tsingy de Bemaraha. All MNP properties that are developed for tourism have a choice of official walking circuits, which might range from a few hundred metres/yards in length to taxing multi-day hikes. These options are discussed in the relevant entry in the places chapter.

In contrast to the situation on mainland Africa, most MNP properties can be explored only on foot (the main exception being marine parks geared to snorkellers and divers). It is forbidden to enter any MNP property without an official guide, to walk in it after dark (night walks are now conducted outside the boundaries), or to build lodges inside it (so accommodation servicing any given park usually stands just outside it). All national parks charge a daily entrance fee, as well as fixed guide fees that are determined in conjunction with the local guides association and often depend on the length of walk and degree of skill (specialist bird guides, for instance, often charge more). Almost without exception, all charges are clearly itemised at the park's ticket office, and arrangements can be made on the spot.

In addition to the MNP properties, Madagascar hosts a number of other government-run, community-managed or private conservation areas, notably the admirable community-run Réserve d'Anja (famed for its ring-railed lemurs) and popular Réserve de Berenty (a private initiative set on a sisal plantation). In most cases, these operate a similar basis to MNP properties, charging entrance as well as guide fees, but rates tend to be lower and timings more flexible.

Depending to some extent on seasonal factors, which reserve you are visit, and how far you want to walk, it is advisable to wear solid walking shoes or hiking boots on all walks and hikes, and to carry waterproof gear, drinking water, a snack and possibly a walking stick.

are the 2,876-metre (9,436ft) Pic Maromokotra in the Réserve Naturelle Intégrale de Tsaratanana, and the 2,658-metre (8,720ft) Pic Boby in the Parc National d'Andringitra.

The prevailing southwesterly trade winds ensure that rainfall is highest in the east and north, which receives up to 3,000mm (118in) annually. By contrast, the semi-arid far south-west receives less than 500mm (20in) of rainfall annually. The wettest months islandwide coincide with the monsoon season of December to March, but whereas the west has a highly sea-

families and genera (10 and 260 respectively). Certain emblematic families are particularly well-represented: six of the world's nine bao-babs are endemic to Madagascar, and the island also hosts 170 types of palm (three times as many as mainland Africa) and an astonishing 960 species of flowering orchid. Although the flora of Madagascar is probably most strongly affiliated to Africa, it also possess strong links to Asia, most strikingly in the form of two car-nivorous species of Nepenthes pitcher plant, a genus unknown from Africa.

A typical Madagascar snapshot: baobab trees at sunset, Mandrare River Camp.

sonal rainfall pattern, the east coast and escarp-ment would seldom go more than a few days without some solid precipitation. Madagascar is frequently battered by cyclones, typically along the east coast over the monsoon season, but they might hit any part of the coast at any time of year.

VEGETATION

Madagascar's floral diversity is practically impossible to enumerate. The total number of described plant species stands at more than 11,000, at least 90 percent of which are endemic, and it is thought this number might eventually rise to 20,000 – more than half the tally for mainland Africa. The country is second only to Australia when it comes to endemic plant

Of the world's nine species of baobab, all but three are endemic to Madagascar. Most impressive of these is the splendid Grandidier's baobab Adansonia grandidieri, whose cylindrical smooth-barked trunk can attain a height of 30 metres (100ft).

The varied ecosystems of Madagascar are largely determined by altitude and local rainfall patterns. As might be expected, the well-watered eastern lowlands and highlands are swathed in dense evergreen rainforest, while the more

seasonal northwest coastal belt is dominated by deciduous woodland, and the heavily cultivated central highlands still support pockets of indigenous heath, grassland and forest. By contrast, the semi-arid southwest supports a bizarre cover of spiny forest dominated by the towering octopus trees of the Didiereaceae and various other weird and wonderful xerophytic succulents.

These designations are, of course, rather simplistic. The eastern rainforest, for instance, can be broken up into at least four distinct communities whose composition is determined swamps and lakes. The many rivers that rise in the highlands also play an important role in nurturing diversity, since they form formidable barriers to the spread of more sedentary species. Sadly however, Madagascar's endemic flora is increasingly threatened by human activity, most overtly the clearing of forest and other vegetation to make way for cultivation, but also more insidious threats such as pollution, a decrease in the numbers of pollinators and seed-carrying animals, and the spread of invasive introduced species of acacia, eucalyptus and cactus.

A spiny forest of octopus trees.

largely by altitude and soil type. Inundated coastal sands support a specialised littoral forest of salt-tolerant, cyclone-resistant species. Immediately inland, this intergrades with a more diverse lowland rainforest whose tallest canopy trees stand up to 60 metres (197ft) above the ground. At the 750-metre (2,460ft) contour, lowland forest gives way to a lower-canopied montane forest rich in orchids and other epiphytes, then at around 1,250m/4,100ft) it intergrades into a more stunted mist-swathed cloud forest.

Other factors that have influenced Madagascar's floral abundance include a varied collection of niche habitats, not only the aforementioned mountains and outcrops, but also a wide range of brackish coastal wetlands and freshwater

⊘ OCTOPUS TREES

The most otherworldly of Madagascar's peculiar plants is the 11 octopus tree species of the endemic family Didiereaceae. Dominant in the surreal 'spiny forest' of the south, these tangled and rather untidy trees typically have woody euphorbia-like trunks lined with spine-like arrangements of small deciduous leaves and rows of long narrow protective thorns. Most impressive are the two giant species of the genus Alluaudia, whose skeletal trunks stand up to 20 metres (65 ft) high and totter haphazardly above the main canopy like a forest of misshapen rugby posts – an effect that is especially eerie on a moonlit night walk.

Guide climbing up the roots of a banyan tree inside the Belobaka caves, Boeny region.

Male fossa in the Parc National Andasibe-Mantadia.

MAMMALS

From the puma-like fossa to various hedgehog-, otter- and mole-mimicking tenrecs, Madagascar's non-primate mammal fauna includes some fascinating examples of convergent evolution.

The indigenous terrestrial fauna of Madagascar includes around 210 known mammal species, about 95 percent of which are endemic to the island. This mammal checklist is dominated – both numerically and in terms of impact on tourists – by the lemurs, which are represented by 100-odd species, but it also includes around 10 carnivore, 31 tenrec, 46 bat and 30 rodent species. The island's only known shrew, the near-endemic Madagascan pygmy shrew (*Suncus madagascariensis*) rivals the Etruscan pygmy shrew (*S. etruscus*), which some authorities regard to be conspecific, as the world's smallest mammal measured by mass. The largest non-domestic on Madagascar is the African bushpig (*Potamochoerus larvatus*), an introduced species that has gone feral in some areas and weighs up to 150kg (330lb).

In addition to these terrestrial mammals, the waters off Madagascar are home to 30-plus species of cetacean (whales and dolphins) and the manatee-like dugong (*Dugong dugon*).

CARNIVORA

Represented by 10 living and one extinct species, the endemic family Eupleridae, sometimes referred to as Madagascar carnivores, are all descended from one common ancestral pair of mongoose – or civet-like creatures that rafted over from Africa around 20 million years ago. As is the case with most of their mainland cousins, the Euplerids of Madagascar are all shy and secretive nocturnal hunters seldom seen by visitors unless actively searched for. Of six species of mongoose, the most common and widespread is the ring-tailed vontsira (*Galidia elegans*), which might be seen in

The elusive lowland streaked tenrec.

Madagascar's most recently discovered carnivore, the aquatic and presumably very localised Durrell's vontsira (Salanoia durrelli) was described in 2010 after researchers observed an individual swimming in Lac Alaotra five years earlier.

national parks such as Ranomafana and Montagne d'Ambre, and has a distinctive red coat and black tail rings. More likely to be seen than any mongoose, however, is the fanaloka (*Fossa fossana*), a pretty cat-sized nocturnal often referred to as the Malagasy civet but

RECENT MAMMALIAN EXTINCTIONS

Madagascar's megafauna would be far more diverse today were it not for the extinction of most of the island's bulkiest mammal species over the past two millennia.

Giant lemur skulls, including the Archaeoindris.

A rich and tantalising array of sub-fossils (bones of animals that died too recently for fossilisation) gives some idea of how much more diverse Madagascar's mammalian fauna must have been at the time of its colonisation by humans some 1,500–2,500 years ago, or indeed when the first Europeans landed there in the 16th century. At least 30 endemic species of mammal have become extinct during this comparatively short time span, either as a result of hunting or habitat loss, and a great many were significantly larger than any living survivors.

More than 15 lemur species have been described based solely on sub-fossil evidence, and several must have become extinct within the past 500 years. The gorilla-sized Archaeoindris, the largest mammal ever known to have lived on Madagascar, is one of eight species of giant 'sloth lemur' placed in the extinct family Palaeopropithecidae. Also significantly bulkier than any extant lemurs were the predominantly terrestrial 'monkey lemurs' (family Archaeolemuridae), which filled a baboon-like niche, and the strictly arboreal 'koala-lemurs' (family Megaladapidae), whose elongated nasal region and enlarged upper lip would have given them a rather rhino-like facial appearance. Another extinct creature known only from sub-fossils is the giant aye-aye (*Daubentonia robusta*), which must have been at least twice as heavy as its modern namesake.

The only ungulates ever known to have occurred naturally on Madagascar were hippos (family Hippopotamidae), which probably swam across the Mozambique channel in at least three separate colonisation events, resulting in the evolution of three different species. The hippos of Madagascar were all smaller that the common hippopotamus of mainland Africa, and they evidently lived a more terrestrial lifestyle, probably due to the lack of large predators and bovid competition. The most recent hippo sub-fossils are around 1,000 years old, but oral evidence and folklore suggest that small numbers might have survived until as recently as the 1870s.

Bibymalagasia is a taxonomically enigmatic order of endemic insectivores sometimes referred to as Malagasy aardvarks. Known only from a few sub-fossil skeletal bones, the most recent of which are around 2,000 years old, the Bibymalagasia were initially thought to be related to the African aardvark when first described in 1895, but are probably more closely affiliated to the tenrecs. At least two species have been described, both placed in the genus Plesiorycteropus, and thought to have fed mainly on termites and ants, and to have weighed up to 18kg (40lb).

Among the carnivores of Madagascar, the only recent extinction is the giant fossa Cryptoprocta spelea, which was morphically very similar to the common fossa C. ferox, but significantly larger. The giant fossa has been recognised as a distinct species since 1935, based on sub-fossils found at scattered sites all around the island, and it most likely became extinct at around the same time as the giant lemurs, which presumably formed its main item of prey. However, occasional reports of unusually large individuals do leave room for hope that a small population of giant fossa still survives deep in the island's forests.

closer in appearance to the genets of mainland Africa.

Half-cat, half-dog is the tagline most often applied to the fossa (*Cryptoprocta ferox*), an atypical Euplerid that ranks as Madagascar's largest mammalian carnivore. In truth, this handsome brown creature, complete with retractable claws, looks more like a genet crossed with a puma, and is comparable in size to a lynx or caracal. The fossa is said to be the world's most arboreally agile carnivore, which is hardly surprising given that it feeds mainly

IUCN red list, with a declining island-wide population estimated at 2,500 adults.

TENRECS

Very few visitors to Madagascar are fortunate enough to see a wild representative of the island's most peculiar and ancient mammal lineage. This is the tenrecs, a group of small nocturnal insectivores and omnivores whose ancestors most likely crossed from the African mainland on a raft of floating vegetation some 40 million years ago. Placed in the family

Ring-tailed mongoose, Parc National de Marojejy.

on leaping lemurs, and although mainly nocturnal, it is often active by day, especially during the breeding season. It is too small to pose a serious threat to humans, except perhaps when cornered, which makes its reputation for ferocity among the Malagasy people difficult to explain except as a lingering folk memory of the closely-related but much larger *Cryptoprocta spelea*, which fed mainly on large terrestrial lemurs prior to becoming extinct, and might well have transferred its sights to humans. A notoriously secretive creature of forest interiors, the fossa is unlikely to be seen except in the Réserve Forestière de Kirindy, where a few semi-habituated individuals lurk on the fringes of the camp. It is listed as Vulnerable on the

Tenrecidae, the tenrecs are Madagascar's only terrestrial representatives of the Afrotheria, a superorder that also includes elephants, aardvarks, elephant-shrews, hyraxes and dugongs, and was first proposed in 1998 based on DNA sequence analysis. A total of 34 tenrec species are recognised, with all but three being endemic to Madagascar (the exceptions are a trio of localised otter-shrew species endemic to equatorial Africa).

Even more so than lemurs, tenrecs have evolved to fill a remarkable variety of ecological niches, as borne out by their descriptive common names. The aquatic web-footed tenrec (*Limnogale mergulus*) leads an otter-like lifestyle, foraging for prey in mountain

streams, while the mole-like rice tenrec (*Oryzorictes hova*) spends much of its time in self-dug burrows, and the spiky-coated greater hedgehog tenrec (*Setifer setosus*) and lesser hedgehog tenrec (*Echinops telfairi*) both bear a strong resemblance to their namesakes, and roll themselves into a tight defensive ball when threatened. The most diverse genus is the shrew tenrecs (*Microgale spp*), rather mouse-like forest-floor creatures represented by 22 recognised species, eight of which were described since 1990. Most tenrecs have a

as well as the giant jumping rat (*Hypogeomys antimena*), a nocturnal rabbit-sized creature that lives in burrows, can leap almost 1 metre (3ft) in the air, and has a tiny range focussed on the Réserve Forestière de Kirindy north of Morondava. Far more conspicuous than any indigenous rodent are three introduced species – the black rat *Rattus rattus*, brown rat *R. norvegicus* and house mouse *Mus musculus* – that represent something of an ecological problem in certain urban areas.

Madagascar is home to 36 endemic and 10

Lesser hedgehog tenrec in the spiny forest.

The rabbit-sized giant jumping rat.

rather localised distribution, but not so the tailless tenrec (*Tenrec ecaudatus*), which is the family's largest species, weighing up to 2.5kg (5.5lb), occurs throughout the island, and has also been introduced to Mauritius (where it is eaten as bush meat), Réunion, Comoros and the Seychelles.

BATS AND RODENTS

The world's most cosmopolitan mammalian orders, the Rodentia (rodents) and Chiroptera (bats) are both well represented on Madagascar. The island's indigenous rodents are placed in the endemic subfamily Nesomyinae, which includes around 30 small, inconspicuous and unremarkable mouse-like species

other indigenous bat species, split across 22 genera and 8 families of African or Asian origin. Most impressive and conspicuous among these is the Madagascar flying fox (*Pteropus rufus*), a frugivore that has a wingspan of up to 125cm (50in) and is likely to be seen flying overhead at dusk anywhere on the island, but might also be observed by day in large and noisy communal treetop roosts. Two other megabats often encountered on the island are the Madagascar fruit bat (*Eidolon dupreanum*) and Madagascar rousette (*Rousettus madagascariensis*), both of which are more localised and somewhat smaller than the flying fox. Most other bats on Madagascar are small cave- or crevice-dwellers, and difficult to tell apart.

Madagascar flying fox hanging about in the Réserve Privée de Bérenty.

Verreaux's sifaka in the spiny
forest, Mandrare River Camp.

LEMURS

Lively, engaging and ceaselessly entertaining, the lemurs of Madagascar are not only a major draw for wildlife enthusiasts but also constitute the second-largest primate diversity of any country on earth.

Descendants, in all probability, of one pair of bushbaby-like pioneers who unwittingly rafted across the Indian Ocean on floating vegetation at least 30 million years ago, the lemurs rank as the most charismatic of Malagasy endemics, with their soft round eyes, beautifully marked woolly coats, impossibly gentle and delicate fingers, and a trademark aura of equanimity that should put most so-called higher primates to shame. Lemurs tend to be the most conspicuous mammalian inhabitants of all the island's rainforests, spiny forests and other uncultivated habitats, and a full 101 species are recognised, placing Madagascar second only to Brazil (114 species) when it comes to primate diversity, and far ahead of the next closest rival Indonesia (44 species).

Most lemur species have limited ranges defined by natural obstacles such as rivers, mountains or gaps in the forest cover. Populations have been further reduced by deforestation and hunting since humans first settled Madagascar around 2,000 years ago. Indeed, sub-fossil remains indicate that at least three families and 30 species of lemur have become extinct in this short space of time. Of the five extant lemur families, the Cheirogaleidae (five genera, at least 34 species), Lepilemuridae (one genus, at least 26 species) and Daubentoniidae (one genus, one living species) are comprised entirely of nocturnals, while the Indriidae (three genera, at least 19 species) and Lemuridae (give genera, at least 21 species) contain a mix of nocturnal and more conspicuous and generally larger diurnal species.

The prognosis for most living lemur species is less than glowing. A full 73 species are IUCN red-listed as endangered or critically endangered, and another 25 are regarded to be

An inquisitive ring-tailed lemur.

vulnerable, near threatened or data deficient. By contrast, only three species – the nocturnal and widespread fat-tailed dwarf lemur (Cheirogaleus medius), reddish-grey mouse lemur (Microcebus griseorufus) and grey mouse lemur (Microcebus murinus) – are accorded 'least concern' status. Furthermore, the most recent edition of the IUCN Primate Specialist Group's list of the World's 25 Most Endangered Primates includes six of Madagascar's lemurs. Most immediately threatened among these are probably the silky sifaka (Propithecus candidus), northern sportive lemur (Lepilemur septentrionalis) and blue-eyed black lemur (Eulemur flavifrons) – in all cases with populations that might have dropped below the 500 mark.

TRUE LEMURS

Wherever you travel in Madagascar, the most conspicuous lemurs tend to be whichever diurnal representatives of the Indriidae and Lemuridae occur locally. These include a dozen species of so-called 'true lemur' (*Eulemur spp*), most of which are medium-sized and mousy-brown in colour, with non-prehensile tails as long or longer than the body, weaselly snouts and some tufting on the cheeks or crown. Almost exclusively arboreal, the true lemurs can leap long distances between trees and they are unusually mobile on the ground, running on all four legs with a rather cat-like gait.

True lemurs tend to be very sociable, and tend to display strong dimorphism in colouration, most strikingly in the case of the black lemur (*E. macaco*) and closely allied blue-eyed black lemur (*E. flavifrons*), where the jet black male contrasts with the light brown, white-tufted female. Most true lemurs have their main population centre in the north, where the common brown lemur (*E. fulvus*) is the most widespread species. The red-fronted brown lemur (*E.

A sociable golden-crowned sifaka.

⊘ LEMUR BEHAVIOUR

Nocturnal lemurs, almost without exception, move alone or in pairs, but most diurnal species are highly sociable, typically living in tightly bonded troops of up to 15 related individuals. Unusually among primates, most lemur species have female-dominated social structures. Indeed, dominant females often display significant aggression towards males, particularly when feeding, and almost invariably the response will be submissive.

Lemurs are highly tactile, using both mouth and hands to groom each other when greeting, waking up, resting or making sexual advances, an activity that plays an important role in easing intra-troop tensions and reinforcing relationships. The most explosive and memorable of lemur vocalisations is the booming banshee wail of the indri, but other diurnal species generally possess an extensive repertoire of alarm calls, and maintain intra-troop communications with sporadic soft chatterings that might easily be mistaken for birdcalls.

Most lemur species also make extensive use of scent-marking to demarcate territorial boundaries, and to communicate information about sex and reproductive status during brief reproductive seasons that are timed to make the most of seasonal availability of food and other resources.

rufifrons) is the most common member of the genus in the south.

SIFAKAS

Ranking among the most gorgeous and charismatic of all lemurs, sifakas (*Propithecus spp*) are also larger than any other extant species, bar the closely affiliated indri. With their bold coat patterns, silky fur and long narrow tails, sifakas are superficially reminiscent of the colobus monkeys of mainland Africa, especially when troops sit upright in the canopy foraging

> *Since 1990, the lemur species count has trebled from 32 to 101, largely due to new research in remote areas and to DNA studies of cryptic genera. However, it also reflects a trend towards splitting taxa formerly treated as subspecies.*

on leaves. Until recently, only two species were recognised, the diademed sifaka (*P. diadema*) of the eastern mountains and Verreaux's sifaka (*P. verreauxi*) of the west and south, but these have now been split into four and five species respectively, most of them with very limited ranges. The various species differ most obviously in their coat patterns, which range from the all-white silky sifaka (*P. candidus*) to the all-black Perrier's sifaka (*P. perrieri*) but are mostly a combine black, white and gold to striking effect.

All sifakas have shortish forelimbs and long powerful hind legs, an unusual body designed to facilitate a unique vertical 'clinging and leaping' mode of arboreal locomotion. Rainforest species typically avoid descending to the ground almost as avidly as humans do climbing trees. However, species living in more arid climates – most strikingly, Verreaux's sifaka of the spiny forests of the southwest, and Von der Decken's sifaka (P. deckenii) of the Tsingy de Bemaraha – are forced to makes regular forays to the ground. Here, instead of walking or crawling, they performs a spectacularly comical dance, bouncing upright between the trees like a furry flamenco dancer, with head facing forward, body flipped sideways, arms flouncing aloft, and heels clicking in the air.

OTHER DIURNAL LEMURS

Madagascar's largest living lemur, the strictly arboreal indri (Indri indri; see page 92), most easily seen in and around the Parc National Andasibe-Mantadia, looks like the progeny of a tailless colobus monkey and a panda, while its far-carrying eerie call conjures up images of helium-snorting whales flirting with a rusty hinge.

Among the largest and most handsome of lemurs, the black-and-white ruffed lemur (Varecia variegata) and red ruffed lemur (V. rubra) are both characterised by their gentle disposi-

Black-and-white ruffed lemur.

tion, sociable nature and striking yellow eyes, but have a very limited distribution and are listed as critically endangered. The red ruffed lemur, easily distinguished by its predominantly chestnut-red coat offset by black face, black tail and white skull patch, is essentially restricted to the Masoala Peninsula. The black-and-white ruffed lemur, split into three subspecies, inhabits the montane forest of the northeast as well as the island of Nosy Mangabe.

Bamboo lemurs, represented by five relatively small Hapalemur species as well as the rather hefty greater bamboo lemur (*Prolemur simus*), are rather nondescript diurnal primates that feed mainly on bamboo shoots and roots, and are most likely to be seen in the vicinity of it. The

greater bamboo lemur is a critically endangered species that was actually thought to be extinct prior to the discovery in 1986 of a remnant population now protected in the Parc National de Ranomafana, where groups of up to 20 are regularly spotted by hikers.

A charmer of note, the ring-tailed lemur (Lemur catta) was the first lemur species known to western scientists, and the second part if its Latin binomial, coined in 1758, refers to its long cat-like (or more accurately genet-like) tail. The most terrestrial and habitat tolerant lemur, and highly sociable, it looks and behaves rather like a vervet monkey, and is readily distinguished by its grizzled grey coat, white face, banded tail, inquisitive foxy face, and scampering disposition. A characteristic of this endearing species is a predilection for sunbathing on rocks or on the ground with arms half-raised as if supported by an invisible side-rest. Known locally as the maki, it is widely distributed and common in southern Madagascar, where it is most often associated with relatively arid habitats such as spiny and deciduous forest and rocky slopes.

Eastern lesser bamboo lemur.

The weird-and-wonderful aye-aye, feeding on a coconut.

⊘ THE ENIGMATIC AYE-AYE

The most anatomically deviant of lemurs, the nocturnal aye-aye (*Daubentonia madagascariensis*) was initially classified as a rodent on account of its squirrelly tail, scraggly coarse fur, unusual ear-bone structure, and rat-like incisors that grow throughout its life. It is now unambiguously recognised as a primate, but its relation to other lemurs remains conjectural. According to recent molecular analysis, the Daubentoniidae – the family of which the aye-aye is the sole living representative – is basal to all other lemur families. Yet based solely on morphic grounds, many primatologists believe it to be the last relict of a separate prosimian colonisation event.

However you classify it, this large and elusive oddball ranks among the world's weirdest creatures. As indicated by its bat-like ears, it is the only primate to use echolocation, while its long skeletal middle finger is designed to extract wood-boring larvae from dead branches. Thanks to its somewhat diabolical appearance, the aye-aye is persecuted by locals as a harbinger of death. IUCN-listed as endangered and once feared to be extinct, it was rediscovered in 1957, and is now known to be among the most widely distributed of lemurs. The best places to see it are the Île au Coq on the Pangalanes, Aye-Aye Island near Mananara, and the Kianjavato Research Station near Ranomafana.

NOCTURNAL LEMURS

Around 70 percent of Madagascar's lemur species are entirely or primarily active by night. The largest and most widespread of these nocturnal foragers is the bizarre aye-aye (*Daubentonia madagascariensis*), an elusive forest-dweller so peculiar and distinctive it is placed in the monospecific family Daubentoniidae (see page 94). All other nocturnal lemurs are small or medium in size, rather nondescript in colour with uniform grey, grey-brown or brown coats, and possess large round eyes that enhance their night vision and

Among the most easily distinguished of nocturnal lemurs, the fork-marked lemurs (Phaner spp) all of possess a vertical black spinal stripe that forks behind the neck. Some also have bold black face markings.

24 species countrywide. All are tiny and tend to creep mouse-like along tree branches, but Madame Berthe's mouse lemur (*M. berthae*), which

Female black lemur, Palmarium Reserve.

further their resemblance to the prosimian bushbabies of the African mainland. A large number of new species have been recognised in most of the main nocturnal genera in recent years, which might theoretically create room for confusion when it come to visual identification, except that most locations host only one species in any given genus, and local guides will usually know which it is. Unsurprisingly, nocturnal lemurs are most likely to be seen on guided night walks, but in some locations, the guides are skilled individuals roosting in regularly used sites by day. Many species are very vocal, emitting an array of shrieks and squeals, especially in the breeding season.

The smallest nocturnal lemurs are the mouse lemurs of the genus Microcebus, which comprises

was discovered in the Réserve Forestière de Kirindy in 1992 and described in 2000, has the distinction of being the world's smallest primate, with a body length of up to 10cm (4in). Not much larger are the so-called giant mouse lemurs of the genus Mirza (2 species), the dwarf lemurs of the genera Allocebus (1 species) and Cheirogaleus (7 species) and the more boldly-patterned fork-marked lemurs of the genus Phaner (4 species). Similar in size but given more to leaping between trees than to crawling along branches are the aptly-named sportive lemurs of the genus Lepilemur (24 species). Slightly larger than other nocturnal lemurs, and with an upright posture that betrays their closer affinity to the sifakas and the indri, are the nine woolly lemur species of the genus Avahi.

📷 LEMUR DIVERSITY

The poster boys for Madagascar's diverse and unique wildlife, lemurs are a charismatic group of predominantly arboreal primates represented by at least 100 species split across five families and 15 genera, all of which are endemic to the island.

Accounting for roughly 15 percent of the world's primate species, the lemurs of Madagascar also represent the most significant example of island-bound radial evolution among mammals, ranging in size from the 30g (1.1oz) Madame Berthe's mouse-lemur (the world's smallest primate) to the gorilla-sized and recently extinct Archaeoindris, and embracing a wide diversity of adaptations to ecological niches filled elsewhere in the world by non-primates. The main reason for this diversity probably boils down to the lemur's lack of terrestrial mobility (most species are either strictly arboreal or rather clumsy on the ground) and inability to swim, leap or stone-hop across the many wide rivers that incise the Malagasy landscape, a scenario that has created a large number of forest pockets sufficiently isolated from each other to encourage speciation. As a result, many lemur species have very restricted ranges, and are highly vulnerable to habitat loss – indeed, more than more than 70 lemur species now appear on the IUCN Red List as endangered or critically endangered, and several more are categorised as vulnerable.

The most terrestrial and monkey-like of extant lemurs, the ring-tailed lemur (Lemur catta) – the Malagasy equivalent of the mainland vervet monkey – is easily distinguished by its long ringed tail and foxy face.

The quirky aye-aye (Daubentonia madagascariensis) fills a woodpecker-like niche, using echolocation and an elongated middle finger to retrieve wood-boring grubs from trees.

Named for their small size, the diminutive and strictly nocturnal mouse lemurs (Microcebus spp) are also rather mouse-like in their colouration and manner of running along branches.

Closest in appearance and habit to their bushbaby-like ancestors, the sportive lemurs (Lepilemur spp) are strictly nocturnal feeders often seen resting in holes in tree trunks by day.

Lemur evolution

Lemurs are classified as prosimians, a group of primates which, as their name suggests, came into being long before monkeys, apes and humans (collectively known as simians) and is traditionally regarded to be more primitive than them. However, the lemurs of Madagascar are not actually thought to be ancestral to humans or other simians, as is often claimed, but would have evolved independently from a long-extinct common prosimian ancestor. Astonishingly, DNA testing and morphological comparisons suggests that the island's modern diversity of lemurs is the result of one single random colonisation event – most likely a pair or group of animals that inadvertently crossed from the African mainland on a temporary islet of floating vegetation around 30 million years ago, when the Mozambique Channel was somewhat narrower than it is today, and currents would have been more favourable to such a voyage. These pioneers probably bore a close resemblance to the modern-day bushbabies, a group of small African nocturnal prosimians that has diversified less than the lemurs, largely as a result of competition with monkeys and apes.

The largest extant lemur, the Indri (Indri indri) is also the only tailless species, and the most vocal, with a call that can sometime be heard 3km (2 miles) distant.

The most glamorous of the lemurs, sifakas (Propithecus spp) cannot walk in the conventional sense, but cover short distance on the ground by hopping sideways with arms held aloft – a clumsy but rather beautiful action often referred to as dancing.

Helmet vanga nesting in the Parc National de Masoala.

BIRDLIFE

A long list of weird and wonderful endemic species makes Madagascar a unique and spectacularly rewarding destination for specialist birdwatchers.

Madagascar ranks among the world's most alluring ornithological destinations. True, the national checklist of almost 290 species is relatively modest for a tropical island of its considerable size. Furthermore, by comparison to most parts of mainland Africa, Madagascar's birdlife seems to maintain a strangely low profile, partly because most species are unusually silent. Amply compensating for these caveats, however, is the island's unusually high level of endemicity, which embraces at least four families, 36 genera and 105 species found nowhere else in the world, along with another two families and 20 species shared only with the islands of the Comoros or Seychelles.

The most diverse of those bird families endemic to Madagascar and nearby islands is the Vangidae, represented by 22 species in 16 genera, 10 of which are monotypic. At the opposite end of the spectrum, the cuckoo-roller (*Leptosomus discolor*) is the only species in the Leptosomidae, a non-passerine family so distinct from any other that some taxonomists think it should be placed in its own order Leptosomatiformes. Displaying strong sexual dimorphism (the male is grey-blue, the female speckled rusty-brown), this top-heavy medium-large bird is named for the stunning aerial displays it performs above the forest canopy, accompanied by a loud and distinctive three-part call.

The other four endemic families are the tiny but iridescently colourful asities and sunbird-asities of the Eurylaimidae (four species), the spectacularly marked but secretive ground-rollers of the Brachypteraciidae (six species), the primitive-looking ground-dwelling mesites of the Mesitornithidae (three species) and the rather more nondescript warbler- and greenbul-like small

The yellow-bellied asity feeds mainly on fruit.

Only in 2010, based on DNA testing, was the Bernieridae formally recognised as a cohesive family endemic to Madagascar. Prior to that, its 11 species were variously regarded to be warblers, babblers or bulbuls on morphological grounds.

birds of the Bernieridae (11 species). Two other endemic genera are of particular interest to visitors. The vasa parrots (*Coracopsis spp*), represented by only two species, are bulky white-billed, black-feathered parrots often seen and heard flying above the forest canopy. The ten species of coua (*Coua spp*) are large and rather colourful

ground- and tree-dwellers most closely related to the cuckoos but also rather similar in appearance and habits to the turacos of mainland Africa.

SEASHORE AND WETLANDS

Around 110 bird species recorded on of offshore of Madagascar could be classified as marine or aquatic species. A high proportion of these are seasonal migrants or oceanic wanderers and a relatively low number are endemic to the island. Most marine species are rather gull- or tern-like in appearance and many are likely to be seen only on offshore boat trips. Notable exceptions include the spectacular red-tailed tropicbird (*Phaethon rubricauda*), large numbers of which roost colonially on the island of Nosy Ve, near Toliara, and the related white-tailed tropicbird (*Phaethon lepturus*), which is often seen soaring above the cliffs of Cap Mine near Diego Suarez. Other striking marine birds include the long-billed greater and lesser frigatebirds (*Fregata spp*) and seldom seen albatrosses (*Diomedea spp*).

Probably the most characteristic birds of Madagascar's inland waters are the herons,

Humblot heron and his entourage in the Parc National d'Ankarafantsika.

⊘ VASA PARROTS

Outwardly frumpish with their uniform off-black feathering and seasonal baldness, the vasa possesses possibly the keenest sex drive in the avian world. Unusually, the female is larger than the male, and sexually dominant, distributing her favours among a modestly-sized harem of eager courtiers. No less unusual is the male's 2–3cm (1in) long erectable hemipenis – a cloacal adaptation common in reptiles but unique among birds – or that vasa intercourse, far from being the usual brisk and cheerless avian affair, endures for up to an hour, frequently attracting an excited flock of voyeurs and hopefuls.

bitterns and egrets of the family Ardeidae. The largest and most eagerly sought of these is the 1.1 metres (3.6ft) tall Humblot's heron (*Ardea humbloti*), an endangered near-endemic with a total population of around 750 breeding pairs centred on Madagascar, though it is occasionally recorded as a vagrant on the Comoro Islands. Far more common however are the familiar grey heron (*A. cinerea*), the lovely purple heron (*A. purpurea*), dainty striated heron (*Butorides striata*) and various all-white or all-black egrets (*Egretta spp*). Other relatively common aquatic birds include the hammer-headed hamerkop (*Scopus umbretta*), greater and lesser flamingo (*Phoenicoparrus spp*), white-faced whistling duck (*Dendrocygna viduata*), knob-billed duck

(*Sarkidiornis melanotos*), common moorhen (*Gallinula chloropus*), and a subset of the resident and migrant waders associated with mainland Africa, the latter usually seen in non-breeding plumage.

Endemic water birds, most of them uncommon and/or very localised, and many listed and critically endangered, include the Madagascar Sacred Ibis (*Threskiornis bernieri*), Bernier's teal (*Anas bernieri*), Meller's duck (*Anas melleri*), white-throated rail (*Dryolimnas cuvieri*), Madagascar rail (*Rallus madagascariensis*), Madagascar flufftail (*Sarothrura insularis*), Madagascar Jacana (*Actophilornis albinucha*), Madagascar snipe (*Gallinago macrodactyla*) and Madagascar plover (*Charadrius thoracicus*). The Alaotra grebe (*Tachybaptus rufolavatus*) is an endemic waterfowl last observed on Lake Alaotra in 1985 and declared extinct in 2010. By contrast, the endemic Madagascar kingfisher (*Corythornis vintsioides*) is a small gem-like bird likely to be seen hawking from low fringing vegetation alongside almost any freshwater body.

BIRDS OF PREY

Of 17 recorded raptor species, nine are endemic to Madagascar and two are otherwise only known from nearby islands such as Réunion or the Comoros. Most conspicuous among these is the Madagascar kestrel (*Falco newtoni*), a dashing small falcon-like bird that comes in two colour morphs, one with black-on-white speckled underparts and the other (less common) with bright rufous chest and belly. Widespread and common except in forest interiors, this habitat-tolerant kestrel is often seen perching openly on bare trees and telephone lines. The much larger peregrine falcon (*F. peregrinus*) is resident but uncommon, and most likely to be seen in the vicinity of the cliffs and rocky outcrops where it breeds, while the migrant dark grey sooty falcon (*F. concolor*) and striking chestnut-bellied Eleonora's falcon (*F. eleonorae*) are common summer visitors from Africa.

Several endemic raptors are primarily associated with forest fringes and interiors. The Madagascar serpent-eagle (*Eutriorchis astur*) is the largest, most localised and rarest of these, listed as endangered and confined to a few specific rainforest pockets in the east. Less bulky and more widespread forest raptors include Henst's goshawk's (*Accipiter henstii*), Madagascar sparrowhawk (*A. madagascariensis*) and the much smaller and more streamlined Frances's sparrowhawk (*A.*

francesiae) and banded kestrel (*Falco zoniventris*).

Three large raptors are associated with more open country. The Réunion harrier (*Circus maillardi*) is a distinctive slender-tailed and predominantly black bird usually seen flying a few metres above the ground with slow, deliberate wing flaps as it scans for prey. The Madagascar buzzard (*Buteo brachypterus*) is a typical old world buzzard with a variable brown and white plumage. The spectacular Madagascar harrier-hawk (*Polyboroides radiatus*) is a habitat-tolerant grey, black and white raptor with a striking bare yellow face

Madagascar fish eagle taking flight, Nosy Be.

The black egret (*Egretta ardesiaca*) is also known as the umbrella bird on account of its unusual foraging technique, which entails holding both wings out to form a curving canopy and create a patch of shade to attract fish.

mask and uniquely modified inter-tarsal joints that allows it to flex its leg in both directions as it climbs trees and extracts nestling birds – its favoured prey – from crevices and other holes.

The largest and most eagerly sought of the island's raptors is the Madagascar fish eagle (*Haliaeetus vociferoides*), which has a body length

of up to 80cm (31ins) and is known for its thrilling vocalisations (a duet reminiscent of the related African fish eagle). Associated with tree-lined open waters in the northeast of Madagascar, this magnificent bird is now listed as critically endangered, with a global population estimated at between 40 and 100 pairs.

Madagascar is home to four endemic and two more cosmopolitan species of owl, all of which are nocturnal and most likely to be located by call. These range from the buzzard-sized Madagascar long-eared owl to the tiny Madagascar scops owl

to be located by call. Four of the five extant species, including the brilliantly colourful pitta-like ground-roller (*Atelornis pittoides*), have a range confined to the forests of eastern Madagascar.

A number of other unusual birds are mainly associated with forest habitats. One such is the Madagascar crested ibis (*Lophotibis cristata*), a large forest-dweller easily recognised by its long decurved bill, chestnut-brown feathering offset by bold white wings, bare red face and wild glossy green and white head crest. The Madagascar pygmy kingfisher (*Corythornis madagascariensis*)

The tiny Madagascar scops owl.

(*Otus rutilus*). The rarest species is the red owl (*Tyto soumagnei*), a northeastern forest endemic that rather resembles an orange-washed variation of the familiar barn owl (*T. alba*), which is also present on Madagascar.

FORESTS

The moist rainforests that cover much of eastern and northern Madagascar are probably the island's most rewarding habitat in terms of avian diversity. It is a particularly important stronghold for the ground-rollers, an endemic family of medium-large near-passerines related to the kingfishers, bee-eaters and rollers. Shy and highly terrestrial birds that stick to forest interiors, they nest in holes in the ground and are most likely

is a diminutive orange-and-white insectivore usually seen perching unobtrusively in the mid-strata of the forest interior. The island's two species of sunbird-asity (*Neodrepanis spp*) both have bright blue-and-yellow feathering, large iridescent caruncles around the eye, and long decurved for feeding on nectar.

Many other forest birds are essentially Malagasy variations on common African or Asian species, a list that includes the pretty Madagascar green pigeon (*Treron australis*), confiding Madagascar magpie-robin (*Copsychus albospecularis*), iridescent Madagascar green sunbird (*Cinnyris notatus*) and utterly gorgeous Madagascar paradise flycatcher (*Terpsiphone mutata*) with its long orange or white tail.

A good location to look for forest birds is the Parc National Andasibe-Mantadia, which hosts all four of the forest-associated ground-rollers, has plenty of experienced local guides, and forms a popular goal for a one- or two-night excursion from Antananarivo. Equally worthwhile is the Parc National de Ranomafana, which hosts a similar range of species to Mantadia. Even more rewarding, but a lot less accessible, is the vast Parc National de Masoala, which also forms a stronghold for the iconic helmet vanga (*Euryceros prevostii*), the highly localised Bernier's vanga (*Oriolia bernieri*) and the distinctive red-breasted coua (*Coua serriana*).

OTHER HABITATS

Almost as rewarding to visiting birdwatchers as the moist rainforests of the north and east and the more arid succulent-dominated spiny forests of the southwest around Toliara. This is the stronghold for several very localised dry-country endemics, most of which are rather more easy to locate than their rainforest counterparts. Four species of largely terrestrial

The Madagascar pygmy kingfisher is a likely encounter.

⊘ A DIVERSITY OF VANGAS

Like a colourful Malagasy variation on Darwin's finches, the 22 species of the near-endemic Vangidae represent a classic example of island-bound adaptive radiation. Evolved from a single founding population of shrike-like passerines from mainland Africa, the family is now so morphically diverse that some of its 16 genera were recognised as vangas only as a result of recent DNA analysis. Conservative species such as the stunning blue vanga (*Cyanolanius madagascarinus*) and hook-billed vanga (*Vanga curvirostris*) retain a shrike-like appearance and stance. More extreme are the helmet vanga (*Euryceros prevostii*), a breathtaking rainforest dweller with the beak of a nascent toucan, and the sickle-billed vanga (*Falculea palliata*), whose long decurved bill allows it to fill a woodpecker-like niche. By contrast, the four species of the genus Newtonia are so warbler-like they were classified with the Sylviidae (Old World warblers) until as recently as 2001. Other recent additions are the tylas (*Tylas eduardi*), Crossley's vanga (*Mystacornis crossleyi*) and Ward's flycatcher-vanga (*Pseudobias wardi*), which were respectively lumped with the greenbuls, babblers and old-word flycatchers. The only extralimital family member is the Comoro blue vanga (*Cyanolanius cormorensis*), a Cormoran endemic once treated as a subspecies of its Madagascar namesake.

coua, including the magnificent 60cm (2ft) giant coua (*Coua gigas*), are more-or-less confined to the southwest. Other regional specials include subdesert mesite (*Monias benschi*), Madagascar sandgrouse (*Pterocles personatus*), thamnornis-warbler (*Thamnornis chloropetoides*), subdesert brush warbler (*Nesillas lantzii*), red-shouldered vanga (*Calicalicus rufocarpalis*) and the quirky long-tailed ground-roller (*Uratelornis chimaera*).

Although much of Madagascar is now covered in grassland, lightly wooded savannah, cultivation and exotic plantation forest, these habitats tend to support a limited avifauna. However, certain more tolerant species thrive in these artificial habitats, among them the devastatingly beautiful green-and-red Madagascar bee-eater (*Merops superciliosus*), the equally striking long-crested Madagascar hoopoe (*Upupa marginata*) and the convivially chatty Madagascar bulbul (*Hypsipetes madagascariensis*). Other variation-on-a-theme endemics instantly recognisable to most European visitors are the Madagascar stonechat (*Saxicola sibilla*), Madagascar wagtail (*Motacilla flaviventris*) and Madagascar lark (*Eremopterix hova*).

A pair of Madagascar hoopoe in the Parc National de l'Isalo.

ⵔ ELEPHANT BIRDS

The largest feathered creature ever to roam the earth was probably the elephant bird (family Aepyornithidae), a flightless ratite endemic to Madagascar. Standing more than 3 metres (10ft) high, this massive bird was twice as bulky as an ostrich, weighing in at 400kg (880lb), though DNA evidence suggests it was more closely related to the kiwi of New Zealand. The egg of the elephant bird was the largest single cell found in nature, weighing around 10kg (22lb) – sufficient, in chicken terms, to make a two-egg omelette for almost 100 people. Several intact elephant bird eggs have been discovered, most now on display in overseas museums such as the Denver Museum of Nature and Science in Colorado and the Grant Museum of Zoology at London University. However, most specimens on display within Madagascar have been pasted together from arbitrary pieces found on the beaches of the south. The elephant bird still roamed the island in the mid-17th century, when Governor Étienne de Flacourt of Fort Dauphin wrote of an ostrich-like bird called the vouropatra. It almost certainly became extinct as a result of human activity, though it's an open question whether the main contributing factor was direct hunting, the collection of eggs as food, or the spread of introduced diseases via imported poultry.

An egg of the extinct elephant bird is on display at the Musée Cedratom in Toliara.

Now you see me, now you don't:
a perfectly camouflaged mossy
leaf-tailed gecko in the Réserve
Spéciale d'Analamazaotra.

REPTILES AND AMPHIBIANS

Madagascar supports a staggering diversity of reptiles and amphibians, with around 700 species described, more than 90 percent of which are endemic to the island.

Far more conspicuous here than on most parts of the African mainland, Madagascar's reptiles are represented by almost 400 known species of lizards, snake, chelonid and crocodile, though it seems likely that many more still await discovery. No less diverse is the island's amphibian fauna, which comprises around 310 described frog species, and another 200 first identified since the turn of the millennium though a laboratory process known as DNA barcoding. Astonishingly, this means that considerably more than 5 percent of the world's 7,000-odd amphibian species are endemic to an island that accounts for less than 0.5 percent of its surface area.

CROCODILES AND SNAKES

The only reptile that represents a genuine threat to humans, the Madagascar crocodile (*Crocodylus niloticus madagascariensis*) is a subspecies of the Nile crocodile that most likely colonised the island following the extinction of an endemic crocodilian *Voay robustus* a few thousand years ago. The world's second-largest crocodile, this rapacious creature can attain a length of 6 metres (20ft) and it inhabits many lakes and other freshwater bodies islandwide.

One of the pleasures of exploring the rainforests of Madagascar is the knowledge that none of the island's 80-odd species of snake is sufficiently venomous to pose a threat to people. The island's largest snakes are the three species of boa of the endemic subfamily Sanziniinae, all of which grow to around 2–3 metres (6–10ft) in length, have rich and cryptically marked coats, and kill their prey by constriction rather than envenomation.

Tomato frog in the Parc National Andasibe-Mantadia.

Other distinctive and commonly observed snakes include the back-fanged giant hognose (*Leioheterodon madagascariensis*), which has a distinctive black and yellow scale pattern and grows up to 1.5m (5ft) long, and the nocturnal cat-eyed snakes (*Madagascarophis colubrinus*), which are quick to bite but only mildly venomous, and are named after their vertical eye pupils.

LIZARDS

The island's most diverse reptile group, lizards are represented by at least 210 species, a checklist that is rapidly growing as a result of fresh fieldwork in remote areas as well as improved DNA analysis. Madagascar is

renowned as an important centre of chameleon diversity, with almost half of the world's 200-odd species being endemic to it. Chameleons are likely to be seen on most guided day or night walks in the forests, and it's the giants and extroverts that tend to garner the most attention. The heavyweight Oustalet's chameleon (*Furcifer oustaleti*) and Parson's chameleons (*Calumma parsonii*) both regularly attain a body length of 60cm (2ft), thus vying with each other for the title of world's largest chameleon, while the breeding male

Giraffe-necked weevil.

of the slightly smaller panther chameleon (*Furcifer pardalis*) takes the gong when it comes to uninhibited gaudiness. No less fascinating, however, is the island's array of smaller and more unobtrusive species, and they don't come any smaller or obtuse than the inch-long *Brookesia micra*, an astonishing miniature that could set up a commune in a matchbox if it so chose, but more normally inhabits leaf litter on the offshore island of Nosy Hara.

Less familiar than chameleons, the leaf-tailed geckos of the endemic genus *Uroplatus* are equally bizarre, with their wide eyes, large colourfully-lined mouths, delicate fingers and spatulate tails. The most remarkable aspect of these nocturnal forest-dwelling lizards is their capacity to render themselves near invisible to diurnal predators such as the rapacious cuckoo-roller, as well as all but the most attuned of human eyes. By day, these peculiar geckos rest motionless on tree trunks with their head facing the ground and body flattened, while their elaborately mottled scaling, enhanced by subtle colour changes, provides an almost perfect camouflage against the bark. The giant leaf-tailed gecko is the largest of 14 described species, frequently attaining a length of 30cm (1ft), and reputedly possessing more teeth than any other living creature. When it comes to masterful disguise, however, the mossy leaf-tailed gecko is truly extraordinary, with its lichen-like green, grey and brown scaling, and frilled

⊙ OUTRAGEOUS INSECTS

Madagascar's insects certainly are a weird and wonderful lot.

There are giant stick insects (*Phasmatodea*) so perfectly camouflaged that you can stare at a bare tree for five minutes and still not distinguish the odd twig out.

There's the spectacular comet moth (*Argema mittrei*), named for the finger-length orb-tipped pennants that trail behind its thrush-sized wings, and Morgan's sphinx moth (*Xanthopan morganii*), whose foot-long tongue is the longest relative to body size of any known animal.

For those who prefer their creepy-crawlies to be a

touch more freakish, there is the Madagascar hisser (*Gromphadorhina portentosa*), a flightless 15cm (6in) -long cockroach named for its habit of hissing loudly at all who dare intrude upon its domain.

But for complete off-the-wall idiosyncrasy combined with natural engineering prowess, it's difficult to beat the giraffe-necked weevil (*Trachelophorus giraffa*), which – with its bright red chassis and hinged black neck – doesn't actually resemble a giraffe so much as a miniature crane mounted on a toy fire engine. In the case of the male, the neck is more than double the body length, and is used to roll a leaf case in which the female lays its egg.

underparts that erase any shadow when it is flattened against a tree.

Uroplatus is one of a dozen genera of gecko represented on Madagascar. Others include the brightly-coloured day geckos of the genus *Phelsuma*, the most striking of which is the foot-long giant day gecko (*P. grandis*) with its brilliant red-on-green spotted scale pattern. Most other geckos are nocturnal and can be distinguished by their bug-eyes and ability to run up and down walls, windows and other smooth vertical surfaces. House geckos

> *Most of Madagascar's lizards have clear African origins, but not so the Opluridae, an endemic family of medium-large spiny-backed dry-country iguanids most closely related to their counterparts from the Pacific islands and Americas.*

are often found in hotel rooms and make for entertaining roommates that also contribute to controlling mosquitoes and other pests.

TORTOISE AND TERRAPINS

Madagascar supports nine species of terrestrial and freshwater chelonids, five of which are endemic to the island. These endemics are all listed as critically endangered and actually rank among the world's most threatened reptile species, though several are now protected in two well-run breeding programmes: Le Village des Tortues in Mangily (north of Toliara) and the Chelonian Captive Breeding Centre in the Parc National d'Ankarafantsika.

The ploughshare tortoise or angonoka (*Astrochelys yniphora*), considered to be the world's rarest chelonid, is represented by a few hundred wild individuals whose range is centred on the Parc National Baie de Baly.

The other endemic species are radiated tortoise (*Astrochelys radiata*), flat-tailed tortoise (*Pyxis planicauda*), spider tortoise (*Pyxis arachnoides*) and the freshwater-associated Madagascan big-headed turtle (*Erymnochelys madagascariensis*).

FROGS

At night, the Malagasy rainforest comes alive with a bewildering repertoire of clicking, clacking, squeaking, squawking and other odd noises whose colourful amphibious sources are often traceable by torchlight. Madagascar is one of the world's most important centres of frog speciation with a checklist of 300-plus species that grows with every passing year, and includes only two species of non-endemics, the Asian common toad (*Duttaphrynus melanostictus*) and Asian bullfrog (*Hoplobatrachus tigerinus*) – both

The radiated tortoise is endemic to Madagascar.

of which are thought to be recent introductions that pose a threat to indigenous competitors. Most widely represented are the mantellids of the genus *Boophis*, which is endemic to Madagascar and Mayotte and comprises 80 described species, most of them small and exquisitely coloured nocturnals that typically call from flat leaves which they grip with their delicate wide-tipped fingers. Arguably the island's most spectacular amphibian, however, is are the three species of tomato frog (*Dyscophus spp*), which resemble a ripe tomato not only in colour but also in size and rotundity – though they fall short on the lettuce-compatibility front by secreting a noxious white fluid that can gum up a predator's mouth for several days.

📷 MARINE WILDLIFE

Although lemurs and other terrestrial endemics tend to hog the limelight, Madagascar – as might be expected of a tropical island surrounded by myriad coral reefs – also supports a wonderful diversity of marine wildlife.

One of its most renowned marine spectacles is the several thousand humpback whale Megaptera novaeangliae that gather to breed over July and September in Antongil Bay, where they are most easily seen from the Réserve Spéciale de Nosy Mangabe, but more than 30 species of Cetaceans (whales and dolphins) have been recorded offshore, along with the seaweed-guzzling manatee-like dugong (*Dugong dugon*). In addition, five of the world's eight marine turtle species inhabit Malagasy waters, the most common being the green turtle Chelonia mydas and hawksbill Eretmochelys imbricata, both of which are quite frequently encountered by snorkellers. Coral reefs off the coast of Madagascar are renowned among snorkellers for supporting a dazzlingly kaleidoscopic menagerie whose numbers include includes surgeonfish, damselfish, butterfly fish, clownfish, parrotfish and devil's firefish. Nosy Be is widely regarded to be the best place in Madagascar for viewing marine wildlife, thanks to its profusion of offshore reefs and wide choice of well-equipped dive and boat operators. Other good sites include the reefs either side of Toliara, Île Sainte-Marie, Baie de Sainte Luce and Plage de Ramena near Diego Suarez.

Coral reefs off Madagascar often host green turtles (Chelonia mydas) and hawksbills (Eretmochelys imbricate). Both species occasionally come ashore onto sandy beaches to lay eggs.

The devil firefish (Pterois miles) ranks among the most spectacular denizens of Madagascar's coral reefs, but beware its fin spines, which are highly venomous.

The humpback whales (Megaptera novaeangliae) might be seen breaching anywhere off the coast of Madagascar between May and December.

The most spectacular of several dozen marine birds associated with Madagascar, the red-tailed and white-tailed tropicbirds (Phaethon rubricauda, Phaethon lepturus) are often seen near coastal cliffs.

A gentle giant

The world's largest fish, the whale shark Rhincodon typus, is easily distinguished by its combination of immense bulk, wide mouth and spotted skin pattern. An adult typically attains a length of 12 metres (40ft) and weighs up to 35 tonnes, but can be 50 percent larger than that. It only matures at around 30 years of age, and its potential lifespan is thought to exceed one century, making it one of the world's longest living creatures. Despite its intimidating size, the whale shark is a filter-feeder whose main diet is plankton and other microscopic organisms, and it is essentially harmless to humans (though snorkellers or divers who get too close to its powerful tail fins risk being swiped). An estimated global numerical decline of at least 60 percent since the turn of the millennium, mainly as a result of overfishing, led to the whale shark being IUCN-listed as endangered in 2016. Despite this, it is quite common off the coast of Madagascar, and often seen by snorkellers or divers around Nosy Be, which is considered to be something of a hotspot for this gentle giant.

Whale shark getting lunch.

Possibly the most conspicuous aquatic mammal off Nosy Be, the spinner dolphin (Stenella longirostris) regularly moves in schools of several hundred individuals and is named for its spectacular habit of rotating longitudinally as it leaps through the air.

The always spectacular
Allée des Baobabs.

A sweeping view of the
Réserve d'Anja.

Idyllic Île Sainte-Marie.

Fishing boat on the beach in Morondava.

INTRODUCTION

Exploring Madagascar can be a challenge, but the rewards –
idyllic Indian Ocean beaches, steamy tropical jungles alive
with lemurs and birds, and bizarre succulent-dominated
'spiny forests' – more than justify the effort.

*Red tsingy landscape
near Antsiranana.*

Madagascar is the world's fourth-largest island, its vast-
ness exaggerated by a patchy road and rail infrastructure.
Most visitors land at the historic capital Antananarivo, which
stands right in the island's centre, surrounded by edifices dating back to the precolonial heyday of the Imerina kingdom.
This agreeable highland city also boasts a discernible French
cultural influence and comfortable climate, and it lies within
a half-day's drive of Andasibe-Mantadia, a justifiably popular
national park whose rich lemur diversity includes the ador-
able diademed sifaka and caterwauling panda-like indri. No
less importantly, Antananarivo is the hub of a domestic flight network that
allows one to reach more remote attractions without losing
too much time to road travel.

Madagascar has two main tourist circuits, and visitors with
limited time usually stick to one or the other. The lynchpin
of the northern circuit is the lovely offshore island of Nosy
Be, a popular beach destination that attracts a fair amount
of fly-in package tourism. Important attractions within striking distance of Nosy Be include the dramatic karstic tsingy
landscapes of Ankarana, the moist endemic-rich rainforest
of crater-pocked Montagne d'Ambre, and the charming old
harbour city of Diego Suarez.

Getting ready for adventure.

Southern Madagascar doesn't lack for luscious beaches,
but its tourist circuit is more about active engagement with
various cultural, wildlife and scenic attractions. These
include the artisanal city of Antsirabe and the Unesco-recognised woodcarving tradition of Pays Zafimaniry, the fluffy lemurs and colourful birds
that inhabit the montane forests of Ranomafana, the stunningly eroded
sandstone sculptures of Isalo, and the towering octopus trees that proliferate in the so-called spiny forest of the semi-arid southwest.

For those who want to explore further, Madagascar boasts a remarkable
assemblage of remote attractions, many quite unique to this vast island. From
Morondava's photogenic Allée des Baobabs to the mysterious rainforest interior of Masoala (the country's largest national park), from the atmospheric
Pirate Cemetery on lovely Île Sainte-Marie to the southerly windswept cape
of the same name, the opportunities for exploration are practically endless.

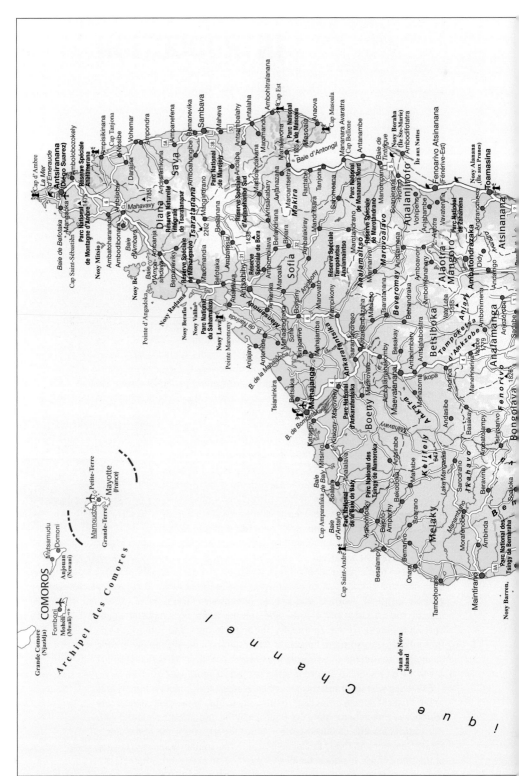

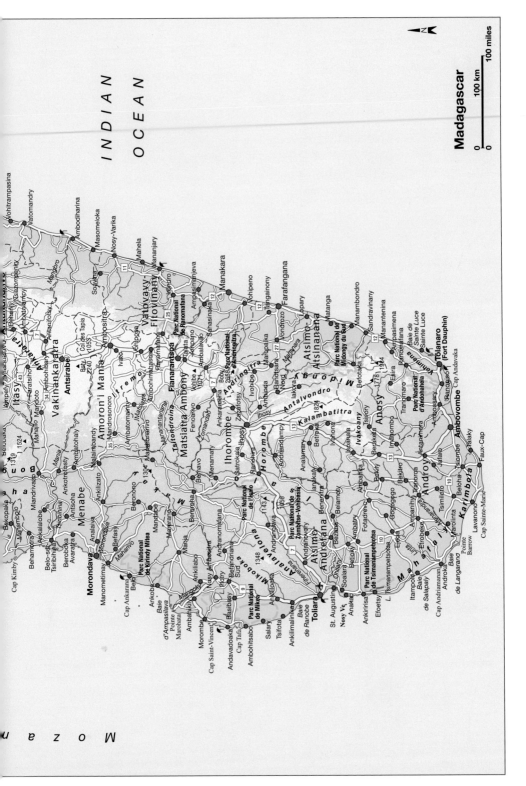

Madagascar

INDIAN OCEAN

Mozam

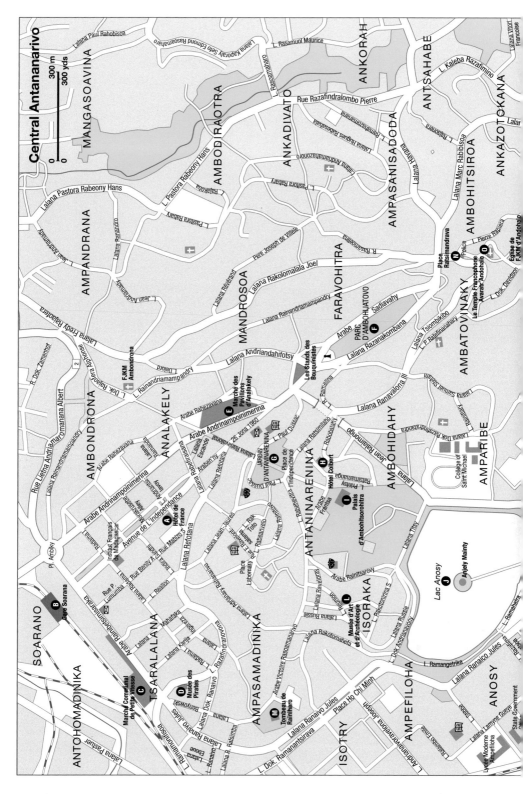

Central Antananarivo

300 m
300 yds

ANKORAHOTRA

AMBANIDIA

AMBOHI-
MIANDRA

VOLOSARIKA

Rabibisoa

Lalana Printsey Kamamy

MIANDRARIVO

Rue Razakarivony Arthur

The Church of Jesus Christ
of Latter-day Saints

AMBOHIMITSIMBINA

Rue Razakarivony Arthur

AMBOHIPOTSY

L Hazafimaheta

ANKADIBEVAVA

MANJAKAMIADANA

Musée d'Andafiavaratra
(Prime Minister's Palace)

Palais de Justice
d'Ambatondrafandrana

ANKADINANDRIANA

FJKM Rasalama
Maritora Ambohipotsy

Ratsimba

Maison de
Jean Laborde

Lycée Galiléni
d'Andohalo

Eglise
d'Ambonin'Ampamarinana

Rova Antananarivo

Rova Viewpoint

Lalana Ramboatiana

Lalana Ramboatiana

Lalana Ramboatiana

Ecole Normale

Arabe Rabozaka

ANKADILALANA

Lalana Kasanga Fernand

TSIMBAZAZA

Arabe Mahatma Gandi

Stade Municipal
de Mahamasina

MAHAMASINA

Marché de
Mahamasina

FJKM Atsimon'i
Mahamasina

AMBOHIJANAHARY

Fort Voyron

PARC BOTANIQUE ET
ZOOLOGIQUE DE TSIMBAZAZA

Ministère de
l'Enseignement Supérieur

MANANJARA

FIADANANA

L Rabary Pierre

Lalana Rakotonirainy

Hôpital Général
de Befelatanana

Maternité
Befelatanana

Toby Ratsimandrava
Sports Complex

BEFELATANANA

Palais du Sénat

ANDAVAMAMBA

Joseph Ravoahangy
Andrianavalona Hospital

Ministry of
Foreign Affairs

Rue Pavoahangy Andrianavalona

ANOSIBE

AMBOHIBARY

Market day in Antananarivo.

ANTANANARIVO AND SURROUNDS

Political centre of Imerina since 1610, Madagascar's bustling capital offers an alluring combination of ancient history, French architectural and culinary flair, and modern Malagasy pizzazz.

Madagascar's tongue-twisting capital, Antananarivo – frequently abbreviated to 'Tana' and still sometimes referred to by the ephemeral French misnomer Tananarive – has been the island's largest centre of population since the early 18th century and it now supports a population of roughly 1.6 million. Situated in the heart of the temperate central highlands, the city spans altitudes of 1,280–1,480 metres (4,200–4,856ft), and comprises a series of naturally wooded ridges and hills interspersed with low swampy valleys used to grow rice and watercress. This proliferation of slopes and wetlands makes for a rather confusing but appealingly quaint layout of roads that seem to turn back on themselves and frequently return newcomers back to the same place they started.

Captured c.1610 by King Andrianjaka of Imerina, Antananarivo was traditionally known as Analamanga, a name that was revived after independence and now applies to the 16,911-sq-km (6,529-sq-mile) administrative region of which it is capital. The city centre is conventionally divided into three loosely-defined and prosaically named parts: the modern commercial and administrative districts of Ville Basse and Ville Moyenne, and the lovely historic quarter of Haute-Ville. All three districts possess a certain degree of charm, but ridge-top

Haute-Ville is by far the most interesting to visitors, thanks to its far-reaching views and wealth of pre-colonial royal edifices. By contrast, the flattish sprawl of bland residential areas, low-rise industrial and scruffy paddies that makes up suburban Antananarivo is almost totally lacking when it comes to tourist attractions or any other compelling attributes.

Ivato International Airport, 15km (9 miles) north of central Antananarivo, is probably the most significant port of entry to Madagascar (despite

Main Attractions

Musée d'Andafiavaratra
Rova Antananarivo
Parc de Tsarasaotra
Rova Ambohimanga
Rova Ambohidrabiby
Rova Ilafy
Réserve d'Anjozorobe-Angavo
Lemurs' Park
Geysers d'Andranomandraotra
Chutes de la Lily

Maps on pages 122, 136

The Andafiavaratra Palace.

the growing importance of Nosy Be as a stand-alone beach holiday destination) and unquestionably the main hub of the domestic flight network. The surrounding area has plenty to offer visitors with time to spare. For the historically and culturally minded, the highlight is the 12 Sacred Hills of Imerina, in particular Ambohimanga (now a Unesco World Heritage Site) and to a lesser extent Ambohidrabiby and Ilafy. For wildlife enthusiasts, the little-visited Réserve d'Anjozorobe-Angavo, home to nine lemur and 74 bird species, makes for a satisfying indri-spotting alternative to the busier Andasibe. And hikers seeking some fresh air and attractive scenery might like to head west to the volcanic landscapes in the vicinity of Lac Itasy.

CENTRAL ANTANANARIVO

Often referred to as the Ville Basse (Lower City), Antananarivo's relatively grid-like CBD, situated at the northwestern base of the ridge that houses the more ancient royal capital of

Taxis line up on Avenue de l'Indépendance.

Imerina, is essentially a French colonial creation, established in the early years of the 20th century. The most important central thoroughfare is the six-lane Avenue de l'Indépendance, which was laid out in 1912 under the name Avenue Armand Fallières (after the then President of France), renamed Avenue de la Libération in 1945 to mark the end of World War II, and given its present name in 1960. Landmark buildings along this wide and busy avenue include the **Hôtel de France (A)**, an attractively faded colonial edifice whose wide colonnaded terrace – complete with time-warped signposts reading Avenue de la Libération – is as good as place as any to watch the city bustle past over a coffee or beer.

The city centre's grandest colonial relic, situated at the northwest of Avenue de l'Indépendance, is the **Gare Soarana (B)**, a railway station built in French rural style on the site of a spring (Soarana means 'Good Water') over 1908–10. The old station building now houses a shopping

centre containing several craft shops, while the old diner has been converted to the chic Café de la Gare, a popular spot for a light meal or drink. A block to the west, the lively **Marché Communal de Petite Vitesse** , specialising mostly in electronics and other imported good, spills out into Rue Rainibertsimisaraka, and has something of a reputation for bag-snatchers and pickpockets. About 50m/yards to the south, the intriguing **Musée des Pirates**  (Pirates Museum; Rue de Liège; tel: 020-2262527; Mon–Fri 9am–5pm) is a private endeavour that documents the history of piracy off the coast of Madagascar (and the controversial republic of Libertatia) with some well-researched displays (French only, but English translation sheets are available), and artefacts such as cannons and treasure chests.

The southeast end of Avenue de l'Indépendance is dominated by the **Marché des Pavillons d'Analakely** , where neat rows of slightly oriental-looking red-tiled wooden kiosks (the 'pavillons' in question) sell everything from fruits and vegetable to clothing, stationary and pirated DVDs. Analakely means 'Place of the Small Forest', in reference to a plantation that was cut down to make way for what is now the city centre's largest market. For bibliophiles, the **Marché des Bouquinistes** 100m/yards further south is an excellent place to seek out second-hand or out-of-print titles about Madagascar. Just past this, the **Parc d'Ambohijatovo** , shaded by jacarandas and other exotic trees, is overlooked by a tall stele erected in 1987 to commemorate the 40th anniversary of the Malagasy Uprising of 29 March 1947. The park is also the site of a smaller plaque dedicated to the many Christian martyrs who were burnt alive, thrown off cliffs or poisoned to death during the tyrannical 19th-century reign of Queen Ranavalona I.

THE MIDDLE TOWN

Slotting between the commerce-driven city centre and more sedate Haute-Ville in terms of both location and feel, the Ville Moyenne is a relatively posh administrative quarter founded by the French in the early colonial era. It runs roughly southward from the **Jardin d'Antaninarenina** , a small elevated wedge-shaped park and linked to the southeast end of Avenue de l'Indépendance by the pedestrian-only stairs of Escalier Ranavalona I. Also known as Place de l'Indépendance, the leafy Jardin d'Antaninarenina is adorned with monuments to Queen Rasalimo, the Sakalava princess who married King Radama I in 1823, and their son Princess Rabobalahy. The park also contains a large-scale version of the popular Malagasy board game *fanorona*, and a useful tourist office operated by the **Office Régional du Tourisme d'Analamanga** (ORTANA; tel: 020-2227051; www.tourisme-antananarivo.com; daily 9am–5pm).

A block further south, on Rue Printsy Ratsimamanga, the historic

Gare Soarana.

Café de la Gare.

Lac Anosy with the Monument aux Morts, a French monument to those fallen in World War I.

Two landmarks in central Antananarivo, Lac Anosy and the Stade Municipal de Mahamasina.

Hôtel Colbert  first opened its doors in 1940 and its strong period character – grand reception hall with marble and granite floor, leather chairs and classical art on the walls – makes it an excellent place for a drink or meal break. Rue Printsy Ratsimamanga then runs past the **Palais d'Ambohitsorohitra** ❶, or Presidential Palace, a grand colonial edifice whose ornate facade can only be seen from a distance though a tall boundary fence. It was constructed over 1890–92 as the residence of Charles Le Myre de Vilers, who served two terms as Resident-General of Madagascar between 1886 and 1895, and later served at the French Embassy prior to being handed over to the Malagasy government in 1975. Now under heavy guard, it serves as the symbolic rather than actual residence of the president since being captured by the military in the coup of March 2009.

Although it abuts the southern end of the Presidential Palace gardens, the jacaranda-fringed **Lac Anosy** ❶ stands in a rather insalubrious neighbourhood where you'd be ill-advised to walk unaccompanied at night or at any time carrying valuables. It was established during the reign of Queen Ranavalona I, who commissioned Jean Laborde to fashion an artificial lake from an area of swampland formerly notorious as a breeding ground for mosquitoes. Laborde constructed a small island in the middle of the heart-shaped lake, as well as a causeway connecting it to the southern shore. The island originally housed a blacksmith's workshop, and was later used an armoury, in both cases to protect the surrounding wood and thatched roofs from exposure to fire. Since 1927 it has been the site of a prominent stele dedicated to the Malagasy soldiers who died fighting for France in World War I. Added in 1935, the black-winged angel that tops the stele is the work of the prominent French sculptor Charles-Georges Barberis. Excellent views of the lake can be enjoyed from several spots in Haute-Ville.

Constructed in 1986 a short distance southeast of Lac Anosy, the

22,000-seater **Stade Municipal de Mahamasina**  regularly hosts rugby and football matches, as well as live music concerts, and in 2007 it was the venue of the seventh edition of the Indian Ocean Island Games. It stands on an area of former swampland that was reclaimed as a royal military ground at the command of Queen Ranavalona I in 1833 and served as the coronation site if King Radama II in 1861. The name Mahamasina dates back to this time and refers to an ointment-yielding plant that grew there.

From Lac Anosy, you can return to the city centre via the characterful old suburb of Isoraka, whose narrow roads house several handsome colonial-era buildings now restored as boutique hotels. Isoraka is also the site of the Université d'Antananarivo's **Musée d'Art et d'Archéologie** (Rue Dok Villette; tel: 020-2232639; daily 9am–4pm; donation), which includes a small but interesting selection of artefacts from archaeological sites all around the island. These include fossilised bones from the extinct elephant bird and pygmy hippo, and a reconstruction of a *teza betsilio* (a type of wooden tomb from southern Madagascar) complete with tall, triangular-tipped phallic pillar.

About 500 metres/yds west of this, the **Tombeau de Rainiharo** on Avenue Victoire Rasoamanarivo is the city's most impressive tomb, a striking Hindu-influenced arched mausoleum constructed by Jean Laborde to house the remains of Prime Minister Rainiharo, who served under Queen Ranavalona I from 1833 until his death in 1852. The tomb is also the final resting place of Rainiharo's two sons and successors Rainivoninahitriniony and Rainilaiarivony, who respectively served as prime minister from 1852–64 and 1864–95.

HAUTE-VILLE

Historically the most important part of Antananarivo, Haute-Ville occupies a long narrow hill that rises to 1,480 metres (4,856ft) immediately east of the city centre. It was upon this lofty ridge

Streetlife in Haute-Ville.

IMERINA'S ROYAL CITY

Antananarivo is one of the few inland African capital cities to boast a long pre-colonial pedigree.

Formerly the site of a Vazimba village called Analamanga (Blue Forest), the present-day Haute-Ville was captured by King Andrianjaka c.1612 to become the first and most enduring capital of Imerina. Andrianjaka chose the elevated ridge-top site partly for its defensibility but also because the flanking wetlands were ideal for rice cultivation. King Andriamasinavalona (r.1675–1710) later renamed the site Antananarivo ('City of the Thousand') in reference to the 1,000-strong garrison that traditionally guarded it.

The Rova at Antananarivo dates back to the reign of Andrianjaka, who constructed a trio of royal residences and a burial site there. Under King Andrianampoinimerina (r.1787–1810), more than 20 buildings stood in the Rova. The oldest surviving structures today date to the early 19th-century reign of Radama I. For much of its history, Antananarivo's Rova has enjoyed a complementary relationship to its counterpart at nearby Ambohimanga (see page 138), with the former serving primarily as the political capital of Imerina, while the latter is its main spiritual hub.

Antananarivo remained the primary royal seat until 28 February 1897, when the Imerina monarchy was abolished, and Queen Ranavalona III was evicted from her palace and exiled to Réunion. By this time, the rova incorporated nine tomb houses, arranged with great cosmological significance, contained the remains of various Imerina monarchs and other royals, among them the city's founder Andrianjaka. With characteristic disrespect, the French colonial authorities not only rearranged the royal burial ground, but supplemented it with the reinterred remains of several monarchs originally buried at Ambohimanga. A tomb for Ranavalona III, who died in exile in Algiers in 1917, was added to the Rova in 1938.

On November 1995, most tombs and other buildings in the Rova were destroyed or damaged in an arson attack. Mysteriously, the body of Ranavalona III appeared in a public square in the city centre on the same night. Such was the extent of the fire damage that efforts to list the Rova as a Unesco World Heritage Site were abandoned and Ambohimanga – where Ranavalona III is now interred – was inscribed in its place in 2001.

Statue of Ranavalona III at the royal palace complex.

that King Andrianjaka established the first Imerina capital some 400 years ago, and here too that a succession of powerful monarchs reigned over their kingdom until Queen Ranavalona III was evicted by the French colonists in 1897. Haute-Ville today remains the most attractive part of Antananarivo, partly for the same views once enjoyed by King Andrianjaka and his successors (albeit somewhat more urbanised than all those centuries ago), but also for the rich sense of history embodied in the narrow cobbled brick alleys and flanking hotchpotch of pre- and early colonial stone or wood edifices.

Haute-Ville's architectural highlights mostly lie along or close to Rue Ramboatiana, a narrow road with narrower pavements that winds uphill to the hill crest from **Place Ratsimandrava** . Here, a prominent triangular stele commemorates President Richard Ratsimandrava, who served for a mere six days prior to his assassination, by persons unknown, whilst driving home from the Presidential Palace on the evening of 11 February 1975. From here, the alley-like Rue Raharinosy winds uphill past the arched face-brick **Temple Francophone Avaratr'Andohalo** ⊙, a Protestant church that was founded just outside the original city walls in 1864, in keeping with an edict prohibiting the construction of non-royal buildings with them. Embellished with a brick tower in 1892, the church served as a post office between 1897 and 1903, when it was re-sanctified and graced with an extant 16-pipe organ shipped over from London.

After about 300 metres/yds, you enter the bounds of the old walled city at the **Place d'Andohalo** ⊙, which is now overlooked by the **Cathédrale de l'Immaculée Conception d'Andohalo** (www.cathedraleandohalo.com), a rather austere sandstone edifice whose arched entrance is guarded by a pair of fort-like turrets. Inaugurated in

1890, this is the city's preeminent place of worship, graced with a visit by Pope John Paul II in 1989. Outside the cathedral is a small but popular chapel dedicated to the Blessed Victoire Rasoamanarivo (1848–94), a Malagasy women who devoted her life to tending the sick and needy, and was beatified in 1989. Immediately alongside the cathedral, Rue Justin Rajaro is flanked by the **Maison de Jean Laborde** ⊙ (tel: 033-1416725), a beautifully restored wide-balconied wooden house that was constructed in 1863 by its namesake engineer and royal confidante as the first French Embassy in Antananarivo.

Place d'Andohalo has reputedly served as a public square since the days of King Andrianjaka and it is flanked to the east by the triangular **Jardin d'Andohalo** ⊙, which served as the city's main market in the early days. Enclosed by tall leafy trees, the Jardin d'Andohalo was the coronation site of Radama I and most subsequent monarchs, and it still contains the horseshoe-shaped amphitheatre from

A backstreet in Haute-Ville.

⊙ Tip

An excellent place to break for lunch between sightseeing in Haute-Ville, perched opposite the Palais de Justice d'Ambatondrafandrana, is the Grill du Rova (Rue Ramboatiana; tel: 020-2262724). After hours, Lokanga Boutique Hotel (Rue Ramboatiana; tel: 034-1455502; www.lokanga-hotel.mg), is an alluring sundowner spot offering fine views over the Lac Anasy and the city centre and excellent French/Malagasy fusion cuisine. In both cases, booking is recommended.

Musée d'Andafiavaratra.

where Ranavalona III used to address her subjects. It now hosts occasional all-day *hira gasy* musical performances and competitions, most usually on Saturdays. The garden is flanked by several imposing colonial edifices. The Lycée Gallieni d'Andohalo, founded in 1909 as the city's premier school, is immediately to the south, while the attractive Eglise de FJKM d'Andohalo and Anglican Cathédrale Saint Laurent d'Ambohimanoro, both of a similar vintage, stand opposite it to the north.

Another 300m/yards uphill along Rue Ramboatiana, the **Musée d'Andafiavaratra** ⑤ (Mon–Sat 10am–6pm) is housed in a striking baroque ridgetop building notable for its conical turrets, massive ceremonial inner courtyard complete with sky-lit veiling and heavy darkwood doors, and front and back balconies supported by ornate columns on all three floors. Most recently restored in 2000, this is the so-called Prime Minister's Palace, built in 1876 as the residence of the nobleman Rainilaiarivony, a moderniser and noted diplomat who served as *ipso*

facto Prime Minister of Imerina from 1865–96, through the rather unusual expedient of marrying three successive queens: Rasoherina, Ranavalona II and Ranavalona III. The museum itself consist of a weird and rather mismatched miscellany of royal paraphernalia – original 19th-century treaties between France and Imerina, ceremonial guns and cannons, traditional astrological artefacts, a jug of royal circumcision water, and oil portraits of Radama I and most subsequent monarchs – salvaged from the fire that almost destroyed the Rova in 1995.

Another 100m/yards past this, the fenced-in **Palais de Justice d'Ambatondrafandrana** ⑦, a courthouse styled like a misplaced Greek Temple, is perched on a natural stone base on the left side of Rue Ramboatiana. Also known as the Fitsarana Gasy, this unusual building was constructed for Queen Ranavalona II by the British architect John Parrett *c.*1881, and comprises 16 ionic stone columns set around three sides of a small open pavilion with a closed roof and back

⊙ THE TANGENA ORDEAL

Imerina's favoured form of traditional justice was the tangena ordeal, wherein the accused was forced to imbibe a dose of poison extracted from the toxic tangena nut, together with three pieces of chicken skin, and either vomit it up – in which case they were deemed innocent – or perish first. Originally, the poison was dispensed to an animal owned by the accused, but from the time of King Andrianjaka onwards, it was administered to the actual person. Trial by poison reached genocidal proportions during the reign of Ranavalona I, when it claimed many thousands of deaths annually, with most of the victims being alleged Christians or sorcerers. In 1863, two years after its most enthusiastic practitioner died, the tangena ordeal was outlawed by Radama II.

wall. Ambatondrafandrana means 'Stone of Rafandrana', the latter being the name of an important Vazimba family who lived at the site prior to its annexation into Imerina in the early 17th century. Indeed, prior to the Christianisation of the Imerina court under Ranavalona II, this stone was where the Imerina monarchs dispensed traditional justice, subjecting the accused to the tangena ordeal (see box) to determine their guilt or innocence. It was also at Ambatondrafandrana, in 1849, that the fanatically anti-Christian Queen Ranavalona I notoriously ordered the execution of 14 recent local converts, whose punishment was to be marched to a cliff 100m/yards west of the courthouse, and dangled over the edge on a rope that was cut when they persisted in refusing to renounce their faith. The Anglican **Eglise d'Ambonin'Ampamarinana**  was inaugurated in 1874 on the site where the 14 martyrs plunged to their death; a commemorative stone was erected there in 2009 to mark the event's 150th anniversary.

THE ROVA ANTANANARIVO

The highest point in Haute-Ville – and indeed all of the city – is capped by the **Rova Antananarivo** (tel: 034-0552049; Mon–Sat 9am–5pm), the royal residential compound that was founded by King Andrianjaka c.1610 and gutted by fire in 1995, since when partial restoration has taken place. Situated 100m/yards uphill of the Palais de Justice, the ticket office stands in front of an arched gateway built by James Cameron in 1845 to resemble a simplified miniature of the Arc de Triomphe, and adorned with a bronze *voromahery* (eagle) donated by Napoleon I as well as a phallic stone symbolising circumcision. Once inside, the 1ha (2.5-acre) complex offers splendid views over the town centre and surrounding hills, with the Lac Anasy and Stade Municipal de Mahamasina prominent in the foreground.

The dominant building in the Rova, visible for miles around, is the three-storey **Palais de Manjakamiadana**, which dates to the reign of Ranavalona

A bronze eagle gifted by Napoleon guards the main gate of the Rova Antananarivo.

Stone columns at the Rova.

> **ⓘ Tip**
>
> Tana Waterfront (www.centre-commercial-tanawaterfront.com) is an enclosed shopping mall abutting the RN3 just north of the city centre. Centred on a small lake that attracts plenty of aquatic birds, the complex also incorporates the highly-regarded Hôtel Tamboho, a well-stocked Shoprite supermarket, and several other book, spice and craft shops. The squeaky-clean food court, comprising more than a dozen outlets, offers the city's most cosmopolitan eating experience – but note that no alcohol is served.

The Parc Botanique et Zoologique de Tsimbazaza.

I and is often referred to as the Queen's Palace. Engineered by Jean Laborde over 1839–40, Manjakamiadana started life as an elaborate hardwood structure – some 30 metres/yds long, 20 metres/yds wide and 37 metres (121ft) high – topped by a steep pitched shingle roof that extended its height by another 15 metres (49ft). It took its present-day form in 1867, when Queen Ranavalona II commissioned James Cameron to encase the original structure with a multiple-arched stone facade and quartet of fortress-like turrets comprising an estimated 70,000 granite blocks held together by an egg-white and crushed eggshell cement. Following the eviction of Ranavalona I in 1897, the palace was converted to a college for Malagasy civil servants employed by the French colonists.

As with most other buildings in the Rova, Manjakamiadana suffered intensive fire damage in 1995, and it has been unsafe to go inside ever since. Restoration work – mostly using cement instead of wood and stone – commenced in 2006 but was stalled by the 2009 coup and seems unlikely to resume in the foreseeable future.

The building least affected by the fire was the **Fiangonana** (Royal Church), an impressive stone Anglican edifice built for Ranavalona II by William Pool over 1869–80. Essentially a private chapel reserved for the use of the royal family, this handsome church nevertheless comprises more than 35,000 hand-chiselled granite blocks and is large enough to seat 450 worshippers. Other features include the 34-metre (112ft)-high slate-roof clocktower, one surviving stained-glass window and a pipe organ imported from England, and a rosewood royal pew crafted by local artisans. Behind the main palace, the **Fitomiandalana** is a collection of seven ancient tomb houses, the oldest of which was constructed above the tomb pit of King Andrianjaka in 1630. Other noteworthy features of the complex include the stand-alone tombs built for King Radama I in 1828 and Queen Rasoherina in 1868, and a swimming pool commissioned by Ranavalona III and overlooked by her sculpture.

SUBURBAN ZOOS AND PARKS

Situated about 1km (0.6 miles) south of the city centre, the **Parc Botanique et Zoologique de Tsimbazaza** ⓦ (PBZT; Rue Kasanga Fernando; tel: 033-1260670; http://pbzt.recherches.gov.mg; daily 9am–5pm) makes for an interesting though less than essential open-air outing. Stronger on the botanique than the zoologique front, the pretty green grounds contain the country's largest herbarium, recreations of several different Malagasy habitats (including spiny desert), and a scattered collection of stone and wooden tomb markers from all around the country. Two ornamental ponds originally dug by Radama I now support a large and noisy heronry whose inhabitants (all free-ranging) are dominated by dimorphic herons, but also include the more secretive black-crowned night heron, black egret and gem-like Madagascar kingfisher. Half-a-dozen lemur species, including the charismatic ringtailed, are split between a few cramped cages and some rather more appealing islands (from which they cannot escape as they are unable to swim). There is also a rather shabby and depressing vivarium containing a few species of chameleon, snake and tortoise.

Attached to the PBZT, the Musée de Tsimbazaza contains the country's most extensive collection of fossils, ranging from Jurassic-era dinosaur skeletons to more recently extinct giants such as the elephant bird and koala lemur.

The capital's top birdwatching spot, situated only 3km (2 miles) north of the city centre, is **Parc Tsarasaotra** ❶ (off Colonel Ratsimandrava Parkway; tel: 033-1244127; www.boogiepilgrim-madagascar.com, daily 6am–6pm) a private 5-hectare (12-acre) wetland that was made a Ramsar site in 2005. Dominated by two small lakes, the well-wooded wetland has a checklist of 66 bird species, most of them aquatic, and it is the only site in the central highlands that offers a decent chance of spotting endemics such as the Endangered Meller's duck and Madagascar pond heron and Vulnerable Madagascar grebe. Other endemics present include Madagascar harrier and Madagascar sparrowhawk. The Parc de Tsarasaotra is managed by Boogie Pilgrim, and you need to drop by their office in Tana Waterfront to pay entrance fees and arrange access. Since the most productive time to visit is early morning ideally within an hour or two of sunrise, this is best done at least a day in advance.

IVATO

Situated about 15km (9 miles) north of central Antananarivo, **Ivato** is a large and distinct suburb that sprawls in all directions around the shallow Lac Ambohibao. Separated from the rest of the city by a narrow belt of green paddies and industry, it is reached along Rue Général Andrimahazo (technically the most southerly stretch of the RN4), a perennially congested trunk route that can take up to two hours to

⊙ TSIMBAZAZA'S CHEQUERED PAST

In Imerina's heyday, Tsimbazaza was an important sacred site. Located immediately below the Rova, it was for many years reserved for a ceremony wherein zebus were sacrificed to mark the end of the mourning period after the death of a member of the royal family. A pair of small lakes dug there by King Radama I c.1810 initially served as a place for his soldiers to bathe before presenting themselves for review. Queen Ranavalona I would later use the lakes to drown any nobles she condemned to death, thereby circumventing a *fady* on shedding their blood. The land was confiscated by the French colonial administration in 1896 and distributed among a few select Malagasy leaders, among them Prime Minister Rasanjy, who built an imposing villa that now houses an entomological reference collection and library. In 1925, the 23-hectare (57-acre) site was resuscitated as the Botanical Garden of Tananarive, and it has since doubled as a centre for research into the island's natural, social and cultural environment. Tsimbazaza literally means 'place where children are forbidden', a name that dates back to pre-colonial times, but the restriction on children no longer applies. On the contrary, Tsimbazaza today is a very family-friendly set-up, with an elaborate children's playground to boot.

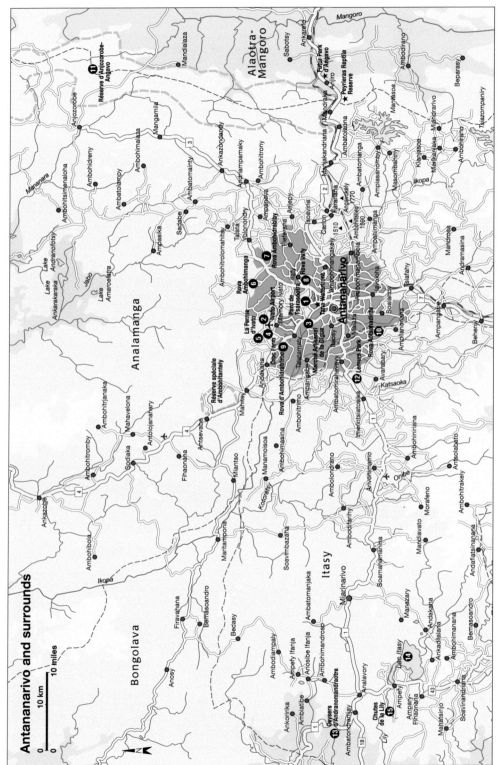

Antananarivo and surrounds

0   10 km
0   10 miles

cover on a bad day. Ivato is best-known as the site of **Ivato International Airport ❷**, which is the main port of entry to Madagascar, and is now serviced by an excellent selection of hotels catering to overnight fly-in, fly-out visitors who don't particularly want to face the tedious stop-start drive along Rue Général Andrimahazo in both directions. Though it's unquestionably convenient in this respect, Ivato does lack the historic ambience of the city centre.

Set on the banks of the Ikopa Canal halfway along the main road between the city centre and Ivato, the **Marché Artisanal de la Digue ❸** is Madagascar's largest handicrafts market, comprising more than 100 stalls selling pretty much every conceivable memento and curio, from colourful fabrics, handsome wooden carvings and basketware to cute hand-made toy trucks and every spice under the Malagasy sun. About 6km (3.7 miles) further north, the junction of the RN4 and main road leading east to Ivato International Airport is the site of a ground-level mall that forms a useful one-stop shop for new arrivals – in addition to an excellent Shoprite supermarket, it includes representatives of the country's major mobile/data network providers, and stands close to several major banks and ATMs.

The best-known tourist attraction in Ivato is the **Croc Farm ❹** (tel: 020-2200715; daily 9am–5pm) situated about 3km (1.8 miles) out of town past the airport. Set on an attractively landscaped slope run through by a clear paved footpath, this active crocodile farm supports free-ranging populations of (introduced) Coquerel's sifaka and several (naturally occurring) aquatic birds, while open-air cages house a variety of tortoises, snakes, chameleons and other reptiles, as well as a rather unhappy looking fossa. The footpath ends at a small lake overlooked by a stilted wooden viewing platform from where you'll see some fearsomely ginormous Nile crocodiles showing off their daunting dentition. Amenities include a restaurant specialising in crocodile-meat dishes, and a good craft shop.

A morning stop at the Croc Farm could be followed up by a visit to **La Ferme d'Ivato ❺** (tel: 032-1159495/6; www.lafermedivato.com; daily 10am–3pm) a few minutes drive to the north. This working farm specialises in organic produce and offers guided 30- to 60-minute tours detailing their production methods and crops. The rustic restaurant is set in a pine planation serves lunch to small parties at noon by prior arrangement (ideally at least three days' notice).

SACRED HILLS OF IMERINA

Antananarivo stands at the heart of Imerina, a powerful highland kingdom founded in the mid-16th century by King Andriamanelo (r.1540–75) but named by and consolidated under his son Ralambo (r.1575–1612). Ralambo's son and successor Andrianjaka (r.1612–30), the first king first to settle

⊙ Tip

Outdoor activities on offer in the vicinity of Ivato include horseback trips at the **Ferme Equestre du Rova** (tel: 032-0703904; www.cheval-madagascar. com), which is based on the shore of Lake Andranotapahina, just off the RN4 some 4km (2.5 miles) northwest of the Shoprite Centre. The 18-hole **International Golf Club du Rova** (tel: 020-2201190) is the only golf course in Tana; established in the colonial era it lies along the RN4 about 10km (6 miles) further northwest.

Nile crocodiles at the Croc Farm.

on Antananarivo as capital, is credited with first implementing the concept of the 12 sacred hills of Imerina, elevated sites that were chosen for their significance as a former royal capital, or on account of being the birth or burial place of an important political or spiritual leader.

Several of the sacred sites designated by Andrianjaka were later replaced by subsequent kings, most notably during the reign of King Andrianampoinimerina (r. 1787–1810), whose 12 wives were each allocated one sanctified hill as their residence. The total number of sacred hills remained constant, however, presumably to maintain the sites' spiritual link with the 12 lunar months that form the bedrock of Malagasy cosmology. As a result of this, more than 20 different hills in the vicinity of Antananarivo now have some sort of claim to being counted among the sacred dozen, and while many have little concrete to show for their exalted status, others are genuinely steeped in history and of great interest to visitors.

Foremost among the latter category is the **Rova Ambohimanga** ❻ (www. ambohimanga-rova.com; daily 9am–4pm), a forested rocky outcrop that stands some 23km (14 miles) north of central Antananarivo. This hill was probably first settled by the Merina people in the 15th century, and its royal association dates to the late 16th or 17th century, when it became the home of a prince called Andriamborona, who named it Ambohitrakanga ('Hill of Guinea Fowl'). Renamed Ambohimanga ('Blue or Great Hill') by King Andriamasinavalona (r. 1675–1710), it served as the regional capital of eastern Imerina for several decades prior to becoming spiritual capital of the whole kingdom during the unifying reign of King Andrianampoinimerina (r. 1787–1810), who established a palace there. An important royal residence and spiritual site ever since, Ambohimanga was in 2001 inscribed as the island's only cultural World Heritage Site, with Unesco citing it as 'the most significant symbol of the cultural identity of the people of Madagascar' and 'an exceptional example of

Part of the royal complex atop the sacred Rova Ambohimanga.

a place where, over centuries, common human experience has been focussed in memory, ritual, and prayer'.

Ambohimanga is entered via Ambatomitsanaga Gate, which features an excellent example of a *vavahady*, a traditional circular stone disc door that would be rolled into place by several dozen slaves when the complex was under threat. From here a 500-metre/yd walk or drive ascends through lushly forested slopes to the modern gate and ticket office, which stands outside the main compound wall, a tall defensive structure built with rocks and concrete made with egg albumin and shell. In front of this, a heart-shaped stone called the Kianja Fidasiana was used for royal sacrifices during the reign of Andrianampoinimerina.

There are three main buildings in the compound. The smaller and older but more traditional is Mahandrihono Palace, a single-roomed one-storey wooden structure whose original steep-angled thatch roof, built in 1788 by King Andrianampoinimerina, was later replaced by wooden tiles by Jean Laborde. At the centre of the building, a tall supportive rosewood trunk, reputedly carried up from the coast by a caravan of 2,000 slaves, is carved with a pair of women's breasts to symbolise Andrianampoinimerina's virility. When guests arrived, the king would clamber up the pole into the rafters, and signal his willingness to formally receive them by dropping a small stone to the floor. Andrianampoinimerina's palace is now a museum displaying traditional household utensils, furniture, weapons and other artefacts associated with its royal builder. It is probably the most sacred site in the compound and several of Andrianampoinimerina's successors made regular visits to make contact with his spirit. It is customary to enter the house right-foot-first to exit backwards out of respect for its royal builder.

Next to this stands a tight pair of more elaborate two-storey buildings that originally formed the summer residence of Queen Ranavalona II. These are the Tranofitaratra ('House of Glass'), constructed in 1862 using panes imported by an Englishman named Parrett, and Fandriampahalemana Palace, which was designed by Jean Laborde in 1870. The two buildings are connected by a maze of ornate wooden balconies and their wallpapered interiors are cluttered with antique French display cabinets, four-poster beds, wall mirrors, banquet tables and other 19th-century items that stand in stark contrast to rest of this otherwise down-to-earth site. The wooden tombs of Queens Ranavalona I and II and Kings Andriantsimitoviaminiandriana, Andriambelomasina and Andrianampoinimerina are lined up behind this like a row of windowless beach huts.

OTHER SACRED HILLS

Roughly 10km (6 miles) east of Ambohimanga by road, the little-visited **Rova Ambohidrabiby** ⑦ (daily 9am–4pm; donation), former capital of King

☉ Tip

Although most visitors limit their exploration of Ambohimanga to the main compound, a choice of three guided walking trails around the slopes of the forested hill is offered to energetic travellers. The longest and most rewarding of these is a 3–4 hour grand tour that takes in two smaller walled royal compounds, the fern-covered Grottes d'Andranomatsatso, the sacred Lac d'Amparihimasina, and Andakana Gate, the most interesting of the ancient *vavahady* stone disc entrances to the royal hill.

The main entrance, Ambatomitsanaga Gate.

Posters in the museum at Ambohidrabiby hill.

Traditional Merina house at Ambohidrabiby.

Ralambo, has a strong claim to being the oldest capital of Imerina. The story is that Ambohidrabiby (Hill of Rabiby) is named after Ralambo's grandfather, an Arab astrologer called Habib who arrived there from the coast circa 1520, married the daughter of a local chief, and had his name bastardised to Rabiby. Ambohidrabiby reputedly supported a population of 5,000 in its 16th-century heyday, but it was abandoned by King Andrianjaka (Ralambo's son and successor) in favour of Antananarivo c.1610. It reputedly enjoyed a revival in the early colonial era and today several impressive French-style two-storey houses overlook the old royal site. The stone tombs of Rabiby and Ralambo can still be seen at the site, and the small and moderately illuminating museum is undermined by the lack of English or even French labels.

Now a small forested suburban enclave situated 15km (9 miles) southwest of Ambohidrabiby and only 9km (5 miles) northeast of central Antananarivo, the short-lived **Rova Ilafy** ❽ (daily 9am–noon and 2–5pm) was founded in 1861 as the part-time capital of King Radama II, who was buried there upon his death two years later. The two-storey wooden house built for Radama II is now an excellent little ethnographic museum boasting a great collection of traditional musical instruments – from the stringed *sodina* to the rattle-like *korintsina* and *piripity* drums – as well as board games, and household and farm implements. Of particular interest is the upstairs collection of wooden funerary totems: women balancing items on their heads, men displaying amply proportioned erections, and both together coupling in positions of which no missionary would approve. The original tomb of Radama II now stands empty (his body was subsequently reinterred in Antananarivo's Rova), but the small wooden structure is guarded by a few zebu skulls.

A relatively minor but very accessible component of the 12 sacred hills, the **Rova d'Ambohidratrimo** ❾ stands on the left side of the RN4 just 3km (2 miles) north of the prominent junction with the road to Ivato International Airport. The birthplace of King Radama I's mother, the forested hill contains a few relics of its heyday, including some well-maintained royal tombs and stone trenches, and a breast-shaped rock where local women hoping to become pregnant leave offerings to the ancestors. Another relatively little-known site is **Rova Antsahadinta** ❿ (literally 'Above the Valley of Leeches'), which overlooks the plains immediately southwest of Antananarivo. Founded by Prince Andriamangarira in 1725, it served as the capital of the western division of Imerina and houses several impressive royal tombs as well as a large wooden palace built in 1860 and reminiscent of its counterpart at Ilafy.

THE FORESTS OF ANJOZOROBE

Anjozorobe is a substantial highland town (altitude 1236 metres/4055ft) situated at the terminus of the surfaced

RN3 as it runs 90km (55 miles) north-east from Antananarivo. It was founded in the late 18th century as a place of retreat for King Andrianampoinimerina of Imerina, who named it both for the reeds (zozoro) that proliferate in the area, but also in reference to its spiritual location northeast (zoro) of the capital (this being the angle from which Malagasy traditionalists communicate with the ancestors). More recently, the remote highland village of Anosivol-akely, about 50km (30 miles) further north, has been dubbed the Lourdes of Madagascar, and emerged as an important Catholic pilgrimage site, following the supposed apparition there of the Virgin Mary – in flowing white robe, barefoot, and speaking fluent Malagasy – in 1990.

For tourists, the main attraction of Anjozorobe District, some 10km (6 miles) east of town along a very poor 4x4-only road, is the 665-sq-km (247-sq-mile) **Réserve d'Anjozorobe-Angavo** ⓫ (http://association-fanamby. org; tel: 020-2263661) which incorporates the country's largest extant tract of highland forest. Despite its low profile, however, Anjozorobe-Angavo offers some excellent wildlife viewing, with nine lemur species present, among then the charismatic indri and diademed sifaka, and Goodman's mouse lemur, a nocturnal species first described in 2005. A checklist of 74 bird species includes 43 forest and marsh-associated endemics, notably Madagascar snipe, Meller's duck, Madagascar partridge, Madagascar long-eared owl, grey emu-tail, Crossley's babbler and velvet asity. There are also 38 amphibian, 36 reptile and 75 orchid species.

The closest major wildlife sanctuary to Antananarivo, Anjozorobe-Angavo is privately-managed for sustainable tourism by the NGO Association Fanamby, and serviced by only one small eco-lodge, the highly regarded Saha Forest Camp (http://sahaforestcamp.mg). Consequently it retains a very untrammelled and off-the-beaten-track feel, certainly when compared to the better-known likes of Andasibe and Rana-mofana. A number of guide hikes are

Exhibits in the ethnographic museum inside Rova Ilafy.

offered. These include the 2.7km (1.5 mile) Source Trail, which usually takes around two hours and offers a good chance of spotting indri and rufous-headed ground-roller, a 1.5km (1 mile) hike to a sacred waterfall, and a full-day 14km (9 mile) hike that incorporates wildlife viewing and local cultural visits. Night walks offer a good chance of seeing nocturnal lemurs, chameleons and frogs.

THE RN1 WEST TO LAC ITASY

The main surfaced road running west from Antananarivo, the RN1 is traversed by relatively few tourists, but it does offer access to a few worthwhile goals for day or overnight trip. Foremost among these is **Lemurs' Park ⑫** (tel: 033-1125259; www.lemurspark.com; daily 9am–5pm), a small zoo-like set-up set in well-maintained 5 hectares (12.3 acres) gardens bounded by a bend in the wide, muddy Katsaoka River only 23km (14 miles) from the capital. Established in 2000 as an education facility and rehabilitation centre for confiscated pet lemurs, the park is also a popular self-standing day excursion for visitors who don't expect to be seeing lemurs in the wild. It supports introduced free-ranging populations of seven diurnal primate species, namely crowned and Coquerel's sifaka and mongoose, brown, ring-tailed, eastern lesser bamboo and black-and-white ruffed lemur. It also contains around 70 endemic plant species and a variety of naturally-occurring birds, chameleons and other reptiles. The best time to visit is around 10am, when all seven lemur species are active and likely to be seen. Other amenities include a well-appointed restaurant and a well-stocked gift shop selling fluffy toy lemurs and the like.

Roughly 105km (63 miles) west of Antananarivo, the RN1 arrives at **Analavory**, a small crossroads town that services a region studded with three dozen crater lakes and various other relics of quaternary volcanic activity. Analavory is the springboard for visits to the **Geysers d'Andranomandraotra ⑬**, a surreal landscape that can be reached by following the RN1b west

Fisherman on Lac Itasy.

out of town for 4km (2.5 miles), turning right onto a rough dirt road that arrives at a car park on the east bank of the Mazy River after 8km (5 miles), then finally crossing a short footbridge to the west bank. Spouting up to 50cm (20 ins) into the air from a fantastic stalagmite-like quartet of multihued 4-metre (13ft) -tall tufa mounds, the geysers at Andranomandraotra are not, as might be expected, steaming hot, but actually comprise cool carbonated water rich in ferric and lime deposits.

Straddling the surfaced RN43 10km (6 miles) south of Analavory, the small town of **Ampefy** has an attractive location on the mouth of the Sakay River as it flows into Lac Kavitaha, a small crater lake connected the much larger **Lac Itasy ⑭** by a short channel. The third largest lake in Madagascar, Itasy was formed when an ancient lava flow blocked a riverine valley and it extends over 35 sq km (13.5 sq miles) and gives its name to the smallest (and second most densely populated) of the country's 22 administrative regions. Easily explored by canoe or on foot, Itasy

and its shore support a rich aquatic birdlife, notably various herons and rallids, and the lake also offers good fishing, especially between April and November. An interesting goal for a day outing is the **Îlot Sacré Amboh-iniazy**, which houses the tomb of the 17th-century King Andriambahoaka and is also the site of an impressive fruitbat colony.

Reached along a 7km (4-mile) dirt road that branches west from the RN43 2km (1.3 miles) north of Ampefy, the **Chutes de la Lily ⑮** is a pretty 20-metre (65ft) -high waterfall set on the Sakay River as it cascades into a ravine characterised by pocked black volcanic rocks and lush *Ficus* trees. You'll need to weave through a barrage of aspirant guides and women selling painted rocks and other handicrafts, then walk for about five minutes, to reach the waterfall, but it's worth the effort. A second larger and more impressive waterfall can be reached by following the river downstream, past several babbling rapids, for almost 1.6km (1 mile).

⊙ **Tip**

Imerintsiatosika, a substantial Merina town with a bustling Friday market 4km (2 miles) past Lemurs' Park, is best-known these days as the site of Serena Racing Karts (SRK, tel: 033-1231700; http://srk.mg; Tue–Sun 10am–6pm). SRK's winding 1,750-metre/yd go-kart track stands on the eastern outskirts of town, and a range of four different modern karts cater to different age groups and levels of experience.

Chutes de la Lily.

Namorona waterfall inside the
Parc National de Ranomafana.

THE RN7 TO TOLIARA

The long road connecting Antananarivo to Toliara is the spine of a tourist circuit whose attractions range from Ranomafana's rainforests and Isalo's rockscapes to the artisanal city of Antsirabe and historic Fianarantsoa.

Madagascar's longest road and arguably its most heavily touristed, the RN7 between Antananarivo and Toliara is surfaced for its entire length of 980km (609 miles), bisecting six of the country's 22 administrative regions en route. Starting in the fertile and moist central highlands before it gradually descends into the lower-lying and drier coastal belt, it offers direct or indirect access to several of Madagascar's key attractions, from national parks such as Ranomafana and Isalo to the historic old towns of Antsirabe and Fianarantsoa. Theoretically, you could cover the full length of the RN7 in two days of more-or-less non-stop daylight driving, but if sightseeing is a priority, then it's worth allocating at least a week, better 10 days, to the trip, and it offers enough stops and diversions to keep one busy for the best part of a month. In addition, many sites along the RN7 immediately south of the capital would make for ideal self-standing day or overnight trips out of the capital.

TOWARDS ANTSIRABE

Having cleared the congested outskirts of Antananarivo, the RN7 passes through undulating highlands dotted with neat two-storey Merina homesteads and wide riverine valleys partially submerged below bright green rice paddies. Overlooking the right side of the road 37km (22 miles) out of the capital, **Iharanandriana ❶**, also known as the Casque de Behenjy, is a prominent helmet-shaped rock formation whose steep but climbable 1,690-metre (5,545ft) summit offers fabulous views over the surrounding countryside. Over the next 6km (4 miles), the RN7 follows the pretty Ambondrona River south to **Behenjy**, a small town with a reputation as something of a culinary hotspot, tempting passing travellers with its excellent *menakely*

⊙ **Main Attractions**
Antsirabe
Pays Zafimaniry
Soatanana
Parc National de
  Ranomafana
Fianarantsoa-Côte Est
  (FCE) Railway
Fianarantsoa
Réserve d'Anja
Parc National de l'Isalo
Parc National Zombitse-
  Vohibasia

⊙ Map on page 146

Silk scarves for sale in Ambalavao.

(doughnut-like pastries), homemade sausages and *foie gras*.

Another 14km (8 miles) further south, an unsignposted 2km (1.2-mile) dirt road branches west to **Andriambilany ❷**, a ridge-top hamlet renowned in the 19th century as the place where the Imerina monarchs crossed the Ambondrona River en route between Antananarivo and the south. Since 1923, the river below Andriambilany has been spanned by an impressive 10-arched stone-brick railway bridge with a total length of 160 metres/yds and maximum height of 25 metres (82ft).

A substantial highland town with a population estimated at 30,000, **Ambatolampy ❸** straddles the RN7 another 10km (6 miles) further south. It is renowned as a centre of metalwork and aluminium pots, as well as foosball tables (known locally, with potential room for confusion, as 'baby foot'). An excellent but anonymous aluminium foundry can be visited by turning left from the RN7 into the market and continuing for another 200 metres/yds or so. A souvenir shop here sells miniature pots along with other aluminium cast items such as baobab trees, zebus, lemurs and chameleons. A memorial to the dead of World War I stands in the town's central square.

About 15km (9 miles) west of Ambatolampy, the deeply incised slopes of the massif known appropriately as Ambohimirandrana (Braided Mountain) support the 30-sq-km (11.5-sq-mile) **Forêt**

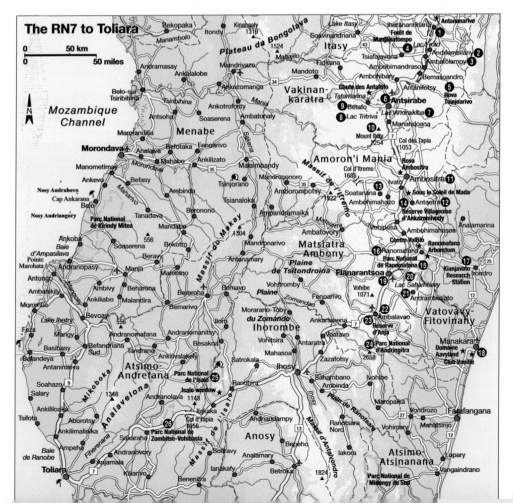

de **Manjakatompo** ❹ (daily), roughly 20 percent of which comprises natural forest and the remainder plantation. This sacred mountain is an important traditional sacrificial site, legendarily inhabited by invisible evil dwarfs known as Vazimba, and it is *fady* to bring pork meat onto its slopes, or to wear shoes or talk in a few specific areas. A network of hiking trails run through the reserve, starting at the pretty Lac Froid (which supplies water to Ambatolampy) at the eastern base. Immediately east of Manjakatompo stands Madagascar's third-highest summit: the 2,642-metre (8,668ft) **Mount Tsiafajavona** (roughly translated as 'Place of Permanent Cloud').

Another possible diversion from Ambatolampy, **Rova Tsinjoarivo** ❺, 45km (27 miles) to the southeast, is the site of a restored five-building summer palace built for Queen Ranavalona I over 1832–6 and subsequently used as a retreat by Ranavalona II and III. The first Ranavalona chose the site for its fabulous location on a forested promontory bordered on three sides by the Onive River; it is said that one of her favourite amusements whilst holidaying at Tsinjoarivo was instructing her underlings to throw a zebu into the water and then watching it plummet helplessly to its death over a series of cascades that includes the Andriamamovoka ('Mighty Sand-maker') and Ambavaloza ('Mouth of Danger') Falls. The high ridges west of Tsinjoarivo support some of the country's most undisturbed and little-visited montane rainforests. Eleven primate species are present in the area, notably the diademed sifaka, brown lemur, red-bellied lemur, giant bamboo lemur, and the only known population of Sibree's dwarf lemur, a critically endangered species first described in 1896 based on a museum specimen, and long assumed to be extinct until its rediscovery here in 2010.

Heading along the RN7 south of Ambatolampy, some large painted Merina tombs can be seen on the roadside after about 16km (10 miles) on the northern outskirts of Ambohimandraso. A few kilometres further south, Bemasoandro (literally Big Sun) is the

Cast aluminium souvenirs for sale at Ambatolampy.

Village women selling local produce in a highlands market.

⊙ Tip

Although Rova Tsinjoarivo is only 45km (25 miles) from Ambatolampy, the rough road usually takes around three hours to traverse, so it makes sense to plan on an overnight stay at the adjacent Gîte du Rova (tel: 033-8118971). This community-run gîte is managed by a local guides association, and visits to the nearby waterfalls and lemur-rich forests are offered in collaboration with Sababe (www.sadabe. org), a dynamic NGO named after the Malagasy for diademed sifaka.

site of a few roadside stalls selling handmade musical instruments and beautifully crafted pinewood replica trucks, tankers, *taxis-brousse* and other vehicles. About 40km (24 miles) south of Ambatolampy, the RN7 skirts past **Antanifotsy**, which is the eighth-largest town in Madagascar, with a population now estimated at 100,000, but has little to show for it in terms of tourist attractions. From Antanifotsy, it's another 75km (45 miles) southwest to the larger town of Antsirabe.

ANTSIRABE

Situated 170km (105 miles) south of Antananarivo, **Antsirabe** ❻ is the capital of Vakinankaratra, an administrative region whose borders approximate those of an eponymous kingdom (also known as Andrantsay) that was founded in the early 17th century and incorporated into Imerina following its conquest by King Andrianampoinimerina 200 years later. Madagascar's third-largest city, it supports a population estimated at 250,000, and boasts an unusually vibrant economic feel (at least for Madagascar) thanks partly to its thriving industrial sector (it's the site of the country's main beer, cotton and tobacco factories) and artisanal ingenuity. Situated an altitude of 1,500 metres (4,921ft) amidst fertile and well-watered volcanic soils, Antsirabe is also an important centre of agricultural production, well suited to growing anything from potatoes and pumpkins to apples and plums.

The Malagasy name Antsirabe means 'Place of Big Salt' and dates back hundreds of years, back to when it was just a small market village renowned for selling salt extracted from its potash-rich soils and thermal springs. It was these same springs, combined with a refreshingly temperate highland climate, that led to the foundation of the modern town in 1872, originally as a hill retreat and spa for Norwegian missionaries, and under French colonial rule it went on to replace the traditional royal capital at Betafo as the administrative centre of Vakinankaratra. The hot springs of Antsirabe are also alluded to in its

Traditional Merina house, near Antsirabe.

popular nicknames Ville d'Eau and Visy Gasy (Vichy of Madagascar).

Antsirabe is particularly worth visiting on Saturday mornings, when the colourful open-air Tsena Sabotsy (Saturday market), set in a large walled hilltop compound on the southwestern outskirts, is at its busiest and most chaotic. The wide avenues of the town centre are dotted with attractive early 20th-century architectural relics, among them the imposing Marian **Cathédrale Notre-Dame-de-la-Salette**, whose ornate multi-turreted five-storey bell tower dominates the skyline of Avenue de l'Indépendance, and the 1920s Gare d'Antsirabe at the east end of Grande Avenue. A more contemporary landmark, standing totem-like in the square in front of the railway station, is the **Fahaleovantena (Independence) Monument**, which is engraved with scenes associated with Madagascar's 19 main ethnic groups, and also features a bronze zebu head and inscription of the first two measures of the national anthem.

Set in a massive suburban garden at the west end of Grande Avenue, the magnificent **Hôtel des Thermes** (tel: 034-6548761; www.sofitrans-sa.com), built c.1897, is a three-storey pile notable for its colonnaded facade and time-worn colonial-style interior, as well as the agreeably characterful Le Pousse-Pousse Café, complete with terrace seating overlooking the swimming pool. Somewhat more industrial in feel are the free guided tours offered by the **Star Brasserie** (tel: 020-4487171; Tue–Thu 9am and 2pm), which was founded on the Betafo Road, about 1km (0.6 mile) west of the town centre, back in 1947.

Antsirabe's artisanal wealth is well worth exploring. A recommended first stop is **Maminirina Corne de Zébu** (Parc de l'Est; tel: 034-3190581; daily 7am–7pm), an ingenious cottage industry dedicated to manufacturing richly-textured and multihued souvenirs from zebu horns. Visitors are treated to a free demonstration of the process used to transform the horns into a malleable sculpting material, and can then visit a shop selling a wide variety of artefacts made on site, from salad bowls, drink coasters and ashtrays to pretty jewellery and lively miniature figurines of lemurs and birds. Next door, the Broderie et Miniature Mamy (Parc de l'Est; tel: 020-4496120; Mon–Sat 8am–6pm), founded in 1990, manufactures and sells miniature cars, bicycles, rickshaws and other items made from recycled metal.

AROUND ANTSIRABE

The most popular goal for an outing from Antsirabe is the **Lac Andraikiba ❼**, which lies just 7km (4 miles) west of town, practically alongside the R34. One of several crater lakes that stud the volcanic countryside around Antsirabe, it has a diameter of around 1km (0.6 miles), and is enclosed by steep wooded slopes, especially on the eastern side. It is also something of a victim of its own success, attended by large numbers of persistent hawkers

Colourful zebu-horn jewellery at Maminirina Corne de Zébu, Antsirabe.

and aspirant guides, for which reason many people now prefer head to the smaller, steeper and quieter **Lac Tritriva** , set in the middle of a pine plantation another 10km (6 miles) to the southwest along a fair dirt road. Walking trails run around both lakes but locals say that those who transgress an ancient *fady* on swimming in Lac Tritriva will drown. Either or both form an excellent goal for a bicycle or scooter trip out of Antsirabe; reliable vehicles can be rented from Rando Raid Madagascar (Rue Stavanger; tel: 020-490021; http://randoraidmadagascar.fr).

In precolonial times, **Betafo** ❾, 22km (13 miles) west of Antsirabe on the R34, was not only the capital of Vakinankaratra, but it also ranked – as suggested by its name (literally, 'Many Roofs') – as one of the largest settlements anywhere in the country's. Now an attractive country town of 30,000 inhabitants, it incorporates some excellent examples of traditional Merina homesteads, solid-looking double-storey clay-brick constructions supported by thick wooden pillars, as well as the tomb of Vakinankaratra's last monarch Andriatomponitany, whose name means 'King of the Earth'. Only 500 metres/yds north of the town centre, Lac Tatamarina is a pretty small lake with a backdrop of three volcanic hills. Another 4km (2.5 miles) to the northeast, the pretty Chutes d'Antafofo snake down a forested ravine into a pretty pool where swimming, once again, is *fady*.

Rising starkly to the west of the RN7 south of Antsirabe, the 2,254-metre (7,395ft) **Mont Ibity** ❿ is a prominent shale and quartzite massif renowned for its wealth of rare reddish and bluish gems including rubellite, tourmaline, amethyst and rose quartz. Ibity is also known for its immense floral (and in particular succulent) wealth, which embraces 242 species, more than 10 percent of which are endemic to this one specific massif, among them several aloes and the yellow-flowered dwarf elephants foot *Pachypodium brevicaule*. The usual starting point for Ibity hikes is Manandoana, a large village bisected by the RN7 about 24km (14 miles) south of Antsirabe. The steep and largely shadeless trail to the summit starts at the Manandoana Rova (possibly the only palace in Madagascar still inhabited by people of royal descent), takes around three hours in either direction, and is suited only to fit travellers.

AMBOSITRA

Sprawling organically across a patchwork of paddy-flanked hills 92km (55 miles) south of Antsirabe, **Ambositra** ⓫ (pronounced am-*boo*-stra) is an attractive town of around 30,000 predominantly Betsileo inhabitants and administrative capital of Amoron'i Mania Region. Ambositra means 'Place of Many Zebus', but today the town is best-known as the centre of the unique Zafimaniry woodcrafting tradition. The sloping, winding alleys of the town centre are lined with craft shops selling wooden sculptures, many housed

Cathédrale du Coeur-Immaculé-de-Marie, Ambositra.

in run-down old colonial buildings whose intricately carved balconies are another facet of the Zafimaniry woodcraft legacy. The most imposing single building is the hilltop brick-faced Cathédrale du Coeur-Immaculé de Marie on Rue du Commerce.

About 500 metres/yds north of the town centre, the **Monastère des Bénédictines de Sainte Bathilde** (www.benedictines-ste-bathilde.fr) is a convent founded in 1934 by a French nun whose husband had died in World War I. The large and beautiful brick-faced church has an intricately decorated interior comprising bold patterns of orange, black and white bricks. Services are held at 6.30am daily and a shop (Mon–Fri 8am–4.30pm, Sat 6am–noon, Sun 2–4.30pm) sells delicious cheeses and other homemade goodies produced by the nuns.

Set on a craggy mini-peak about 4km (2.5 miles) drive or walk southwest of the town centre, the old **Rova Ambositra** is an 18th-century palace built by the Betsileo monarch Mpanalina II. The original was all but destroyed when

King Radama I of Imerina captured Betsileo in 1811, but the two main wooden buildings, both ornately carved with a tiled roof, have since been restored, and one now houses a small museum dedicated to the palace's history. Other surviving features at the untended site include two large stone royal tombs, a sunken courtyard, and a large boulder from which the king would address his subjects. Even if you've no interest in historic ruins, the walk out is lovely, and the attractively terraced slopes offer some fine views back to town. The best route is to follow the RN7 south from the town centre for about 500 metres/yds, then turn onto a dirt road that branches west opposite the *taxi-brousse* station (just before the hospital). The road crosses a paddy then after 1km (0.6 miles) hits a T-junction where you need to turn left. After another 300 metres/yds, turn left again at the oddly angled fork opposite a prominent brick tomb, and you'll reach the site after another 2km (1.2 miles). On foot, allow up to 90 minutes in either direction. By car, a 4x4 is required.

Rova Ambositra.

Zafimaniry woodcarving workshop.

⊙ Tip

If you don't have time to head deep into Pays Zafimaniry, do drop into Ambositra's Chez Victor, a workshop of Malagasy arts on Rue du Commerce opposite the Grand Hôtel. Here you will discover the intricate process of marquetry, using a kind of homemade jigsaw to fashion pieces of different coloured wood with such precision they interlock without glue. A second workshop features sculptors who work up to 20 wood types. A fabulous selection of marquetry products and wooden sculptures is for sale.

Zafimaniry wooden crafts souvenirs, Ambositra.

SOUTH OF AMBOSITRA

Set in the chilly forested highlands of southeast Amoron'i Mania, the **Pays Zafimaniry** is the main stronghold of an eponymous ethnic group whose traditional woodcraft skills and knowledge are recognised as the only Madagascan inclusion on Unesco's Intangible Cultural Heritage List. The Zafimaniry build their houses entirely from timber, without using nails, and they decorate the exterior, as well as all furniture therein, with geometric patterns that reflect their ancient Indonesian heritage as well as a more recent Arab influences. They also form one of the last ethnic groups in Madagascar to continue the traditional practice of erecting stone obelisks to commemorate their ancestors. In recent decades, the combination of deforestation and land pressure relating to population growth has caused many Zafimaniry to abandon woodworking in favour of subsistence farming, but still the tradition remains very much alive, boosted somewhat by the opportunity to sell carvings and other products via the tourist trade.

Even today, the rugged terrain of the mist-swept Pays Zafimaniry is best explored over two to five days on foot, hiking between villages along steep forested footpaths that evoke something of Madagascar as it must have been in precolonial times, overnighting in a network of simple homestays set in traditional wooden homesteads. The road gateway to the region is **Antoetra** ⑫, a relatively large Zafimaniry settlement situated at an altitude of 1,650 metres (5,415ft) about 40km (24 miles) southeast of Ambositra along a dirt road that diverges left from the RN7 at the crossroads village of Ivato 15km (9 miles) south of town. Hikes can be arranged through any hotel in Ambositra or at the well-organised Sous le Soleil de Mada (tel: 033-0734414; http://souslesoleilde mada.monsite-orange.fr), a traditional-style lodge set about halfway along the feeder road between Ivato and Antoetra.

A picturesque village of earthy traditional two-storey Merina houses surrounded by tall granite outcrops, **Soatanana** ⑬, 40km (24 miles) southwest of Ambositra, is renowned for

producing some of the country's finest handcrafted silk scarves and other products. Around 200 villagers here, most of them women, derive their income either from silk production or from weaving scarves and cloths on traditional wooden looms. Local guides at Soatanana will demonstrate the silk-production process from start to end, and the village is also an excellent place to buy hand-crafted silks direct from source. To get there from Ambositra, follow the RN7 south for 15km (9 miles) to Ivato, then turn right onto the erratically surfaced RN35 and continue for another 15km (9 miles) to Anjoman Akona (also known as Tsarafandry). Here you need to turn left onto a red earth road, then right after another 6km (4 miles) just before the village of Ambohimahazo, from where it's about 4km (2.5 miles) from to Soatanana.

Flanking the RN7 about 20km (12 miles) south of Ambositra, the **Réserve Villageoise d'Ankazomivady** ⓮ (tel: 034-8161869; http://lemursankazomivady forest.over-blog.com; daily 8am–5pm) opened in 2014 to protect a 6-sq-km

(2.4-sq-mile) tract of primary forest threatened among other things by illegal clearance to make way for geranium plantations. Guided walks last from 30 minutes to two hours and come with a good chance of spotting red-fronted brown lemur along with various forest chameleons and birds, ideally leaving between 7 and 10am. Night walks to look for the forest's three nocturnal lemur species can also be arranged.

RANOMAFANA

Practically all tours heading south divert to the **Parc National de Ranomafana** ⓯ (www.parcs-madagascar.com; daily 7am–4pm) which protects of 416 sq km (160 sq miles) of lush rainforest-swathed slopes flanking the RN25 about 20km (12 miles) east of its junction with the RN7 and almost 400km (240 miles) south of Antananarivo. One of the most biodiverse protected areas in Madagascar, Ranomafana is home to seven species of diurnal lemur, namely Milne-Edward's sifaka, black-and-white ruffed lemur, red-fronted brown lemur,

Silk weaver in Ranomafana.

☉ MALAGASY SILK

The hilly countryside around Soatanana supports the island's largest remaining stands of tapia tree *Uapaca bojeri*, which in turn forms the staple diet and breeding ground of the Madagascar silkworm *Borocera madagascariensis*. The cocoons of this endemic moth, harvested in the wild over March to June, produce a highly prized form of 'wild silk' unique to the island. This is supplemented in most places by the lighter-coloured and softer-textured cultivated silk of the domestic Chinese silkworm *Bombyx mori*, which locals breed in their houses, feeding them mulberry or other similar leaves, to harvest over October to March.

The transformation from cocoon to silk is an elaborate process. It involves gently drying the cocoons for one week, then simmering them in boiling water, together with a soap made from zebu-fat and ash, for three days in order to separate the fibres, which must then dry in the sun for another week before a dye is applied. Most dyes used in Madagascar are natural – passion fruit leaf for green, turmeric for yellow, waterlily roots for grey, wild mushrooms for brown, and a type of tree bark for red – but purists should note the dye used for blue silk is artificial. The entire process can be seen at the silk-producing village of Soatanana outside Ambositra, or at Atelier Soalandy in Ambalavao, both of which also sell excellent local silk products.

Fanaloka or Malagasy striped civet (Fossa fossana), Parc National de Ranomafana.

The road through the Parc National de Ranomafana.

red-bellied lemur, greater bamboo lemur, grey bamboo and golden bamboo lemur (the latter a critically endangered species first discovered in 1986 and the raison d'être for the creation of the national park five years later). Other wildlife includes five nocturnal lemur, 115 bird, 98 amphibian and 58 reptile species, along with a variety of seldom seen nocturnal carnivores.

A diverse selection of day trails run through the park, the most popular – and best for general lemur viewing – being the demanding 15km (9-mile) Circuit de Varibolema and 11km (7-mile) Circuit de Edena, both of which start at the Varibolo Ticket Office on the RN25 some 30km (18 miles) southeast of the junction with the RN7. Adjacent to the ticket office, the privately-run Varibolo Resto (tel: 034-9082303; www. varibolo.com; 7am–8pm) not only serves good and well-priced meals, but also which operates expertly guided kayaking trips on the Namorona (aka Andriamamovoka) River, departing at 9am daily and taking around three hours. More ambitiously, the 28km (17-mile)

Circuit de Soarano, which starts further west at the village of Ambatolahy, involves camping overnight deep in the forest at a chilly altitude of 1,770 metres (5,810ft). Birdwatchers with time on their hands will also find it highly rewarding to wander along the RN25 as it runs through the park, since no guide is required nor is any fee levied, and it offers clearer and less neck-craning views into the canopy than any of the trails into the forest interior. Another interesting excursion is the 45-minute tours offered by the **Centre ValBio** (tel: 034-1358171; www.stony brook.edu/commcms/centre-valbio; Mon–Fri 9–11am and 4–5pm), a research and educational centre with links to the Smithsonian Institute, Stony Brook University and several other international academic institutions.

Some 6km (4 miles) east of Varibolo, the RN25 emerges from the forested national park to bisect the attractively sprawling village for which is named. **Ranomafana** ⑯ is Malagasy for 'hot water' and the village did indeed start life as a spring-fed thermal bath complex that formed its main attraction in the colonial era. Still operational today, the Ranomafana Thermal Baths (Wed–Mon 6am–noon and 1–5.30pm), reached from the village via a rickety wooden bridge across the Namorona River, are set in a large, leafy and attractively ramshackle grounds that close every Tuesday in order that the main swimming pool can be cleaned and refilled. Ranomafana village is well equipped with restaurants and hotels but its only other attraction is the **Famoiva Weaving Cooperative** (tel: 033-0984402; daily 7am–6pm), which produces cotton items on site using traditional looms and also sells silk scarves from Soatanana. The town is busiest on Sunday when it holds its main market.

Situated on the south side of the RN25 about 2km (1.2 miles) past the village, the **Arboretum Ranomafana**

(tel: 034-9916466; Mon–Sat 8am–5pm; Sun 2–5pm) was established in 1994 as a trial site for plantations of indigenous tree species and transformed into an arboretum in 2007. Pride of place here goes to the only known wild specimen of *Dypsis robusta*, a type of palm named in 2005 based on a tree cultivated from seed in Hawaii, and now regarded to be the world's rarest tree. Four other critically endangered palm species are present, most notably *Tahina spectabilis*, which is the tallest of the island's 170 indigenous palms, standing up to 18 metres (59ft) high, and also ranked among the world's 100 rarest plants, with a total wild population of around 30 mature individuals. An attractive feature of the arboretum is that you can walk around unguided at your own pace, and the most interesting trees are all well labelled.

TOWARDS MANAKARA

Situated on the outskirts of the eponymous village alongside the RN25 60km (37 miles) east of Ranomafana, the **Kianjavato Research Station** ⑰

(tel: 032-0378008; https://madagascar partnership.org) was established in 2010 to protect and study the inhabitants of a patchwork of forest fragments that collectively protect nine species of lemur. Kianjavato is one of only two sites countrywide for Jolly's mouse lemur, an endangered species first described in 2006 and named after the pioneering primatologist Alison Jolly. It also harbours important populations of the critically endangered black-and-white ruffed lemur and greater bamboo lemur, and a population of habituated aye-ayes that offer the best opportunity in Madagascar of seeing these perversely charismatic creatures in the wild (as opposed to on an island where they have been introduced). In addition to its research work, the station has planted more than a million indigenous trees to help create corridors between existing forest fragments, and it is involved in several community projects. A full-day tourist package out of Ranomafana, with a maximum group size of ten, incorporates a guided day and evening walk, and offers a better

Football game, Ranomafana.

⊙ Tip

For beach lovers, a more attractive option than staying in Manakara is to grab a *pousse-pousse* or taxi along the sandy 8km (5 miles) road running south to Club Vanille, which stands in glorious isolation on an idyllic clean beach sandwiched between the open sea and a canal. There are no other developments in the area, just a few small fishing villages whose pirogues line the beach, and a rocky reef right in front of the hotel creates calm swimming conditions.

than even chance of seeing all four key lemur species mentioned above. An onsite tented camp is planned in the near future.

Another 115km (70 miles) southeast of Kianjavato, **Manakara** ⑱ is a sleepy end-of-the-line port town set on an attractive stretch of coast four hours' drive from Ranamofana along the surfaced RN25 and RN12 (which splits at the tiny junction village of Irondro). Capital of Vatovavy-Fitovinany Region, Manakara is primarily of interest as the coastal terminus of the historic and scenic twice-weekly Fianarantsoa–Côte Est railway service (see page 156) but it is a pleasant enough place in its own right, and very untouristy. The town centre comprises two distinct sectors bisected by the Manakara River, which forms a southern extension of the Pangalanes canal system, and connected by a solitary metal bridge. Inland of the canal, low-rise Tanambao, the main commercial and residential sector, is home to the railway station, a few modest hotels, and a large bustling market that sprawls out into the surrounding

A flurry of activity at one of the FCE train stops.

streets. Opposite it, raffish Manakara Be is a spacious, shady and decidedly soporific former colonial administrative centre dominated by a wide waterfront avenue dotted with grassy traffic islands and lined with decrepit government buildings that lend it a compelling aura of faded grandiosity. The only tourist attraction in the vicinity of Manakara is the **Domaine Aavyland** (tel: 032-4465325; daily 9am–5pm), set on the RN12 about 20km (12.5 miles) south of town, is an organic farm that produces cinnamon, cloves, vanilla and other herbs for medicinal products and massage oils, and offers guided tours with a day's notice.

FIANARANTSOA

Straddling a series of hills some 410km (246 miles) south of Antananarivo, **Fianarantsoa** ⑲, the historic capital of Haute Matsiatra Region, is Madagascar's fifth-largest city, with a population estimated at around 200,000. Fianarantsoa's main point of interest is Haute-Ville, whose characterful assemblage of sloping cobbled alleys and 19th-century

⊙ THE FIANARANTSOA-CÔTE EST RAILWAY

One of Madagascar's most appealing public transport options, the FCE between Fianarantsoa and Manakara is an ageing but functional colonial relict laid over 1926–36 using forced Malagasy labour and 19th-century narrow-gauge German rails awarded to France as World War I reparation. The 163km (102 mile) line navigates an incredible 48 tunnels and 65 bridges along its spectacular descent from the highlands to the coast, while passing landscapes embrace montane rainforest, steep waterfalls, tea plantations and subsistence farmland. Trains also stop at 17 colonial-era railway stations whose platforms transform into impromptu markets for the occasion.

In theory, coast-bound trains leave Fianarantsoa at 7am on Tuesday and Saturday, taking anything from 12 to 24 hours to complete the journey, and the return trip out of Manakara departs at 7am on Wednesday and Sunday. In practice, delays are not so much commonplace as utterly inevitable, so the trip is only worth considering if you've a reasonably flexible schedule. Fruit and other snacks can be bought from local vendors en route, but you might prefer to bring your own food, and should carry enough drinking water to last the duration. Tickets can be bought cheaply on the spot and it is emphatically worth paying extra to travel first-class, which won't be quite what you are used to in Europe or North America, but still beats second-class hands down.

buildings resembles a scaled-down but more architecturally cohesive variation on its namesake in Antananarivo. According to the World Monuments Fund (www.wmf.org), which placed Fianarantsoa on a 2008 watch list of the world's 100 Most Endangered Sites, the old town incorporates 500 houses constructed between 1868 (when Queen Ranavalona II lifted an edict forbidding commoners from using permanent building materials) and the turn of the 20th century, many in poor state of repair but still occupied by the descendants of their original inhabitants. The old town's main square is overlooked by the **Cathédrale d'Ambozontany**, an imposing brick-faced Catholic edifice constructed in 1890 with two tall white-domed clock towers. Leading uphill from this, Rue du Rova is flanked by two more modest but older Protestant churches: FJKM Antranobiriky and FLM Trinitie Masombahoaka, which respectively date back to 1859 and 1885. Rue de Rova terminates at the top of Ivonea Hill, formerly the site of a 1830s palace built by Governor Rafaralahindraininaly, now home to a

sealed reservoir but still worth a visit for the fantastic views it offers over the lower town and surrounding hills.

A popular overnight base or lunch stop in the vicinity of Fianarantsoa, **Lac Sahambavy** ⑳ is a pretty artificial lake surrounded by pine plantations and overlooked by the legendary Lac Hôtel (tel: 020-7595906, www.lachotel.com). The lake is in the village of Sahambavy, which is also a stop on the FCE Railway, and home to the 330ha (815 acre) Sidexam Tea Estate (Mon–Fri 9am–4pm) which is the only such agricultural concern in Madagascar, and offers 30-minute tours when a guide is available. A wilder and more off-the-beaten-track goal for a rail excursion is **Andrambovato** ㉑, which lies some 45km (25 miles) from Fianarantsoa along the FCE line. Here, a community-based ecotourism organisation called COBA Soamiray (tel: 032-6319711 or 033-0163942) offers a range of affordable day and overnight hikes through the jungle to visit waterfalls, look for birds, or summit a spectacular rock outcrop called Tsitondroina.

Church in the old town of Fianarantsoa.

Fisherman mends his net in Manakara.

⊘ Eat

There's no better place to soak up the atmosphere of Fianarantsoa's old town than Snack Imanoela (tel: 034 6172613; www.facebook.com/SnackImanoela; Mon–Sat 9am–6.30pm), which occupies a well-maintained traditional homestead with a pretty terrace garden on Rue du Rova. In addition to serving wholesome and affordable meals made with locally sourced products, the friendly folks here can arrange homestays with local families in the heart of Haute-Ville.

Artisan at the Fabrique de Papier Anaimoro, Ambalavao.

AMBALAVAO

A steep 54km (32-mile) descent along the RN7 from Fianarantsoa leads to **Ambalavao** ㉒, a neat town of 30,000 set in a hilly basin intermediate in feel between the moist highlands to the north and the drier low country to the south. Coming from the north, Ambalavao is visible from a long way off, and it is customary for private vehicles to stop at a viewpoint marked by a memorial to the six victims of a fatal accident wherein an overloaded French military aeroplane crashed into a ridge 300 metres (985ft) above town on 4 October 1947, leaving just one survivor. Signposted off the road from Fianarantsoa, about 4km (2.5 miles) before you enter Ambalavao, the renowned **Soavita Winery** (tel: 020-7534197; Mon–Sat 7–11am and 1–5pm), run by the same family since it opened in 1973, offers informative and enjoyable wine-making and -tasting tours.

Ambalavao itself is busiest and most engaging on Wednesdays, when a small hill to the south of the town centre hosts the country's largest livestock market. This vibrant and exciting event runs from dawn to dusk, but zebu-trading activity tends to peak between 9am and noon. At other times, the main attraction within the town limits is the **Atelier Soalandy** (tel: 033-1498745; www.facebook.com/soalandy.ambalavao; daily 7am–5pm), which offers fascinating 20-minute demonstrations of silk production as well as selling handmade scarves and other products. Also worth a visit, in the grounds of the popular Aux Bougainvillées hotel, is the **Fabrique de Papier Antaimoro** (tel: 032-4368069, 7.30–11.30am & 1–5pm Mon–Sat), which manufactures organic paper from the bark of the endemic *avoha* tree using a traditional Arab method.

On the south side of the RN7 about 12km (7 miles) west of Ambalavao, the 37ha (91 acre) **Réserve d'Anja** ㉓ (tel: 032-2087651; http://anjareserve.angelfire.com; daily 7am–5pm) was designated by the government in 1999 and opened to visitors two years later. Protecting a pocket of natural forest and small heart-shaped reservoir at the base of an imposing domed granite inselberg, this community reserve was created

⊘ CITY OF LEARNING

Fianarantsoa was founded as the administrative centre of Betsileo following its conquest by Queen Ranavalona I of Imerina in 1830. Under Governor Rafaralahindraininaly, who served there over 1831–42, the hilltop town emerged as the ipso facto political capital of southern Madagascar. Often shortened to Fianar, the town's name roughly translates as 'Good Education', and aptly so, since it rivals Antananarivo as the island's main intellectual and academic centres, housing the county's oldest Lutheran seminary as well as the Université de Fianarantsoa, which was founded in 1992 and now has 11,000 students. Fianarantsoa's reputation for sophistication extends to its role as the joint centre (together with nearby Ambalavao) of the country's low-key wine industry.

to protect a population of ring-tailed lemurs that has increased from around 150 individuals to an estimated 400 since its inception. Guided walks are best undertaken in the early morning or late afternoon, when these enchanting monkey-like creatures tend to be most sociable and active, often sunning themselves on the rocks or coming to the reservoir to drink. Visitors can choose between a short (90 minutes) walk to the forest at the rock base, or a longer (up to six hours) hike that ascends to a viewpoint near the summit and also goes past the caves where the lemurs sleep (along with bats and owls) and some traditional tombs. Supported by more than 200 local community members, Anja prides itself on being the country's most popular community-managed eco-tourist site, attracting around 1,000 visitors monthly.

Ambalavao is the springboard for visits to the 311-sq-km (120-sq-mile) **Parc National d'Andringitra** ㉔ (tel: 033-1234081; www.parcs-madagascar.com; daily 6.30am–3.30pm), a hiker-friendly destination that protects the upper slopes of the eponymous granite massif 47km (28 miles) south of town. Andringitra boasts the greatest mammalian diversity of any protected area in Madagascar: more than 50 species have been recorded, among them eight carnivore, nine diurnal lemur and five nocturnal lemurs, notably Milne-Edward's sifaka, brown lemur, red-fronted brown lemur and ring-tailed lemur. Other wildlife includes more than 100 bird, 75 amphibian and 50 reptile species. Andringitra was set aside as a strict nature reserve since 1927, upgraded to national park status in 1999, and included as a component of the Rainforests of the Atsinanana Unesco World Heritage Site upon its inscription in 2007.

Geared mainly towards properly equipped hikers, Andringitra is traversed by five hiking trails that collectively explore all its major habitats. Most challenging and popular with peak-baggers is the Circuit d'Imarivolanitra, a 28km (17 mile) two-day round hike that leads to the 2,658-metre (8,720ft) summit of Pic Boby, a spectacular bare granite prominence

Ring-tailed lemur at the Réserve d'Anja.

Highland scenery near Ambalavao.

> **◎ Tip**
>
> Momotrek (tel: 032-4418790; www.isalo-trek.com) is a Ranohira-based company dedicated to showing off the more remote corners of Isalo. It arranges several multi-day treks including a five-day, four-night portered camping excursion that starts at Andriamanara in the park's little-visited north, then heads back to Ranohira in a succession of manageable legs (the longest day is 13km/8 miles).

that ranks as the country's second-tallest peak (and the highest that can be scaled without specialist climbing gear). The 14km (9 mile), eight-hour Circuit d'Imaitso is the best trail for general lemur viewing and birdwatching, while the 13km (8 mile), 10-hour Circuit de Diavolana leads through high meadows sprinkled with seasonal wildflowers to a rocky moonscape inhabited by a distinct high-altitude morph of ring-tailed lemur with an unusually thick and rusty coat. For more reluctant hikers, the relatively undemanding 6km (4 mile), four-hour Circuit d'Asaramanitra, which leads through dense forest past the impressive Riambavy Falls, is worth considering.

TOWARDS TOLIARA

The 460km (276-mile) drive along the RN7 between Ambalavao and Toliara is marked by a gradual drop in altitude and ecological trend towards the semi-arid climate and succulent-dominated dry-country flora typical of the island's far southwest. The road is surfaced in its entirety and can easily be covered in one

day, but most tours punctuate it with a one- or two-night stop at the small and rather impermanent-looking 'wild west' town of **Ranohira**, which lies almost precisely halfway between Ambalavao and Toliara and forms the springboard for visits to the popular Parc National de l'Isalo as well as expeditions to the more remote Makay Massif.

Running north from the RN7 as it passes through Ranohira, the **Parc National de l'Isalo** ㉕ (tel: 033-1317258; www.parcs-madagascar.com; daily 6.30am–4.30pm) was gazetted in 1999 to protect a 815-sq-km (314 sq-mile) tract of semi-arid low-lying grassland from which a vast massif of contorted water- and wind-eroded sandstone formations rises to a maximum altitude of 1,268 metres (4,160ft). The evocative rockscapes of Isalo include all manner of otherworldly eroded strata and spine-like formations dotted with jagged peaks and balancing rocks, and support a wealth of suitably bizarre succulents, including the bulbous elephant's foot *Pachypodium rosulatum* and unique red-flowering *Aloe isaloensis*. The park is also a stronghold

The rocky landscape of the Parc National de l'Isalo.

for the Bismarck palm, a tall, fire-resistant, large-leafed endemic placed in its own monotypic genus *Bismarckia*, while the streams that run though its deep shady canyons feed ribbons of riparian woodland. Verreaux's sifaka, red-fronted brown lemur and ring-tailed lemur are all common and easily seen on day hikes, and the park also supports four nocturnal lemur species. The most eagerly sought of 83 bird species is the conspicuous Benson's rock thrush, an Isalo endemic that was once regarded to be a full species but is now thought to be a dry-country subspecies of forest rock-thrush. Permits and guides can be arranged at the national park ticket office and local guides association office, which stand opposite each other at the junction for the main park entrance in Ranohira. The most popular option is a 12km- (7-mile), four-hour circular day hike to a beautiful palm-fringed natural swimming pool set oasis-like near the base of the rocky massif.

If you arrive at Ranohira in time for a short late afternoon foray, it's worth following the RN7 another 15km (9 miles) west to the **Reine de l'Isalo**, a spectacular roadside balancing rock formation now, unfortunately, scarred by graffiti. Just past this, a short dirt track runs north to **La Fenêtre de l'Isalo**, an elevated rock arch that offers spectacular and very photogenic views, especially at sunset. Heading on towards Toliara, dusty **Ilakaka**, 21km (13 miles) past Ranohira, has mushroomed from a hamlet of half-a-dozen houses to a bona fide boomtown since the discovery of sapphires there in 1997. The story is that the boom started after a local sold a pretty stone to a passing backpacker in a *taxi-brousse*, and this was later identified to be a sapphire. Ilakaka today wouldn't win any awards for town-planning or beauty, but it's a thriving place, and plenty of gem dealerships line the main road if you're interested in looking around, or brave enough to buy.

Another 63km (38 miles) past Ilakaka stands the roadside reception area of the little-visited but highly accessible 3.6-sq-km (1.4-sq-mile) **Parc National Zombitse-Vohibasia** ㉖ (www.parcs-madagascar.com; daily 8am–4pm), which

○ THE MAKAY MASSIF

Situate to the north of Isalo, Makay is a vast and little-visited sandstone massif boasting similar scenic qualities and flora to the more southerly national park, but at a lower altitude, and with notably hotter temperatures and far more of a wilderness feel. Bisected by the Mangoky River, it supports a mixture of woodland and open vegetation, and is incised with deep forested river canyons and scattered with beautiful natural lakes. Supporting an exceptional variety of birds along with red-fronted brown lemur and Verreaux's sifaka, Makay is likely to be made a national park at some point in the future, but for now the massif remains the country's last and largest unprotected wilderness area, making it a beacon for adventurous travellers wanting to get away from an established tourist track. Expeditions usually start at Ranohira, from where it is a long, tough full-day 4x4 drive to the base of the massif, and might involve anything from five more days to two full weeks of hiking and camping rough. Access is limited to the dry season, with May to July being the optimum months climatically. A reliable specialist operator running regular portered hikes into the massif is Ranohira-based operator Momotrek (tel: 032-4418790; www.isalo-trek.com).

La Fenêtre de l'Isalo, a popular spot at sunset.

Sandstone formations in the Parc National de l'Isalo.

was created in 1997 to protect three small pockets of transitional moist-spiny forest set on gently undulating sandstone hills flanking the RN7. The park is of particular interest to birders as the best place to see Appert's tetraka, a Vulnerable and highly localised grey-headed, yellow-breasted species first described in 1972, initially as a type of greenbul or a warbler, but now ascribed to the Bernieridae. Also notable and regularly observed among the 98 bird species identified in this small national park are the giant coua, Coquerel's coua, white-browed owl, Madagascar cuckoo-roller, blue vanga and rufous vanga. Verreaux's sifaka, ring-tailed lemur, red-fronted lemur are quite commonly seen, five nocturnal lemur species live here, and it is the only known locale for *Grammangis spectabilis*, a stunning pink-flowered epiphytic orchid that blooms in January. The pick of three short trails is the flat and easy 2.5km- (1.5-mile) Circuit de Mandresy, which offers a good chance of spotting Appert's tetraka if you take it slowly (allow two hours) and also passes a trio

of large baobabs. The very short (800 metre/yd) Circuit de Ritakala is perhaps better suited to serious birders (again, allow an hour or two), while the longer, 3km (2-mile) Circuit de Lobo offers a more genuine leg stretch and is usually good for lemurs and chameleons.

West of Zombitse-Vohibasia, the last stretch of the RN7 passes initially through a landscape studded with impressive baobabs before emerging at Toliara after 145km (87 miles). The route is punctuated by urban settings, including **Sakaraha**, another booming but rather scruffy sapphire-production centre situated just 16km (10 miles) past the reception of Zombitse-Vohibasia. Look out for the boat-shaped Mahafaly tomb, complete with cannons, to the right of the RN7 as you exit the town. A larger collection of elaborately-painted Mahafaly tombs – depicting everything from baobabs and zebus to mermaids and football players – flanking the south side of the RN7 about 42km (25 miles) before Toliara. Only 12km (7 miles) before Toliara, you could divert to the highly worthwhile Arboretum d'Antsokay (see page 179).

Miners looking for alluvial sapphire, Ilakaka.

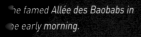
The famed Allée des Baobabs in the early morning.

MORONDAVA AND SURROUNDS

The iconic Allée des Baobabs, spectacular tsingy rockscapes of Bemaraha, and navigable Tsiribihina and Manambolo Rivers are highlights of the wild countryside around the port of Morondava.

Situated on the west coast roughly 660km (400 miles) by road from Antananarivo, sleepy **Morondava** ❶ is not generally visited as a destination in its own right but as the springboard for excursions to the Allée des Baobabs, the Parc National des Tsingy de Bemaraha and the Réserve Forestière de Kirindy. Despite this, it is an attractive enough place, albeit one whose appealing tropical seaside character isn't subsidised by much in the way of prescribed sightseeing. The old town centre stands on a small virtual island bounded to the northwest by a wide sandy beach and the open ocean, to the south by the delta-like mouth of the Morondava River, to the southeast by the Canal Hellot (dug in 1930), and to the east by a muddy alluvial estuary. In recent decades, however, the town has expanded eastwards across the estuary in order to accommodate an ever-growing population that now stands at around 70,000.

The name Morondava derives from the Malagasy *morona lava*, meaning 'long beach' or possibly 'long distance'. It is the administrative capital of Menabe, a region named after the eponymous Sakalava kingdom (literally 'Big Red', in reference to its predominantly laterite soils) founded by King Adriamandazoala *c.*1540. Menabe emerged as the island's most powerful polity under King Andriandahifotsy,

whose six-decade reign ended in 1685, but a succession of Imerina invasions in the early 19th century culminated in defeat at the hands of Queen Ranavalona I's army in 1846 and the incorporation of Menabe into her highland kingdom. Today, Morondava is populated mainly by people of the Sakalava and Vezo ethnic groups, but it also supports a substantial Indian, Chinese and European community whose forbears settled there in the colonial era.

The most popular and efficient way to travel from Antananarivo is by air, a

⊙ Main Attractions

Tsiribihina and
   Manambolo river trips
Allée des Baobabs
Réserve Forestière de
   Kirindy
Parc National des Tsingy
   de Bemaraha
Parc National de Kirindy-
   Mitea

Map on page 166

Salt evaporation ponds near Belo-sur-Mer.

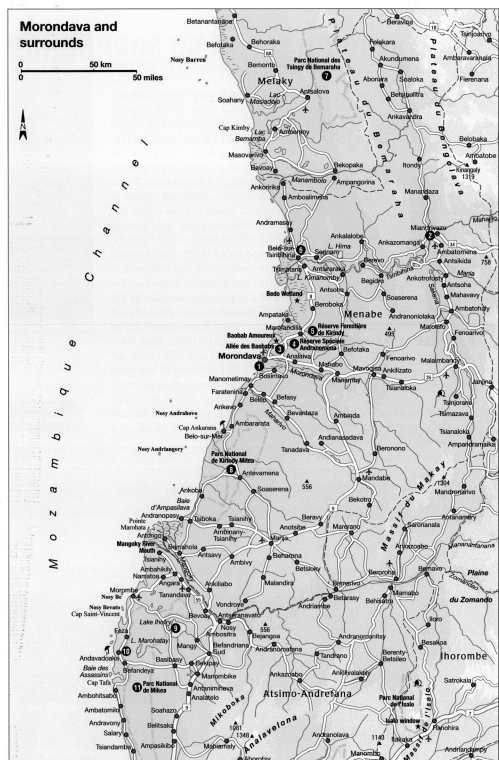

Morondava and surrounds

0 — 50 km
0 — 50 miles

Mozambique Channel

Betanantanana
Beravina
Tsinjoarivo
Behoraka
Folakara
Befotaka
8A
Akundumena
Ambaravaranala
Nosy Barren
Parc National des
Tsingy de Bemaraha **7**
Fierenana
Bemonto
Abonara
Soaloka
Melaky
Antsalova
Betsipolitra
Lac
Masiadolo
Soahany
Ankavandra
Belobaka
Cap Kimby
Lac
Ambereny
Ambatobe
Bemamba
Kinangaly
Masovarivo
Bekopaka
Itondy
1319
Bevoay
Ampangorina
Manandaza
Ankoririka
Manambolo
Amboalimena
Mahajilo
Andramasay
Miandrivazo **2**
Ankalalobe
34
L. Hima
Ankazomanga
Ambatomena
Belo-sur- **6**
Serinam
Antsikida
Tsiribihina
Berevo
758
Tsimatana
Antsiraraka
Begidro
Ankotrofosty
Antsoha
Kimanomby
Mania
Antsoha
Mahavavy
Bedo Wetland
Beroboka
Soaserena
Ambatohaly
Ampataka
Menabe
Andranoniolaka
Marolefo
Marofandilia
Fenoarivo
Baobab Amoureux
Réserve Forestière **5**
de Kirindy
495
Allée des Baobabs
Réserve Spéciale **4**
Andranomena
3
Morondava
Befotaka
Malaimbandy
1
Analaiva
Fenoarivo
Mahabo
Mavogisa
Ankilizato
35
Manometimay
Bosimavo
Morondava
Manamby
Tsinjorano
Faratenina
Beleo
Befasy
Tsianaloka
Tsimazava
Ankevo
Maharivo
Bevantaza
Ambinda
Nosy Andrahovo
Ambararata
Andianasadava
Tsianaloka
Cap Ankarana
Beronono
Ampandramaika
Belo-sur-Mer
Tanadava
Nosy Andriangory
Parc National
Mandabe
T304
de Kirindy Mitea
Mandronarivo
8
Antevamena
556
Ankoba
Soaserena
Bekotro
Baie
d'Ampasilava
9
Antanamary
Andranopasy
Tsiboka
Tsianihy
Beravy
Saronanala
Pointe
Anotsibe
Marerano
Ankazoabo
Marohata
Ambinany-
Manja
Mananantanana
Antongo
Tsianihy
Mangoky River
Bemahola
Antsavy
Beharona
Bemarivo
Beroroha
Bemavo
Mouth
Ambivy
Betsioky
Plaine
Tsianihy
Malandira
Zomando
Ambahikily
Bemarivo
du Zomando
Namatoa
Angara
Ankiliabo
Mamabo
Moromba
Tanandava
Vondrove
Behisatra
Nosy Be
55
Betarasy
Nosy Bevato
Bevoay
Andriambe
Iloro
Cap Saint-Vincent
Antseranavato
Besakoa
Lake Ihotry
Nosy **9**
Ihorombe
Feza
Ambositra
556
L. Marohatay
Mangy
Bejangoa
Andranomanitsy
Andavadoaka
10
Befandriana
Andranomafana
Berenty-
Baie des
Basibasy
Sud
Tandrano
Betsileo
Assassins
Bekipay
Ankazoabo
Satrokala
Cap Tafa
Manombike
Ankilivalakely
Ambohitsabo
Parc National
Antanimiheva
Parc National
Ambatomilo
11
de Mikea
Analatelo
de l'Isalo
Andravony
Soahazo
9
7
Mikoboka
Atsimo-Andrefana
Isalo window
Salary
Belitsaka
1081
Ranohira
Tsiandamba
1348
Andranolava
1143
Ampasikibo
Mahiamaly
Ilakaka
Andriandampy
Analavelona
Aborotsy
Manombo

one-hour flight that lands at Morondava Airport, on the town's eastern outskirts about 5km (3 miles) inland of the old centre. Driving between Antananarivo and Morondava, following the RN7 to Antsirabe then heading west along the RN34 through Miandrivazo and Malaimbandy, is a more appealing prospect than it was a few years back, thanks to recent road upgrades, but you need to allow two days for the 660km (400-mile) trip. The best place to stop overnight, about 390km (235 miles) out of Antananarivo, is **Miandrivazo ❷**, a hot but pretty town set on the south bank of the Mahajilo River, a large tributary of the Tsiribihina. Known for its busy Wednesday market, Miandrivazo is also the springboard for boat trips along the Tsiribihina River to Belo-sur-Tsiribihina.

BAOBAB AVENUE AND KIRINDY

Arguably the most iconic scenic landmark anywhere in Madagascar, the **Allée des Baobabs ❸**, 30 minutes' drive northeast of Morondava, is a short stretch of road lined on either side by around two dozen Grandidier's baobabs, the highest of which stand about 30m (98ft) tall. The avenue is best visited at dusk (or less conveniently at dawn), when the smooth trunks of the trees glow orange-brown in the golden light, and they also usually make a strikingly photogenic silhouette against the setting (or rising) sun. Thought to be up to 800 years old, the baobabs here rank among the tallest extant specimens on the island, and were accorded temporary protected status in 2007, but have yet to be incorporated into the national network of national parks and reserves. To get there from central Morondava, take the RN35 east for 13km (8 miles), then turn left onto the RN8 and follow it for another 6km (4 miles).

About 10km (6 miles) north of the Allée des Baobabs, the RN8 passes through the **Réserve Spéciale Andranomena ❹** (www.parcsmadagascar.com; daily 8am–4pm) a 64-sq-km (25 sq-mile) tract of deciduous coastal scrub interspersed with several small lakes and tall stands of

⊙ Fact

Only 7km (4.3 miles) northwest of the Allée des Baobabs stands a remarkable pair of Adansonia za baobabs with intertwined trunks. Known as the Baobabs Amoureux, these twin baobabs legendarily contain the spirits of two star-crossed lovers whose parents forced them into arranged marriages against their will. The couple were never united in their own lifetime, but after their death, God reincarnated them as a pair of baobabs locked together in an eternal embrace.

Traditional fishing in the Morondava River.

⊙ RIVER TRIPS IN WESTERN MADAGASCAR

A truly adventurous way to travel partway between Antananarivo and the Morondava region is by local pirogue or motorboat, a one-way trip that requires the best part of a week. Two main options are available. The more established is the descent of the wide, flat, rust-coloured Tsiribihina, which starts near Miandrivazo on the RN34 and terminates just inland of the river mouth at Belo-sur-Tsiribihina. More offbeat, but growing in popularity, is the trip along the Manambolo River from Ankavandra to Bekopaka, the gateway village to the Parc National des Tsingy de Bemaraha.

Either river trip entails a full day's drive from Antananarivo and at least three days, preferably five, on the water, setting up overnight camp on the sandbanks. The main attractions are the unspoilt riverside scenery and the wildlife (in particular birds), both of which are more easily appreciated from a silent pirogue than from a larger motorised boat. Of the two, the Manambolo river is the less heavily touristed and the more scenic, passing as it does through an imposing eroded sandstone gorge frequented by Decken's sifaka, and is especially recommended to anyone who plans on visiting Bemaraha.

Boat trips through western Madagascar can be arranged through any operator, but the reputed specialist, based at Morondava's Chez Maggie hotel, is Remote River Expeditions (tel: 020-9552347, www.remoterivers.com).

baobab. Due partly to illegal tree fell-ing and poaching, the population of Verreaux's sifaka that once inhabited the reserve is probably no longer, but it still supports seven other lemur species, including Madame Berthe's mouse lemur, a nocturnal forager first discovered in 1992 and now regarded to be the world's smallest primate, weighing in at around 30g (1.1oz). The reserve's lushly-vegetated lakes are home to Madagascar jacana, Madagas-car pond heron and Madagascar grebe, while terrestrial specials include red-capped coua, white-breasted mesite and Schlegel's Asity. Easily visited as a day trip out of Morondava, the park offers a choice of three easy guided walks, all around two to three hours in duration, with the Circuit des Trois Lacs being the pick for birds and the Circuit Andranohazo best for baobabs and lemur-spotting.

Not to be confused with the Parc National de Kirindy-Mitea, the **Réserve Forestière de Kirindy** ❺ (tel: 020-9593811; www.kirindyforest.com) is a small privately-managed conservancy and research centre that runs east from the RN8 about 65km (39 miles) north of Morondova. Kirindy is renowned as the most reliable site for seeing the fossa, Madagascar's largest carnivore. This striking nocturnal hunter is most conspicuous during the mating season (September to November) but the few individuals that routinely scavenge from around the camp are likely to be seen throughout the year, and often make an appearance during daylight hours. The reserve is also the main strong-hold of the oddball Malagasy giant rat, an endangered endemic that grows as large as a rabbit, is capable of leaping almost a metre (3ft) in the air to escape predators, and whose total range is now restricted to a 20-sq-km (7-sq-mile) territory between the between Tomitsy and Tsiribihina rivers. Guided day walks through Kirindy tend to be most productive in the early morning and come with a good chance of spot-ting several of the 45 bird, 30 reptile and seven lemur species (including the 'dancing' Verreaux's sifaka) recorded to date. You need to spend at least one

Fossa, a likely encounter at the Réserve Forestière de Kirindy.

Ⓞ FITAMPOHA CEREMONY

Every few years, Belo-sur-Tsiribihina hosts a colourful ceremony known as the *fitampoha* (bath of the royal relics). This is an ancestral cleansing ritual wherein the *dady* (preserved body parts such as teeth, fingernails or hair) of ancient Sakalava kings are removed from the sacred *zomba* house to be immersed in the waters of the Tsiribihina River. Nine former kings are represented in total, the oldest being Andriamisara I, whose two sons founded the two main Sakalava dynasties (Menabe and Boina) in the 16th century. Though the regularity and timing of the *fitampoha* is dictated by a bouquet of *fadys*, it is usually held every five to 10 years, in July or August, invari-ably on a Friday and over a full moon, both auspicious times to perform a royal ceremony.

night in the rather basic camp to stand a solid chance of encountering a fossa, Malagasy giant rat or the diminutive Madame Berthe's mouse lemur.

At Beroboka about 12km (7 miles) north of Kirindy, the RN8 crosses the Mandroatsy River as it flows into the **Bedo Wetlands**, a Ramsar site that incorporates the 4-sq-km (1.5-sq-mile) Lac Bedo along with 15 sq km (6 sq miles) of marshland and other freshwater habitats. Home to flamingos and a wide variety of migrant waders, Bedo is also an important site for several localised aquatic endemics, among them the Critically Endangered flat-tailed tortoise and Madagascan big-headed turtle, the endangered Bernier's teal and Humblot's heron, and the Vulnerable Madagascar plover.

Continuing north from Beroboka for another 33km (20 miles), the RN8 reaches the south bank of the Tsiribihina opposite **Belo-sur-Tsiribihina** ❻, a dusty little riverside town with an airstrip, a Lutheran Church and a few very basic hotels and restaurants. Coming from the south, the motor ferry crossing downriver to Belo-sur-Tsiribihina takes up to 30 minutes (in the opposite direction, it's more like 60 minutes, travelling against the flow). Belo-sur-Tsiribihina is primarily of interest to tourists as the endpoint of the three- to five-day river trip from Miandrivazo, but it's also a popular lunch stop en route to the Parc National des Tsingy de Bemaraha. Locally, the sleepy small town is renowned as the home of surviving princes and princesses of the Menabe Sakalava dynasty founded almost 500 years ago by King Adriamandazoala, and as the site of the important Fitampoha ceremony.

THE TSINGY OF BEMARAHA

North of Belo-sur-Tsiribihina, the RN8 deteriorates to become a rough 4x4-only track that emerges after 90km (55 miles) at the south bank of the Manambolo River opposite **Bekopaka**. More overgrown village than town, Bekopaka is of note primarily as the gateway to the Parc National des Tsingy de Bemaraha, but also as

Malagasy shooner moored at Belo-sur-Tsiribihina.

Getting on the ferry in Belo-sur-Tsiribihina.

Tourists on a trip down the Manambolo River aboard a traditional outrigger canoe.

Rope bridge across the stone forest in the Parc National des Tsingy de Bemaraha.

the terminus of the thrillingly remote three- to five- boat trips that follow the Manambolo downriver from Ankavandra. Coming by road from Morondava, the track north of Belo-sur-Tsiribihina is usually impassable during the rainy season (November to March) and even when it is dry, you are looking at up to 10 hours' drive to cover the full 190km (115 miles) in a private 4x4, and at least two days by *taxi-brousse*.

Ample justification for this energy-sapping drive comes in the form of the singularly spectacular 725-sq-km (280-sq-mile) **Parc National des Tsingy de Bemaraha ❼** (www.parcs-madagascar. com; May–Nov 6.30am–4.30pm) which was inscribed as a Unesco World Heritage Site in 1990, together with the bordering 666-sq-km (257-sq-mile) Réserve Naturelle Intégrale des Tsingy de Bemaraha. The centrepiece of this vast protected area is the world's largest 'stone forest', the so-called Grand Tsingy, a labyrinthine karstic formation that stretches almost 100km (60 miles) from north to south, and whose jagged black limestone pinnacles

are incised with neat linear valleys to resemble endless rows of city blocks when viewed from the air. Despite being referred to as a stone forest, the Tsingy of Bemaraha possesses many desert-like qualities, with daytime temperatures on the exposed stone canopy frequently soaring above 50°C (122°F) and what little rain does fall tending to put straight down the bare rock slopes into tall narrow valleys up to 100m (330ft) deep. In recent centuries, the formation has been practically unpopulated, but in times gone by it was home to Vazimba hunter-gatherers whose sculpted katrafay-wood coffins are still found on the more remote caves and ledges.

Inhospitable as it might look, this jagged rock archipelago supports a xerophile flora and fauna as diverse as it is predictably rich in endemics. The succulent-dominated plant life includes the beautiful red-flowering *Euphorbia viguieri*, the spiky cactus-like *Euphorbia enterophora*, the bulbous yellow-flowered elephant's foot *Pachypodium rosulatum*, the tall-stemmed

dragon tree *Dracaena xiphophylla*, and the magnificent bulbous-trunked vine *Cyphostemma laza*. The star among 13 recorded lemur species, often seen crossing the tsingy pinnacles in small family parties, is the magnificent Von der Decken's sifaka, with its long creamy-white coat offset by a black face mask and prominent yellow eyes. A bird checklist of 103 species includes 72 national endemics, and the park is also home to 120 reptile and amphibian species. The plentiful limestone caves of Bemaraha are also home to several uniquely adapted species including the ground gecko *Paroedura homalorhina*, with its partially depigmented skin and large eyes.

Set aside as a strict nature reserve in its entirety in 1927, Tsingy de Bemaraha remained off-limits to non-scientific visits until as recently as 1994 when, following its inscription as a World Heritage Site, roughly half of the formation was redesignated as a national park and developed for eco-tourism. Although 4x4 trails run through the park, it is best explored on foot, which can be a relatively strenuous exercise due to the extreme heat, difficult underfoot conditions and vertiginous edges. The most accessible hiking circuits run through the so-called Petit Tsingy, which lies about 5km (3 miles) east of Bekopaka, and can also be accessed by pirogue from the Manambolo River Gorge. More impressive but also more challenging are the trails that run through the Grand Tsingy about 20km (12 miles) further north. Most trails involve crossing suspension bridges and some mild clambering, but longer outings that include abseiling down the pinnacles, or harnessed climbing up them, are offered. Most visitors explore on one or more day hikes out of a hotel in Bekopaka, but it is also possible to arrange an overnight hike, sleeping in the park's Ankidroadroa campsite.

SOUTH TOWARDS TOLIARA

Roughly 350km (210 miles) apart as the crow flies, Morondava and the more southerly port of Toliara are connected by a seasonal coastal road that requires a 4x4 at the best of times (and is usually completely impassable between November and May) and takes at least three days to cover in full. The first port of call, about 60km (36 miles) south of Morondova, is **Belo-sur-Mer**, an isolated but rather idyllic seaside village known locally as a centre of traditional dhow-building and salt production. Only four hours drive from Morondava, or two to three hours by motorboat, Belo-sur-Mer is blessed with a scattering of low-key eco-lodges, while the uninhabited offshore islands of Nosy Andrahovo are fringed with coral reefs that offer fine snorkelling. Some 15km (9 miles) to the south stands the entrance gate to the little-visited **Parc National de Kirindy-Mitea** ❽ (www.parcs-madagascar.com; May–Nov daily 8am–4pm), which protects a 722-sq-km (279-sq-mile) tract of coastal woodland and Ramsar

Vezo man and his canoe, Belo-sur-Mer.

wetlands inhabited by eight lemur species and plentiful birds.

It takes the best part of a day to cover the roughly 160km- (100-mile) road running south from Belo-sur-Mer to **Morombe**, a small seaside town whose isolated feel is only partly alleviated by the presence of a small airport. Inland of Morombe, the **Lac Ihotry** , focal point of the Complexe de Zones Humides Mangoky-Ihotry, is a green-hued saline lake that extends over roughly 100 sq km (38 sq miles) depending on the season, and forms an important refuge for aquatic birds such as Bernier's teal and Humblot's heron. Also protected with the complex, Madagascar's largest mangrove ecosystem stands at the mouth of the Mangoky River.

Only 45km (27 miles) south of Morombe stands **Andavadoaka** ⑩, a pretty coastal fishing village that won the UNDP's Equator Prize in 2007 for piloting a pioneering octopus-closure scheme (which entails the periodic temporary closure of the local octopus hunting grounds) that has now been replicated by more than 30 other communities in Madagascar. Andavadoaka is the administrative centre of the **Velondriake Locally Managed Marine Area** (LMMA; https://blueventures. org), which was created in 2006 to protect some 800 sq km (309 sq miles) of marine and terrestrial habitats along the nearby coast. Velondriake literally means 'to live with the sea' and its integrated community-based approach to sustainable management of local fisheries, supplemented by small-scale aquaculture, has resulted in one of the most pristine marine habitats anywhere in Madagascar.

Established to the south of Andavadoaka in 2007, the 1,846-sq-km (712-sq-mile) **Parc National de Mikea** ⑪ (www.parcs-madagascar.com; daily 8am–4pm) is named after the Mikea hunter-gatherers who inhabit the western coastal hinterland between the Mangoky and Manombo River. It protects a tract of dense red sand woodland with affiliations to the deciduous forest to the north and spiny forest to the south. More than 300 plant species have recorded, including some impressive stands of Grandidier's baobab, and it also incorporates several salt pans and lakes. The most conspicuous mammals are Verreaux's sifaka and red-fronted brown lemur, but low densities of ring-tailed lemur are present, and it also supports five nocturnal lemur species. A checklist of 63 bird species includes the only officially protected populations of the localised ground-dwelling sub-desert mesite and long-tailed ground roller.

Another 65km (40 miles) south of Andavadoaka along a rough road skirting the intriguingly-named Baie de Assassins lies the small and very beautiful resort village of Salary. From here, it is another 70km (42 miles) or so south along a gradually improving road to Mangily-Ifaty, a busy resort village that lies firmly within the orbit of Toliara, being only 30 minutes' drive away along a newly surfaced road.

The always-photogenic baobab tree.

The clear waters of the lagoon at Andavadoaka.

📷 TOMBS AND TOTEMS

The importance of ancestral spirits in traditional Malagasy religion is reflected in the high physical and cultural prominence of tombs and sacred clan burial grounds all over the island.

Such is the prominence of tombs in Malagasy culture that it is customary among many ethnic groups for an important person to spend more money on, and pay greater attention to, the construction of their tomb than that of their house, since the latter is viewed as an ephemeral dwelling, while the former will become their permanent abode when they transform to an ancestral spirit. Funerary traditions vary from one area to the next. The Sakalava, for instance, traditionally bury their dead below a pile of rocks hemmed in by a rectangular wooden fence and totems on each of the four corners. By contrast, the Mahafaly traditionally mark tombs with carved aloalo sculptures that stand up to 2 metres (6.5ft) high and are often topped with zebu horns, while the Merina build square wooden or stone houses above a burial pit, and decorate them with geometric patterns. Common to most Malagasy cultures is a tradition of exhuming the deceased at regular intervals, the best known among these being the famadihana (turning of the bones), a celebratory Merina and Betsileo ceremony that allows the living to communicate with their beloved ancestors.

The most revered burial place in Madagascar, the Fitomiandalana at Rova Antananarivo, incorporates seven ancient tomb houses, the oldest originally built for King Andrianjaka of Imerina in 1630.

Dating to the 16th and early 17th century, the stone tombs of Prince Rabiby and King Ralambo at Ambohidrabiby are the oldest surviving tombs in Madagascar.

The totems on Sakalava tombs often represent the deceased naked, with enlarged genitals or in an explicitly erotic embrace with a partner of the opposite sex, as a symbol of fertility.

This Antanosy clan burial site near Fort Dauphin is huddled with funerary obelisks whose height indicates the importance of the deceased.

The sacred zebu

The most sacred animal in most Malagasy cultures is the zebu (Bos taurus inidicus), a striking humpbacked breed of ox that originated in India but most likely arrived on the island via East Africa. The zebu is strongly associated with many Malagasy funerary customs. At least one zebu is usually sacrificed before a funeral, and the meat is apportioned among those who attend according to strict rules, with the hump, which is regarded to be the finest cut, being reserved for immediate family members of the deceased. The zebu's distinctive lyre-shaped horns are often painted on tombs or carved at the top of funerary totems. Zebus are also invariably sacrificed in the course of exhumation ceremonies such as the famadihana, both to honour and to appease the ancestral spirit. As a result, among some cultures, the number of zebu skulls hung or piled onto any given tomb is a reliable indicator how influential and important was the deceased.

The influence of Christianity is clearly seen at some of the more modern graves in this traditional Antandroy burial site in a hill covered with spiny forest overlooking the Mandrare River.

Painted Mahafaly tombs are a common sight along the RN7 road near Toliara.

A sacred symbol of royalty throughout Madagascar, the zebu is often depicted in funerary art such as this Mahafaly tomb marker.

Pousse-pousse is the best way to get around in Toliara.

TOLIARA AND THE SOUTHWEST

The characterful seaport of Toliara offers access to
a fine stretch of coast as well as the bizarre spiny
desert and its wealth of endemic flora and fauna.

The capital of the Atsimo-Andrefana region, **Toliara** ❶ is a timeworn seaport set on the southwest coast about 10km (6 miles) north of the Tropic of Capricorn and 5km (3 miles) south of the sandy Fiherenana Delta. Toliara is still often referred to by the pre-1975 French spelling Tuléar; both are pronounced identically and probably derive from the Malagasy phrase *toly eroa*, which one early foreign visitor misunderstood to be a specific place name rather than generic advice to 'moor your boat there'. The modern city was founded and laid out by the French colonists in the late 1890s and has since expanded to be the island's sixth-largest, with a rapidly growing population now thought to be approaching the 200,000 mark. Despite this, unemployment is high even by Madagascan standards, and downtown Toliara, though strikingly hassle-free and friendly, possesses an aura of slight abandonment and past-it's-prime, end-of-the-road tropical ennui.

Toliara stands at the north end of the Baie de Saint-Augustin in a region dominated by the semi-arid spiny forest typical of southern Madagascar. The earliest account of the area was provided by the English explorer Walter Hamond, who circumnavigated much of Madagascar in 1630. According to Hamond, Saint-Augustin was then entrenched as 'the place where English ships bound for India usually put in both outward and homeward to take in their wood, water and other provisions, and refresh and cure their sick people' and its inhabitants were 'the happiest people in the world'. In the early 1640s, Hamond returned to Saint-Augustin, together with 140 compatriots, to found an English colony and trade outpost, but after most of his party had fallen swift prey to malaria, dysentery or attacks by local people, the few dozen survivors abandoned the site.

Main Attractions

Arboretum d'Antsokay
Ifaty and Mangily beaches
Anakao
Aire Protégée d'Amoron'i
  Onilahy
Réserve Spéciale du Cap
  Sainte-Marie

Map on page 178

What to expect at the Arboretum d'Antsokay.

Impressions of Toliara tend to be made by how one travels there. Being the southwestern coastal terminus of the RN7's 980km (610-mile) passage through the interior, Toliara comes across as a well-equipped destination in its own right to travellers who drive down from Antananarivo over several days. By contrast, those who fly directly from the capital tend to view sleepy old Toliara as little more than a springboard for further exploration, whether it be inland along the RN7 to the Parc National Zombitse-Vohibasia and the Parc National de l'Isalo, or to other more isolated coastal resorts. Either way, most visitors find Toliara itself to be a far less attractive prospect than the more resort-like seaside villages of Ifaty, Mangily and Anakao, all of which are equipped with plenty of beach hotels and restaurants.

EXPLORING TOLIARA

The torpid town centre doesn't lack for tropical backwater character. Cars are surprisingly few, but pedestrians and *pousse-pousse* bicycle-rickshaws are plentiful, and life seems to amble along at a wobbly cyclist's pace. Wide pothole-scarred avenues are lined with faded colonial relicts in the Art Deco and other early 20th century architectural styles, while market stalls spill out onto pavements shaded by leafy tamarinds. Opportunities for formal sightseeing are limited, but the sprawling central market in Rue du Marché is

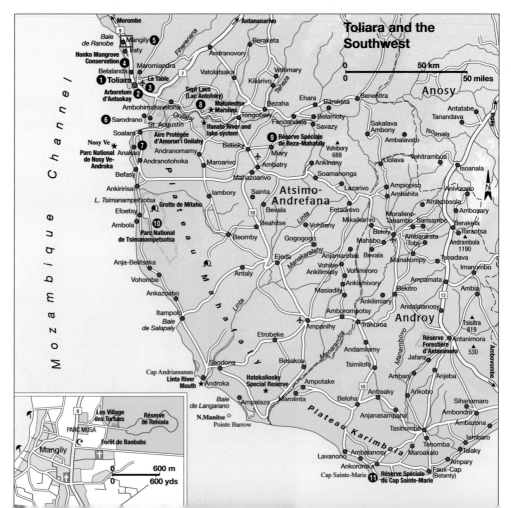

certainly worth a look, as is the small but chaotic loading beach – complete with ox-carts carrying goods on and off twin outrigger pirogues – on Rue du Port next to the Manatane hotel.

Established by the Université de Toliara in 1984, the **Musée Cedratom** (Rue Philibert Tsiranana; tel: 032-5377631; Mon–Sat 7.30–11.30am and 2.30–5.30pm) contains a small but interesting ethnographic collection dominated by funerary items. These include replicas of traditional Mahafaly and Sakalava tombs – the former made mainly of stone and colourful, the latter more sombre and wooden – as well as a Mikea mask made with genuine zebu teeth, and a Vezo totem statue with an outsized penis. Other items on display include traditional musical instruments and household objects, and an elephant bird egg. Overall the museum seems cramped and dusty, and the limited displays don't quite justify the asking price, so a planned move to newer and larger premises, should it ever actually happen, would be welcome indeed.

Situated about 5 minutes' walk south of the town centre, the **Musée de la Mer** (Avenue de France; tel: 033-2120971; Mon–Sat 8am–noon and 2.30–5.30pm) is another university-run museum but its main focus is natural history. Pride of place goes to half-a-dozen stuffed specimens of the coelacanth, an impressively hefty 'living fossil' that has been caught off the shore of Toliara on several occasions. The museum also includes displays about coral, whales and various marine invertebrates.

On the south side of the RN7 12km (7 miles) southeast of central Toliara, the highly worthwhile **Arboretum d'Antsokay** ❷ (tel: 032-0260015; www.antsokayarboretum.org; 7.30am–5.30pm) was established in 1980 by the Swiss botanist Hermann Petignat to help protect the unique succulent-dominated flora of southwest Madagascar. Of more

than 900 indigenous plant species represented in the 40-hectare (100-acre) gardens, 90 percent are southwestern regional endemics and 80 percent have known medicinal properties. A well-maintained labelled botanical trail introduces visitors to some of the southwest's more interesting plants, including young baobabs from Morondava, various colourful orchids, the arbre vazaha or European tree *Commiphora apprevalii*, whose bark peels like sunburnt skin, and the velvet elephant-ear *Kalanchoe beharensis*, which is also known as Napoleon's hat on account of its unusual shape. The checklist of 30-plus bird species includes running and red-capped coua, and night walks can be arranged to look for mouse lemurs, tenrecs and warty chameleons. A good interpretative centre and restaurant are attached.

About 3km (2 miles) further east along the RN7, **La Table** ❸ is Toliara's very own miniature Table Mountain, a smallish flat-topped hill so strikingly symmetrical that it looks artificial – like a transplanted mine dump

⦿ Shop

An excellent goal for curio hunters, situated off the waterfront end of Boulevard Gallieni, is the small handicraft market in the alley behind the Alliance Française (itself housed in an intriguing Art Deco building). And when you are ready for a drink or snack, head around the corner to the bar-restaurant Bo Beach (tel: 032-9277476), a Toliara institution with a fabulous beachfront terrace, an equally attractive interior, and the town's most tempting seafood and cocktail menu.

Zebu cart, Toliara.

– rather than the natural formation it actually is. A clear 15–20 minutes walking trail leads from the roadside to the summit, which offers fabulous views towards the coast around Toliara and Baie de Saint-Augustin. The area around La Table is the typical locality and probably the best place to look for the red-shouldered vanga, a stocky sparrow-like southwestern endemic associated with thorn trees and first described as recently as 1997.

Ambondrolava, on the R9 about 12km (7 miles) north of central Toliara, is home to **Honko Mangrove Conservation** ④ (tel: 032-7046504; www.reefdoctor.org; daily 8am–5pm), a highly-regarded community-based reserve protecting an extensive tidal mangrove habitat running north from the Fiherenana mouth. A variety of short excursions are guided by locals. These include a 2km (1.2-mile) board-walk tour that ends at an elevated wooden viewing platform above the mangroves, as well as forest walks, kayak and pirogue trips, a village tour, and specialist ornithological trips to seek out some of the 74 bird species recorded in the mangroves and sur-rounding salt pans.

IFATY-MANGILY

The most developed beach resort in the vicinity of Toliara, the twin villages of **Ifaty** and **Mangily** ⑤ lie about 25km (15 miles) north of town on the newly surfaced RN9. Confusingly, while Man-gily, the more northerly of the two vil-lages, is by far the larger and more developed for tourism, the area as a whole is more normally referred to as Ifaty. By any name, however, this is a lovely stretch of coast, and its white sandy beaches, protected by offshore reefs and lined with swaying palms and casuarinas, offer safe swimming in calm waters at high tide (but tend to be too shallow for swimming at low tide). Mangily's beach also supports a compact cluster of agreeably laidback sandy-floored, thatch-shaded restau-rants and bars, where local children good-naturedly hawk seashells and fruit, and women offer open-air beach massages (all *à bon prix*, naturally).

⊘ TOLIARA'S LIVING FOSSIL

An order of fish that recognisably took its modern form 400 million years ago, coelacanths are regarded by evolutionists to be one of the most significant 'missing links' in the fossil record, since they are less closely related to cartilaginous or ray-finned fish (that is to say, pretty much all other extant species of aquatic fish) than they are to lungfish and the tetrapod vertebrates (i.e. amphibians, reptiles, birds and mammals). The first fossil coelacanth was described by Louis Agassiz in 1839, and for a century after that, it was assumed that the order had become extinct around 66 million years ago, a victim of the same late Cretaceous event that accounted for the dinosaurs. Then, remarkably, a solitary live coelacanth was caught off the coast of Port Elizabeth (South Africa) in 1938, confirming that these remark-able 'fossils' were still very much a living concern. Two extant spe-cies are now recognised: the bright blue 2-metre (6ft) -long African coelacanth *Latimeria chalumnae*, a denizen of deepwater habitats off the southeast coast of Africa and various Indian Ocean islands including Madagascar, and the smaller and rarer Indonesian coela-canth (*L. menadoensis*), which was first identified from a dead speci-men at an Indonesian market in 1997. Both are IUCN red-listed as critically endangered.

Ifaty and Mangily stand on the shallow **Baie de Ranobe**, a marine biodiversity hotspot protected by a 30km- (18-mile) -long coral reef shelf up to 10km (6 miles) offshore. Since 2007, the British NGO Reef Doctor (www.reefdoctor.org) has been instrumental in the establishment of two marine protected areas along the reef. These are the Massif des Roses (also known as the Rose Garden) opposite the Hôtel Solidaire Mangily, and the more remote Ankaranjelita about 30 minutes' boat ride further north. All three offer great conditions for snorkelling and scuba diving on coral formations inhabited by dense populations of colourful reef fish as well as moray eels, electric rays and marine turtles. Between June and October, boat trips on the Baie de Ranobe offer an opportunity to see migrant humpback and southern right whales. Reef Doctor also recently created a new protected area called Andabotira to protect the seagrass that attracts feeding turtles close to shore.

In addition to its beaches and marine wildlife, Mangily is home to a cluster of small but worthwhile private terrestrial reserves, all situated at the north end of the village. Best known among these is the **Réserve de Reniala** (tel: 032-0251349; https://reniala-ecotourisme.jimdo.com; daily 5.30am–5.30pm), which is named after the hundreds of ancient specimens of the fony baobab *Adansonia rubrostipa* (the largest with a 13-metre /42ft circumference) that form such an impressive component of the 60 hectares (148 acres) of spiny forest it protects. Guided walks through the reserve take up to 90 minutes and offer a possibility of seeing sportive lemurs and various localised birds. There are also caged ring-tailed lemurs at the entrance.

Just outside Reniala, the separately managed 7-hectare (17-acre) **Village des Tortues** (tel: 032-0207275; www.villagetortues.com; daily 9am–5pm) is designed as a breeding programme for the radiated tortoise (*Astrochelys radiata*), a large and beautifully marked species with a lifespan of up to two

Sarongs for sale on Ifaty beach.

Palm-fringed Ifaty beach.

⊙ Tip

Several Mangily-based operators offer all-inclusive snorkelling and diving trips all year through. Both the Massif des Roses and Ankaranjelita support a great diversity of fish, with the latter being quieter human-wise and more productive fish-wise, but also more expensive to visit as it is further away. Whale-watching trips generally run from July to October only. Recommended operators include Mangily Scuba (tel: 034 6478176; www.ifatyscuba.com) and Atimoo Plongée (tel: 034 0252917; www.atimoo.com).

Going out fishing in Anakao.

centuries, and the smaller spider tortoise (*Pyxis arachnoides*). Listed as critically endangered, both species are threatened by poaching for food and body parts and illegal trafficking for the pet trade, and bred here for release into the wild.

Almost adjacent to Reniala and protecting a broadly similar habitat of baobab-studded spiny forest, the 50-hectare (123-acre) **Parc Musa** (tel: 033-1913928; daily 5am–5pm) and 70-hectare (173-acre) **Forêt de Baobabs** (tel: 034-7199921; daily 6am–6.30pm) are better suited to birdwatchers as the guides pay special attention to locating several avian species whose range is more-or-less restricted to the far southwest. These include the relatively easy-to-locate sub-desert mesite, long-tailed ground-roller and running coua as well as the more elusive green-capped coua, thamnornis-warbler, Archbold's newtonia and Lefresnaye's vanga. Parc Musa is particularly recommended due to its birding-friendly opening hours, but best to make arrangements the day before to ensure the guide is there at 5am sharp.

ST AUGUSTINE'S BAY AND THE ONILAHY RIVER

The centrepiece of the 40km (24-mile) -long Baie de Saint-Augustin, the wide, sandy mouth of the Onilahy River, 25km (15 miles) southeast of Toliara as the gull flies, is overlooked by the tiny fishing village of Sarodrano. An attractive but sandy road runs along the bay all the way from Toliara to **Sarodrano ❻**, branching right from the RN7 just before La Table, then continuing south for another 20km (12 miles), looking out for the localised red-shouldered vanga, before crossing the Tropic of Capricorn at a prominent marker decorated with zebu horns. Hemmed in by a narrow rocky 1,000-metre/yd -long peninsula, the sandy village is of interest mainly as the site of the **Grotte de Sarodrano**, a beautiful transparent turquoise natural swimming pool that supports some giant fish. An unusual feature of this pool is that the upper level, fed by a subterranean freshwater stream, is warm and mildly brackish, whereas the heavy lower layer is colder and comprises salty seawater.

Vying with Toliara as the main tourist focus on Saint-Augustin, **Anakao** ❼, 15km (9 miles) southwest of the Onilahy mouth, is a picturesque Vezo fishing village, where the gorgeous swimming beach is protected by a shallow offshore reef. Anakao is lined with low-key beach hotels and offers a similar range of marine activities to the more accessible Ifaty-Mangily, but has a more isolated feel and is correspondingly more difficult of access (the only option from Toliara is a motorboat across the bay). There are some interesting painted concrete Vezo tombs on the southern outskirts of town.

Opposite Anakao, the flat and rather scrubby island of **Nosy Ve** (probably a mistransliteration of Nosy Be, i.e. Big Island) served as a refuge for pirates back in the 17th century and in 1888 it became the site of a short-lived French settlement now survived by a few graves. Uninhabited today, it is held sacred by the Vezo residents of Anakao, who cross over once a year to sacrifice a zebu to the ancestors. Rather aptly, given its location just past the Tropic of Capricorn, Nosy Ve also supports the southernmost breeding colony of the red-tailed tropicbird, a spectacular marine bird protected by local *fady*.

The Onilahy River forms the northern border of the 1,021-sq-km (394-sq-mile) **Aire Protégée d'Amoron'i Onilahy**, a recently-created protected area managed by local communities from 11 communes with the aim of promoting biodiversity through ecotourism and other sustainable means. The semi-arid reserve protects a cover of spiny desert and harbours 27 mammal, 79 bird and 55 reptile species, many of which are southwestern regional endemics. Tourist development here is in its infancy, but the lovely inland region known as the **Sept Lacs** ❽ can easily be visited as a long day trip out of Toliara, or better perhaps as an overnight camping excursion. Fed by the Onilahy River and various tributaries on their descent from the highlands, this fragmented 220-hectare (543-acre) wetland is held sacred locally, and it is *fady* to cut down the fringing trees, so the odds of seeing Verreaux's sifaka and ring-tailed lemur are good, and it also supports a wide variety of birds.

Sept Lacs is accessible by 4x4 only (it may be completely off-limits in the rainy season) and getting there is something of an expedition. Coming from Toliara, it's a three- to four-hour drive in either direction. To get there, follow the RN7 east for about 16km (10 miles) past La Table, then turn right onto the 13km (8-mile) dirt road for the riverside village of Ambohimahavelona. From Ambohimahavelona, a rough track follows the north bank of the Onilahy for 25km (15 miles) to Lac Antofoky. The other lakes are up to 15km (9 miles) further downriver.

SOUTHEAST TO CAP SAINTE-MARIE AND FORT DAUPHIN

One of Madagascar's wildest and most remote road trips runs from Toliara to

⊙ **Tip**

There's no viable road route between Toliara and Anakao, but several companies motorboat back and forth across the Baie de Saint-Augustin daily, typically taking around 90 minutes in either direction and leaving Toliara from the beach next to the Manatane Hotel. The most reliable service is Anakao Express (tel: 034-6007261; www.anakaoexpress.com), which leaves Anakao at 7.30am and starts the return trip from Toliara two hours later.

Sand dunes at Sarodrano.

isolated Cap Sainte-Marie, the island's most southerly point, then veers east towards the Mandrare River Valley and Fort Dauphin. Strictly for 4x4s only, this long bumpy drive could be undertaken in three days at a push, using the most direct inland route (about 600km/360 miles along the RN10 and RN13, bypassing Cap Sainte-Marie) but to make the most of it, you'd be better off allocating a full week to the trip. Note that upon leaving Toliara, you first need to head 67km (40 miles) inland along the RN7 to Andranovory, before turning right onto the unsurfaced RN10, which crosses the Onilahy River about 60km (36 miles) further south at Tongobory.

Betioky, straddling the RN10 about 25km (15 miles) south of the river crossing, is the springboard for exploring the 6-sq-km (2.3-sq-mile) **Réserve Spéciale de Beza-Mahafaly** ❾ (www.parcs-madagascar.com; daily 8am–4pm) 35km (21 miles) to its east. Primarily set aside for scientific research and educational purposes, this small reserve is also open to tourists, who can make use of the rooms at the research centre when they are available. The comprises two separate blocks, one dominated by spiny forest and the other by tamarind-dominated riparian forest fringing the Sakamena River (a tributary of the Onilahy) and it is run through by six day trails of up to 12km (7 miles) in duration. Ring-tailed lemur and Verreaux's sifaka are both easily observed, the fossa is sometimes encountered after dark, and a riverside hide offers a chance of seeing several of the park's 100-plus recorded bird species.

An inauspicious junction 20km (12 miles) south of Betioky, just past the blink-and-you'll-miss-it village of Mahazoarivo, marks the biggest decision point on the long drive to Fort Dauphin. If your primary objective is getting from A to B as directly as possible, then keep going straight along the relatively well-maintained RN10, but if you want to continue along the rough (and seasonally impassable) coastal 4x4 track to Cap Sainte-Marie, then turn right, and brace yourself for adventure.

Woman with a masonjoany mask, Toliara.

⊘ MASONJOANY MASKS

In most coastal regions of Madagascar, but particularly around Toliara, you'll regularly encounter women whose faces are painted with a thick layer of white, yellowish or orange paste. This is not, as many visitors first assume, some sort of ritual mask, but a cosmetic beauty mask that not only enhances the wearer's immediate appearance but also has the long-term benefit of softening the skin and protecting it from the sun. The paste is created by rubbing the bark of the masonjoany (sandalwood) tree *Santalina madagascariensis* against a coral stone to produce a fine powder, then adding water and possibly a natural floral extract for colour. The masonjoany paste is usually applied as a plain monochrome mask, but it has become fashionable, especially among girls and young women, to use two or three different colour pastes to create floral or abstract patterns. The origin of this practice is unknown, but the fact it is most widespread on the west coast, and a similar paste called *musiiro* is applied by the Makua people on the facing north Mozambican coast, suggests it is rooted on the African mainland. Internationally, Masonjoany is now being promoted as a natural allergen-free suncream and skin softener. If you want to give it a go, small pouches containing the powder can be bought inexpensively at almost any coastal market countrywide.

A highlight of the coastal route, **Parc National de Tsimanampetsotsa** ⑩ (www.parcs-madagascar.com; daily 8am–4pm) is accessed from the seaside village of Ambola, which is only 90km (56 miles) south of Toliara as the crow flies, but more than 260km (156 miles) by road. Extending over 432 sq km (167 sq miles) of limestone flats, Tsimanampetsotsa was aside as a nature reserve in 1927 and upgraded to national park status in 1966, and its strangely stunted succulent-dominated flora is attributed to the combination of low rainfall (less than 500mm/20ins annually) and calcareous soils.

The park's centrepiece, situated only 5km (3 miles) inland of the coast, is the long, narrow and shallow Lac Tsimanampetsotsa, which is fed by underwater springs and has no outlet other than evaporation, making it too alkaline to support fish (its name literally means 'water where no dolphins live'). A Ramsar site, Lac Tsimanampetsotsa usually hosts large numbers of wading birds, including flocks of greater and lesser flamingo, and it forms an important stronghold for the Madagascan plover. Other wildlife includes 24 mammals species, most conspicuously ring-tailed lemur and Verreaux's sifaka. Night walks also offer the possibility of encountering the endangered and very localised Grandidier's vontsira (aka giant-striped mongoose), an elusive fluffy-tailed 60cm (2ft) -long predator first described in 1986. Tsimanampetsotsa is a fantastic birding site, not only for aquatic species, but for typical dry-country specials. The sacred Grotte de Mitoho hosts an underground lake that form the only known habitat of the blind sleeper goby *Typhleotris madagascariensis* and is also said to be the dwelling place of invisible spirits called Antambahoka.

Heading on south to Cap Sainte-Marie, it's worth breaking up the trip at Itampolo, 75km (45 miles) south of Ambola, then, after crossing the Linta River Mouth (4x4 essential, dry season only), at Lavanono, another 140km (85 miles) to the southeast. From Lavanono, it's another two hours' drive south to the 17.5-sq-km (6.75-sq-mile) **Réserve Spéciale du Cap Sainte-Marie** ⑪ (www.parcs-madagascar.com; daily 9am–5pm), which protects the island's most southerly point, also known as Cap Vohimena. A suitably desolate and windswept headland whose tall cliffs are topped by a lighthouse, the cape supports a strange dwarfish variation on the spiny forest found elsewhere in the region – its stunted condition is attributed to the perpetual wind and chalk soil. Traversed by two short but scenic guided day trails, the reserve is renowned as a stronghold of the radiated tortoise, with a population estimated at 10–20 per hectare, and is also the best place in Madagascar to see elephant bird eggshell fragments in situ. Once you're done, the erratic 230km (143-mile) road running east to Fort Dauphin via Amboasary can be driven in a day.

The lighthouse at Cap Sainte-Marie, the southernmost point of Madagascar.

The rigged coastline of Cap Sainte-Marie.

The view from Fort Flacourt in Fort Dauphin.

FORT DAUPHIN AND THE SOUTHEAST

The oldest French settlement in Madagascar has a wildly beautiful seaside location and offers access to the surreal 'spiny desert' landscapes of the Mandrare River Valley.

Antananarivo

Situated at the base of Pic St Louis, the attractive but rather isolated seaport of **Fort Dauphin ❶** is perched on a hammer-headed peninsula flanked by the Baie de Farodafay to the northeast and smaller Fausse Baie des Galions to the southwest. In 1500, it became the first part of Madagascar to be sighted by a European, when the hopelessly lost Portuguese navigator Diogo Dias sailed past, naming the island in honour of São Lourenço (whose feast day it happened to be). The country's oldest French colonial town, Fort Dauphin was founded in 1643 by Jacques Pronis (who served as the first French Governor of Madagascar over 1642–8) in the wake of his ill-fated attempt to establish a permanent settlement at Baie de Sainte Luce. The town's namesake fort was built under Etienne de Flacourt, who succeeded Pronis as governor of Madagascar in 1648. Today, Fort Dauphin supports a population of 70,000 and is the regional capital of Anosy (literally 'Land of Islands') and the main urban centre of its predominantly Antanosy inhabitants.

In 1975, Fort Dauphin was formally renamed Tolagnaro, which derives from the Malagasy phrase *taolana maro*, meaning 'thousands of skeletons'. Some say that this name dates to the early 19th century, when untold numbers of local Antanosy people were killed during the Imerina conquest of Anosy. Others say that the name is much older and refers to the skeletons buried beneath a poisonous fig tree that once stood on the peninsula and claimed hundreds of victims before it was eventually cut down. Whatever the truth might be, Fort Dauphin is still most often referred by this established French name, both locally and by outsiders.

Among the most scenic of Madagascar's seaports, Fort Dauphin

⊙ Main Attractions
Fort Dauphin
Pointe d'Evatraha and
  Baie de Lokaro
Baie de Sainte Luce
Fort Tranovato
Parc National
  d'Andohahela
Lac Anony
Réserve Privée de Bérenty
Mandrare River Lodge

Map on page 188

Verreaux's sifaka, Mandrare River Camp.

⚲ Eat

Fort Dauphin boasts some great seafront eateries. On Plage de Libanona, Chez Georges is an unpretentious beachfront restaurant with a no-frills seafood-dominated menu. Wander uphill to the crest of the Libanona Peninsula and you'll find yourself at the Talinjoo hotel (www.talinjoo.com), home to Fort Dauphin's smartest and most beautifully sited restaurant. When it comes to value for money, however, the filling and delicious freshly-grilled seafood, zebu and chicken kebabs served at Plage d'Ankoba's Chez Marceline take some beating.

stands on a wildly beautiful stretch of coast whose multiple sandy bays are hemmed in by high cliffs and interspersed with flat rock shelves dotted with tidal pools. The town is largely protected from cyclones by the mountainous Pic St Louis, and its hinterland receives an annual rainfall of around 1,000mm, making it ecologically transitional to the northeastern tropical wet zone and the semi-arid southwest. Agriculture, tourism and mining are all important to the local economy, but development is hampered by the limited road access – in the rainy season, it can take three days to cover the largely unsurfaced 500km (300-mile) RN13 connecting Fort Dauphin to Ihosy on the RN7, and the longer coastal route from Toliara via Cap Sainte-Marie is no better. For all but the most hardy of travellers, this means that access to the southeast is essentially limited to the daily flights that connect Antananarivo to Fort Dauphin (Tolagnaro) Airport, 5km (3 miles) west of the town centre on Rue du Maréchal Foch.

AROUND FORT DAUPHIN

Sloping down to a tall cliff overlooking the old harbour at the south end of the Baie de Farodafay, Fort Dauphin's small town centre has the agreeable feel of a transplanted French seaside village on a sunny summer day, but rather lacks for notable historic landmarks. The one obvious exception is the **Musée du Fort Flacourt** (Avenue Gallieni; Mon–Sat 9–11.30am and 2.30–5pm; no photography) which dominates the narrow peninsula (the northern end of the hammerhead) at the eastern end of the town centre. The museum is housed in the original fort built by Governor Etienne de Flacourt in 1648, which now doubles a military base guarded by armed guards who seem to view interested tourists with mild suspicion. The building is quite well-preserved, and outer fortifications offers some stirring views over the old harbour towards Pic St Louis. The museum itself includes a portrait of Etienne de Flacourt, some interesting colonial-era photographs

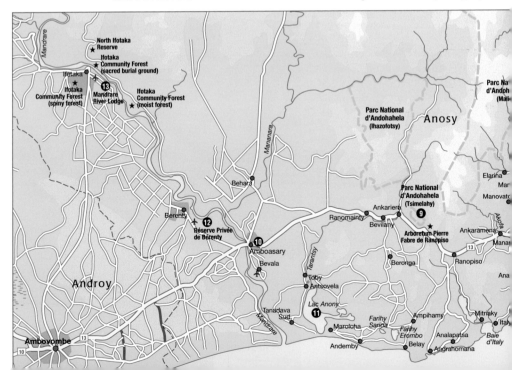

and maps, a life-size wooden replica of an elephant bird skeleton (complete with obligatory glued-together egg), and musical instruments and other artefacts relating to the local Antanosy culture, as well as photographs of their traditional hairstyles and tattoos.

A delightful scenic walk follows the clifftop Rue de la Corniche south out of town for 1.5km (1 mile) to the south end of the hammerhead and the pretty **Plage de Libanona**, which stretches for 500 metres/yds along a curving bay offering views all the way west across the Fausse Baie des Galions to the new deepwater harbour at Ehoala. The sheltered sandy bay here is usually safe for swimming, though strong currents can pose a genuine threat, and it also offers good conditions for surfing. A less sheltered suburban beach, but better for surfing, the **Plage d'Ankoba** lies on Fausse Baie des Galions about 2km (1.2 miles) west of the town centre, on the south side of Rue Circulaire as it runs towards the airport.

DAY EXCURSIONS NORTH AND EAST OF FORT DAUPHIN

The prominent peak rising to the immediate north of Fort Dauphin, the 529-metre (1,735ft) **Pic St Louis** ❷ forms an obvious goal for a half-day hike out of town. The ascent typically takes around two hours and can be tougher than it looks, especially in the heat of the day, but hikes will be rewarded with stunning views over Fort Dauphin and the surrounding bays and lakes. The easiest trail to the summit leaves from opposite the Société Industrielle de Fort-Dauphin (SIFOR) Factory about 4km (2.4 miles) out of town.

Flanking the east side of the RN12a some 2km (1.2 miles) north of the SIFOR Factory, the **Parc Botanique de Saïadi** (tel: 032-0541698; www.madagascar-resorts.com; daily 8am–5pm) is under the same management as the more remote Réserve de Bérenty. It offers the opportunity to walk and canoe through 20 hectares (50 acres) of landscaped lush gardens that support a variety of orchids and birds as well as introduced

Mural of Etienne de Flacourt at Fort Flacourt.

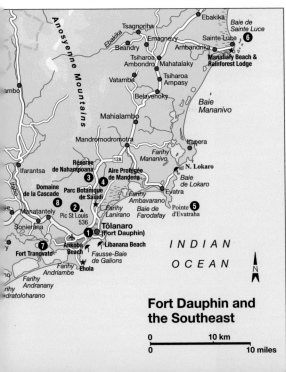

Fort Dauphin and the Southeast

⊙ Tip

The path up Pic St Louis isn't well marked, there's always a slight risk the mountain will live up to its Malagasy name *Be Zavuna* (Big Fog), and armed robberies are a perennial concern. For all of these reasons, tourists are advised against carrying valuables up the mountain, or making the ascent without a reputable local guide.

You'll be able to get up close to Verreaux's sifakas at the Réserve de Nahampoana.

larger wildlife such as ring-tailed lemur and Nile crocodiles.

Only 2km (1.2 miles) north of Saïadi, the similar but more established and in most respects superior **Réserve de Nahampoana ❸** (tel: 020-9221224; www.nahampoana.com; daily 8am–5pm) is an attractively landscaped and well-maintained former botanical garden that extends over 50 hectares (123 acres) on the eastern foothills of Pic St Louis. Five self-guided trails run through the reserve and it is also possible to take a boat trip along the river that runs along its boundary or to arrange a night walk. For most, the main attraction is the introduced but free-ranging (and very tame) troops of Verreaux's sifaka, ring-tailed lemur and brown lemur, but the less demon-strative southern bamboo lemur and various nocturnal lemurs are also present. It can also be rewarding for birding, though the range of spe-cies is restricted by the dominance of introduced trees – not only indig-enous palms but also exotics such as tropical mangos and jacarandas and temperate-zone araucarias and eucalyptuses.

Another 1.5km (1 mile) north of Nahampoana, the 220-hectare (543-acre) **Aire Protégée de Mandena ❹** (tel: 033-1281504) was established by the mining operation QQM to protect an area of wetlands and relatively unde-graded littoral forest within its strip-mining concession to the northeast of Fort Dauphin. A guided four-hour walk and boat trip leads through the reserve, which protects more than 200 plant species (about 10 percent of which are endemic to the area) as well as six species of lemur and a variety of woodland and wetland birds.

The coastline immediately northeast of Fort Dauphin comprises a narrow 12km (8 mile) long network of shallow lakes and interconnecting channels separating the Baie de Farodafay from QMM's Mandena mining concession. Starting at the western shore of the **Lac Lanirano**, only 3km (2 miles) from Fort Dauphin by road, it is possible to take a local pirogue all the way east via the **Lac Ambavarano** to the spectacular Evatraha Peninsula, which hems in the east side of the Baie de Farodafay. It's a lovely trip, gliding through an ethereal landscape of brackish inky black chan-nels covered in floating vegetation and flanked by odd low palm-like plants and white-barked mangroves that harbour plenty of herons and other aquatic birds. When you disembark at the base of the Evatraha Peninsula, you can either walk 2.5km (1.5 miles) south to **Pointe d'Evatraha ❺**, which offers wonderful views across the 10km (6.2-mile) -long Baie de Farodafay to Fort Dauphin, or hike 3km (2 miles) north to the gorgeous sheltered beach at the **Baie de Lokaro**. Easily arranged through any operator in Fort Dauphin, this is a full-day outing, taking around two hours each way by boat, and at least 30 minutes in either direction on foot, so an early start is advised.

BAIE DE SAINTE LUCE

Some 40km (24 miles) northeast of Fort Dauphin (a two-hour drive along the unpaved and undulating RN13a), the **Baie de Sainte Luce** ❻, also known locally as Manafiafy, is one of the most beautiful and isolated stretches of coastline anywhere in Madagascar. Despite this, the bay has a long history of European settlement, having hosted the Portuguese survivors of the shipwrecked *São Ildefonso* in 1527, and later accounting for several Dutch ships including the *Westfriesland* in 1605. It also became the site of the island's earliest French Settlement when Jacques Pronis, newly appointed as the first governor of Madagascar, established a short-lived trading post there in 1642, landing on 13 December, the day dedicated to Saint Lucia (or Luce) of Syracuse. Within months, however, 26 of the 40 settlers had died of tropical ailments such as malaria and dysentery, and Pronis decided to abandon the swampy site and its unhealthy air for Fort Dauphin.

This remote bay's main terrestrial attraction is the **Sainte Luce Reserve** (tel: 034-9317588; www.sainte-luce-reserve.com), an Australian-initiated community-based project founded in 2009 to conserve one of the rarest habitats in Madagascar. Also known as the Ambatoatsignana Forest Zone, the reserve incorporates 17 pockets of east coast littoral forest, with a total extent of 13.6 sq km (5.25 sq miles). Inhabitants include the endangered collared brown lemur, a recently described species restricted to this part of Madagascar, along with the nocturnal southern woolly, brown mouse, fat-tailed dwarf and greater dwarf lemurs. At least 70 reptile and amphibians have been recorded, while an extensive checklist of forest birds including Madagascar crested ibis, giant coua, and the exquisite Madagascar pygmy kingfisher (the latter often seen on night walks, sleeping on a branch above the footpath). Guided walks into the largest of the reserve's forest blocks (Sector 9) can be arranged out of the rustic Antanosy village of Manafiafy, which is also renowned for its powerful local shaman and as a centre of traditional *mangaliba* music.

⊘ Fact

In 2007, QIT Madagascar Minerals (QMM), a joint venture between the government of Madagascar and the multinational Rio Tinto, signed a 40-year contract to extract ilmenite (titanium) and zircon from heavy mineral sand in the Mandena concession northeast of Fort Dauphin. The presence of QMM has boosted employment, and it led to the construction of a modern deepwater harbour at Ehoala (5km/3 miles from the town centre), but it has also caused significant deforestation in the area of operation.

Baie de Lokaro near Taolagnaro.

Net-casting spider,
Manafiafy Lodge.

In tourist terms, Sainte Luce is more-or-less synonymous with **Manafiafy Lodge** (tel: 020-2202226; www.madaclassic.com), a superb exclusive beach idyll set on an exquisite small bay whose steep-sloping palm-fringed sandy beach is sheltered by a rocky entrance. In addition to expertly guided day and night hikes in the forest reserve, all-inclusive packages at the lodge include snorkelling excursions off a nearby coral-fringed beach, kayaking between the rocky islands, and motorboat trips into the mangroves. It also offers seasonal whale-watching from June to December, when migrant populations of humpback and southern right whales join the resident dolphins.

DAY EXCURSIONS WEST OF FORT DAUPHIN

Around 8km (5 miles) west of the town centre by road, **Lac Andriambe** (also known as Vinanibe) is the largest and most easterly of a series of shallow lagoon-like lakes and channels separated from the breakers by a narrow sandy beach less than 200 metres/

Wood carvings at
Manafiafy Beach.

yd wide in places. Arguably the most intriguing feature associated with Andriambe is a mysterious stone ruin known as **Fort Tranovato** ❼, which stands on the Ilha de Santa Cruz, among a maze of low-lying islands in the delta formed by the Efaho (aka Manampanihy) River as it flows into the lake's northern shore. A modest squarish stone fort whose surviving walls are more than a metre thick and overgrown with lush green trees, Tranovato almost certainly dates to the early 16th century, which would make it the first European building ever constructed on Madagascar. The only way to get there is by pirogue from the lake's eastern shore.

Set in the western foothills of Pic St Louis 11km (7 miles) from central Fort Dauphin, the 125-hectare (310-acre) **Domaine de la Cascade** ❽ (tel: 032-0767823; www.domainedelacascade.net; charge) is reached by following the RN13 to Manatantely, then turning right onto a well-signposted 1.5km (1-mile) dirt feeder road. This private estate, complete with large vanilla and lychee plantation, as well as 50

⊘ THE ENIGMATIC HOUSE OF STONE

The existence of Tranovato – a Malagasy name meaning 'Stone House' – was first documented in 1613 by a Portuguese expedition whose leaders were told it had been founded by 'gente branca' (white people) several decades earlier. According to the 1613 expedition, the fort then boasted two doors, a stone tower, and a marble standard inscribed with a crucifix on one side and the Portuguese coat-of-arms and phrase *Rex Portugalensis* on the other. Tranovato was still active in 1656, when it was mapped by Governor de Flacourt, who depicts a reasonably substantial settlement surrounded by orchards, pastoral fields, and two (possibly Christian) cemeteries, one on the island, the other on the facing northern mainland. Despite this, little concrete is known about the provenance of Fort Tranovato. It is often, but controversially, claimed that it was built by a group of Portuguese sailors who were shipwrecked off the Anosy coast in 1504, and intermarried with locals to establish a mixed-race community that persisted for up to a century after the last of its foreign founders perished 16 years later. No contemporary documentation exists to support this story, and it seems just as likely that the fort was originally built by mediaeval Swahili settlers from East Africa, but a few Portuguese adventurers washed up there at a later date.

honey-producing beehives, is named after a small but pretty waterfall that can be reached in two hours along a well-laid footpath. It also contains patches of primary forest, two natural swimming pools, attractively rustic accommodation and a small restaurant. Wildlife includes Verreaux's sifaka, brown lemur and various forest birds.

The only botanical conservatory dedicated to the unique flora of southeast Madagascar, the 2.2-hectare (54-acre) **Arboretum Pierre Fabre de Ranopiso** (www.pierre-fabre.com/en/heart-madagascar) stands within a larger area of protected natural forest whose species composition is transitional to the moist southeast and dry southwest. More than 350 plant species are represented, among them 200 that are endemic to spiny desert habitats in the arid south, including various types of aloe, euphorbia, baobab and octopus tree. It is also a good spot to look for endemic dry-country birds. The arboretum flanks the RN13 near the village of Ranopiso some 40km (24 miles) west of Fort Dauphin.

Past Ranopiso, the RN13 skirts what is by far the smallest and also comfortably the most accessible of the three disjunct sectors that comprise the 760-sq-km (293-sq-mile) **Parc National d'Andohahela** ❾ (www.parcs-madagascar.com; daily 7.30am–5.30pm), which was set aside as a strict nature reserve in 1939 and made a national park in 1988. The transitional moist forest in this small sector of the park covers a mere 5 sq km (2 sq miles) but is the only place in the world with a naturally occurring population of the unusually-shaped triangle palm *Dypsis decaryi* (which, though widely cultivated elsewhere, is represented by no more than 1,000 specimens in the wild).

Three guided trails run into Andohahela, and permits and guides for all must be arranged at the prominent ticket office on the south side of the RN13 about 5km (3 miles) west of Ranopiso. The most popular option is the 3.7km (2-mile) Circuit de Tsimelahy,

which leaves from the village of the same name (8km/5 miles north of the RN13) and passes through some interesting vegetation (including many triangle palms and a venerable baobab) and also offers a good chance of spotting Verreaux's sifaka, ring-tailed lemur and possibly some of the other 10 lemurs recorded in the park. Andohahela lacks for overnight accommodation other than unequipped campsites, and the park's two other more remote sectors are difficult to explore as a day trip out of Fort Dauphin.

MANDRARE RIVER VALLEY

The most compelling attraction in the vicinity of Fort Dauphin, and primary reason for most tourist visits, is the surviving 'spiny forest' associated with the hinterland of the Mandrare, southern Madagascar's principal river, about four hours' drive west of town. This most easterly region of spiny forest is heavily planted with sisal and thus less pristine than some similar semi-arid habitats further west, but it is also the main home of the surreal landscape's most eye-catching

Cooling down in the Parc National d'Andohahela.

Octopus tree in the spiny forest, Mandrare River Camp.

Life along the Mandrare River.

feature, the bizarre multi-tendrilled octopus tree *Didierea madagascariensis*. For tourists, the sisal-dominated Mandrare River Valley offers a choice of two largely self-sufficient goals: the world-famous Réserve de Bérenty and the rather more upmarket Mandrare River Lodge. Both locations offer a great opportunity to see the endearing ring-tailed lemur, the dancing Verreaux's sifaka and a long list of localised avian endemics including giant coua, running coua, sub-desert brush-warbler and thamnornis-warbler. Mandrare River Lodge also effectively offers exclusive access to the otherwise little-visited Ifotaka Community Forest Reserve.

. The road gateway to the region is **Amboasary** ⑩, which straddles the RN13 on the east bank of the Mandrare River some 75km (45 miles) west of Fort Dauphin. A low-rise settlement with a population estimated at 27,000, Amboasary is one of the principle towns of the Antandroy ethnic group, an offshoot of the Sakalava whose name literally means 'People of the Thorns' in reference to the barbed trees typical of

their semi-arid homeland. Economically dependent mainly on the surrounding sisal plantations and a low-scale mica mining industry, the town has a busy daily market that positively thrives with semi-rural mercantile activity on Saturdays, the main market day. At its western end, the 416-metre (1,365ft) Mandrare River Bridge is reputedly the third-longest construction of its type in Madagascar.

An interesting diversion from the RN13 about 7km (4 miles) before you reach Amboasary is the 15km (9-mile) 4x4-only road that runs south to the bleakly beautiful **Lac Anony** ⑪. This large shallow and brackish tadpole-shaped lake is separated from the Mandrare River Mouth 5km (3 miles) to its west by a field of magnificent sand dunes, and its shore of crushed seashells often throws up egg segments of the extinct elephant bird – which evidently favoured sandy habitats. The main avian attraction at Anony today is the flocks of hundreds, sometimes thousands, of greater and lesser flamingos that aggregate in its shallows. Endemic birds associated with the scenic lake include Madagascar grebe,

Humblot's heron and the very localised littoral rock-thrush.

The main tourist focus along the Mandrare, around 10km (6 miles) by road past Amboasary, is the **Réserve Privée de Bérenty** ⑫ (tel: 032-0541698; www. madagascar-resorts.com), a private 2-sq-km (0.75-sq-mile) sanctuary set in the middle of the 60-sq-km (23-sq-mile) sisal estate founded in 1936 by the de Heaulme family, and still under their ownership. In some respects more like an open-air zoo than a genuine eco-destination, the reserve is centred on the midrange Bérenty Lodge, which stands alongside a large tamarind copse on a wide bend in the river. Ring-tailed lemurs are more-or-less resident in camp, and the spectacular Verreaux's sifaka dance through daily as they cross between their foraging grounds and the riverine forest. Night walks in a nursery-like plantation of octopus trees offer the opportunity to see nocturnal lemurs, and the site also harbours the largest fruit bat colony in southern Madagascar, a checklist of more than 100 birds, and a small ethnographic museum.

Altogether more alluring but aimed at deeper pockets, the **Mandrare River Lodge** ⑬ (tel: 020-2202226; www.mada classic.com) also stands in a tamarind copse on the west bank of the eponymous river. Offering accommodation in spacious tented units, it has the feel of an all-inclusive African safari camp, and operates in much the same way, offering guests a range of guided activities to explore various strands of woodland protected by ancient *fady* or modern community consensus as part of the patchwork Ifotaka Community Forest Reserve. Excursions and activities include a boat trip to a sacred kokolampo (traditional burial site) on a forested hill on the eastern riverbank, a visit to a large patch of tamarind forest to look for naturally-occurring troops of ring-tailed lemur, day and night walks in a large taboo-protected spiny forest inhabited by Verreaux's sifaka and a wide range of semi-arid avian endemics, sun-downers at a spectacular forest, and a thrilling traditional Antandroy drum and dance performance.

Antandroy dancer, Mandrare River Camp.

⊘ SISAL AND CACTUS

The ecology of the Mandrare Valley is threatened by the spread of two invasive desert plants introduced from Mexico. The most conspicuous of these is sisal *Agave sisalana*, a spiky 2-metre (6ft) -high succulent whose fibrous leaves are used to make rope, twine and to a lesser extent paper and cloths. Sisal was first planted in Madagascar in the early 1920s and it had become a major export crop by the late 1930s, with the main areas of production being around Fort Dauphin and Toliara. The plantations at Toliara have long since closed, but those in the Mandrare Valley now extend over more than 300 sq km (116 sq miles) and produce almost 20,000 tonnes annually, making it the world's fifth-largest producer (after Brazil, Kenya, Tanzania and Mexico). In addition to the direct loss of habitat caused by sisal plantations, this hardy plant is also highly invasive and specimens can be seen infiltrating most of the region's extant patches of spiny forest. Even more pernicious perhaps is the rapid spread of the prickly pear *Opuntia monacantha*, a type of cactus introduced by the French colonists as a natural fence to protect military forts and gardens, but now widely cultivated by the Antandroy both for its fruit and as a cattle feed in times of drought. As is the case with sisal, prickly pears are now a depressingly common sight throughout the Mandrare Valley, and can be found infiltrating the fringe of most natural forest stands.

All eyes on you – a common brown lemur at the Parc National Andasibe-Mantadia.

ANDASIBE AND SURROUNDS

Half-a-day east of the capital, forested Andasibe-Mantadia – home to the charismatic indri and a host of other wildlife – is Madagascar's best-equipped national park.

Antananarivo

Blanketing the hilly eastern escarpment 145km (90 miles) from Antananarivo along the RN2, the **Parc National Andasibe-Mantadia** ranks among Madagascar's most convenient and popular one-stop wildlife destinations, boasting a good selection that collectively attracts more than 20,000 foreign visitors annually in recent years. The rainforest here is the main stronghold of the indri, which is renowned both as Madagascar's largest lemur and for its eerie far-carrying call, and can be seen with reasonable ease on a guided forest walk out of the park headquarters. Andasibe-Mantadia also supports 13 species of smaller lemur, including the handsome diademed sifaka, giant bamboo lemur, black-and-white ruffed lemur, and Goodman's mouse lemur, the latter a local endemic only discovered in 2005. The park also ranks as one of the country's key ornithological destinations, with more than 110 species recorded, and it supports a wide variety of colourful orchids. Popular night walks along the main road through the forest offer a great opportunity to see nocturnal lemurs, chameleons and an array of colourful tree-frogs.

THE RN2 FROM ANTANANARIVO

Although it's a well-maintained asphalt road, the RN2 between Antananarivo

and Andasibe usually takes around four hours flat to drive, thanks partly to its winding nature and the sloping terrain, but also due to the prolific truck traffic bound to or from the busy port of Toamasina. The drive could also easily be stretched over a full day with a few strategic diversions and stops.

Coming from the capital, the small lakeside town of **Mantasoa ❶** is reached by turning right onto a 13km (8-mile) feeder road signposted at Ambatoloana, 57km (35 miles) along the RN2. Mantasoa played an important role in

◉ Main Attractions

Lac Alaotra
Parc National de Zahamena
Réserve Spéciale d'Analamazaotra
Parc Mitsinjo
Parc Le Vondron'olona Ifotony Mitia sy Miaro ny Ala (Le Voi MMA)
Parc National de Mantadia
Réserve de Torotorofotsy

Map on page 198

Tree frog, Réserve Spéciale d'Analamazaotra.

> **☉ Tip**
>
> Although it stands at a lower altitude than Antananarivo, Andasibe is notoriously chilly at night. And as might be expected of a rainforest, it receives rain on two out of three days over the course of the average year. June to September are the driest months, but also the coolest, so it's worth bringing a couple of sweaters or sweatshirts and a waterproof jacket at all times.

Madagascar's history. It was here that the resourceful French adventurer Jean Laborde built a county residence for Queen Ranavalona I in 1833, as well as an industrial complex – comprising an ammunition factory, a foundry, and facilities to manufacture weapons, glass, ceramics, bricks and silk – that heralded the island's first modest industrial revolution. Several of the buildings constructed by Laborde were destroyed during a slave rebellion in 1951, and others were submerged under a 20-sq-km (7.7 sq-mile) artificial lake created in 1931. Surviving relics of Mantasoa's heyday include the restored **Maison Jean Laborde** (daily 8am–4pm), parts of the old cannon factory and foundry. Also still standing, the handsome Tomb

of Jean Laborde was designed and built by the man himself before his death in Antananarivo in 1878 (an event marked by a national funeral at the decree of Queen Ranavalona II).

Only 3km (2 miles) past Ambatoloana, **Mandraka Park** (tel: 020-2243127) is a self-styled 'biodiversity park' that sprawls across 50 hectares (123 acres) of well-tended wooded grounds that host a wealth of orchids and is bisected by the babbling Manambolo River. A fair amount of wildlife can be seen here, notably brown lemur, eastern woolly lemur, various frogs and 60 bird species including Madagascar long-eared owl. A popular snack bar specialises in pizzas and omelettes.

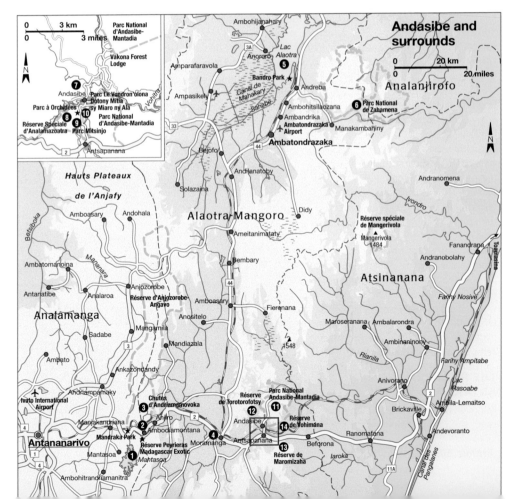

A scenically winding 12km (7-mile) descent from Mandraka Park leads to **Ambodiamontana ❷**, a modest town set in a lush valley that supports a small hydroelectric plant fed by water piped down from the surrounding hills. Ambodiamontana is best known as the home of the **Réserve Peyrieras** (tel: 033-1575165; daily 7am–5pm daily), a small private zoo that offers a great opportunity to get close to and photograph a variety of reptile and amphibians, including the spectacular bright-red tomato frog. The pine forest behind the zoo supports three introduced but free-ranging groups of Coquerel's sifaka as well as a few brown lemurs. Allow 45 minutes to see the zoo and up to two hours if you also want to look for the sifakas.

Known for its bustling Saturday market, Anjiro, straddling the RN2 some 6km (4 miles) east of Ambodiamontana, is the springboard for a side trip to the **Chutes d'Andriamamovoka ❸**, a lovely jungle-fringed waterfall that plunges 120m (395ft) down a sloping rock face about 5km (3 miles) to the north. You can drive to within a few hundred metres/yds of the perennial waterfall along a winding dirt road that also leads past the Tombeaux d'Andranomena, a cluster of royal tombs 1km (0.6 mile) out of town, and the nearby Pierre Sacrée d'Ambatotsarahasina, a massive stone erected in the name of unity among the local people. An attractive natural swimming pool above the main waterfall is said to have been the bathing place of the King of Bezanozano in the 18th century.

MORAMANGA

Traditional capital of the Bezanozano ethnic group, **Moramanga ❹**, 110km (66 miles) east of Antananarivo, is a centuries-old market town that today supports a population of around 30,000 and thrives as a centre of the pine timber industry. Moramanga is often translated as 'Cheap Mangoes', but more likely – especially as mango trees aren't especially

conspicuous in the vicinity – the name derives from a 19th-century vernacular phrase meaning 'Cheap Slaves'. Indeed, the area around Moramanga was ruthlessly exploited as a source of both slaves and unpaid porters – the latter required to transport goods along the arduous caravan route between the Toamasina and Antananarivo – following the subjugation of the Bezanozano by King Radama I of Imerina in 1817.

Historically, Moramanga is now mainly remembered for the pivotal role it played in the so-called Insurrection Malgache, a nationalist uprising against colonial rule initiated on 29 March 1947 by a series of coordinated MDRM attacks on French military bases and plantations in Bezanozano territory. Five weeks later, on 6 May, Moramanga was the site of the unprovoked massacre of an estimated 150 unarmed MDRM officials and activists who were detained by the French military then mowed down by machine guns. A concrete monument in the traffic circle in front of the railway station honours the many local victims of the uprising, and

⊙ Fact

The nomenclature of the destination widely referred to Andasibe can be confusing. Andasibe (formerly Périnet) is the correct name of the village that services it, but the abutting national park is actually called Andasibe-Mantadia, and it comprises two disjunct components, neither of which has ever been officially known as Andasibe. The southerly Réserve Spéciale Analamazaotra, bordering Andasibe village, is where most visitors to Andasibe are taken to look for indris, while the more remote and northerly Parc National de Mantadia is generally only visited by specialist birding tours.

Monument to the 1947 uprising against French colonial rule, Moramanga.

a museum commemorating these historic events is also in the works.

On the town's southwestern outskirts, the recently renovated museum in the grounds of the **Ecole Supérieure de la Gendarmerie** (Tel: 034-9692856; Mon–Fri 8–11.30am and 1–5pm; Sat–Sun 9–11am and 2–4pm; no photography) that hosts an unexpectedly interesting and eclectic selection of displays covering the transport, military and police history in Madagascar since the 19th century. Pride of place goes to a cannon given as a gift by King George III to Ramada I c.1817, when the British crown entered into a formal alliance recognising the latter as the King of Madagascar.

ALAOTRA AND ZAHAMENA

Not to be undertaken casually, a 160km (100 mile) diversion from Moramanga along the RN44 leads north to **Ambatondrazaka**, a substantial highland town founded in the late 18th century by a queen called Randriambololona and named after her youngest son Razak, and now known as the country's most bountiful centre of rice production.

A river runs through the jungle of the Parc National Andasibe-Mantadia.

Another 34km (20 miles) to the north along the RN44, the smaller town of **Ambatosoratra** is the northern terminus of the MLA (Moramanga–Lac Alaotra) railway, which was laid over 1914–23 and still operates a twice-weekly passenger service today.

Ambatosoratra is a gateway town to the 900-sq-km (348-sq mile) **Lac Alaotra** ➎, which ranks as the largest freshwater body in Madagascar. It stands at the centre of a vast Ramsar wetland whose reedbeds form the sole refuge of the Lac Alaotra bamboo lemur. First described in 1975, this localised bamboo lemur, known locally as the bandro, is probably unique among primates in that it lives almost entirely on papyrus leaves. It is now listed as critically endangered, having suffered a population decline from 11,000 individuals in 1990 to fewer than 3,000 today. The easiest place to see the Lac Alaotra bamboo lemur is **Bandro Park** (tel: 034-1014760; www.madagascar-wildlife-conservation.org), a community-run initiative situated just outside the lakeshore village of Andreba, which straddles the RN44 just 10km (6 miles) south of

⊘ ALAOTRA'S AVIAN RARITIES

The Alaotra Basin's status as the rice basket of Madagascar has come at a heavy environmental price. Likewise, its significance as the country's most important inland fishery has had a huge impact on the lake's ecology. Today, the lake hinterland is dominated by rice paddies, which has led to the silting up of many channels and former shallows. The area's environmental integrity has been further compromised by the rampant colonisation of introduced eating fish such as *Oreochromis macrochir* (from mainland Africa) and *Channa maculata* (from Asia) and the spread of the water hyacinth, a highly invasive species from South America. The effect on Lac Alaotra's once prolific populations of endemic waterfowl has been devastating. The near-flightless Alaotra grebe, once endemic to the lake and environs, hasn't been seen since 1985 and was officially declared extinct in 2010. Alaotra was once the main stronghold for the Madagascar pochard, a species of duck that had been thought extinct since the late 1990s until a second small population was reported from Lake Matsaborimena in northern Madagascar in 2006. The lake still remains an important refuge for Meller's duck, but numbers of this endangered endemic are also in rapid decline, partly rough hybridisation with domestic waterfowl.

Ambatosoratra. Park Bandro operates an inexpensive rustic camp and also offers pirogue trips into the reedbeds to look not only for bamboo lemurs (about 80 are resident) but also for aquatic birds.

Situated about 25km (15 miles) east of Ambatosoratra, the little-visited **Parc National de Zahamena ❻** (www. parcs-madagascar.com; daily 9am–5pm) protects a 423-sq-km (248-sq-mile) tract of medium- to high-altitude forest that forms part of the Rainforests of the Atsinanana Unesco World Heritage Site. Glibly, this lush mountainous park might be described as a larger, wilder, more rugged and more remote counterpart to Andasibe-Mantadia, since it protects a broadly similar habitat and range species, including substantial numbers of indri and 12 other lemur species. It is possibly the country's single most important site for forest birds, with a checklist of 112 species, 67 of which are Madagascar endemics, most notably perhaps Madagascar red owl, Madagascar serpent eagle, red-fronted coua, rufous-headed ground-roller, velvet asity, helmet vanga and red-tailed newtonia. Three guided walking circuits have been established. The 6km (3.7 mile) Ankosy Circuit is especially good for lemur viewing and also offers great views over Lac Alaotra and a stop at a natural swimming pool, but the shorter (4km/2.5 mile) and less steep Ambarihely Circuit is better suited to less fit travellers.

ANDASIBE

The focal point of tourist activity at Andasibe-Mantadia, the village of **Andasibe ❼** (sometimes referred to by the old French name Périnet) lies 3.5km (2 miles) north of the RN2 along a signposted feeder road from the junction village of Antsapanana, 25km (15 miles) east of Moramanga. Bisected by the River Vohitra and surrounded by forest, it is a pretty little village, its muddy main road lined with creaky two-storey houses and timeworn colonial buildings, most notably an old FJKM church,

post office and railway station – the latter more-or-less disused but notable for the free-tailed bats that roost inside it by day and flock out to hunt insects at disk. Amenities in Andasibe are limited to a few hotels and small local shops; there is no bank, ATM or supermarket.

The smaller and more accessible of Parc National Andasibe-Mantadia's two components parts, the **Réserve Spéciale d'Analamazaotra ❽** (www. parcs-madagascar.com; daily 6am–4pm) extends across 8 sq km (3 sq miles) of lushly forested hills immediately east of the feeder road between Antsapanana and Andasibe village. Named after a river that flows along its border, Analamazaotra has been the site of a forestry station since 1902, but its eastern half was upgraded to become a special reserve in 1970, largely to protect the population of several dozen indris that forms its main attraction today. Guided hikes into the forest run from the Madagascar National Parks ticket office and entrance gate roughly halfway along the Antsapanana-Andasibe road, and the earliest possible start is recommended

The aptly named comet moth.

Typical dwelling in Andasibe village.

⊘ Tip

A guided night walk at Andasibe provides a great opportunity to see a variety of nocturnal lemurs, chameleons and tree frogs. It is forbidden to enter the national park after dark, so most night walks are conducted along the 2km (1.2 mile) main road between the railway station and national park office, dropping in at Parc à Orchidées (often good for chameleons). If you prefer to walk in the forest interior, the Parc Mitsinjo and Voi MMA also both offer night walks.

in order to locate the indris before the tour groups trudge in en masse. Two overlapping main circuits run east from the entrance: the short (3.5km/2 mile) and long (4.5km/3 mile) Indri Trails, the main difference between them in practice being how long the guide will be prepared to spend in the forest (around two hours on the short trail and three hours on the long one). You are almost certain to see indris – their far-carrying call makes them easy to locate – and there is also a good chance of encountering the spectacular diademed sifaka and duller brown lemurs and giant bamboo lemur.

Managed as a community project by a local guides association, the **Parc Mitsinjo** ❾ (tel: 034-1290482; https://associationmitsinjo.wordpress.com; daily 7am–4pm) comprises the 7-sq-km (2.7-sq-mile) portion of the former Analamazaotra Forestry Station that lies to the west of the Antsapanana-Andasibe road. More heavily utilised for logging than the eastern part of Analamazaotra, it now supports a cover of secondary forest and abandoned timber plantation currently in the process of being rehabilitated by planting with indigenous trees. Despite this, it protects a broadly similar fauna to the abutting special reserve, including indri (seven family groups are resident), brown lemur and greater bamboo lemur. Guided hikes leave from a clearly signposted and well-run ticket and information office on the east side of the road a couple of minutes' walk south of the national park office, and take from one to six hours, depending on which circuit you choose. Indris are almost certain to be seen, and it tends to attract fewer tour groups than Analamazaotra, but the vegetation is less pristine. The Parc Mitsinjo is also the base for Across Branch, a grassroots organisation that offers two adventure activities: zip-lining from a 25-metre (82ft) -high platform along a 100 metre (330ft) cable starting, and climbing a tree 15m (50ft) into a canopy to relax in a hammock and look for wildlife (including indris).

The public road flanked by the Réserve Spéciale d'Analamazaotra and Parc Mitsinjo can be walked unguided and it offers much to first-time birdwatchers looking to familiarise themselves with more widespread forest and woodland species such as Madagascar buzzard, Madagascar blue pigeon, Madagascar coucal, blue coua, common sunbird-asity, Madagascar magpie-robin, common jery, blue vanga and Madagascar cuckoo-shrike. There's a good chance of seeing brown lemur from the road, too, and it is worth dropping into the **Parc à Orchidées**, on the west side of the road between the national park office and Andasibe village, especially over October to November, when most of the 100-plus orchid species associated with Andasibe-Mantadia are in bloom.

Situated about 100 metres/yds east of the main road almost as you enter Andasibe village, the **Parc Le Vondron'olona Ifotony Mitia sy Miaro ny Ala** ❿ (usually abbreviated to Parc Voi MMA; tel: 034-1570496; daily 7am–4pm) is a tiny (32-hectare/79-acre) community-based

A rather curious red-fronted brown lemur at Lemur Island.

reserve that abuts the national park and supports two groups of indri along with brown lemur, giant bamboo lemur and eastern wooly lemur. Though less pristine than the Réserve Spéciale d'Analamazaotra, this small park has a fee structure that's far more amenable to single travellers, and the guides are also adept at locating localised birds such as Madagascar wood rail, Madagascar crested ibis, red-breasted coua, Madagascar long-eared owl and Madagascar pygmy kingfisher. An exciting activity offered by the Parc Voi MMA are self-paddled or guided kayak trips upstream along the Analamazaotra River into the forest, or downstream to its confluence with the Vohitra a short distance east of Andasibe Railway Station.

The upmarket Vakona Forest Lodge, 5km (3 miles) north of Andasibe, is home to **Lemur Island** (020-2262480; www.hotelvakona.com; daily 7am–5pm) a rather contrived set-up that nevertheless offers the opportunity to get up close with a variety of lemurs that have the run of a small island covered in non-indigenous eucalyptus trees (but cannot leave as they are unable to swim). Species represented include black-and-white ruffed lemur, diademed lemur, brown lemur, giant bamboo lemur and (way outside their natural range) ring-tailed lemur. The adjoining crocodile farm, included in the entrance fee, is basically a zoo where you can see caged crocodiles, fossa and various birds. Also based at Vakona Forest Lodge, Les Ecuries de Falierada (tel: 033-6697471) is a stable offering well-priced horseback trips ranging in duration from 30 minutes to two hours.

MANTADIA AND THE OUTLYING RESERVES

By far the larger and more ecologically diverse and pristine of Andasibe-Mantadia's two component parts, the **Parc National de Mantadia** ⑪ (www.parcs-madagascar.com; daily 6am–4pm) extends for roughly 158 sq km (61 sq miles) across an almost unbroken sequence of forested hills that start about 7km (4 miles) north of Andasibe village and run all the way north to Zahamena. Mantadia protects almost

Crossing over to Lemur Island.

⊙ Fact

Andasibe is renowned for its diversity of endemic frogs, with more than 100 species recorded within 30km (18 mile) of the village. The regional flagship species is the golden mantella (*Mantella aurantiaca*), a tiny (up to 25mm/1 inch) critter named for its uniform bright gold (or occasionally orange) colour. Confined to three wetlands countrywide, this delightful but critically endangered amphibian is now being bred for release back into the wild at a facility at the Parc Mitsinjo

all the vertebrate species found in Analamazaotra, including large numbers of indri, along with plenty that aren't – notably black-and-white ruffed lemur and a wide variety of iconic birds associated with primary forest interiors. However, its relatively remote location means it is far less frequented, except by dedicated birdwatchers, for whom the main draw is a quartet of shy and localised ground-rollers (scaly, pitta-like, rufous-headed and short-legged). Permits and guides must be arranged at the national parks office at the Réserve Spéciale d'Analamazaotra, from where the 23km (14-mile) drive along a rough road through Andasibe village to the main trailhead usually takes around 90 minutes. The most rewarding trail for birders, the Circuit de Tsakoka (the Malagasy name for pitta-like ground roller) is only 2.8km (1.6 miles) long but can take four hours or longer to work thoroughly. For less specialised visitors, the two-hour Circuit des Chutes offers a good chance of seeing indris and other lemurs, as well as leading to the sacred waterfall for which it is named.

Exploring the Parc National de Mantadia.

Situated about 10km (6 miles) northwest of Andasibe village, the **Réserve de Torotorofotsy** ⑫ (tel: 034-1290482; https://associationmitsinjo.wordpress.com), a community initiative under the same private management as the Parc Mitsinjo, protects the largest and most intact natural marsh in eastern Madagascar. Declared a Ramsar wetland in 1975, Torotorofotsy is named after the white (fotsy in Malagasy) morph of the Madagascar scops owl (torotoroka) that legendarily haunts the marsh verges. Among birdwatchers, however, it is renowned as a key site for endemic aquatic birds such as the Madagascar snipe and the endangered slender-billed flufftail and Meller's duck. It is also a good place to look for endemic frogs such as golden, yellow and painted mantella, while greater bamboo lemur and black-and-white ruffed lemur are more often herd than seen in the fringing rainforest. Guided day trips can be arranged through the information office at Parc Mitsinjo.

The 100-sq-km (38-sq-mile) **Réserve de Maromizaha** ⑬, which lies immediately south of the RN2 about 3km (2 miles) east of Antsapanana junction, protects a broadly similar fauna to Andasibe-Mantadia, including at least 13 lemur and 85 bird species. Tourist development here is limited and wildlife tends to be shyer than elsewhere in the vicinity, but no entrance fee is charged, it retains a true wilderness feel, and visits can be arranged with the guides at the national park office at Analamazaotra. The forested corridor connecting Maromizaha to the Parc National de Mantadia is protected in the 16-sq-km (6-sq-mile) **Réserve de Vohimana** ⑭ (http://madagascar-environnement. org), a private ecotourism site that boasts about 20km (12 miles) of hiking trails and offers the opportunity to get close to various birds and lemurs as well as the lance-nosed chameleon, a very localised reptile with a distinctive long, narrow proboscis.

FATHER OF MEN

The panda-like indri is Madagascar's largest living primate but it pales in size by comparison to the giant lemur that roamed the island a few thousand years ago.

The charismatic Indri is a black-and-white fur-ball placed in the monotypic genus Indri, and distinguished from the closely-related sifakas by a combination of its greater bulk, big yellow eyes, large tufted ears and stumpy tail. It ranks among the most strictly arboreal of lemurs, seldom descending from the trees, and feeds almost exclusively on leaves, clinging vertically to branches while it feeds, and using its muscular legs to propel itself upright from trunk to trunk.

A unique feature of the indri is its distinctive eerie call, which sounds like a pod of whales might were they high on helium and armed with megaphones. Incredibly loud for a relatively small animal, this cry of the indri lasts for up to three minutes, resonating through the forest for up to 4km (2.5 miles) from its point of origin, and is positively ear-shattering when heard up close. The indri is most vocal, and thus easiest to locate, in the early to mid-morning, which is also when it might be seen 'sunbathing' with arms wide open, behaviour traditionally interpreted by locals as a form of sun worship.

The origin of the name indri is open to conjecture. The animal's Malagasy name is babakoto, literally 'father of man', reflecting the widespread belief it is an ancestral spirit. One legend has it, for instance, that the first indri and first human were brothers who lived together in the forest until the latter decided to come down to cultivate the land, leaving the former to howl in mourning for his missing sibling from the treetops. This ancestral status means that a widespread fady exists on killing indris.

Weighing in at up to 10kg (22lb), the indri vies with the fossa (a type of carnivore) as Madagascar's largest living mammal. Both, however, are only a fraction of the size of the extinct Archaeoindris (Ancient indri), a robust tailless terrestrial lemur that would have weighed around 160kg (350lb), making it larger than an adult female gorilla and comparable in bulk to a giant panda. Known from fossils unearthed at a single site in the central highlands north of Antananarivo, Archaeoindris probably roamed the island until 2,000 years ago, when its extinction was precipitated by the arrival of humans, and resultant habitat loss and hunting

The indri today faces similar threats. Once more widespread, it is now confined to inland rainforests in the northeast of Madagascar, and is listed as critically endangered, with the total population estimated at a few thousand. The main threat to its survival is not direct hunting, but habitat loss and fragmentation associated with logging and slash-and-burn agriculture. It doesn't help the indri's prospects that it is a very slow breeder, with females usually giving birth to a single infant every two to three years – or that it has thus far failed to reproduce, or even to live significantly longer than a year, in captivity.

Screaming indri at the Réserve Spéciale d'Analamazaotra, Andasibe.

Woman washing dishes at sunset in the Canal des Pangalanes.

THE EAST COAST NORTH TO MASOALA

The northeast coast's varied attractions range from the atmospheric Canal des Pangalanes and kilometre-high forested Masoala Peninsula to the idyllic offshore Île Sainte-Marie and Nosy Mangabe.

A large and logistically incohesive region focussed around the seaport of Toamasina, the northeast coast incorporates two predominantly fly-in destinations – the resorty offshore Île Sainte-Marie and altogether more wild and remote Masoala Peninsula – but it can also be explored using a combination of road transport and boat as an extension of an overland visit to Andasibe. Coming from Andasibe, access is along the RN2, the surfaced 360km (220 mile) trunk route that connects Antananarivo to Toamasina, though most tourists divert eastward to explore the lovely Canal des Pangalanes by boat. Heading north of Toamasina, the trunk road you need is the RN5, which is surfaced and in reasonable condition for the first 165km (103 miles) as far as Soanierana Ivongo, the mainland ferry port for boats to Île Sainte-Marie. By contrast, the more northerly 225km (140 miles) of the RN5 connecting Soanierana Ivongo to Maroantsetra and the Masoala Peninsula is legendarily awful and might easily take two or three days to cover, longer in the rainy season.

EXPLORING THE PANGALANES

The gateway to the Pangalanes, **Brickaville ❶** is a district capital and riverport that sprawls untidily along the RN2 some 255km (158 miles) east of Antananarivo. Now officially but

less memorably known as Ampasimanolotra, it owes its peculiar name to the twin-masted square-rigged merchant ships – known as brigs or bricks – that sailed up the Rianila River to dock on its west bank in the 19th century. Now an important centre of sugar production, Brickaville no longer sees much naval traffic, and the main port serving the southern Pangalanes is **Manambato ❷**, which is reached by following the RN2 north for another 10km (6 miles) and turning right onto a rough 7km (4 miles) that might well

◎ Main Attractions
Canal des Pangalanes
Fort Manda
Île Sainte-Marie
Île aux Nattes
Aye-Aye Island
Nosy Mangabe
Parc National de Masoala

📍 Map on page 209

Idyllic Île Sainte-Marie.

⊙ **Tip**

Dedicated to promoting ecotourism in Fetraomby (inland of Brickaville), the Centre Lambahoany (Boulevard de la Libération; tel: 032-7193869; www.lambahoany. org) is an NGO that also runs language classes for locals, and promotes occasional cultural events in Toamasina. It's a great place to organise well-priced guided city tours and excursions, whether by boat to the Île aux Prunes or by road to the Parc Ivoloina. Its speciality is multi-day hikes in and around Fetraomby.

require a 4x4 after rain. Decidedly modest in terms of both population and infrastructure, Manambato has a lovely setting on a palm-lined jungle-fringed white beach on the west shore of the Lac Rasoabe, and it's serviced by a few rustic low-cost beach lodges where, in the right frame of mind, one could spend a very agreeable few days doing not very much at all.

Manambato is the main southerly boat pickup point for visitors headed deeper into the Pangalanes to stay at one of several small resorts that line the shores of Lac Rasoamasay and the more northerly Lac Ampitabe. The only genuine protected area in the Pangalanes is the 20-sq-km (7.7-sq-mile) **Réserve de Vohibola ❸**, which stands on the north shore of Lac Ampitabe and protects one of the last two stands of littoral rainforest on the east coast. Managed by the NGO Man And The Environment (MATE) in collaboration with the local Andranokoditra community since 2003, this reserve is home to six naturally occurring lemur species, including Milne-Edward's sifaka and red-bellied lemurs,

along with 50 bird, 20 reptile and 19 amphibian species. It can be explored on three different guided trails.

The most enjoyable and popular overnight base in the Pangalanes is the **Palmarium Reserve and Hotel ❹** (tel: 034-1772977; www.palmarium.biz), standing in densely-wooded 50ha (123-acre) grounds on the west shore of Lac Ampitabe. It supports a varied selection of free-ranging and very habituated – and photogenic – lemurs, most of which have been introduced and are not actually indigenous to this part of Madagascar. These include diurnal black-and-white ruffed, crowned, black, brown and red-bellied lemur, which have the run of the property and spend a lot of time lurking around the main hotel buildings hoping to snatch fruit and other food of guests' plates. Guided forest walks deeper into the forested property offer the opportunity to see the more dignified and elusive Coquerel's sifaka and the all-black morph of indri, as well as a host of forest birds. Night walks focus on naturally-occurring nocturnal lemurs and birds.

Crowned lemur, Palmarium Reserve.

A must-do for those staying over-night at Le Palmarium is the two-hour dusk excursion to **Île au Coq**, a private reserve onto which six aye-ayes were introduced in 2003. With its initial population now supplemented by a couple of individuals born there, Île au Coq is the most reliable site anywhere in Madagascar for these most unique and fascinating of lemurs, admittedly because they are lured to a few specific feeding sites by coconuts, so they don't need to be actively sought.

From Lake Ampitabe, tourists head-ing back towards Antananarivo gener-ally return to Manambato by boat, but it is also possible to follow the most atmospheric stretch of canal north all the way to Toamasina, from where one can fly to Antananarivo or Île Sainte-Marie, or continue driving northward along the RN5.

TOAMASINA

Still sometimes referred to by its old French name Tamatave, **Toamasina ⑤** is Madagascar's second-largest city, supporting an estimated population of 300,000-plus, and its most impor-tant seaport, accounting for around three-quarters of the island's maritime trade, thanks partly to its good trans-port links to Antananarivo. Boasting a deep natural harbour protected by an offshore reef, it has a long history as a centre of maritime trade and piracy, and appears on most 17th-century maps under the name Port aux Prunes or variant spellings of Tamatave. Back then, the port was also known infor-mally as the Europeans' Graveyard, thanks to the high incidence of malaria and other tropical diseases.

Toamasina's rise to modern pre-eminence dates to the reign of King Radama I (1816–28), when its relative proximity to the Imerina capital led to its development as the island's main slave emporium. It overtook Mahajanga as the island's busiest port in the early years of the French colonisation, and has

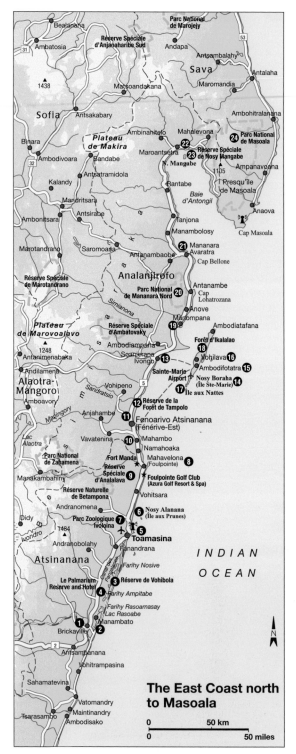

The East Coast north to Masoala

CANAL DES PANGALANES

Created to transport cargo in the late 19th century, the labyrinthine Canal des Pangalanes now transport tourists back to an older and more rustic way of life.

One of the world's longest artificial waterways, the Canal des Pangalanes runs along the east coast from the port of Toamasina south all the way to Farafangana, a distance of almost almost 650km (404 miles). The canal is typically separated from the ocean by a sandbar of a few hundred metres/yards in width, and it flows through 18 shallow natural lagoons, yet the inflow of around 10 major rivers and innumerable minor streams ensures that, though brackish in parts, it is essentially a freshwater ecosystem, and it also means that the water level shows little seasonal or tidal variation.

The excavation of the earliest canals was initiated by the Imerina monarchy in the pre-colonial era as the first leg of an inland transport route connecting

A heavy cargo on the Canal des Pangalanes.

the port of Toamasina to the royal capital at Antananarivo. The network was vastly expanded and upgraded under Governor Genera Joseph Gallieni after Madagascar became a French Colony in 1896. By 1901, an uninterrupted 95km (57-mile) canal connected Toamasina to Andevoranto, a small coastal port from where cargo barges could continue inland on the Rianila River to Brickaville. After World War II, the canal was further upgraded with the construction of a proper riverport at Toamasina, and the addition of a 65km (39-mile) southern extension from Andevoranto to Vatomandry. Plans to expand the network of small canals running south from Vatomandry all the way to Manakara via Mananjary to carry 30-tonne barges were shelved in the 1950s, and the entire canal system started to silt up through lack of maintenance in the early post-colonial era.

Major renovations were undertaken in the 1980s, including the dredging of the silted-up canals between Toamasina and Andevoranto, and the construction of new warehouses at several strategic ports, with a view to reviving the Pangalanes as the first leg of a modern transportation route between the country's largest port and the capital city. This plan never quite came to fruition, but the canal is still heavily utilised by local traffic, primarily to transport timber, charcoal, dried fish and agricultural produce on overladen flat-bottomed barges that also double as public transport between the canalside villages.

The Canal des Pangalanes – or at least the stretch between Manambato and Toamasina – also remains an important wildlife sanctuary, fishery and tourist attraction. More than 60 species of fish have been recorded, a long list of aquatic and woodland birds includes yellow-billed stork, black egret, hamerkop, white-faced whistling duck, knob-billed duck, Madagascar kingfisher, grey-headed lovebird, red-fronted coua and hook-billed vanga. Larger wildlife includes Nile crocodile, Malagasy ground boa and a variety of lemurs, including habituated aye-ayes on Île au Coq. For tourists, travelling by boat along the calm tree-shaded canals and open lakes that comprise this literal backwater, gliding past old-fashioned stick-and-rope fish traps and rustic fishing villages lined with dugout canoes, also provides a fascinating glimpse into local Malagasy life away from the towns and highways.

retained this role ever since, despite the almost total destruction of the city centre and harbour facilities by a cyclone in 1927. In the wake of this disaster, a Franco-German consortium built the first deep-water port at Toamasina, and the city centre was laid out along its modern lines, with the seafront Boulevard Ratsimilaho arcing northward from the harbour, and the main commercial thoroughfare Boulevard Joffre running parallel and inland if it.

Toamasina today has a relatively modern bustling feel, though there's also no shortage of old colonial buildings in various states of disrepair to give it an underlying raffish quality. Traffic is dominated by *pousse-pousses*, which stream along the main suburban thoroughfares like anarchic wildebeests. It's worth taking a stroll down **Boulevard Ratsimilaho**, which offers fine views across a pretty (but rather dirty) palm-lined beach to the harbour and its multitude of container boats on the opposite side of Ivondro Bay. The beach here is lined with a clutter of rickety wooden beachfront bars, local eateries and fresh coconut stalls where you can watch the passing parade over a chilled beer or seafood snack. Surprisingly, there's even a small and little-used funfair!

Toamasina offers little in the way of formal tourist attractions. Housed in a fantastically rundown two-story building, the compact **Musée Régional de l'Université de Toamasina** (cnr boulevards de la Libération & Joffre; 8–11am and 2.30–5pm) displays a reasonably interesting selection of archaeological and ethnographic artefacts. On the opposite side of the city, situated inside the harbour entrance, the **Musée du Port** (Mon–Fri 8am–noon and 2–5pm; donation) details the maritime history of the city and its port. A couple of blocks back from this, **La Place Bien-Aimée** is a small open square, favoured by local *pétanque* enthusiasts, shaded by massive multiple-trunked banyan trees,

and surrounded by decaying colonial and Creole buildings. For maps and further information about Toamasina, visit the **Office Régional du Tourisme de Toamasina** (Boulevard Joffre; tel: 020-5334395; Mon–Fri 9am–5pm).

Situated about 3.5km (2 miles) offshore to the north of Toamasina, **Île aux Prunes** ❻ is a small island fringed by lovely sandy beaches and coral reefs that offer fine snorkelling. The island supports a dense cover of forest and large colonies of the Madagascar flying fox, an endangered species with a 1.25m (4ft) wingspan. Its only human inhabitant is the caretaker of a prominent 60-metre (197ft) -high lighthouse, which ranks as Africa's tallest such structure, being about 1m (3ft) taller than the nearest mainland contender, at Port Said in Egypt. The island is also known as Nosy Alanana and while the significance of the plums alluded to in its old French name is obscure, it presumably derives from Port aux Prunes, an old name for Toamasina. Île aux Prunes stands about 15km (9 miles) from Toamasina by boat

⊙ **Fact**

An oft-repeated local tradition holds that the name Toamasina was coined by King Radama I of Imerina, who had never visited the sea before arriving at the port, and upon tasting its water exclaimed: '*Toa masina!*' – literally, 'It's salty'. However, since Toamasina first appeared under that name on a marine chart compiled in 1768, a full 25 years before Radama's birth, this popular legend must either be untrue, or else relate to an earlier monarch.

Place de la République, Toamasina.

Shoes off on the muddy trail from Maroantsetra to Antalaha.

Lookout at the Parc Zoologique Ivoloina.

and snorkelling excursions can be arranged through any operator there.

A popular day trip out of Toamasina, the **Parc Zoologique Ivoloina ❼** (tel: 020-5393168; www.parcivoloina.org; daily 9am–5pm), only 15km (9 miles) north of the city centre, was established in 1963 as an educational facility and refuge for wildlife confiscated by the authorities. It comprises a small zoo containing 12 species of lemur (including aye-aye and blue-eyed black lemur) and a few other indigenous creatures in cramped but clean cages, and a 280-hectare (690-acre) area of forest and wetland habitats set around the Lac Fulgence. The park is traversed by around 5km (3 miles) of trails, which can be explored with or without a guide, as you prefer, and include stops at a stilted birdwatching hide on the lake and a small but pretty waterfall. Introduced but free-ranging populations of brown, crowned, red-bellied, great bamboo and black-and-white ruffed lemur might be seen, and the lake attracts plenty of birds including Madagascar pond heron, white-faced duck, Madagascar kingfisher and grey-headed lovebird. There's a decent handicraft shop and snack bar at the entrance. To get to Ivoloina, follow the RN5 north out of Toamasina for 12km (7 miles) as far as Ambodihariha, then turn left onto a signposted dirt road that follows the south bank of a wide river before veering sharp to the left and arriving at the entrance gate after roughly 3km (2 miles).

HOPEFUL FOULPOINTE

Foulpointe ❽, now officially called Mahavelona, is scruffy little resort village whose string of modest lodges caters mainly to weekenders from Toamasina, 60km (36 miles) further south along the RN5. Ironically, its rather uninviting name actually derives from the English 'Hopeful Point', most likely as coined by Captain Thomas White, an English pirate who settled there briefly, marrying a Malagasy woman, *c.*1706 (another version of events is that Hopeful was the name of an Indian ship that stopped there to trade cloth for gold with the locals). Foulpointe subsequently emerged as an important maritime trade centre and slave emporium, though it was largely superseded by Toamasina in the early 19th century. Today, despite its low-key feel, Foulpointe boasts a lovely shallow swimming beach whose calm waters are protected by an offshore reef, while the swanky out-of-town Azura Golf Resort & Spa (tel: 032-0342066; www.azuragolf.mg) is home to the **Foulpointe Golf Club**, whose 9-hole seaside course is open to day visitors.

Foulpointe also boasts a genuine historical curiosity in the form of **Fort Manda** (daily 9am–noon and 2.30–4.30pm), which was built by King Radama I to defend his realm against foreign naval attacks following the annexation of the east coast to Imerina in the early 19th century. Constructed over eight years, the circular fort has an imposing 9-metre (15ft) -high, 6-metre (10ft) -thick outer stone wall,

held together with a cement made from egg-shell and albumin, with a circumference of almost 200 metres (655ft), and it reputedly house more than 20,000 soldiers from Imerina in its prime. Correctly known as Fort Mahavelona (Manda is simply the Malagasy word for fort), it was captured in 1898 by a French occupational force that found it completely unmanned – possibly because its inhabitants all managed to escape through a secret subterranean tunnel that has since been buried. The site was heavily looted during the colonial era, but the fern-draped outer wall, topped with several cannons, is still standing, and can be walked around in its entirety, offering fabulous views over the surrounding scrubland to the ocean. The former military barracks, kitchen and prison are also still standing, along with several shady mango trees. The fort stands about 100 metres/yds from the RN5 at the north end of the small town, and is clearly signposted.

Situated about 8km (5 miles) southwest of Foulpointe, the **Réserve Spéciale d'Analalava** ❾ (tel: 032-5392378; www.analalavareserve.org; 8am–5pm) is reached along the same road that leads past Fort Manda – one that deteriorates in quality as you get further out if town, and that may be totally impassable after rain. Established as a community reserve in 2006, it extends over 229 hectares (566 acres) of moist lowland rainforest and protects more than 350 plant species, including 25 of the island's 188 endemic palm species. Wildlife includes the diurnal white-headed lemur and eastern bamboo lemur, along with three nocturnal lemur, 51 bird, 35 reptile and 24 frog species. Two short (2–3km/1.2–2 miles) guided day trails run through the reserve, and night walks are also offered to people staying overnight in the rustic camp, which comprises half-a-dozen simple bungalows set in a forest clearing, and a tall wooden watchtower.

TOWARDS SOANIERANA IVONGO AND ÎLE SAINTE-MARIE

Probably the most convincing beach resort on the northeast coastal mainland, sleepy **Mahambo** ❿ lies 30km (18 miles) north of Foulpointe at the

Ruins of Fort Manda.

ISLAND OF PIRATES

Its proximity to the main shipping lanes between India and Africa made Île Sainte-Marie a popular base for pirates in the 17th and 18th centuries.

Little is known about Île Sainte-Marie's early history, though it's been suggested that its Malagasy name Nosy Boraha – Island of Abraham/Ibrahim – alludes to a medieval Arabic, Swahili or Jewish settlement there. The name Sainte-Marie was bestowed on it by Portuguese navigators who narrowly escaped being shipwrecked there on Assumption Day (the principal feast day dedicated to the Virgin Mary) of 1506. One participant in this expedition, De Constantin, wrote that the islanders, far from displaying obvious Islamic or Jewish cultural traits, wore 'a cleverly woven garment of coloured reeds' and carried 'four javelins trimmed with silver points... and large shields of wood that cover them wholly when they fall'. De Constantin was impressed by the island's verdancy and beauty, and noted that it comprised two landmasses (the other being Île aux Nattes).

The infamous pirate Henry 'Long Ben' Every.

One map from 1733 simply refers to Île Sainte-Marie as 'Island of Pirates'. It started in 1685, when Adam Baldridge, an Englishman who fled Jamaica to escape charges of murder, took control of the bay immediately south of present-day Ambodifotatra. Not satisfied with his regular piratic hauls, Baldridge imposed a tax on all ships that docked on Sainte-Marie, as well as maintaining a harem of Malagasy women and a pool of willing ship-hands to service them. Baldridge's tenure on Sainte-Marie ended in 1697, when local Malagasy leaders chased him out by for selling others of their number to slave traders. By then, however, the Baie aux Forbans – literally 'Pirates' Bay' – was entrenched as retreat for hundreds of rogues and profiteers, among them William 'Captain' Kidd, Henry 'Long Ben' Avery (the subject of Daniel Defoe's *The King of Pirates*) and Olivier Levasseur (nicknamed *La Buse* – The Buzzard – because of the ruthless efficiency with which he executed his attacks).

The most influential buccaneer to settle on Île Sainte-Marie was Thomas Tew, who reputedly wed a Malagasy princess called Antavaratra Rahena and fathered King Ratsimilaho, the charismatic founder of the Betsimisaraka Kingdom. Shortly before his death, Ratsimilaho ceded his throne to his daughter Bity and instructed her to sign a treaty of protectorateship that granted Île Sainte-Marie to France provided it didn't interfere with Betsimisaraka sovereignty on the facing mainland. The treaty was signed in 1750, after which the island served as a penal colony for some years.

It wasn't until 1821 that Sylvain Roux established the island's first formal French settlement, an ill-fated venture that resulted in 85 of the 200 settlers dying of fever within a year of their arrival, and most of the rest being evacuated to La Réunion. Another settlement was established in 1837 by Rev. Pierre Dalmond, a Jesuit missionary who baptised more than 1,000 islanders prior to his death in 1847, and also compiled the first French-Malagasy dictionary. Even after the formal annexation of Madagascar in 1896, Île Sainte-Marie technically remained a part of France, as opposed to a colony. It retained this status until 1960, when it was ceded to the newly independent Malagasy Republic, though all inhabitants born before 1960 are recognised as French citizens, while those born prior to 1972 have dual nationality.

end of a long arcing bay that offers fine conditions for swimming, surfing and snorkelling. The established focal point of tourism at Mahambo is La Pirogue, a mid-range hotel situated about 2km (1.2 miles) east of the RN5 along a feeder road lined with budget lodges, eateries, craft stalls and surf schools catering mainly to backpackers and a local clientele. More lived-in village than tarted-up resort, Mahambo is a refreshingly affordable and untouristy beach destination in its own right. Logistically, it makes for a convenient and comfortable overnight springboard for the daily boat services that connect Soanierana Ivongo to Île Sainte-Marie – as well as forming an agreeable alternative to the island when weather intervenes with the ferry schedule.

Most people heading north from Mahambo are bound for Soanierana Ivongo, the mainland terminus for boats to Île Sainte-Marie, 80km (50 miles) further along the RN5 – in which case an earlyish start is required, and there won't be time for prolonged stops. The largest town en route, only 15km

(9 miles) past Mahambo, is **Fénérive-Est ⑪**, aka Fenoarivo Atsinanana, the former capital of the Betsimisaraka Kingdom, whose founder Ratsimilaho – reputedly the son of the pirate Thomas Tew – was born there circa 1695. Now an important centre of clove production, this town of 20,000 doesn't have much to show for its long history, but the large, lively market is worth a look, and travellers using *taxi-brousse* might well end up changing vehicle here.

Situated just 800 metres/yds east of the RN5, the super-accessible **Réserve de la Forêt de Tampolo ⑫** (www.lemur reserve.org/madagascar; daily 7am–5pm) protects 6.75 sq km (2.6 sq miles) of literal forest and marshland only 10km (6 miles) north of Fénérive-Est. The forest station incorporates a good information centre (labelled in French only) and arranges guided day and night walks into the forest. Day walks take about four hours and offer a good chance of spotting brown lemur, eastern bamboo lemur and forest birds such as Madagascar crested ibis and blue vanga. Night walks are likely to throw up

Crowd gathering at Soanierana Ivongo for the crossing to Île Sainte-Marie.

nocturnal lemurs, of which five species are present, including aye-aye.

There's a definite end-of-the road feel to **Soanierana Ivongo ⓭**, a small and down-at-heel but unexpectedly lively riverport sandwiched between the Indian Ocean and the south bank of the Marimbona perhaps 2km (1.2 miles) upstream of its mouth. Soanierana Ivongo is best known as the mainland port of embarkation for boats to Île Sainte-Marie, but it also forms the terminus of the surfaced southern sector of the RN5, and travellers planning on taking a 4x4 further north must first take a motor ferry across the Marimbona. Short on amenities but strong on tropical riverport character, Soanierana Ivongo is dominated by a hectic market that sprawls either side of the road connecting the town centre to the port, with stalls selling everything from fresh produce, chilled beers and used clothes to pirate DVDs, plasticware and mini-solar panels. Also in Soanierana Ivongo is the office for the **Réserve Spéciale d'Ambatovaky**, an alluring 600-sq-km (232-sq-mile) tract of montane forest that's renowned for its birdlife (92 species, including 55 Madagascar endemics) and theoretically accessible by boat along the Marimbona, but currently open to researchers only.

ÎLE SAINTE-MARIE

Often billed as the east coast's answer to Nosy Be, **Île Sainte-Marie ⓮** is a 222-sq-km (86-sq-mile) granitic island situated 7km (4 miles) offshore of the closest mainland peninsula. Officially known but seldom referred to as Nosy Boraha, the sliver-like island stretches almost 60km (36 miles) from north to south, but is nowhere significantly more than 5km (3 miles) wide, and its maximum altitude is a relatively modest 114 metres (374ft). As is the case with Nosy Be, Sainte-Marie offers great swimming, snorkelling, diving and whale-watching opportunities, and while it lacks the spectacular volcanic scenery and lemur-filled forests of its western counterpart, it compensates by being less overtly touristy and considerably more affordable. Weather

Humpback whales off the coast of Île Sainte-Marie.

permitting, daily motorboat shuttles run back and forth between the mainland riverport of Soanierana Ivongo and the island's principal town Ambodifotatra, a 30km (18-mile) crossing that takes up to 90 minutes. However, most visitors opt to fly there from Antananarivo or Toamasina, landing at Sainte-Marie Airport at Ankarena, about 13km (8 miles) south of Ambodifotatra.

Ambodifotatra ⑮, the island's largest settlement, stands on its southeast coast overlooking the shallow Baie aux Forbans (Pirate's Bay), a former piratic stronghold punctuated by the tiny Île aux Forbans and larger Îlot Madame. At the south end of town, the Colline d'Ambodifotatra is a low hill dominated by the **Old Fort**, an arched double-storey building constructed by the French in 1753, making it the oldest extant structure on Sainte-Marie. About 100 metres/yds to its south, the neat **Eglise Notre-Dame-de-l'Assomption**, distinguished by its blue shuttered windows, colonnaded portico and cast-iron altar donated by Eugénie de Montijo (the last Empress of France) is Madagascar's oldest Catholic church, built in 1857 on the site of the Jesuit mission founded by Rev. Pierre Dalmond 20 years earlier.

A 250-metre/yd causeway leads from the north shore of Baie aux Forbans to **Îlot Madame**, the small built-up island that guards the harbour entrance. The Madame in question is Queen Bity of Betsimisaraka, who signed a treaty ceding Sainte-Marie to France there in 1750, and went on the live there with her husband, a French officer. It was here that Sylvain Roux established an ill-fated French settlement in 1822, and a magnificent Governor's Residence built there in 1871 has for some years been under renovation and will eventually open as a local history museum called the Musée de l'Îlot Madame.

Another bridge leads from Îlot Madame to the south shore of the bay, where the scenically located **Cimetière**

Saint-Pierre (daily 8am–5pm), better known as the Cimetière des Pirates (Pirates' cemetery), houses 30-odd tombstones marking the graves of 18th-century pirates (some complete with skull-and-crossbones) and 19th-century missionaries. The cemetery overlooks Île aux Forbans, a tiny circular island which, as its name suggests, reputedly served as the base of several of the most infamous pirates to visit Sainte-Marie, and was traditionally where their freshly returned boats would dock to divide their spoils. There's absolutely no truth in the oft-repeated local legend that the cemetery's largest tombs houses William 'Captain' Kidd, buried in a seated position as punishment for his sins (in reality, Kidd was tried and found guilty of murder and piracy in London in 1701, then hanged at Wapping's Execution Dock, after which his gibbeted body was left to rot alongside the Thames for three years as a warning to other pirates). Whether or not the small gateway-like semi-circular ruin on Île aux Forbans is an alignment marker

⊙ Tip

Several motorboats ply back and forth between Île Sainte-Marie and Soanierana Ivongo, usually leaving the island before 6am, reaching the mainland 90 minutes later, and returning at 10am. The *Gasikara* (tel: 020-5398749; www.sainte-marie-tours.com) and *El Condor* (034-7043301, www.bluemarine-madagascar.com) also operate a connecting road shuttle to/from Toamasina. You could also overnight at Mahambo, or at one of two very basic lodges in Soanierana Ivongo. Especially between May and September, rough weather frequently forces the cancellation of all boat crossings.

Pirates' cemetery, Île Sainte-Marie.

pointing to Kidd's legendary buried treasure is a matter of conjecture.

AROUND SAINTE-MARIE

Vohilava , on the west coast 15 minutes' drive south of Ambodifotatra, lies at the heart of Sainte-Marie's most developed tourist strip, a 3km (2-mile) stretch of beach lined with a dozen or so hotels, among them the peerless Princess Bora Lodge & Spa. All these lodges offer a wider range of marine activities: snorkelling in the shallow coral reefs of the sand cays; scuba diving alongside turtles, manta rays and the like at the 30-metres (100ft) -deep Barracuda and Treasure Islands; day visits to the east coast's utterly gorgeous and unspoilt Baie d'Ampanihy; or whale-watching excursions in search of the 16-metre/yd-long humpbacks that lob-tail and calve offshore during the southern winter months, most visibly over July to September. Also in Vohilava, the **Parc Endemika d'Ambodiforaha** (tel: 032-5189666; daily 8am–5pm) is a small private zoo and botanical garden inhabited by endemic flora and fauna such as lemurs, chameleons, tortoises and other rescued animals.

Sainte-Marie Airport, on the far south of the island, overlooks the narrow channel that divides it from the 2.8-sq-km (1.1-sq-mile) **Île aux Nattes** , or Nosy Nato, named after a type of endemic tree that once proliferated there. More even than Sainte-Marie, the white sandy beaches of Île aux Nattes fulfil every expectation of an Indian Ocean island idyll, and the islet's northeast and northwest coast are lined with a burgeoning collection of attractive resort hotels. It is also possible to walk around the entire Île aux Nattes over two or three hours, stopping en route at Phare Pointe Blévec, a small lighthouse that stands at the island's highest point and offers fine views in all directions.

On a hilly slope overlooking the west coast 10km (6 miles) north of Ambodifotatra, the 4-sq-km (1.5-sq-mile) **Forêt d'Ikalalao** is the largest surviving tract of the primary forest that once covered most of Île Sainte-Marie. Too small and isolated to support any of the larger diurnal lemurs, it is nevertheless home to the localised nocturnal Boraha mouse lemur as well a wide variety of birds, chameleons and other reptiles. It can be visited in combination with the **Cascade d'Antanandava**, a small but pretty waterfall that runs down a rock face on the forest edge.

THE RN5 NORTH OF SOANIERANA IVONGO

Back on the mainland, a short ferry ride from Soanierana Ivongo carries you to the north bank of the Marimbona and the start of a notoriously rough – after rain, often impossible – 225km (140-mile) stretch of RN5 that terminates at Maroantsetra. The first opportunity to break up the trip, 45km (27 miles) north of Soanierana Ivongo, is **Manompana** , an attractive small

Negotiating a small wooden bridge on the rural road to Maroantsetra.

seaside town set on the north bank of a shallow and well protected bay that offers good swimming and surfing from a handful of basic beach lodges. Manompana is also the gateway to the 65-hectare (160-acre) **Forêt d'Ambodiriana**, a community-run conservation area set on the banks of the Manompana River about 5km (3 miles) to the west. Activities on offer at Ambodiriana include an hour-long guided forest walk to look for lemurs, birds and frogs, and visit a waterfall that cascades into a natural swimming pool, as well as a kayak trip through the mangroves.

The pretty beachfront village of Sahasoa, 46km (28 miles) north of Manompana, is the best base for exploring the little-visited **Parc National de Mananara-Nord** ㉑ (www.parcs-madagascar.com; 8am–4pm), which protects some 230 sq km (89 sq miles) of mostly forested land along with a 10-sq-km (3.8-sq-mile) marine sector focussed on the small twin islets called Nosy Atafana. The park office in Sahasoa arranges boat trips Nosy Atafana, which

lies about 2km (1.2 miles) offshore and supports an impressive colony of Madagascar flying foxes as well as an immense variety of fish in the surrounding reefs. The terrestrial part of the park can be explored along two relatively strenuous 16–20km (10–12.5-mile) trails out of Sahasoa that take a full day to complete. The reward is a botanically diverse forest (1,200 plant species including almost 50 palms and many seasonal orchids) that counts indri, diademed sifaka and aye-aye among its 13 lemur species, and that also hosts 77 bird species including lesser vasa parrot, helmet vanga and red-tailed vanga.

The largest and best-equipped town along the RN5 between Soanierana Ivongo and Maroantsetra, **Mananara** ㉑ supports a population of around 20,000 at the delta-like mouth of the eponymous river, which flows into the south end of the 70km- (42-mile) long Antongil Bay. Mananara's main attraction, affiliated to the central Hôtel Chez Roger, is a nocturnal visit to **Aye-Aye Island** (tel: 033-1276897), which stands in the Mananara River a short pirogue

⊙ Fact

The largest and most beautiful of Madagascar's orchids, *Eulophiella roempleriana* is an epiphyte whose stunning pink, purple and white flowers are clustered at the end of a long spike. This rare orchid's natural range is confined to the east coast of Île aux Nattes and one remote forest north of Toamasina. It is quite easy to locate in the wild in season (it blooms over December and January) but several hotel gardens on Île aux Nattes contain cultivated specimens.

The azure-blue waters surrounding Île aux Nattes.

ride upstream of the town centre. As its name suggests, the island hosts a small population of introduced and semi-habituated aye-ayes, and it ranks as one of the few places where these bizarre coconut-chomping creatures can be seen in a more-or-less natural state. From Mananara, it's another 106km (63 miles) north along a very rough stretch of the RN5 – offering some lovely views across Antongil Bay – to remote Maroantsetra.

MAROANTSETRA AND THE MASOALA PENINSULA

A contender for the hotly contested title of Madagascar's ultimate end-of-the-road town, **Maroantsetra** ② is an isolated and time-warped seaport situated at the mouth of the Antainambalana River as it flows into the sheltered northern end of Antongil Bay. Maroantsetra is connected to Soanierana Ivongo by the occasional taxi-boat and the arduous RN5, but there is no road access from the west or north, and the overwhelming majority of visitors fly in, either with the (increasingly

Market day in Maroantsetra.

unreliable) scheduled service offered by Air Madagascar or (with increasingly frequency) by charter flight. Despite its remoteness, Maroantsetra is an unexpectedly prosperous town, thanks largely to its suitability to vanilla and cinnamon production, and the busting market at the north of town is well worth a visit.

Only 2km (1.2 miles) offshore of Maroantsetra, the 5.2-sq-km (2-sq-mile) **Réserve Spéciale de Nosy Mangabe** ㉓ (www.parcs-madagascar. com) protects Antongil Bay's largest island, a lovely forested protrusion that rises to a summit of 332 metres (1090ft) above the surrounding turquoise waters. As suggested by its name (literally 'Big Slave Island'), Nosy Mangabe, like Sainte-Marie to its south, was once a popular refuge for pirates, and it was later a quarantine for sick sailors and a major space and slave trading centre. Relicts of this long history can be seen in the form of 16th-century Dutch engravings on the northerly Plage des Hollandais and a cemetery with old stone tombstones

near the summit. Nosy Mangabe was originally set aside as a reserve to protect an introduced population of aye-aye (it was visited by Douglas Adams, of *Hitchhiker's Guide to the Galaxy* fame, in the course of researching the BBC documentary *Last Chance to See*) and other wildlife likely to be seen along its well-marked trail network includes black-and-white ruffed lemur, white-fronted lemur and a wide variety of birds, reptiles and frogs. The island is particularly worth visiting between July and September, when several thousand humpback whales gather in Antongil Bay to breed, and they can frequently be seen breaching and lob-tailing. Day visits or overnight camping trips to Nosy Mangabe must be arranged through the national park office in Maroantsetra.

The main attraction close to Maroantsetra, situated about 20km (12 miles) further east, is the **Parc National de Masoala** ㉔ (tel: 034-4941538; www.parcs-madagascar.com), which protects the forests and mountains on the spectacular Masoala Peninsula. Unbreached by roads, Masoala is Madagascar's largest national park, with a total area of 2,400 sq km (927 sq miles), and a key component of the Rainforests of the Atsinanana Unesco World Heritage Site. Rising from a succession of stunning uninhabited beaches to a series of tall peaks (maximum altitude 1,310 metres/4,298ft), the park protects and extraordinary diversity of wooded and wetland habitats, and it is an important stronghold for several localised birds, notably Madagascar serpent eagle, Madagascar red owl, running coua, pitta-like ground-roller, rufous-headed ground-roller, Bernier's vanga and helmet vanga. Other wildlife includes 15 species of lemur, the spectacular tomato frog, and the gorgeous day-flying Madagascar sunset moth, whose iridescent wings have a span of up to 10cm (4in). Alluring though it is, Masoala is accessible only by boat and is best suited to fit and adventurous travellers willing to embark on a 3–14 day hiking trip between the official national park campsite and cottage.

⊙ Tip

For those on a generous budget, the award-winning Masoala Forest Lodge (tel: 032-0541587; www.masoalaforestlodge.com) is an intimate (up to 14 guests) wood-and-thatch ecolodge set in a 10-hectare (25-acre) beachfront concession within Masoala National Park. The last word in rustic luxury, it is also perfect located for snorkelling, swimming, whale-watching, birding, hiking in the primary rainforest, and seeking out the otherwise seldom seen aye-aye.

Stream in lowland rainforest, Parc National de Masoala.

The white-and-yellow cathedral in Mahajanga.

MAHAJANGA AND BOENY REGION

A sleepy but historic port on the island's northwest coast, Mahajanga is the main gateway to Boeny Region's diverse selection of underrated national parks and remote beauty spots.

Antananarivo

The administrative centre of Boeny Region, Mahajanga is a cosmopolitan port town situated 550km (340 miles) from Antananarivo at the northern terminus of the RN4. It is situated on the north bank of the mangrove-lined Bombetoka Bay, the country's largest estuary, its waters tinged rusty-brown with topsoil carried down from the highlands by the 525km (326-mile)-long Betsiboka River. Mahajanga offers ready access to some agreeable beaches, but it is arguably of less interest in itself than as a springboard for exploring some of the country's least publicised or visited conservation areas. The most popular regional attraction is the Parc National d'Ankarafantsika, which lies about 110km (68 miles) back along the RN4 and is readily accessible by public transport. Boeny's other top sites are mostly only accessible on organised 4x4 expeditions and include the spectacular subterranean labyrinths of the Grottes d'Anjohibe, the bird-rich Complexe Mahavavy-Kinkony and bizarre tsingy landscape of the Parc National des Tsingy de Namoroka.

THE RN4 FROM ANTANANARIVO

Most foreign visitors to Mahajanga take one of several flights weekly from Antananarivo. However, the two towns are also connected by the surfaced

RN4, a well-maintained road that carries relatively light traffic and can be covered in one very long day by taxi-brousse or in a private vehicle, though there are also plenty of opportunities to break the journey.

Firarazana, 125km (75 miles) north of Antananarivo, stands at the junction of the rough 12km (7.5-mile) 4x4-only road that runs east to the 56-sq-km (21.5-sq-mile) **Réserve Spéciale d'Ambohitantely ❶** (www. parcs-madagascar.com; 8am–4pm). Straddling elevations of 1,300–1,660 metres

⚙ Main Attractions

Parc National
  d'Ankarafantsika
Mahajanga's Corniche
Cirque Rouge
Grottes d'Anjohibe
Katsepy Peninsula
Complexe Mahavavy-
  Kinkony
Parc National des Tsingy
  de Namoroka

Map on page 224

Dhow at sea, Mahajanga.

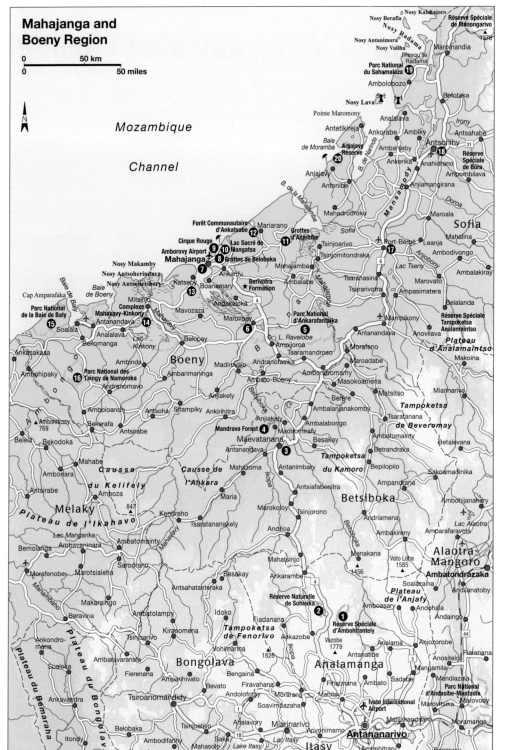

Mahajanga and Boeny Region

0 ——— 50 km
0 ——— 50 miles

N

Mozambique

Channel

Nosy Kalakajoro
Nosy Berafia
Nosy Radama
Réserve Spéciale de Manongarivo
1878
Nosy Antanimora
Nosy Valiha
Presqu'île Radama
Maromandia
Parc National du Sahamalaza **19**
Ambolobozo
Befotaka
Nosy Lava
Pointe Maromony
Analalava
Analalava
Antetikireja
Ankorabe
Ambiky
Antsahabe
Irony
Antsohihy **31**
Baie de Moramba
Anjajavy Réserve
Ambanjeby
Ankerika
Anahidrano
Réserve Spéciale de Bora **18**
20
Anjajavy
Ampombilava
Anjiamangirana
Antonibe
Mahadrodroka
Doroa
B. de la Mahajamba
Maroala
Sofia
Mahadrodroka
Forêt Communautaire d'Ankatsabe **12**
Mariarano
Grottes d'Anjohibe
Sofia
Port-Bergé **17**
Leanja
Mahalina
Cirque Rouge
Lac Sacré de Mangatsa
Grottes d'Anjohibe **11**
Tsinjoarivo
Ambodivongo
Lac Sacré de Mangatsa **9** **10**
Mahajanga
Tsinjomitondraka
6
Ambalakiray
Amborovy Airport **8**
Grottes de Belobaka
Mahajamba
Marovato
7
Ankarifu
Tsarahasina
Ampasimatera
Berivotra Formation
Katsepy
Boanamary
Tsararivotra
Belalanda
13
Andakaloka
Ambalabe
Réserve Spéciale Tampoketsa Analamaintso
Nosy Makamby
Parc National d'Ankarafantsika
Nosy Antsoherindava
Mavozaza
Anovilava
Nosy Antsoheribory
Plateau d'Analamaintso
Cap Amparafaka
Baie de Bay
Mitsinjo
Baie de Boeny
Marovoay
Mampikony
Makoina
Complexe Mahavavy-Kinkony
14
6
L. Ravelobe
Parc National de la Baie de Baly
Antananandava
Ampijoroa
Antananandava
Miarinarivo
15
Soalala
Bekomanga
Analalava
Lac Kinkony
5
Tsaramandroso
Morafeno
Ankasakasa
Bekipay
Andranofasika
Maroadabe
Matsitso
Tampoketsa
Ambohipaky
Ambinda
Boeny
Madirovalo
Masokoamena
de Beveromay
Parc National des Tsingy de Namoroka **16**
Ambarimaninga
Ambato-Boeny
Ambondromamy
Tsaratanana
Andranomavo
Anjiakely
Berere
Ambalanjanakomby
Tsaratanana
Amboloande
Antsoha
Sitampiky
Ankirihitra
Ambalabongo
Ambatomainty
Betalevana
Ambohitrosy 769
Bekerafa
Antsirabe
Anjiakely
Madiromirafy
Besakay
Betrandraka
Sakoamadinika
Beleia
Bekodoka
Mandrava Forest **4**
Tampoketsa
Bepilopilo
Mahabe
Maevatanana
Antanimbaty
du Kamoro
Ampandrana
Ambohijanahary
Ambonara
Antanandava
3
Antsirabe
Causse du Kelifely
Causse de l'Ankara
Mahazoma
Ampoza
847
Antanimbaty
Andriamena
Lac Alaotra
Amparafaravola
Plateau de l'Ikahavo
Kendreho
Maria
Marokoloy
Tsinjorono
Ambakirany
Betsiboka
Andrioa
Manakana
Alaotra Mangoro
Lac Mangarika
Ambatomainty
Vato Loha 1585
Soalazaina
Bemolanga
Ambavaninara
Sarodrano
Mahatsinjo
Ankarambe
1456
Ambatondrazaka
Morafenobe
Marotsialeha
Plateau de l'Anjafy
Ambositra
Andilanatoby
Makaraingo
Antsahatanteraka
Amboasary
Andohala
Andaingo
Beravina
Ambatolampy
Idoko
Réserve Naturelle de Sohisika
2
Réserve Spéciale d'Ambohitantely
Analaroa
Anjozorobe
Ankondromena
Tsinjoarivo
Kiranomena
Fiadanana
44
Fierenana
Plateau du Bemaraha
Ambatovaranala
Fierenana
Tampoketsa de Fenorivo
Ankazobe
Vazobe 1779
Antanatibe
Anositelo
Soaloka
Ankavandra
Vohimarina
1826
Mangamila
Marovoay
Itondy
Plateau du Bongolava
Bongolava
Bengaina
Firavahana
Mahitsy
Sadabe
Mandiazala
Moramanga
Fierenana
Amparihivato
Bevato
Andolofotsy
Morarano
Ambato
Ivato International Airport
Manjakandriana
Marovitsika
Manambolo
Tsiroanomandidy
Soavimbazaha
Beparasy
Belobaka
Tsinjoativo
Analavory
Arivonimamo
Antananarivo
2
Mahasolo
1
Saka
Lake Itasy
Antananarivo
Kinangaly 1319
Imanga
Soavinandriana
Lac Itasy
Itasy
Ambohitran-Diamanitra
Lakato
18
Miarinarivo

(4,265–5,445ft), little-visited Ambohitantely – literally, Honey Mountain – protects an isolated vestige of secondary and primary forest renowned for its proliferation of orchids, some 40-plus species of which bloom between November and March. The reserve also protects important populations of the critically endangered black-bark tree *Asteropeia amblyocarpa* and the localised Manambe palm *Dypsis decipiens*. The diurnal brown lemur and nocturnal brown mouse lemur and eastern woolly lemur are also present, along with 75 bird species, including Madagascar marsh harrier and Madagascar crested ibis, and the locally endemic frog *Anodonthyla vallani*. Three guided walking trails run through the reserve, the most interesting and challenging being the 6km (3.6-mile), four-hour Loop Circuit to the summit. There is a campsite in the reserve but the closest accommodation is a very basic hotel at Ankazobe, which straddles the RN4 about 30km (18.5 miles) south of Firarazana.

Only 7km (4 miles) north of Firarazana, Ankafobe is the site of the community-run **Réserve Naturelle de Sohisika** ❷ (tel: 033-132480) though far smaller than Ambohitantely at mere 30 hectares (74 acres), is also far more accessible to casual passers-by. Comprising a relict forest patch in a valley 30-minutes' walk from the signposted office on the west side of the RN7, it was set aside to protect the namesake sohisika *Schizolaena tampoketsana*, a critically endangered central highland endemic that grows up to 15m (49ft) high, has a twisted trunk and pinkish-white flowers, and is regarded to be one of the world's rarest trees, with fewer than 300 mature specimens left in the wild. A well-maintained walking trail runs through the forest, which also harbours a conspicuous population of brown lemur, the nocturnal Goodman's mouse lemur, an unspecified and possibly unique dwarf lemur, 35 bird species, and an attractive waterfall.

North of Ankafobe, the RN7 winds uphill though cool, rolling, thinly-populated highlands covered in open grassland and occasional pine and eucalyptus plantations, reaching a maximum elevation of 1,650 metres (5,400ft). Scenically, it's unexpectedly reminiscent of the Ethiopian highlands, with an expansive vista of layered hills and mountains stretching back towards a distant horizon.

MAEVATANANA AND AMBONDROMAMY

At the 175km (110 mile) mark, the RN4 starts the gradual descent to **Maevatanana** ❸, a town of around 25,000 set at an altitude of 70 metres (230ft) on the southeast bank of the Ikopa River 300km (180 miles) north of Tana. Maevatanana means 'Beautiful Town', a misnomer if ever there was one, since it's indubitably one of the scruffiest towns in Madagascar, as well as being notorious for its suffocating heat – and rampant mosquitoes – in midsummer. Despite this, it forms a convenient and popular pit stop for northbound

⊙ Tip

Andranovelona, a small town bisected by the RN4 some 40km (24 miles) out of Antananarivo, literally means *Place of Living Water*, a reference to the nearby freshwater springs that are bottled and marketed as the popular *Eau Vive* brand of mineral water.

Children carting water to the village, Andranofasika.

⊘ Tip

Travelling along the RN4 north of Maevatanana, do hop out of the car to walk across the metallic bridge that spans the mud-brown Betsiboka River some 30km (18 miles) out of town. The bridge offers views across a fantastic rockscape flowed across by an aquatic labyrinth of seething whitewater rapids, explosive waterfalls and massive potholes created by erosive swirls.

Ankarokaroka Canyon, Parc National d'Ankarafantsika.

taxi-brousse, and it boasts a few decent restaurants as well as a couple of somewhat less appealing hotels. It is also the capital of Betsiboka, an administrative region named after the large river whose confluence with the Ikopa lies about 30km (18 miles) further downstream. The closest thing to an urban tourist attraction in Maevatanana, tucked away behind the Shell filling station, is a memorial to the French soldiers who died pendant la campagne of 1895.

Altogether more alluring, the **Mandrava Forest ④** (www.sifaka-conservation. org; charge), some 10km (6 miles) north of Maevatanana as the crow flies, has recently been identified as a stronghold for the endangered crowned sifaka, and is under development as a tourist site. Once operational, the reserve will be reachable by taking a local pirogue downstream along the Ikopa past the small town of Madiromirafy, then walking the last 2km (1.2 miles) or so. Although Mandrava's main attraction is its population of 150-plus crowned sifaka, this 200-hectare (495-acre) stand

of dry forest supports three other types of lemur and more than 35 bird species.

Hotter, drier and scrubbier, the countryside north of the Betsiboka, punctuated by mango-shaded villages of simple mud, thatch and bamboo huts, is distinctly African in feel. Finally, a full 410km (245 miles) north of Antananarivo, a massive suspension bridge over the Kamoro River brings you to **Ambondromamy** (Place of Sweet Reeds), a bustling market town that boasts a couple of modest hotels and lies alongside a lake lined by the reeds for which it is named. Here, astonishingly, you're presented with the first opportunity since leaving the capital to take a wrong turn on asphalt – continue straight ahead on the RN4 for Mahajanga (or Ankarafantsika), or turn right at the main central junction to continue northward on the RN6 to Nosy Be or Diego Suarez.

ANKARAFANTSIKA NATIONAL PARK

Extending across 1,350 sq km (521 sq miles) either side of the RN4, the vast

Parc National d'Ankarafantsika ❺ (www.parcs-madagascar.com; 8am–4pm) supports a diverse flora comprising more than 850 plant species (90 percent of them endemic) along with plenty of lemurs and a rich birdlife. It is probably the most popular tourist attraction in the vicinity of Mahajanga, and unusually accessible to independent travellers using public transport. The main entrance gate and official rest camp verge the RN4 at **Ampijoroa** only 45km (37 miles) northwest of Ambondromamy and 112km (67 miles) southeast of Mahajanga, and smarter accommodation is available at Blue Vanga Lodge in the small town of **Andranofasika** (Place of Sandy Water), only 5km (3 miles) back towards Ambondromamy.

The best and most popular of several guided walks out of Ampijoroa is the **Circuit Grande Boucle**, which first runs through an extensive patch of dry deciduous forest notable among other things for a unique and localised *Diplectria* tree whose outer branches grow a white snowy cover in winter to help them from dehydrating. The trail then emerges onto a grassy plateau and continues to the rim of the spectacular 80-metre (260-ft) -deep Ankarokaroka Canyon. This massive sandstone gorge was created by river erosion and is notable for its multiple reddish hues, which glow to best advantage in the early morning and late afternoon. The path to the base of Ankarokaroka, a bizarre spaghetti-western moonscape of angular sandstone pillars and fields of crystalline fairy chimneys, was closed in 2017 due to erosion, but should reopen in 2018.

The mammals most likely to be seen in the woodland are the delightful Coquerel's sifaka and brown lemur, but the park is home to four smaller nocturnal species: Milne-Edwards' sportive lemur, western woolly lemur, and golden-brown and grey mouse lemur. The deciduous forest of Ankarafantsika is the main stronghold of the localised mongoose lemur, a ferret-faced white-bearded frugivore listed as critically endangered by the IUCN red list and unusual in that it tends to be predominantly diurnal in the rainy

Coquerel's sifaka, Parc National d'Ankarafantsika.

⊙ **Fact**

Ankarafantsika protects the world's only population of *Adansonia boenensis*, a type of baobab (sometimes listed as a subspecies of *A. madagascariensis*) that is no longer able to propagate, most likely because whatever creature once foraged on its fruit has become extinct. Two specimens of this tall and handsome tree can be seen on a botanical trail out of Ampijoroa.

season and more active by night at other times. It is also the only place in the world where the greater big-footed mouse, arboreal foot-long rodent first described in 1959 and listed as endangered, has been recorded.

Andranofasika is rightly regarded to be one of Madagascar's top **birdwatching** sites. The deciduous woodland around Ampijoroa is the most reliable place countrywide for the localised Van Dam's vanga and Schlegel's asity (both resident and quite likely to be seen all-year-through, and easily located by call in October and November, the start of the breeding season) and the more elusive and skulkingly terrestrial white-breasted mesite. Other conspicuous woodland birds include Coquerel's Coua, blue vanga, long-billed bernieria and the white morph of Madagascar paradise flycatcher. Boat trips on the sacred Lac Ravelobe, which lies on the opposite side of the RN4 to the entrance gate, are likely to offer sightings of the resident Madagascar fish-eagle, black-crowned night heron and black egret throughout the year, along with

Madagascar paradise flycatcher, Parc National d'Ankarafantsika.

seasonal visitors such as the endemic Humblot's heron, Malagasy pond heron and lily-trotting Madagascar Jacana over October to December.

ON TO MAHAJANGA

The well-maintained stretch of the RN4 between Andranofasika and Mahajanga can be covered in two hours without stops. An intriguing possible diversion, **Marovoay** ❻ (which translates, rather ominously, as 'Many Crocodiles') is a sleepy but substantial riverport set on the east bank of the Betsiboka River immediately before it fans out to become the multi-channelled delta that empties into Bombetoka Bay south of Mahajanga. Marovoay served as the capital of Boina – a Sakalava subkingdom founded by King Andriamandisoarivo in the wake of a succession circa 1690 – for several decades prior to its relocation to Mahajanga in 1778. It remained an important port into the early 20th century, and the waterfront town centre is lined with time-warped colonial heaps and also contains some examples of engraved Indo-Arabic

◎ BREEDING RARE TORTOISES

The Ankarafantsika park headquarters at Ampijoroa houses a Chelonian Captive Breeding Centre (CCBC) established in the 1986 by the Gerald Durrell Wildlife Conservation Trust, primarily as a breeding centre for the critically endangered ploughshare tortoise. Also known by the Malagasy name *angonoka*, this relatively hefty tortoise (45cm/1.5ft long and weighing up to 10kg/22lb) is the world's rarest chelonid, with a wild population estimated at fewer than 400 individuals confined to Parc National de la Baie de Baly (where it is quite easily seen by hikes) and a handful of other localities on the Boeny coast immediately west of Katsepy. The CCBC started its work with a founding population of 17 individual ploughshare tortoises confiscated from smugglers. More than 500 births had been registered by 2011, since when a reintroduction programme has led to 100 individuals being released into suitable habitats. The CCBC has also expanded its breeding programme to help save two other critically endangered chelonids: the flat-backed spider tortoise and Madagascan big-headed turtle. The breeding centre is fenced off and closed to visitors due to ongoing issue with smuggling associated with the global pet trade, but the turtles can be viewed through the boundary fence.

wooden doors. Now supporting a population of 60,000 and the focal point of Madagascar's second-largest rice-growing scheme, Marovoay lies only 11km (7 miles) west of the RN4 along a surfaced road signposted about 32km (19 miles) past the national park headquarters at Ampijoroa.

Another 30km (18 miles) past the junction for Marovoay, the RN4 passes through the **Berivotra (or Maevarano) Formation**, whose exposed 70 to 80 million-year-old strata have yielded a rare wealth of fossils of dinosaurs and other Cretaceous creatures. Among the most significant of these is *Rahonavis*, a 70cm (2.3ft) theropod whose partial skeleton, unearthed in 1995, indicates it was probably capable of clumsy flight and possesses several other anatomical features that evidently confirm the theory that birds evolved from dinosaurs. Interestingly, the dinosaur and crocodilian fossils of Berivotra typically show closer affinities to their contemporaneous counterparts in India and South America than to the African fauna of the Cretaceous era. This suggests that a land bridge connected Madagascar to South America via India and Antarctica some 80–100 million years ago, a particularly warm period in the planet's history. An informative roadside display close to the 53km (33 miles) marker illustrates and describes some of the more interesting creatures unearthed at Berivotra, and some of the fossils are on display in Mahajanga's Musée Mozea Akiba.

MAHAJANGA

Formerly one of Madagascar six provincial capitals, **Mahajanga** ❼ (also known by the French name Majunga) is still the country's fourth-largest city, with a population nearing 250,000. Coming directly from Antananarivo by air, you'll land at the modest Philibert Tsiranana Airport, which lies on the town's northern outskirts 7km (4 miles) from the centre. Mahajanga is well equipped with hotels and restaurants, and the well-organised tourist office (ORT-BOENY, 14 avenue Philibert Tsiranana; tel: 034-0808880; www.majunga.org; Mon–Fri 7am–noon and 2–6pm, Sat

⦿ HISTORIC MAHAJANGA

Settled by Arab traders in mediaeval times, Mahajanga later emerged as the island's largest slave port. It succeeded Marovoay as a regional power focus after Queen Ravahiny of Boina relocated her capital there in 1778. According to one French visitor, the town housed 6,000 Arab, Comoran and Indian settlers by 1792, as well as several mosques and a good school. Ravahiny's death in 1808 precipitated a decline in Boina power and fall of Mahajanga to King Radama I of Imerina in 1824. Boina's last ruler, the teenage Queen Tsiomeko, signed a treaty of French protectorateship with Admiral de Hell after the Imerina monarchy expelled her to Nosy Komba in 1839. Mahajanga was later the launchpad for the 1883–5 military expedition that led to French subjugation of the whole island.

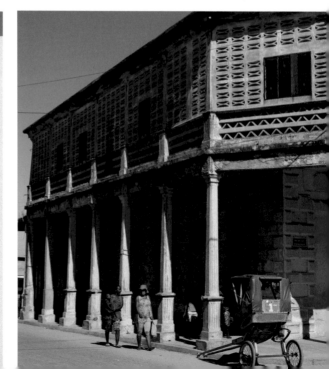

Maison Ismail Jina, in Mahajanga's old dhow port.

7am–noon) stocks maps and brochures covering the whole region.

Developed by the French on reclaimed land, Mahajanga's colonial city centre feels less timeworn and more economically vibrant than most of the country's port towns. Indeed, this is now the island's second busiest cargo port (after Toamasina), with an economy boosted by substantial Indian and Comoran immigrant communities. The old town can easily be explored on foot over a couple of hours. A good starting point is the **old dhow port**, where a couple of dozen large cargo dhows are usually docked, their tall wooden masts flying the white, green and red Madagascar flag. The port is lined by old warehouses and shops, most notably the Blues Rock Café, also known as the **Porte Indo-Arabe**, since it is entered via of the town's finest remaining example of ornately-carved 19th-century Zanzibari-style wooden door and frame. A block behind this, the colonnaded **Maison Ismael Jina**, a large town house built by the Arabic trader Ismael Jina, celebrated its centenary in 2017.

Off-loading in the old dhow harbour.

A short dirt road runs southwest from the dhow harbour to **Pointe de Sable**, site of a simple memorial 'to those lost at sea', and a stumpy 9-metre (30ft) -high cast-iron lighthouse originally erected in 1900 and whose broken weathervane peeks out above a row of spiny-barked *Pachypodium* (Elephant foot) trees that bloom white in winter. This scenic peninsula marks the start of the seafront **Corniche** (which includes the Boulevards Poincarré and Marcoz), whose wide pavement – a popular dusk-time promenade – is planted with palms and white concrete benches where you can sit and watch dhows scoot past a mere 50 metres (165ft) offshore. A clutch of shady terrace restaurants line the boulevard's landward side. Particularly attractive is the **Alliance Française** (tel: 032-0511984; www.facebook.com/afmajunga; 7.30am–10pm), set in a handsome colonial building with a ceramic tiled floor, heavy wooden door, and wide terrace serving light meals and snacks as well as hosting occasional cultural events.

A traffic island at the junction of Boulevard Poincarré and Avenue de France protects a **sacred baobab** claimed to be the island's thickest and oldest tree, with a circumference of roughly 20 metres (65ft), and a probable age of 700-plus years. A truly massive specimen of the African mainland species *Adansonia digitata*, it was most likely planted by Arabic traders, suggesting that Mahajanga has served as a stopover for boats sailing between Africa and Asia. The old baobab has long been an important symbol of Mahajanga and focal point of civic activity: the kings and queens of Boina used to address their subjects from its base, and it later served as a place of execution. A *fady* forbids touching the tree or digging in search of the treasure once reputedly beneath it by the Boina monarchs, and it is said that visitors who walk around it seven times will be blessed on their future travels.

North of the junction with Avenue de France, Boulevard Marcoz, the official name for the northern Corniche, follows the western seaboard uphill to a colonial cemetery and a trio of **war memorials** respectively commemorating the French soldiers who died in the invasion of 1893–5 and World War I, and the Malagasy, French, Indo-Chinese and Algerian victims of World War II. Boulevard Marcoz then descends back downhill to the long, bare, unshaded and defiantly characterless **Plage du Village Touristique** – complete with long pier and life-size dinosaur statue – terminates 3km (2 miles) north of the city centre at **Antsahabingo**, whose lively estuarine harbour is filled with small catamaran-like local fishing dhows.

INLAND ATTRACTIONS

Follow Avenue de France inland from the sacred baobab, then turn left and uphill into Avenue du Rova, and you'll come to the arched gate and last standing 3-metre (10ft) -high wall of the **Doany Mitsinjoarivo Fort**. Built in 1824 by King Radama I, the fort was renovated by the University of Mahajanga in 1995 but has since fallen back into disrepair and is now covered with graffiti and locked to guard a couple of satellite

Indo-Arabian door in the old dhow port.

Mahajanga's sacred baobab is over 700 years old.

Pousse-pousse driver waiting for customers in Mahajanga.

Exploring the Grottes de Belobaka.

towers. About 1km (0.6 miles) inland, on Avenue de la Libération, stands the city's best-known modern landmark, the **Cathédrale du Coeur-Immaculé-de-Marie**, an imposing but rather austere example of post-war Art Deco that dates to 1948 and is now painted white with yellow highlights. Almost directly opposite it, begging to be restored as a museum or boutique hotel, the derelict three-storey **Villa Gustave Eiffel**, with its ornate metal entrance stairway and wraparound balconies, is perhaps the city's finest colonial architectural relict, built *c.*1890 by French engineers inspired by the metalwork of its celebrated namesake. Another 1km (0.6 miles) inland of this, the RN4 bisects the sprawling grid-like alleys of the **Marché de Mahabibo**, the city's largest and most interesting market.

Set within the University of Mahajanga campus about 5km (3 miles) northeast of the city centre, and connected to it by regular *taxi-brousse*, the **Musée Mozea Akiba** (tel: 032-5122943; Mon–Fri 8–11am and 3–5pm, Sat–Sun 3–5pm) packs a surprising variety of artefacts into its small single-roomed interior. It is particularly strong on the dinosaur fossils of Berivotra and the more recent (5,000–8,000-year-old) remains of pygmy hippos, giant lemurs and other extinct mammals unearthed at Anjohibe, but also has some worthwhile history and ethnographic displays, including black-and-white photographs of Malagasy soldiers on zebu-back at Marovoay *c.*1895, and a collection of old *ody* talismans used by traditional healers.

Follow the RN4 for 3km (2 miles) out of town, turning right at the first road after crossing Pont FITIM, and a short dirt road leads to the inauspicious gates of **Univers Reniala** (tel: 034-0276500; 8–11am and 3–5pm), a small eco-park situated within the grounds of the Société Industrielle du Boina, a soap and oil factory established by the Barday Family in 1948. Named after the baobabs (*Reni Ala*, or Mother of the Forest) that proliferate within its confines, Reniala is home to a free-ranging troop of brown lemurs, while a glorified zoo houses four other lemur species in cages, as well as a few crocodiles and a Madagascar fish eagle. A shop sells homemade honey, yoghurt and fruit juices.

An altogether more convincing attraction, particularly if you won't make it to more remote Anjohibe, the **Grottes de Belobaka** 8 (charge) comprises a complex of five sinkhole-like caves set into a wooded limestone hillock about 12km (7.5 miles) inland of Mahajanga. To get there, follow the RN4 for 10km (6 miles) to Belobaka village, then turn left onto an unsignposted 2km (1.2 miles) dirt track that leads to a quarry where you can park and ask around for the caretaker/guide. The cave that is closest to the carpark, though the smallest and least spectacular, is held sacred by locals and still used as a sacrificial site. The other four caves, all at the back of the hill, are much larger and incorporate some fabulous stalactite, stalagmite and other limestone formations,

along with contorted rock figs that climb towards large natural skylights. Back in the 1940s, Belobaka was developed as a tourist attraction, complete with concrete steps, platforms and bridges, some of which are still intact today. The entire complex takes a good hour to explore; for those with limited time, caves four and five, the last ones visited on a full tour, contain the most spectacular formations.

SUBURBAN BEACHES AND CIRQUE ROUGE

The busiest beach near Mahajanga, the casuarina-lined **Petite Plage** runs for about 6km (4 miles) north from Antsahabingo estuary and usually offers calm swimming conditions along its full length. Bounded to the north by low sandstone cliffs, the far end of Petite Plage is very much a working beach, scattered with dhows and fishermen mending nets, while the southern stretch is lined with low-key holiday homes whose Tana-based owners usually take refuge here during midwinter (June to August).

About 5km (3 miles) further north, the **Plage du Grand Pavois** is a lovely palm-fringed swimming beach where local kids kick around footballs on the soft white sand, or play cheerfully in the shallow waves, while traditional dhows sail past, white sails billowing in the wind. The string of unpretentious hotels and seafood restaurants that fronts Grand Pavois is aimed squarely at local weekenders and domestic holidaymakers, but it also makes for a great sundowner or dinner spot for travellers.

An ideal place to work up that thirst or appetite, the **Cirque Rouge** ⑨ (charge) is a spectacular 40-hectare (100-acre) amphitheatre of sedimentary cliffs situated no more than 1km (0.6 miles) north of Grand Pavois. Shaded in many subtle hues of pink, white and orange, the cliffs are a product of riverine erosion and expose a horizontal sequence of ancient laterite and sandstone strata that are at their most beautiful just before dusk, when the last rays of the dying sun enhance the natural colours. A car park offers fine views over the entire formation, or

Plage du Grand Pavois at sunset.

you can walk to the main cliff base in 15 minutes, following a sandy riverbed lined with thick greenery. Look out for the colourful Madagascar bee-eaters that breed in holes in the sandbanks, and old bullet casings and other relicts from when it served as a British military camp and shooting range.

NORTHEAST OF MAHAJANGA

Reached via a sandy 10km (6-mile) road that runs northeast from Philibert Tsiranana Airport, the **Lac Sacré de Mangatsa** ⑩ (8am–6pm) is the focal point of a community ecotourism project that also incorporates a crocodile pond, a sacred spring, a large baobab tree and a forest inhabited by a group of around 10 very habituated Coquerel's sifaka. Legend has it that that the small lake appeared spontaneously – complete with eels and other marine fish – when an important Sakalava chief called Ndramandi took refuge at the site to escape capture by the Imerina army. It remains a Sakalava sacrificial site to this day, and several trees around it are draped with red cloths

and zebu skulls and horns. Dozens of massive carp be seen swimming in the clear water, but fishing (and bathing) are *fady*. The guided trail around the sites can be covered in 45–60 minutes, so allow three hours for the full excursion from Mahajanga.

The most spectacular of several limestone cave systems in the vicinity of Mahajanga, the **Grottes d'Anjohibe** ⑪ (7am–5pm) comprises some 5km (3 miles) of vaulted chambers and narrow tunnels adorned with spectacular stalactites, stalagmites and candelabra-like drip formations, some illuminated by natural cracks in the roof. A subterranean river runs through the part of the cave system that's open to casual visitors, then comes out above ground to water a strip of riparian forest inhabited by Coquerel's sifaka are various birds. Nearby, a lovely clear lake, fed by a waterfall over a protruding rock lip, is safe for swimming. Anjohibe lies almost 90km (56 miles) northeast of Mahajanga and can be reached by following the RN4 east for 21km (13 miles) to Ankarifu junction, then turning left onto a 68km (42-mile) dirt road through the villages of Ambalakida and Antanamarina. The road requires 4x4 and although the travelling is generally given as 3–4 hours, it often takes longer, making it an ambitious goal for a day trip – better to book one of the simple bungalows at the adjacent Ecolodge des Grottes d'Anjohibe (tel: 034-0355480), which also has a restaurant. Access may be impossible from December to March.

A worthwhile 20km (12.5-mile) diversion north from the road to Anjohibe, the **Forêt Communautaire d'Ankatsabe** ⑫ (tel: 033-0553858/034-2053858; email: guidelocauxassociation. aglma@yahoo.com) is a community-owned ecotourism reserve that offers guided walks out of the village of Mariarano. It protects around 28 sq km (10.8 sq miles) of fragmented dry

The red-hued Cirque Rouge.

deciduous forest along with 7 sq km (2.7 sq miles) of coastal mangroves fringing Marosakoa Bay. The 12km (7.5-mile) Matsedroy Circuit offers an opportunity to visit a traditional village distillery and to look for wildlife such as Coquerel's sifaka, crocodile and a profusion of aquatic birds (notably the localised Madagascar fish eagle) associated with a trio of freshwater lakes. The shorter (1.5km/1 mile) Vohikomba Circuit is named after the Malagasy word for a mouse lemur but focusses mainly on chameleons, leaf-tail geckos and other small reptiles and amphibians. Overnight accommodation in simple tents is available, together with locally-prepared meals.

KATSEPY PENINSULA AND BOENY BAY

The largest settlement on the west shore of Bombetoka Bay, **Katsepy** ⑬ is an unpretentious fishing village whose attractive swimming beach, lined with small seafood restaurants, transforms into something of a resort at weekends. It is connected to Mahajanga by at least one motor ferry in either direction daily, a 12km (7.5-mile) crossing that takes up to 45 minutes, but for those without cars, it is easier to cross with one of the private motorboats that serve as the marine equivalent of *taxi-brousse* from around 7am to 3pm. Perched above a cliff 8km (5 miles) north of the village, the 36-metre (118ft) -high **Phare Katsepy** is a circular cast-iron lighthouse prefabricated by the Eiffel Factory in France in 1901 to be erected above the northwest entrance to Bombetoka Bay. The views from the top are fantastic and you can walk there from Katsepy in 90 minutes or so – follow the Mitsinjo Road west for 3.5km (2 miles), then turn right, and bear right again when the road forks after another 1km (0.6 miles).

Situated just 4km (2.5 miles) from Katsepy, the 206-sq-km (79.5-sq-mile) **Aire Protégée d'Antrema** (tel:

034-08088880) was set aside as a protected area in 2000 and opened to the public in 2013. Protecting a mosaic of mangroves, forest and palm savanna, and criss-crossed by a network of guided trails, this is arguably the easiest place to see two of the country's most localised and charismatic lemurs: the crowned sifaka and mongoose lemur, which are respectively listed as endangered and critically endangered. The local Sakalava people revere the crowned sifaka as representatives of the ancestral representatives, so killing them is *fady*, and they are placed under the protection of a local prince (to whom it is customary to pay one's respects before a visit). The protected area also protects 153 plant species (of which 76 percent are endemic), along with 75 bird and 23 amphibian and reptile species, and three types of nocturnal lemur. Lac Sahariaka is a particularly rewarding spot for wetland birds.

The mangrove-lined western shore of the Katsepy Peninsula forms part of **Boeny Bay**, which tradition claims

Coconut seller, Mahajanga.

The spectacular stalagmites and stalactites inside the Grottes d'Anjohibe.

as the site of the original 17th-century capital of King Andriamandisoarivo (Boina's founding monarch) prior to its relocation to Marovoay under one of his successors. Before that, Boeny Bay was treated to an early 16th-century visit by a Portuguese fleet that bombarded an Arab trading outpost on the mainland. Nosy Antsoheribory, a small tadpole-shaped island sheltered within the bay, hosted a Portuguese Catholic mission under Father Luis Mariano over 1613–20. The more northerly and slightly larger island of Nosy Antsoherindava contains the significant coral-rag ruins of a mosque and tiled tombs associated with a significant Islamic settlement visited by the French traveller Sieur Dubois in the late 1660s. Boeny Bay lies some 55km (33 miles) west of Mahajanga, and road access is limited, but its historic islands are sometimes visited by boat.

WESTERN BOENY

Ploughshare tortoises are protected in the Baie de Baly.

Three of Madagascar's most remote, intriguing and little-visited conservation areas are situated within Boeny's two westernmost districts Mitsinjo and Soalala, both of which are named after the small towns that serve as their administrative headquarters. Beyond the reach of public transport, each of these three reserves requires several days to visit from Mahajanga via Katsepy – indeed, you'd need to set aside at least one week to visit them all – and is accessible by 4x4 only. Visits are best scheduled for the dry season (May to November) as roads tend to become completely impassable after heavy rain.

The closest of the three reserves to Mahajanga is the 3,000-sq-km (1,158-sq-mile) **Complexe Mahavavy-Kinkony**  (tel: 032-4124192/034-9052455; email: andriamanandro@yahoo.fr) which is accessed via Mitsinjo town, some 70km (42 miles) west of Katsepy by road. Primarily a wetland reserve, Mahavavy-Kinkony has been recognised as an Important Bird Area since 1999 but was accorded full government protection only in 2015. It is named after the Mahavavy River Delta, which empties into the ocean to the north of

Mitsinjo, and the 140-sq-km (54-sq-mile) Lac Kinkony, the country's second-largest freshwater body, situated about 10km (6 miles) south of town. The complex also incorporates the more westerly Marambitsy Bay, some 20 smaller lakes, and large tracts of mangrove swamp and dry deciduous forest. The main attraction is the birdlife, with more than 140 species recorded, including significant populations of all the wetland species known from western Madagascar, notably Madagascar teal, Sakalava rail, Madagascar sacred ibis and Madagascar Fish Eagle. It is also an important seasonal overwintering refuge for flamingos and various migratory terns and waders including African spoonbill, greater sand plover and Saunders's tern. Other wildlife includes the critically endangered crowned sifaka and Madagascan big-headed turtle.

Soalala is a small fishing port set on a peninsula that juts into the Andranomavo River as it empties into the shallow Baie de Baly 135km (80 miles) west of Katsepy by road. Soalala is the gateway to the 542-sq-km (209-sq-mile) **Parc National de la Baie de Baly** ⑮ (www.parcs-madagascar.com), which extends inland from the west shore of the eponymous bay and was set aside primarily to protect the ploughshare tortoise, the world's rarest chelonid, but it is also a stronghold for the critically endangered Madagascan big-headed turtle, a largely aquatic species. Associated with sandy soils, the ploughshare tortoise is likely to be seen along the 4km (2.5-mile) Angonoka Circuit (Angonoka being its Malagasy name) along with Von der Decken's sifaka, an Endangered denizen of dry deciduous forest, and western bamboo lemur. Marine wildlife includes green, hawksbill and loggerhead turtles, all of which lay their eggs on the bay's wide sandy beaches, while the rare dugong and various dolphins are sometimes seen swimming offshore. Listed as an Important Bird Area, the park supports around 120 avian species and is a particularly important habitat for marine and other aquatic species such as lesser crested tern, Humblot's heron, Madagascar sacred ibis, Madagascar fish eagle and greater and lesser flamingo. The most alluring goal for birdwatchers is Lac Sariaka, the focal point of the 24km (14-mile), two-day Ankoay Circuit.

About 50km (31 miles) inland of Soalala, the spectacular **Parc National des Tsingy de Namoroka** ⑯ (www.parcs-madagascar.com; charge) protects a 222-sq-km (85-sq-mile) expanse of low tsingy whose jagged sandstone clefts and peaks are studded with bulbous baobab trees and elephant's foot (*Pachypodium*) shrubs as well as barbed succulents reminiscent if the more southerly spiny desert. The park can be explored on a trio of guided hiking and 4x4 circuits that lead past clear bubbling springs, caves adorned with stalactite and stalagmites, and the lovely Mandevy River. Wildlife includes 80 bird, 30 reptile and eight lemur

African spoonbills at the Complexe Mahavavy-Kinkony.

⊘ Fact

The caves of the Parc National des Tsingy de Namoroka host one of only two known prehistoric rock art sites in Madagascar. Discovered by speleologists in 2016, the paintings are currently only visitable by special arrangement with the Musée Mozea Akiba.

species, with Von der Decken's sifaka being especially conspicuous.

THE RN6 THROUGH THE SOFIA REGION

Just as most foreign visitors to Mahajanga fly into the city, so too do most of them fly out, either returning to Antananarivo, or winging their way northward to Nosy Be or Diego Suarez. It is also possible, however, for intrepid travellers to continue northward by road, first retracing your tracks along the RN4 as far as **Ambondromamy**, the junction town 150km (90 miles) east of Mahajanga. Once at Ambondromamy, you're also at the southern terminus of the RN6, which heads north through the little-visited Sofia Region before arriving at Ambanja (the junction for boats to Nosy Be) after around 470km (292 miles) then continuing north for another 230km (143 miles) to Diego Suarez.

The RN6 is surfaced more-or-less in its entirety (with growing emphasis on the 'less' as you head further north), but even so it would be wildly ambitious

to try to travel between Mahajanga and Ambanja, Nosy Be or Diego Suarez in one day. The first, and less alluring, of two possible overnight options, straddling the RN6 only 150km (90 miles) past Ambondromamy, is **Port-Bergé** ⑰, a strikingly charmless small inland town also known by the Malagasy name Boriziny. Port-Bergé's misleading name evidently harks back to the distant days when Bemarivo River east of town had to be forded by a ferry now rendered obsolete by the country's longest bridge, which crosses the Sofia River upstream of its confluence with the Bemarivo on the RN6 some 15km (6 miles) north of town.

Time permitting, a more appealing place to break the trip would be **Antsohihy** ⑱, another 120km (72 miles) further north. An agreeable if unremarkable town of around 20,000, Antsohihy stands close to the navigable Loza River and was in times past an important boatbuilding centre (its name refers to the *sohihy* or rosewood tree traditionally used for this purpose). It is also the capital of the

Blue eyes... a blue-eyed black lemur.

⊘ BLUE-EYED BOY

The blue-eyed black lemur *Eulemur flavifrons* was described in 1867 based on a single specimen collected from an unknown locality, and its status remained uncertain until its rediscovery in Sahamalaza in 1983. Remarkably, it is the only primate other than humans to have blue eyes, and the only one at all whose eyes are always this colour. It was once considered a subspecies of the common black lemur, which has more prominent ear tufts and orange eyes, but DNA tests undertaken in 2008 confirmed it to be a distinct species. Hybridisation is reported where the two species' ranges overlap, always producing orange-eyed offspring. The blue-eyed black lemur is listed among the world's 25 most endangered primate taxa, with a global population estimated at a few thousand.

Sofia Region, and serviced by a selection of decent hotels (the Hôtel Sofia Bellevue, on the southern outskirts of town, even has a swimming pool). Otherwise, Antsohihy's main claim to fame is that it – or more accurately nearby Anahidrano – was the birthplace of Madagascar's first president Philibert Tsiranana. A monument to the esteemed Father of Independence now dominates Anahidrano, a tiny village located alongside the RN6 some 3km (2 miles) further south.

Antsohihy is the gateway to the little-visited **Parc National du Sahamalaza** ⑲ (www.parcs-madagascar.com), which protects the hilly Sahamalaza Bay and Radama Archipelago about 120km (74 miles) to its north. Also recognised as a Unesco Biosphere Reserve and Ramsar Wetland, the 260-sq-km (100-sq-mile) park was established in 2007 primarily to protect the critically endangered blue-eyed black lemur, which is unusual and striking insofar as it is the only primate in the world (aside from certain humans) to have blue eyes. The park is also the main

stronghold of the Sahamalaza sportive lemur, another critically endangered species, and first described in 2006. Only accessible in a private 4x4, this remote but scenic park can be explored along three different combined boat, 4x4 and foot circuits, then most popular being the Akomba Manga Maso Circuit, which offers an excellent chance of seeing blue-eyed black lemur along with other wildlife.

Antsohihy is also the closest town to the 750-hectare (1853-acre) **Anjajavy Reserve** ⑳ (www.anjajavy.com), a fabulously remote fly-in sanctuary served by an exclusive owner-managed Relais & Châteaux lodge of the same name. Situated on the west coast 120km (72 miles) north of Mahajanga as the crow flies, Anjajavy ranks among the country's most appealing upmarket beach-'n'-bush destinations, with an idyllic seaside location complemented by the opportunity to explore tsingy formations, fossil-bearing caves and forests inhabited by Coquerel's sifaka, brown lemur, fossa and a wealth of endemic birds.

Dinner by the sea at Le Lodge in Anjajavy.

📷 CHAMELEONS

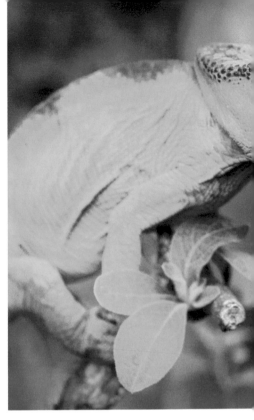

More than half the world's 200 recognised chameleon species are endemic to Madagascar. These range from the thumbnail-sized litter-dwellers to the hulking Oustalet's chameleon.

Arguably the most charismatic of reptiles, the chameleons (family Chamaeleonidae) are confined to the Old World, with all but two of the world's 200 recognised species being restricted to the African mainland or Madagascar. They are best known for their capacity to camouflage themselves by changing colour, a trait that is often exaggerated in popular literature, since most species are broadly green or brown, and have only limited colour variations dictated by mood as much as by environment. Chameleons possess several other remarkable physiological features. One is their independently-swivelling protuberant round eyes, which offer them the potential for 180° vision on both sides. Another is their long sticky-tipped tongue, which can be up to 1.5 times the individual's body length, and uncoils suddenly in a blink-and-you'll-miss-it lunge to catch its prey unawares. Many chameleon species are also adorned with helmets, flaps, horns, spines and crests that enhance their prehistoric appearance. Madagascar is the world's ultimate chameleon hotspot, and the excellent guides associated with most national parks will often show visitors half-a-dozen species – ranging from the cat-sized Oustalet's or Parson's chameleon to various inch-long specimens of the genus Brookesia – in the course of one forest walk.

Chameleons feed on insects, which they catch by darting out their long, sticky tongues at lightning speed.

Camouflaged chameleon on a baobab.

Although chameleons are capable of changing colour, in many cases – for instance, this Labord's chameleon Furcifer labordi – it is stimulated more by mood than by the need for camouflage.

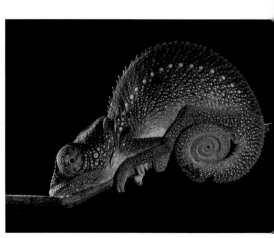

Boasting an island-wide distribution, Oustalet's chameleon (Furcifer oustaleti), reaches up to 68.5cm (27in) in total length, making it the world's longest chameleon.

Chameleon diversity on Madagascar

As recently as the turn of the millennium, the worldwide total of known chameleon species stood at around 130, around half of which were endemic to Madagascar. Since then, however, a flurry of fresh fieldwork and DNA research has caused that number to be revised to around 200, with Madagascar hosting a greater diversity than the rest of the world combined. Many of these newly described chameleons are placed in the genera *Calumma* and *Brookesia*, both of which are endemic to Madagascar and now each comprise around 30 known species, one-third of which were first described after 1995. And the number of species seems certain to keep growing. In 2015, for instance, the University of Geneva announced that fresh DNA research suggested the variably coloured Panther chameleon *Furcifer pardalis*, first described in 1829, was not, as had always been supposed, one morphically diverse species, but might actually comprise more than 11 distinct (and as-yet unnamed) species.

In common with many other chameleon species, the male Calumma malthe has a prominent helmet and horned nose.

The thumbnail-sized Mount d'Ambre leaf chameleon (Brookesia tuberculata) is a litter-dweller with a total adult length of 25–35mm (about 1in). It was often cited as the world's most diminutive reptile prior to the discovery of the marginally smaller Brookesia micra on nearby Nosy Hara in 2012.

The boldly-marked Panther chameleon (Furcifer pardalis) ranges in colour from bright green to orange, though recent DNA research suggests this diversity may be because it comprises not one but several species.

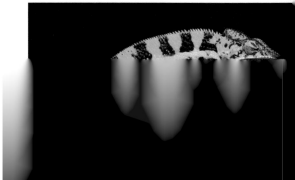

Palm-lined beach.

NOSY BE

Madagascar's most popular beach destination, Nosy Be is a lush tropical island renowned for its relaxed ambience, agreeable year-round weather, superb diving and cuddlesome black lemurs.

Antananarivo

The archetypical Indian Ocean island idyll, Nosy Be is the largest component in an archipelago of partially-submerged Holocene volcanoes that rise from the clear shallow turquoise waters of Madagascar's northwestern continental shelf. Touristically, it functions as something of an island apart, serviced by its own international airport and flights from Europe, South Africa, Réunion and Mayotte – indeed, the majority of visitors are direct arrivals who never set foot on the Malagasy mainland, only 30 minutes away by boat. Pronounced *Noossy Bay*, its name translates somewhat prosaically as 'Big Island', but it also sometimes known as Nosy Manitra (Perfumed Island) in reference to its status as one of the world's two largest producers of aromatic ylang-ylang oil.

Nosy Be's reputation as a tourist trap isn't entirely unjustified, and things do tend to come across as pricey by comparison to the Malagasy mainland, but there is far more to the 312-sq-km (120-sq-mile) island than just another stock tropical beach resort. Scenically, it's a fantastic place, with a backdrop provided by the volcanic cones of the 455-metre (1,492ft) Mont Lokobe and 329-metre (1,080ft) Mont Passot – both in turn dwarfed by the 622-metre (2,041ft) peak of the nearby isle of Nosy Komba. And tourist development is largely focussed on the western seaboard, where the beaches of Ambatoloaka and Ambondrona are lined with swish package resorts and more low-key owner-managed hotels, both typically catering to a predominantly Italian clientele. Elsewhere, the down-to-earth main port of Hell-Ville, the reefs and marine life of Nosy Tanikely, the black lemurs and other wildlife associated with Lokobe and Nosy Komba, the crater lakes that pockmark Mont Passot and the sacred cultural sites at Mahatsinjo and Manongarivo

◎ Main Attractions
Hell-Ville
Ambatoloaka
Mont Passot
Réserve Naturelle
  Intégrale de Lokobe
Nosy Komba
Nosy Tanikely

Map on page 244

Fishermen at sunset.

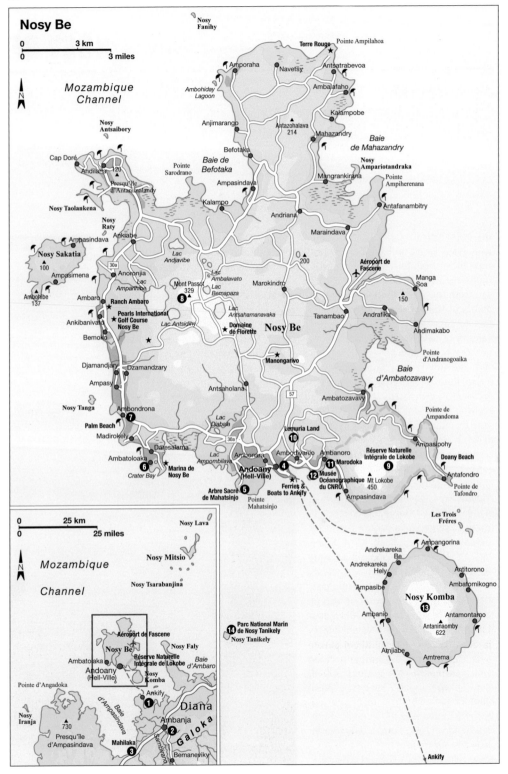

Nosy Be

0   3 km
0   3 miles

N

*Mozambique
Channel*

Nosy
Fanihy

Terre Rouge   Pointe Ampilahoa

Amporaha   Navetsy   Antsatrabevoa

*Ambohiday
Lagoon*   Ambalafaho

Anjimarango   Kalampobe

Antazohalava
214   Mahazandry

Nosy
Antsaibory

Befotaka   *Baie
de Mahazandry*

Cap Doré   Pointe
Sarodrano   *Baie de
Befotaka*   Mangrankirana   Nosy
Ampariotandraka

Andilana   120   Ampasindava   Pointe
Ampiherenana

Presqu'île
d'Antaninalandy   Kalampo   Andriana   Antafanambitry

Nosy Taolankena   Maraindava

Nosy
Raty   Ampasindava   Ankiabe   Manga
Soa

Nosy Sakatia
100   *Lac
Andjavibe*   Marokindro   Aéroport de
Fascene

Ampasimena   30a   Anoronjia   *Lac
Ambalavato*   200   150

*Lac
Amparihibe*   Mont Passot
329   *Lac
Bemapaza*   Andrafika

Ambohibe
137   Ambaro   **8**   Tanambao   Andimakabo

Ranch Ambaro   *Lac
Antsahamanavaka*   Pointe
d'Andranogoaika

Pearls International
Golf Course
Nosy Be   Domaine
de Florette   **Nosy Be**

Ankibanivato   *Lac Antsidihy*

Bemoko   *Baie
d'Ambatozavavy*

Djamandjary   Dzamandzary   Manongarivo

Ampasy   Antsaholana   Ambatozavavy

Nosy Tanga   Ambondrona   **7**   Pointe de
Ampandoma

Palm Beach   *Lac
Diabala*   Lemuria Land   Ampasipohy

Madirokely   30a   **10**   Doany Beach

Daresalama   Ambodiwanjo   Ambanoro   Réserve Naturelle
Intégrale de Lokobe

Ambatoloaka   **6**   *Lac
Ampombilava*   Ambanara   **4**   **11**   Marodoka   **9**   Antafondro

Marina de
Nosy Be   *Crater Bay*   Andoany
(Hell-Ville)   **12**   Musée
Océanographique
du CNRO   Mt Lokobe
450   Pointe de
Tafondro

Arbre Sacré
de Mahatsinjo   **5**   Ferries &
Boats to Ankify   Ampasindava

Pointe
Mahatsinjo   Les Trois
Frères

Ampangorina

Andrekareka
Be

0   25 km
0   25 miles   Antitorono

N   Nosy Lava   Andrekareka
Hely   Ambatomikogno

Mozambique   Nosy Mitsio   Ampasibe

Channel   Nosy Tsarabanjina   **Nosy Komba**
   13   Antamontamo

Ambanio   Antaninaomby
622

Aéroport de Fascene   Parc National Marin
de Nosy Tanikely   **14**   Amjiabe   Amtrema

Nosy Be   Nosy Faly   Nosy Tanikely

Ambatolaka   Réserve Naturelle
Intégrale de Lokobe   *Baie
d'Amaro*

Andoany
(Hell-Ville)   Nosy
Komba

Pointe d'Angadoka

Nosy
Iranja   Ankify   **1**

Diana

730

Presqu'île
d'Ampasindava   Ambanja   **2**

Galoka

Mahilaka   **3**

Bemaneviky   Ankify

should be sufficient to keep the most active and beach-averse of travellers busy for a week.

REACHING NOSY BE

The island of Nosy Be lies about 10km (6 miles) off the northwest coast of Diana Region, opposite the small mainland port of Ankify, almost 900km (560 miles) north of Antananarivo along the RN4 and RN6. Ankify itself stands 17km (10 miles) from the RN6, along a signposted and surfaced feeder road that runs west from Ambanja. Most tourists arrive at Nosy Be by air, either with a domestic flight from Antananarivo or Diego Suarez, or on an international flight from further afield, landing at the **Aéroport de Fascene**, which stands on the island's east shore 10km (6 miles) north of Hell-Ville. However, a significant minority of visitors do cross by boat from **Ankify ❶**, either catching the slow (up to two hours) motor ferry, or chartering a private motorboat, a 30-minute dash enlivened by superb views of the forest- and bamboo-swathed Nosy Komba.

For those coming by road, **Ambanja ❷**, straddling the RN6 about 230km (143 miles) south of Diego Suarez, is quite an interesting place in its own right. Set on the north bank of the Sambirand River, it is the principle town of a fertile region renowned for its natural forests, abundance of fan-shaped travellers palms, and famously productive coffee, cacao and ylang-ylang plantations. It possesses the leafy tropical atmosphere of a West African implant, and a long main road – a 5km (3 mile) stretch of the RN6 shaded by jacarandas that bloom brilliant purple over October and November – lined with a seemingly endless succession of market stalls selling everything from clothes and electronic goods to fresh tropical fruit and *khat*.

Situated on mangrove-lined Ampasindava Bay, just off the RN6 24km (14 miles) south of Ambanja,

the ruined city of **Mahilaka ❸** is arguably the most important archaeological site anywhere in Madagascar. The ruins comprise a 60-hectare (148-acre) walled Islamic port that flourished between the 11th and 15th centuries, when it incorporated a large palace and several mosques, and presumably held trade links to Kilwa and the other Swahili city-states of the East African coast. First discovered and excavated in the 1990s, Mahilaka was pivotal in overturning a long-held assumption that no significant urban settlements existed on Madagascar prior to the 17th century arrival of Europeans.

HELL-VILLE AND SURROUNDS

The largest town on Nosy Be and main mooring point for boats to and from Ankify, **Hell-Ville ❹**, also known by the Malagasy name Andoany, stands on the island's south coast, facing the forested slopes of Mont Lokobe and Nosy Komba. The town's evocative name, far from reflecting any Hadean qualities, is commemorative of Admiral Anne

⊙ Tip

A popular itinerary though northern Madagascar entails flying into Nosy Be, spending a few days there, then crossing to Ankify by boat, driving north along the RN6 to the Réserve de l'Ankarana and the Parc National de la Montagne d'Ambre, then flying back to Antananarivo from Diego Suarez.

Seafood for sale in Hell-Ville.

◎ Tip

Rue Passot is haunted by policemen who stop tourists and demand to see their passport. Fortunately, these guys aren't interested in enforcing the law (it is mandatory to carry ID at all times in Madagascar), so much as securing a bribe. If you don't fancy carrying your passport to town, a photocopy of the main page and visa/entry stamp should suffice. Failing that, suggesting you visit the tourist office to discuss the matter further should settle it quickly enough.

Hell-Ville harbour.

Chrétien Louis de Hell, the French Governor of Isle de Bourbon (now Réunion) whose 1939 treaty of protectorateship with Queen Tsiomeko of Boina led to the formal annexation of Nosy Be to France in 1841. Hell-Ville was established soon after as the island's centre of administration centres and customs, as alluded to in its Malagasy name (*an doany*, the latter derived from the French *douane*, means 'place of customs').

An attractive town of 40,000 residents, Hell-Ville possesses an interesting colonial architectural heritage. This is particularly so on **Rue Passot** (aka Cours de Hell), the wide shady avenue that links the motorboat port to the commercial town centre and also hosts the helpful tourist office (tel: 032-0583700; www.nosybe-tourisme.com; 8am–6pm). The eastern (port) end of Rue Passot, split in two by a green central square dotted with statues, is protected by a pair of cannons that point across the bay towards forested Mont Lokobe, and lined with two- and three-storey colonial

administrative buildings whose down-at-heel state only partially detracts from former pomp.

The smarter west end of Rue Passot is the site of a tall **Catholic Cathedral** with tall wooden doors and brick-faced arched window frames, as well as several banks, including a branch of BFV-SG with an ATM. It's worth diverting south along horseshoe-shaped **Rue Camille Valentin** for splendid views across a shallow mangrove-lined bay to Nosy Komba. Set in an old colonial homestead on the junction with Rue Gouot, **Le Jardin des Sens** (tel: 034-0222323) is a lovely boutique specialising in local spices and massage oils, as well as books about Madagascar and arty postcards; it also offers professional reflexology and massage sessions. Directly opposite, the landmark **l'Oasis** is a retro Parisian-style café with a wide terrace made for people-watching.

Running inland from l'Oasis, the **Boulevard de l'Indépendance** has a more bustling commercial feel but also houses several intriguing old

structures. These include the two-storey **AM Hussanaly et Fils Building**, with its colonnaded facade, shuttered wooden doors, old copper nameplates, filigree balcony and embedded Islamic symbols; the fabulously old-world **Island Trade Merchandises** hardware store; and the Creole-style wooden facade and characterful interior of **Nandipo**, an excellent bar and pizza restaurant a couple of doors down Rue Albert Ier. About 500 metres/yds further inland, the lively **Marché de Hell-Ville**, conspicuous thanks to its bright yellow exterior, is an excellent place to buy fresh produce and local spices, stands next to the 1950s Théâtre Municipal, now home to the **Alliance Française de Nosy Be** (tel: 032-0511967; www.facebook.com/afnos-ybe). The roundabout in front of the market is the best place to pick up charter taxis and *taxis-brousse* to the rest of the island.

The most important cultural site in the vicinity of Hell-Ville is the **Arbre Sacré de Mahatsinjo ⑤** (tel: 034-1941945; 9am–5pm), a sacred banyan *Ficus religiosa* reputedly planted by Indian settlers in honour of the first visit to the island by Queen Tsiomeko of Boina and her 12,000-strong Sakalava army back in 1837. Sprawling across hundreds of square metres, this multiple-trunked tree is draped with red-and-white cloths and the skulls and horns of zebus sacrificed there, and hosts a free-ranging population of black lemurs. The sacred site is overseen by the adjacent **Espace Zeny**, a private ethnographic museum that displays more than 100 old photographs relating to the Sakalava people, along with other cultural and historical objects. Mahatsinjo and its sacred tree stand about 3km (2 miles) from the central market, and can be reached by following the Route de l'Ouest to a roundabout roughly 2km (1.2 miles), then turn left onto the signposted feeder road. You need to remove your shoes before visiting the site and, if wearing shorts, may be asked to wear a wraparound cloth.

⊘ MANONGARIVO: ROYAL BURIAL PLACE

Little known to outsiders but a cultural site of great significance to locals, the *mahabo* (sacred royal cemetery) at Manongarivo lies some 8km (5 miles) inland of Hell-Ville via Antsaholana. The burial place of several Sakalava princes, it is revered primarily as the final resting place of the long-ruling Queen Binao of Bemihisatra (a kingdom that incorporated Nosy Be and the facing mainland). A descendant of the Boina Dynasty, Binao ascended to the throne, aged only 14, following the death of her mother in 1881. Pitted by tradition against the monarchy of the rival Imerina state, she lent her support to the French invasion of 1893–5, and went on to be appointed *gouverneur principal* of Nosy Be, a role she fulfilled for two decades prior to 1917, when a disagreement with the colonial administration led to her being evicted her from her traditional palace at Manongarivo and forced to live in Hell-Ville until her death 1927. Today, Queen Binao's possessions are preserved in a small treasury house next to her tomb, which is the focal point of a ritual commemoration ceremony held at Manongarivo every July. Then as at other times, a cultural site of this significance should be visited only with a local guide who knows the protocol.

For music lovers, the best time to visit Nosy Be is over Pentecost (May or June), which coincides with the annual Donia Festival (www.festival-donia.com) first held in 1993. The week-long festival offers a great opportunity to see Malagasy musicians playing in a variety of traditional and contemporary styles, and it usually attracts a few artists from elsewhere in Africa or the Indian Ocean. *Pétanque* competitions, beauty pageants and a carnival add to the celebratory mood.

The Sakalava people are mostly Muslim.

WEST COAST

The hub of tourist activity on Nosy Be, the idyllic southwestern beaches of Ambatoloaka, Madirokely and Ambondrona collectively stretch for 4km (2.5 miles) along the southwest coast starting about 10km (6 miles) from Hell-Ville along the surfaced Route de l'Ouest. All three beaches have very shallow inclines and are protected by tall headlands, conditions that ensure calm seas and safe swimming condition all year through.

Far and away the most developed of the trio, southerly **Ambatoloaka ❻** is reached along an inauspiciously narrow and hectic feeder road cluttered with stalls, shops, whimsically-parked *taxis-brousse*, weaving bicycles and the like. As you reach the beach, however, small-town Madagascar gives way to a tourist-oriented cluster of hotels, restaurants, cafés, handicraft boutiques, supermarkets, dive centres, tour operators, ATMs, spas, and hopeful taxi drivers and fixers. In direct contrast to the above, a 200-metre/yd stroll further south leads to the gorgeous

Crater Bay, a forest-fringed, near-circular volcanic relict with a diameter of 300 metres/yds and break in the southwest rim forming an inlet to the open sea. The island's only marina stand on Crater Bay, and it has become a popular haunt of yacht-owners and other expats.

Madirokely is essentially a northerly extension of Ambatoloaka – difficult to say where one beach starts and the other ends – but slightly less developed and commercialised. A tall craggy headland separates it from **Ambondrona ❼**, which is probably the island's loveliest beach, totally hassle-free, and lined with more low-key hotels such as the excellent owner-managed Nosy Lodge, whose restaurant and pool literally spill out onto the sand. The more urbanised beach at **Dzamandzary**, separated from Ambondrona by another impressive headland, is distinguished by its location opposite the tiny island of Nosy Tanga, while the more northerly and less developed beaches at **Bemoko** and **Ambaro** face the larger and taller Nosy Sakatia.

Here, **Ranch Ambaro** (Route du Nord; tel: 032-4369178; http://ambaroranchnosy be.blogspot.co.za), which offers family-friendly horseback excursions on the surrounding beaches and slopes.

MONT PASSOT

Dominating the northwestern interior of Nosy Be, the multiple-coned **Mont Passot** ❽ (tel: 032-0293068; email: montpassot@gmail.fr) incorporates the island's second-highest peak – the perfect ending point of a late afternoon excursion to watch the sun set over the west coast and Nosy Sakatia. Named after the French captain who annexed island in 1941, Passot is accessible by all-weather road and its 329m (1,080ft) summit offers splendid views in all directions. A horseshoe-shaped wooden platform, illustrated with paintings of all the visible major landmarks on Nosy Be and beyond, is perfectly positioned to catch the sunset. Behind this stands a row of craft stalls and the inevitable satellite tower.

The ascent road to Passot's summit passes close to eight **crater lakes**, which range in size from pond-like Lac Ambalavato to the 1,200m/yd-wide Lac Amparihibe (the island's largest freshwater body and main source of piped drinking water). A short network of walking trails connecting the summit to the various lake rims can be covered in a couple of hours. Tempting as it may look, swimming in the brilliant green lakes, which are believed to host the spirits of the Sakalava monarchy, is *fady*. There's also a taboo on fishing, or harming the sacred crocodiles that are present in most of the lakes, most numerously Lac Antsahamanavaka, where they have a reputation for enforcing the *fady* on swimming by eating transgressors.

MONT LOKOBE AND THE SOUTHEAST

The far southeast of Nosy Be is dominated by the 8-sq-km (3-sq-mile)

Réserve Naturelle Intégrale de Lokobe ❾ (tel: 020-8692531; www.parcs-madagascar.com; daily 8am–4pm), which protects the island's last remaining stand of undisturbed indigenous forest. It is named after its dominant feature, the volcanic Mont Lokobe, which rises to a high point of 455 metres (1,492ft) only 1km (0.6 miles) from the southern shore facing Nosy Komba. The park is best known for its population of the easily seen and rather glamorous black lemur, but it also provides an important stronghold for the relatively unobtrusive Hawk's sportive lemur and the nocturnal Claire's mouse lemur, both of which are very localised and IUCN-listed as critically endangered. Other wildlife includes the blue morph of panther chameleon, whose striking coloration is restricted to the population centred on Nosy Be and the nearby mainland, and Madagascar pygmy kingfisher and Madagascar long-eared owl.

Prior to 2015, Lokobe was classified as a Strict Nature Reserve, a status that restricted tourist activity to the

Crater lake on Mont Passot, with a view to the sea.

forest periphery. Now a fully-fledged national park, it is traversed by three short (1–2.5km/0.6–1.5 miles) walking trails across rugged terrain that requires some fitness and agility. Most people thus still visit Lokobe on organised tours that follow the 10km (6-mile) road running northeast from Hell-Ville to Ambatozavavy, then proceed by local pirogue to Ampasipohy, a fishing village sandwiched between the beach and the park's eastern boundary.

A tamer and more contrived alternative to Lokobe, **Lemuria Land** ⑩ (tel: 034-0204070; www.lemurialand.com; daily 8am–5pm) is a glorified private zoo aimed squarely at the beach package holiday market. About a dozen lemur species, including black, ring-tailed and various sifakas, are confined to Lemuria's cages and small islands, and it also houses captive tortoises, chameleons, leaf-tailed geckos, crocodiles and other reptiles. Also the site of a rum distillery and ylang-ylang oil extraction plant, Lemuria Land is situated along the Ambatozavavy Road 5km (3 miles) from Hell-Ville.

The Muslim-dominated Sakalava village of **Marodoka** ⑪, set on a lovely palm-lined bay at the base of Mont Lokobe, was Nosy Be's principal town prior to its annexation to France. Then known as Ambanoro, is thought to have been visited by Arab sailors as early as the 9th century, and it emerged as an important trade port in the 16th century, when several Indian and Arab traders settled there to export gold, spices, turtle shells and slaves to places like Goa and Zanzibar. As recently as the 1870s, Marodoka – literally 'many shops' – supported a population of 2,000, but it fell into decline shortly afterwards, partly due to the ascendency of Hell-Ville just 5km (3 miles) to its west, but also due to abolition of the slave trade on which it had thrived. Relics of its heyday include the island's oldest extant mosque, cemeteries containing ornate 17th- to 19th-century Hindu and Muslim tombs, and the so-called Ghost House, an impressive three-storey shell, now overgrown with strangler figs, claimed locally to date to the 15th century (though a

Beach life.

more recent date seems probable). The well-organised **Ravinala Association des Femmes de Marodoka** (tel: 032 4132797, http://ravinala-marodoka.com) offers guided tours of the old town that conclude with a lively demonstration of traditional Sakalava drumming and dancing.

The Saradravay Peninsula, a crooked fingered protrusion into the shallow bay dividing Hell-Ville from Marodoka, is the site of the Centre National de Recherches Océanographiques, an important marine research institute that celebrated its 40th anniversary in 2017. It houses the **Musée Océanographique du CNRO** ⑫ (tel: 032-4202908; http://cnro.recherches. gov.mg/?Service-Musee; Mon–Fri 8am–noon). The museum focuses on local marine animals and plants, as well as traditional fishing techniques and associated materials used in northwest Madagascar. Pride of place, however, is accorded to the *Sarimanok*, the traditional Philippine *vinta* (bamboo trimaran) that Bob Hobman sailed across the Indian Ocean from Bali to Madagascar in 1985. Hobman and his crew of six replicated seafaring techniques, and stuck to a diet of perishable vegetables, in order to demonstrate that such a boat might have carried the first Neolithic humans settlers to Madagascar.

OTHER ISLANDS

Rising from a 25-sq-km (10-sq-mile) base to an imperious altitude of 622 metres (2,041ft), magnificent **Nosy Komba** ⑬ (Island of Lemurs) or, more correctly, Nosy Ambariovato (Island of Rocky Shores) is distinguished by its classic volcanic profile of steep slopes swathed in a multihued green blanket of rainforest and tall bamboo. A popular destination for boat excursions from Nosy Be just 3km (1.8 miles) to its north, it can also be visited directly from mainland Ankify, and all three are connected by a regular public ferry service. Nosy Komba also forms a popular beach destination in its own right, serviced by a handful of thatched palm-shaded seafront lodges whose appealing rusticity stands in defiant contrast to the more mainstream resorts on Nosy Be.

The main tourist focus on Nosy Komba, **Ampangorina** (charge) is the island's largest village, situated on the north shore facing Mont Lokobe. Ampangorina is renowned for its profusion of highly habituated black lemurs, which evidently spend as much time frolicking around the walls of the village, and leaping on visitors in hope of food, as they do foraging in the neighbouring lemur sanctuary. It also has a good craft market. A more challenging but thoroughly rewarding excursion is the steep but scenic hike to **Antagnianaomby**, the highest point on the island. This rock at this sacred summit is said to be the tomb of a legendary queen who reputedly arrived on the island with an entourage of black lemurs and decided to settle there

⊙ Tip

Day trips to Mont Passot, Lokobe, Nosy Komba, Nosy Iranja and Nosy Tanikely can be arranged through any hotel. Failing that, reliable operators include Evasion Sans Frontière (Rue Passot; Hell-Ville; tel: 032-1100596; www.evasionsans frontiere.com) and Nosy Be Original (Bemoko; tel: 032-4052488; http://nosy be-original.com). The main drag through Ambatoloaka is lined with dive and tour operators offering a broadly similar selection of day excursions.

Male black lemur, Nosy Komba.

Ylang-ylang is grown, picked and distilled on the island.

Upmarket beach villas at the Constance Tsarabanjina.

when she saw how much they liked it. As a result, it is a *fady* place, and visits are permitted only on Mondays and Saturdays, and to those wearing a traditional *lambahoany* (printed cotton cloth sarong).

Situated about 8km (5 miles) west of Nosy Komba and a similar distance south of Nosy Be, the **Parc National Marin de Nosy Tanikely** ⓮ (www.parcs-madagascar.com; daily 8am–4pm daily) was created in 2011 to protect the tiny island for which it is named, as well as the sea extending for a radius of 700 metres/yds from its shore. The park's multicoloured coral reefs form one of Madagascar's most popular and finest diving and snorkelling sites, supporting a giddying swirl of colourful reef fish that can easily be explored for quite some distance offshore due to the shallowness of the water. Green and loggerhead turtles are often seen swimming past at close proximity to snorkellers, and dolphins and whale-sharks are occasional visitors. Despite its small size (no more than 500 metres/yds wide in any direction),

Nosy Tanikely (Island of Little Earth) supports a fair amount of wildlife, including flying foxes, panther chameleons and an introduced population of black lemurs. There is also a small lighthouse on its peak. Snorkel gear can be rented on site for those who arrive without it.

Another excellent snorkelling site is mangrove-lined **Nosy Sakatia** (Island of Forbidden Love), which rises to an altitude of 137 metres (450ft) little more than 1km (0.6 miles) offshore of the west coast resort of Ambaro. Somewhat more remote, situated about 35km (21 miles) southwest of Nosy Be, **Nosy Iranja** – actually two forested islets linked by a 1km (0.6-mile) -long sandbar – is an important breeding site for marine turtles and also offers good snorkelling. More remote still, **Nosy Tsarabanjina**, an idyllic islet in the Mitsio Archipelago northeast of Nosy Be, now houses the super-luxurious and equally pricey Constance Tsarabanjina, a five-star destination accessible only by charter flight from Nosy Be.

⊘ THE FRAGRANT YLANG-YLANG

Northern Madagascar, and Nosy Be in particular, vies with Mayotte Island as the world's largest cultivator of ylang-ylang (*Cananga odorata*), a fast-growing medium-tall tree whose yellowish droopy-petalled flowers are distilled to produce an aromatic essential oil. Native to the Philippines, Malaysia and Indonesia, the ylang-ylang's name derives from a Filipino word *ilang* (meaning 'jungle' and it is believed to have aphrodisiac properties in some parts of Asia, where it is customarily spread on the bed of newlyweds. First cultivated commercially by a German sailor called Albertus Schwenger in Manila in 1860, the plant was introduced to Madagascar via Réunion in 1903, and has since become emblematic of Nosy Be – as alluded to in the nickname Nosy Manitra (Perfumed Island). Despite being a rather low-yielding crop – 100kg (220lb) of flowers reduces to just 1 litre (2.1 pints) of oil – this is compensated for by the fact that regularly pruning induces it to blooms throughout the year. Within Madagascar, ylang-ylang essence is mixed with coconut oil to produce a widely available massage oil. It is also exported to Europe as an ingredient of floral perfumes such as Chanel No. 5. and Diorissimo. More improbably, ylang-ylang is now also a popular, though rather floral, flavouring for locally made ice-cream.

Sakalava woman.

Plage de Ramena.

DIEGO SUAREZ AND THE FAR NORTH

Rising from the world's second-largest natural bay, the unspoilt beaches, montane forests and jagged tsingy of the northerly Diana Region can be explored from the relaxed port city of Diego Suarez.

Antananarivo

The most northerly of Madagascar's 22 administrative regions, Diana is also perhaps the most heavily touristed, thanks largely to its incorporation of the perennially popular island resort of Nosy Be. However, while the majority of visitors to Nosy Be are on a fly-in beach package and never set foot off the island, a significant minority do cross over to the Malagasy mainland, typically travelling one-way by road and ferry and the other by air to/from the regional capital Diego Suarez, 250km (155 miles) further north via the stunning tsingy outcrops of the Réserve Spéciale d'Ankarana.

Diego Suarez, overlooking the world's second-largest natural bay, is also as important fly-in travel hub in its own right, being the closest town to the magnificently biodiverse forests of the Parc National de la Montagne d'Ambre, the surreal sandstone sculptures of the Tsingy Rouges, and any number of glorious sandy beaches and sheltered bays. It is serviced by Arrachart Airport, a former French military camp that flanks the RN6 about 7km (4 miles) south of the town centre, and is named after Ludovic Arrachart, pilot of a pioneering postal flight between France and Madagascar in the 1920s.

DIEGO SUAREZ

Among the most agreeable of Malagasy towns, **Diego Suarez ❶** occupies a wide,

tall peninsula that protrudes into the south of the four-chambered 20km- (12-mile) -long bay with which it shares its name. The town is essentially a colonial creation, founded by the French – who had long coveted the easily protected bay and its natural deep-water harbour – shortly after Queen Ranavalona III of Imerina signed a treaty ceding their protectorateship in the wake of the first Franco-Malagasy War of 1883–5. The town centre took its shape under Governor Froger, who laid out Rue Colbert in 1892, and Marshall Joseph Joffre, a

⊙ Main Attractions

Diego Suarez
Montagne des Français
Plage de Ramena
Parc National Marin de
  Nosy Hara
Parc National de la
  Montagne d'Ambre
Tsingy Rouges
Réserve Spéciale d'Ankarana
Aire Protégée de Loky
  Manambato
Parc National de Marojejy

Map on page 256

In the Parc National de la Montagne d'Ambre.

military engineer who reorganised it as a naval base over 1899–1905. A strategically important naval base in World War II, Diego Suarez was captured and occupied by the British in May 1942 in order to prevent the pro-Nazi Régime de Vichy – which had controlled Madagascar since 1940 – from signing a treaty allowing its harbour to be used by Japanese warships and submarines.

The most northerly of Madagascar's six former provincial capitals, Diego Suarez is now the administrative centre of the Diana Region, and the country's seventh-largest settlement, with a population estimated at 120,000. Since 1975, the town's official name has been Antsiranana (Malagasy for 'Place of the Port'), but in practice it is almost ubiquitously referred to as Diego by locals and foreigners alike. The old town centre, at the northern end of the peninsula, comprises a large and sleepy grid of roads lined with old colonial structures, many closed-up or semi-derelict, some with facades livened up by cheerful murals credited to street artists such as Freddy Parole. Others have been converted to chic cafés, hotels, restaurants and shops – and while the low tourist volumes makes it difficult to understand how all these places survive, things falls into place when the occasional cruise ship sails into the harbour, mostly between December and March, to unleash hundreds of eager-spending passengers onto terra firma.

EXPLORING CENTRAL DIEGO

A good place to start a walking tour of the town centre, **Place Foch** is a large central square shaded by palms and other trees, and surrounded by old colonial administrative buildings. Its centrepiece is a bust of Philibert Tsiranana, the first President of Madagascar, and it also hosts a branch of the tourist office (www.office-tourisme-diego-suarez.com; Mon–Fri 8am–noon and 3–6pm). From Place Foch, continue north along Rue Colbert, which was laid out in the 1890s and remains the main commercial road, lined with half-a-dozen cafés and restaurants, as well as a good selection of supermarkets and craft boutiques.

Some 300 metres/yds along Rue Colbert, the two-storey **Maison Cassam Chenai** (now the BMOI bank) was built in 1925 by the eponymous Indian trader, and is notable for the fluted columns that support its grand facade. Another 300 metres/yds to the north, the **Alliance Française** is housed in the former Bazary Be (Big Market), an unusual prefabricated metal structure designed by the Eiffel Workshop and erected in 1925 to replace the original wooden market.

The north end of Rue Colbert is a T-junction with historic Rue Richelieu. On the left side of this junction, the old **Tribunal**, built in 1908, is a still-active courthouse whose classic exterior us rather undermined by the lamentable state of the overgrown ornamental garden in front. Opposite it, **La Résidence** is an attractive two-storey building with a colonnaded and wood-panelled front balcony, a corrugated iron roof and a ship's insignia above the entrance. It was built to replace the original Hôtel du Gouvernement in 1892, and has since served as the mayoral residence and a government administration office.

A few paces west along Rue Richelieu, the once grand **Hôtel des Mines** (aka Hôtel de la Marine) is now a magnificent two-storey arched shell with a palm-shaded central courtyard and some lively street murals on the inner walls. It was built by Alphonse Mortages, a prominent local businessman who made a fortune on the back of his discovery of gold at nearby Andavakoera in

Mural of a pirate ship, Antsiranana.

Ruins of a French colonial building, Diego Suarez.

⊙ DIOGO SOARES AND DIEGO SUAREZ

Diego Suarez is often claimed to be an amalgamation of Diogo Dias and Fernando Suarez, the names of a Portuguese explorer and Spanish sailor who respectively visited Madagascar in 1500 and 1506. More likely, however, the town is named after Diogo Soares de Albergaria, a wanton Portuguese adventurer whose acts of piracy off the Mozambican coast led to a warrant for his arrest being issued by Governor da Gama of Goa in 1540. Fortunately for Soares, he was pardoned when his old friend Martim de Sousa succeeded da Gama in 1542. He was then placed in command of a naval expedition to Madagascar in search of de Sousa's missing brother; he failed in his primary mission but returned to Goa with a shipload of pirated treasures and Malagasy slaves. In 1547, stormy weather forced Soares to land at Portuguese Malacca, where he switched career to become a mercenary and soon rose to be Commander-in-Chief of King Tabinshwehti's army. Soares's last known act of violence, c.1550, was the attempted capture of a wealthy Malaccan merchant's daughter, who he hoped to marry by force, and the murder of a rescue party led by her groom. Soon after, Diogo Soares was arrested, handed over to the merchant's family, and stoned to death by the local townspeople. This much we know, but exactly why and how Soares's name came to be Hispanicised and applied to Madagascar's northernmost city is a matter of conjecture!

Statue of French Marshall Joseph Joffre on Joffre Square.

1905, and was the city's top hotel prior to being sold to the Bank of Madagascar in 1925. It was later sold to the French navy, and restored as a hotel, only to be destroyed by Cyclone Kamisy in 1984. Next to the ruined hotel, the **Kiosque à musique** is an octagonal bandstand – also built by Alphonse Mortages, as a gift to the town – that regularly hosted recitals in the colonial era and stands in a small park that offers fabulous views across the bay.

Rue Richelieu terminates at **Place Joffre**, a small circular clifftop lookout dominated by a bust of Marshall Joseph Joffre attributed to the well-known French sculptor Raymond Sudre and inaugurated in 1933. Once the receiving point for optical telegraph signals from Cap d'Ambre, 40km (24 miles) to the north, the square is now a popular rendezvous lined with benches from where you can watch the harbour lights as the sun sets over the western bay.

From Place Joffre, follow Rue Joffre back east, then turn left into Rue Flacourt, crossing back over Rue Colbert to Rue Albert Joseph Tsiahoana (named

Streetlife in Diego Suarez.

after a former archbishop of the Catholic Archdiocese of Antsiranana who died in 2012). At the north end of this road, **Place Kabary** is a small park sited where traditional trials and *kabary* speeches (formal public addresses known for their liberal use of metaphor, often in a call-and-response dialogue) were held prior the French deposition of Queen Ranavalona III in 1897. Now dedicated to the Malagasy martyrs killed during the 1947 rebellion, the park has a small playground and it's a popular spot for local *pétanque* competitions. A few blocks south of this stands the tall **Catholic Cathedral** built by Bishop Courbet, with floor tiling donated by Alphonse Mortages and a prominent clock tower, which was inaugurated in 1911.

TOWARDS THE BAIE DES FRANÇAIS

About 1km (0.6 miles) south of the town centre, a pair of war cemeteries are the final resting place of the many hundreds of casualties associated with Operation Ironclad, the naval assault on Diego

Suarez undertaken by Commonwealth forces in May 1942. The **Diego Suarez Military Cemetery** on Boulevard Duplex contains the tombs of 921 French, other Europeans and Malagasy killed in action between the 1890s and 1960s, but is dominated by soldiers who fought for Vichy France in 1942. A monument dedicated to the 'glorious memory of the children of Diego Suarez who died for France' stands at its entrance. A block east of this, the well-tended **Diego Suarez War Cemetery** (daily 8am–4pm) contains the graves of 314 Commonwealth soldiers, sailors and airmen – many from eastern or southern Africa, others from the UK – who died in action in Madagascar over 1942–4, as well as one Belgian fatality.

Continue for another 2km (1.2km) south along Boulevard Duplex, past the prominent junction with the RN6, and you'll emerge on a cliff offering lovely views across mangrove-lined tidal flats to Baie des Française and Ramena. The centrepiece of this lovely view is **Nosy Lonjo ❷**, the small but steep 120-metre (393ft) -high island depicted on the back of the 100 ariary banknote, and also known as *Pain de Sucre* (Sugarloaf) on account of its rather tenuous resemblance to the much larger Rio de Janeiro landmark. Nosy Lonjo means 'Island of Strength', in reference to a powerful sacred stone used for rituals invoking the ancestral spirits. However, the forested island remains uninhabited and it is *fady* to step ashore for secular reasons – indeed, it is said than anybody who does so will be destined to die soon afterwards.

MONTAGNE DES FRANÇAIS

Rising to an elevation of 425 metres (1,395ft) above the Baie des Français 5km (3 miles) southeast of central Diego, the tsingy-capped **Montagne des Français ❸** is an important watershed and biodiversity hotspot supporting several localised floral endemics and eight reptile and amphibian species unique to its slopes. Sometimes referred to by its Malagasy name Ambohitra'atsingy (literally Tsingy Mountain), the limestone massif also has a long history of military occupation. In 1828, the Imerina

View from the Montagne des Français over to the Pain de Sucre in the Baie de Diego Suarez.

monarchy built Fort Ambohimerina on the northern slope of the Montagne des Français in order to repel any foreign naval attempts to occupy the bay below. In the wake of the French protectorate-ship treaty of 1885, the imposing colonial Fort d'Anosiravo was constructed on the mountain's northern summit, using rocks carried up by tip-trucks along a short railway through a rock cleft and series of three artificial tunnels. During World War II, the mountain was also a pivotal battleground in the British and Commonwealth defeat of the Vichy government in May 1942. Now adorned with 14 white crosses, the Montagne des Français is now an important Catholic pilgrimage site, attracting thousands of locals worshippers over the weekend a fortnight before Easter.

Designated as a 50-sq-km (19-sq-mile) reserve in 2015, the Montagne des Français is now the focal point of the **Circuit d'Anosiravo** (7am–4pm), a community-based project comprising a guided 2.5-hour, 5km (3-mile) circular nature trail and optional 1km (0.6-mile) historical extension that adds about an hour to the walking time. Starting from a clearly-signposted office abutting the seafront Route de Ramena 8km (5 miles) southeast of central Diego, this superb trail, best undertaken in the cool of the morning, offers fantastic views over the Baie des Français to Nosy Lonjo and the city centre. Look out for the spectacular Suarez baobab *Adansonia suarezensis*, an endangered and highly localised tree distinguished from other members of the genus by its smooth red-brown bark, cylindrical trunk and neat crown of horizontal branches. Other striking vegetation includes some fine examples of the bottle-based, long-tendrilled *Cyphostemma macrocarpa*, the dragon-tree *Dracaena angustifolia* and the endemic rock-loving *Aloe suarezensis*. Wildlife likely to be seen includes crowned lemur, the brilliant green giant day gecko, and up to 60 bird species, among them Madagascar buzzard, crested coua, greater vasa parrot, Madagascar green pigeon, Madagascar spine-tailed swift and Chabert's vanga.

The highlight of the trail is the steep historic extension, which climbs through

Ruins of the Fort d'Anosiravo on the Montagne des Français.

the jagged tsingy to the significant remains of **Fort d'Anosiravo**. The path up incorporates a case of 500-plus concrete steps through the cleft and tunnels formerly traversed by the funicular-style railway use to carry building materials to the top in 1885. Once at the summit, the path leads along what is left of the crumbling stone ramparts to a wooden viewing platform built on the roof of an old optical telegraph signal tower. The sweeping 360° view from the platform offers a fabulous buzzard's-eye view over the bay incorporating such distant landmarks such as Joffreville, Windsor Castle and La Mer d'Emeraude. It then continues to the substantial ruins of the Caserne du Commandant (Commander's Barracks), with its arched facade, semi-intact bathroom and toilet, and stairwell leading to a (now collapsed) roof. The descent incorporates a short walk through a natural limestone tunnel with some interesting drop formation of the walls.

RAMENA AND THE EMERALD SEA

The most popular beach destination in the vicinity of Diego Suarez, **Plage de Ramena ❹** is a compact village situated on the inner (eastern) shore of the peninsula that separates the Baie des Français from the open sea, 5km (3 miles) from the city centre as the gull flies, but more like 18km (12 miles) by road. Supporting a few thousand fisherfolk, the village is geared more towards Diego weekenders than foreign tourists, but it has a fine swimming beach all the same, and a host of welcoming and unpretentious seafood restaurants and bars line the beach either side of the central jetty. For budget-conscious travellers, Ramena is also a lot more wallet-friendly that the likes of Nosy Be or Île Sainte-Marie when it comes to accommodation and eating out.

Ramena is the most popular springboard for day excursions to **La Mer d'Emeraude ❺**, a beautiful pale turquoise lagoon situated on the northeast side of the entrance to Diego Suarez Bay. Only 5km (3 miles) from Ramena by boat, the lagoon owes its distinctive translucent colour to its shallow depth and sandy white base, and it is separated from the open sea by an unbroken 8km (5-mile) -long string of coral reefs and the islets of Nosy Antaly Be, Nosy Diego and Nosy Suarez. In the calm weather that usually prevails between December and April, it offers superb swimming conditions and great snorkelling, but the water might be rougher and submarine visibility lower at other times in year. Half-day trips, inclusive of snorkelling gear and lunch, can be arranged through any operator or hotel in the vicinity of Diego Suarez.

PARC D'ORANGEA AND LES TROIS BAIES

Only 1.5km (1 mile) northeast of Ramena stands the entrance to the **Parc d'Orangea ❻** (7am–6pm), a lovely militarily-controlled reserve that extends across the seaward side

⊙ Tip
It is *fady* to urinate on the Montagne des Français, so make sure you visit a toilet before you hike the Circuit d'Anosiravo. You're also advised to carry drinking water as it can get very hot on the exposed lower slopes.

Fishing boat at sunset, Ramena.

of the same peninsula, protecting a sequence of bays known locally as **Les Trois Baies**. Coming from Ramena, the entrance gate to Orangea brings you directly to the derelict Orangea military camp, set on a sheltered cove below **Cap Miné**, the headland at the peninsula's northerly tip.

Also known historically as Cap Diego (and in Malagasy as Cap Andranomody), Cap Miné forms an imposing natural buttress on the south side of the only oceanic inlet to the immense harbour upon which stands Diego Suarez. This strategic location ensured that the French chose the well-hidden cove at Cap Miné's base as the site of a military camp and naval base almost immediately they took occupation of the area in 1885. Within a year, the cove housed several workshops, barracks and warehouses, as well as a hospital, while a pair of small clifftop forts was supplemented by a lighthouse in 1895. Known as Orangea, the naval base was occupied by Allied forces during World War II, but otherwise remained under French control until 1972, when it was

handed over to the Malagasy navy and began its decline into near-dereliction – assisted, one suspects, by considerable cyclone damage.

A rough road leads uphill from the abandoned camp to the **Phare du Cap Miné**. This clifftop lighthouse started life in 1895 as a prefabricated metal tower set on a square concrete base, but it was later upgraded to the 14-metre (46ft) -high octagonal brick structure that stands there today – and which has been solar-powered since 2009. The surrounding cliffs offer superb views across the bay entrance to the Mer d'Emeraude – its distinctive light green shade visible even at this distance – and are studded with disused cannons and fortification dating to World War II. The spectacular white-tailed tropicbird, easily recognised by its long white tail, is frequently seen gliding gracefully above the cliffs.

The most northerly of Les Trois Baies stands about 1km (0.6 miles) south of the lighthouse. This is the gorgeous **Baie des Dunes**, whose arcing white casuarina-lined beach is hemmed in by a narrow fortified peninsula to the north. From here, a popular option is to have your driver go ahead while you walk southeast along the coast for 4km (2.4 miles) via the equally lovely **Baie des Pigeons**, past the offshore islets of Nosy Angongo and Nosy Tsara, to the breathtaking sweep of **Baie de Sakalava**. Also accessible directly from the main road between Diego Suarez and Ramena (the junction is signposted to the east at the village of Ankorikakely), the windswept Baie de Sakalava is a popular destination for windsurfing and kitesurfing, and gear can be rented (and lessons arranged as required) on the spot.

TOWARDS THE CAP D'AMBRE

Although Diego Suarez is the most northerly town on Madagascar, it actually stands 70km (43 miles) by road from **Cap d'Ambre** ❼, the island's northernmost extremity. Remote and

Delightful Baie des Dunes.

little visited, Cap d'Ambre stands at the business end of an arrowhead of land connected to the rest of the island by a mountainous 20km (12-mile) -long, 5km (3-mile) -wide isthmus flanked by Diego Suarez Bay to the east and the large well-protected Courrier's Bay to the west. The round trip from Diego Suarez to Cap d'Ambre requires a full day, with the earliest possible start, as no accommodation is to be found in the vicinity, and it's a rough 4x4-only road.

A less daunting target for a day trip, **Windsor Castle** ❽ is an imposing fortification set atop a 391-metre (1,282ft) -high rock pinnacle some 50km (30 miles) from Diego Suarez, around halfway up the isthmus towards Cap d'Ambre. The fortifications date to the French colonial era, but have been nicknamed – and widely referred to as – Windsor Castle ever since the British captured it from Vichy France in 1942. The drive from Diego Suarez to the pinnacle base takes up to three hours, and you should allow another couple of hours for the ascent and descent. The castle itself is only of moderate architectural interest, but the views across the isthmus to Diego Suarez Bay and Courrier's Bay are truly breathtaking.

ASCENDING THE MONTAGNE D'AMBRE

Rising to an altitude of 1,477 metres (4,845ft) southwest of Diego Suarez, the **Montagne d'Ambre** is an ancient volcanic mountain named after a type of tree resin believed locally to possess curative qualities.

Thanks to the combination of fertile volcanic soils and a moist cool montane microclimate (the average annual precipitation tops 3,000mm/138 inches), the footslopes of the mountain are an important centre of agriculture, producing an abundance of litchis, bananas and other fruits, as well as being the country's main source of *khat*, a mildly narcotic leaf chewed copiously by many Muslims. By contrast, the uncultivated upper slopes support a cover of lush montane rainforest protected in a 182-sq-km (70-sq-mile) national park and 48-sq-km (18.5-sq-mile) buffer reserve.

⊘ Fact

Nosy Hara, an offshore island in Courrier's Bay, was declared a marine national park in 2012 to protect an endemic chameleon discovered there in 2005. Only 29mm (1.15 inches) long, *Brookesia micra* represents an extreme example of the phenomenon known as island dwarfism – not merely Madagascar's smallest chameleon, it also ranks as the world's tiniest amniote (an evolutionary clade that includes all mammals, birds and reptiles).

Windsor Castle pinnacle.

⊘ THE LIBERTATIA COLONY

A persistent legend relating to Diego Suarez Bay it that it was the site of Libertatia, a utopian pirate colony founded in the 1680s by the French captain James Misson. Governed on democratic lines, Libertatia was anti-state and pro-individual liberties, it opposed wage labour and encouraged the sharing of property and possessions, it was open to all nationalities and races, and its citizens routinely launched Robin Hood-like acts of piracy to free captives on slave ships. According to Captain Charles Johnson, whose influential bestseller *General History of the Pyrates* was first published in 1724, the colony thrived for 25 years before its demise in the wake of a murderous attack by indigenous people from the interior and Misson's subsequent death in a shipwreck.

Diego Suarez Bay sheltered many pirates in the 17th century, and Libertatia, as described by Johnson, might well have been located in the vicinity. The question left begging, however, is whether the colony actually ever existed. Captain Charles Johnson is now thought to be a pseudonym, possibly of the prolific writer Daniel Defoe, of *Robinson Crusoe* fame (1719). Either way, considerable artistic license has been employed in the colourful and often salacious history credited to Johnson, and a lack of corroborating evidence with respect to Libertatia's existence suggests this short-lived utopia was essentially a product of its author's considerable imagination.

The gateway to the Montagne d'Ambre, leafy **Joffreville** ❾ (also known by the Malagasy name Ambohitra, literally 'On the Mountain') lies about 45 minutes' drive from Diego Suarez, and is reached by following the RN6 for 4km (2.5 miles) south of Arrachart Airport then turning west onto a signposted and surfaced 20km (12 mile) feeder road. Perched on the mountain's eastern slopes at a temperate altitude of 635 metres (2,083ft), this resort-like village was established by Governor Joffre in 1902 as a retreat for military personnel stationed at Diego Suarez. Today it comes across as Madagascar's closest approximation of an Indian hill station, its colonial legacy reflected not only in the French-style architecture, but also in a spacious layout dominated by an absurdly wide main road complete with flowering traffic islands.

Joffreville's finest building, the former country residence of Governor Joffre, complete with colonnaded balcony and ornate gables, has been restored as a boutique hotel and restaurant called **The Litchi Tree** (tel: 033-1278454; www.

thelitchitree.com). Also worth a look is the quirkily decorated Village Store, with its bright yellow exterior and informal terrace bar, and the quaint Church of St Michael. Set in 300 hectares (740 acres) of wooded grounds on the village outskirts, **Le Domaine de Fontenay** (tel: 032-1134581; www.lefontenay-madagascar.com; daily 9–11.30am and 2.30–4.30pm) is inhabited by a few lemurs and a very friendly and equally massive Aldabra tortoise thought to be almost 300 years old.

Roughly 3km (2 miles) uphill of Joffreville stands the entrance gate and ticket office to the **Parc National de la Montagne d'Ambre** ❿ (tel: 032-4061450; www.parcs-madagascar.com; daily 8am–4pm), which is Madagascar's oldest national park, established in 1958. Swathed in a liana-draped tangle of 40-metre (131ft) -tall rainforest, the park is also studded with ancient volcanic craters, six of which enclose small emerald-green lakes, and traversed by several mountain streams and associated waterfalls. It can be explored along a 20km (12-mile) trail network offering several day-hiking variations: the roughly three-hour Petit Circuit incorporates a short visit to two waterfalls, while the 4.5-hour Moyen Circuit also visits the tall rim of the beautiful Petit Lac, and the 12-hour Grand Circuit is essentially a return hike to the mountain's summit. The shorter trails are more rewarding for wildlife, simply because they leave more time to stop and search for smaller species, but the longer trail takes you to some worthwhile scenic spots.

Isolated from other similar habitats, the forests of the Montagne d'Ambre are renowned for their floral variety. Indeed, more than 1,000 plant species have been recorded here, among them several flowering orchids, and the epiphytic bird's-nest fern with its 3-metre (10ft) -long fronds. They also boast an extraordinary level of endemism. Of 14 recorded chameleon species, for

The village store in Joffreville.

instance, a full nine occur nowhere else in the world, among then Boettger's chameleon, with its distinctive blue-tipped stub-nose, the heavy-headed Amber Mountain chameleon, and the minuscule Amber Mountain leaf chameleon (a leaf-litter dweller regarded as the world's smallest reptile until an even tinier species was discovered on Nosy Hara in 2005). Montagne d'Ambre also supports the world's greatest diversity of leaf-tailed geckos.

For birdwatchers, a checklist of 75 species includes highlights such as Madagascar crested ibis, pitta-like ground-roller, Madagascar cuckoo-roller, greater vasa parrot and white-throated oxylabes, but the real star is the surprisingly common and confiding Amber Mountain rock thrush, whose entire global population, estimated at around 5,000 individuals, is confined to this one single forest block. Mammals are less conspicuous, but you can expect to see crowned lemur and Sanford's brown lemur (five nocturnal lemur species are also present) and the fossa – the island's largest

carnivore – is quite often encountered on afternoon walks during the main breeding season on November.

THE RN6 SOUTH OF DIEGO

The only surfaced trunk road through northern Madagascar, the heavily potholed 230km (143-mile) stretch of the RN6 between Diego Suarez and Ambanja is frequently traversed by travellers heading to or from Nosy Be. The main attraction along the road is the Réserve Spéciale d'Ankarana, whose spectacular tsingy outcrops and caves are ideally located for an overnight break between Nosy Be and Diego Suarez. The RN6 south of Diego also provides access to the popular Tsingy Rouges and less publicised Lac Antanavo, both of which are easy day trips out of Diego, and it is the springboard for the more remote Réserve Spéciale d'Analamerana and bordering Aire Protégée d'Andrafiamena-Andavakoera.

Justifiably one of the busiest tourist attractions in this part of Madagascar, the **Site Communautaire des Tsingy Rouges ⑪** (7am–5pm) stands

The red tsingy of Antsiranana are natural karsts made of sandstone, marl and limestone.

Red tsingy landscape near Antsiranana.

○ Fact

Ambondromifehy, a small town between Anivorano du Nord and Ankarana, translates as 'Place of Twisted Reeds' and was once a market town for basketwork material. Since the late 1990s, it has transformed into a low-scale mining town, thanks to the discovery of alluvial deposits of yellow and blue sapphires in the hills bordering the Ankarana Massif. As a result, the RN6 through Ambondromifehy is lined with kiosks selling sapphires.

A sacred crocodile on the shores of Lac Antanavo.

about 17km (10 miles) east of the RN6 along a dirt road that's signposted about 40km (25 miles) south of Diego Suarez and offers views to the distant Analamerana Range. Unlike the larger, sharper and harder black tsingy mountains found elsewhere in northern Madagascar, this community-run site protects an otherworldly landscape of curvaceous and crumbly laterite chimneys that typically stand up to 5 metres (16ft) high and possess a texture reminiscent of enlarged coral or lung tissue. Set deep within a riverine gorge, it's a unique, genuinely impressive and madly photogenic phenomenon, and although there are some fine views from the rim, it's worth scrambling down the footpath to the base where several clusters of the ochre tsingy can be inspected up close. The best time to be there is late afternoon or early morning, when the soft light enhances the natural reddish hues of the ferruginous clay, and temperatures tend to be more tolerable. From the Tsingy Route, it is possible to continue for 5km (3 miles) southeast to **Irodo**, a rustic

and attractive fishing village perched alongside the river of the same name.

Straddling the RN6 about 30km (18 miles) south of the junction for the Tsingy Rouges, **Anivorano du Nord** is a bustling little market town and district capital whose name (literally 'Town Surrounded by Water') refers to the sacred **Lac Antanavo** ⑫ (charge) nestled in a volcano crater about 2km (1.2 miles) to its east. Antanavo means 'Village on High' and legend states that the crater used to be the site of a village whose residents refused to give drinking water to a passing sorcerer, who punished them by submerging their homes and transforming them into crocodiles. The crocodiles of Lac Antanavo are now held sacred as ancestral spirits, for which reason it is *fady* to kill or injure them, and they are regularly offered zebu sacrifices by people seeking benediction, usually on a Saturday. The lake is also the centrepiece of an annual festival, usually held on whichever Saturday in November is thought to be most auspicious, during which half-a-dozen zebus might be sacrificed. The near-circular

○ FORESTS OF STONE

A surreal and forbidding landscape characteristic of northern Madagascar, Tsingy – which translates as 'Place you cannot walk barefoot' – is a karstic formation whose deeply-incised clusters or spines of steep, serrated rock needles are often likened to stone forests. These jagged natural sculptures are carved into sedimentary limestone plateaux that formed in a shallow marine habitat in the Jurassic Era, but were subsequently subjected to tectonic uplift, which not only raised them above sea level, but also caused them to develop a grid of vertical and horizontal cracks. Limestone being partially soluble, these linear cracks were then eroded by mildly acid rainwater into larger fissures that eventually exposed the strange striated and pinnacled formations we see today. The tsingy outcrops of Madagascar are also characterised by labyrinthine cave systems typically created by subterranean groundwater erosion of a soft limestone stratum between two harder ones. Madagascar's largest block of tsingy is found in the remote Parc National des Tsingy de Bemaraha, but several smaller formations also exist, with those in Ankarana being the most accessible, since they stand alongside the RN6 between Nosy Be and Diego Suarez. Another popular excursion from Diego, the Tsingy Rouges, though very beautiful in its own right, is rather misleadingly named, as it comprises soft laterite rather than hard limestone, and is much smaller in scale.

lake, measuring around 1,000 metres/yds in diameter, is worth visiting just to see the seriously massive Nile crocodiles that lie along the shore, massive jaws agape, and sharp teeth and cold yellow eyes glistening in the sun. It's a great spot for close-up mug shots, but you won't want to get too close!

IN SEARCH OF PERRIER'S SIFAKA

East of the RN6, Anivorano du Nord District is the site of the remote 347-sq-km (134-sq-mile) **Réserve Spéciale d'Analamerana ⓭** (www.parcs-madagascar.com), which was created in 1956 to protect the tsingy-capped hills bounded by the Irodo River in the north and Loky river in the south. The reserve is home to a number of localised endemics, most famously the striking Perrier's sifaka, a critically endangered lemur distinguished by its dense black coat, long bushy tail and orange eyes. Listed as one of the world's 35 most endangered primate taxa, Perrier's is the rarest of Madagascar's nine recognised sifaka species, and recent reports suggest it now very scarce in Analamerana, possibly even locally extinct.

A more reliable and accessible alternative to Analamerana is the bordering **Aire Protégée d'Andrafiamena-Andavakoera ⓮** (tel: 020-2263661; https://association-fanamby.org), a privately-managed 746-sq-km (288-sq-mile) reserve set aside in 2008 primarily to protect the only remaining wild population of Perrier's sifaka. Although the sifaka is the main attraction of Andrafiamena-Andavakoera, it harbours a broadly similar flora and fauna to Analamerana, notably three species of baobab, seven types of lemur, and an interesting selection of birds including Madagascar crested ibis, white-breasted mesite, sickle-billed vanga and the highly localised Van Dam's vanga. Tourist activity in Andrafiamena-Andavakoera is focussed on Black Lemur Camp (tel: 032-0784344; www.friendlycamp.org),

which lies about 30 minutes along a rough feeder road running east of the RN6 close to Anivorano du Nord.

THE TSINGY OF ANKARANA

The most accessible of Madagascar's major tsingy formations, the **Réserve Spéciale d'Ankarana ⓯** (www.parcs-madagascar.com; daily 7.30am–4pm) extends across an area of 182 sq km (70 sq miles) immediately west of the RN6 at Mahamasina, a village located about 105km (63 miles) south of Diego Suarez. Ankarana 's dominant feature is the immense eponymous limestone formation, which rises from an eastern base set at an altitude to 50 metres (165ft) to a 25km (15 mile) long western wall that peaks at 206 metres (676ft). The massif is renowned for its labyrinthine caverns, which incorporate around 100km (60 miles) of mapped passages, making them the longest cave network in Madagascar, possibly the whole of Africa. The reserve is home to 330 plant, 11 lemur, 96 bird, 44 reptile and 16 amphibian species. Succulents dominate on the bare faces of the tsingy, but the

Tsingy of the Ankarana Massif.

⊙ Tip

The sacred bat caves of Ankarana are protected by several *fadys*. These range from the eminently sensible (it is taboo to touch stalactites or other living rock formations, or to mistreat or remove animals) to the outright bizarre – difficult to imagine any but the most vampiric of visitors being tempted into 'engaging in sexual relations' when there are bats flapping and chirping all over the show, and the unromantic honk of guano hanging heavy in the air!

Exploring the tsingy, Ankarana Massif.

valleys support a cover of dry deciduous woodland where crowned lemur and Sanford's brown lemur are commonly observed. Conspicuous birds include lesser vasa parrot, crested coua, blue vanga and sickle-winged vanga, the latter often revealing its presence with its disturbing infantile call.

Guided day walks into the reserve are best arranged at the main entrance and ticket office in Mahamasina. The shortest circuit, 3km (1.8 miles) in either direction, and usually good both for lemurs and for birds, leads from Mahamasina to the Tsingy Meva and the Grottes des Chauves-Souris, which as its name suggests is home to up to 50,000 bats, and also, more macabrely, the bones of local Antakarana people who took refuge here in the 19th century to avoid persecution by the invading Imerina army. Another short circuit, 5km (miles) in either direction, leads to the Tsingy Ravy and the Perte des Rivières, a massive circular sinkhole where two rivers vanish underground. The more demanding and rewarding Moyen Circuit, running for 10km (6 miles) in either

direction, is a 20km (12-mile) round trip into the Grandes Tsingy, crossing a large ravine via a pair of suspension bridges spanning 22 metres (72ft) and 6 metres (20ft). Slightly longer, at 11km (7 miles) in either direction (allow nine hours for the round trip), is the Grand Circuit, which also takes you to the small but beautiful Lac Vert, set in the base of a wooded ravine. Ankarana can also be explored from two western gates, but these are difficult of access at the driest of times, and usually close completely during the rainy season.

Situated just outside Ankarana's southwestern border, the **Iharana Massif ⑯** is a large isolated tsingy outcrop that rises to 123 metres (403ft) above the pretty lake at its northern base. It is managed as a private reserve by Iharana Bush Camp in collaboration with the local Antsaravibe Community, and can be traversed on an excellent three-hour guided walking trail, complete with rope ladders and small bridges across the tsingy peaks. The trail culminates with a stunning 45 minute, 600-metre/yd walk through a cave adorned with a wealth of limestone drop formations: giant stalactites and stalagmites, abstract natural sculptures resembling an elephant or dinosaur, and smaller coral-like polyps on the roof and walls.

FROM AMBILOBE TO THE SAVA REGION

An acronym of its four main towns Sambava, Antalaha, Vohemar and Andapa, the Sava Region runs along the eastern littoral south from Diego Suarez to the mountainous Masoala Peninsula, which isolates it from the coast further south. Renowned as Madagascar's major producer of the high quality 'Bourbon' export strain of vanilla, Sava is also one of the country's most intriguing and remote travel destination, juxtaposing a lush agricultural coastal belt dominated by vanilla and coconut plantations with a wild mountainous interior blanketed in rainforest.

The few tourists who do head to Sava tend to fly in from Antananarivo or Diego Suarez to the regional capital Sambava, but it is also possible to drive there along the RN5a, which runs east from the RN6 at Ambilobe, a substantial junction town situated 30km (18 miles) south of Mahamasina and the eastern entrance to Ankarana. The unpaved 160km (100-mile) stretch of the RN5a running east between Ambilobe and Vohemar is rough going and may be impassable after rain. By contrast, the 230km (145-mile) stretch running south from Vohemar to Antalaha via Sambava is surfaced and well-maintained.

Coming by road from the RN6, the first landmark you'll reach, 105km (63 miles) from Ambilobe along the RN5a, is the small town of **Daraina** ⓲, which lies in a hot, dry agricultural region that has suffered considerable deforestation partly as a result of informal surface mining for gold. Daraina is the gateway to the ecologically degraded 2,500-sq-km (965-sq-mile) **Aire Protégée de Loky Manambato** (tel: 020-2263661; https://association-fanamby.org), named after two of the rivers that run through it, protects several important patches of relict forest and savanna as well as a remote marine sector. Loky Manambato is best known as a refuge for the Tattersall's sifaka, an off-white gold-crowned lemur first described as recently as 1988 and now listed as critically endangered, with the entire global population being confined to a few dozen forest patches north of Daraina. The sifaka is easily seen on guided walks arranged out of the NGO-managed Camp Tattersalli (tel: 020-2233623, www.friendly-camp.org) 7km (4 miles) from Daraina. Crowned lemurs and Sanford's brown lemur are also common, and the elusive aye-aye is sometimes seen on night walks. Two species of small nocturnal lemur are regarded to be endemic to Loky Manambato: the Daraina sportive lemur, first described in 2006, and an unnamed species of fork-marked lemur first observed in 2010.

THE VANILLA COAST

Coming from the west, you arrive at the so-called Vanilla Coast at **Vohemar** ⓲,

Golden-crowned sifaka in the Aire Protégée de Loky Manambato.

a sleepy town of 15,000 residents situated at the southern end of a large sheltered bay 55km (33 miles) east of Daraina. An attractive and historic seaport, Vohemar derive its name from the phrase 'Vohitra Maro', meaning 'Place of Many Villages', and it is also sometimes referred to as Iharana. The surrounding coast was the centre of the 7th-century Rasikajy stone-age civilisation, and Vohemar later became one of the first Malagasy ports to be settled by Arabs, as evidenced by the extensive mediaeval necropolis now protected in **Parc Anjoaty** a few kilometres inland. A popular local beauty spot, 4km (2.4 miles) south of the town centre, **Lac Andronotsara** is a green freshwater lake separated from the ocean by a narrow sandbar. Known for its birdlife, Andronotsara also supports a population of sacred crocodiles legendarily descended from the drowned inhabitants of a village that was submerged when a giant marine monster emerged from the sea to dig the lake.

Follow the surfaced RN5a for 150km (90 miles) south of Vohemar and you'll

A zebu enjoying the view over Antalaha.

arrive at **Sambava** ⑲, a coastal port situated on a sheltered bay at the mouth of three smallish rivers. The regional capital of Sava, Sambava is also the region's largest town, with a population estimated at 50,000, and the site of its main airport, which is serviced by scheduled flights from Antananarivo and Diego Suarez. The compact town centre comprises two parallel roads running on a 300-metre/yd-wide sandbar sandwiched between the open sea and a pretty river that flows out of the sacred Lac Andamoty and Lac Andohabe 5km (3 miles) to the south. It boasts little in the way of urban tourist sites, but the main market, connected to the western town centre by two short river bridges, is worth a look, especially on Tuesdays, while the main central beach takes on a carnivalesque air on Saturday nights.

Several sites of interest stud the countryside around Sambava. About 17km (10 miles) north of town, where the RN5a crosses the wide brown waters of the Bemarivo (literally 'Big Shallow') River, the **Volamaitso**

Community Association runs three-hour river trips in a traditional wooden boat, as well as offering tours of a local vanilla plantation. The **Parc Privé de Ranoala** (tel: 032-8160036), 7km (4 miles) south of town, is a small forest-fringed nursery that grows several species of medicinal and other indigenous plants as well as hosting a few introduced but free-ranging lemurs. Visits can also be arranged to the factory of the 50-sq-km (19-sq-mile) **Cocoteraie de la Soavoanio** (tel: 032-0514576; Mon–Fri 8.30am–noon), a vast seafront plantation that surrounds the town and produces more than 10 million coconuts annually.

Set alongside the RN5a about 35km (20 miles) south of Sambava, the **Domaine d'Ambohimanitra** (tel: 032-0741107) is a large vanilla plantation that also produces ylang-ylang, cinnamon, pepper and other spices and arranges fascinating half-day tours. The RN5a terminates 45km (26 miles) further south at **Antalaha** ㉒, a seaport of 40,000 that runs along the coast for several kilometres south of the twin mouth of the rivers Ankavanana and Ankavia. Economically dominated by the vanilla industry, Antalaha is also an important ancient centre of dhow production, and traditional shipbuilders can still be seen plying their craft at the shipyard at the south end of town. As you enter Antalaha from the north, the **Sentier Botanique Macolline** (tel: 032-0716101; https://macolline.org), though still recovering from cyclone damage inflicted in March 2017, protects a small wooded hill on the south bank of the Ankavanana River, and is run through by variety of walking trails highlighting its botanical variety and small wildlife such as chameleons and birds.

MAROJEJY AND THE SAVA INTERIOR

Sava's most compelling wildlife attraction, situated inland of Sambava, is the 605-sq-km (234-sq-mile) **Parc National de Marojejy** ㉑ (tel: 020-8807027; www.marojejy.com; daily 7am–4pm), which was set aside as a strict nature reserve in 1952, redesignated a national park in 1998, and inscribed as part of the Rainforests of the Atsinanana Unesco World Heritage Site in 2007. The park protects the rugged slopes of the Marojejy Massif, which rises from a base of 75 metres (245ft) to a maximum elevation of 2,132 metres (6,995ft), and incorporates a diversity of forested habitats and microclimates. As such, it incorporates a quite astonishing floral diversity, including more than 275 fern and 35 palm species, many of which are endemic to the massif.

Marojejy is equally impressive on the faunal front. The checklist of 118 bird species includes 75 forest-associated species endemic to Madagascar (more than any other protected area), notably the stunning and very localised helmet vanga, while the 147 reptile and amphibian species include 18 known only from this one national park. Its mid to upper slopes are also the main stronghold for

○ **Tip**

Marojejy is a genuine wilderness destination suited to well-equipped and reasonably fit travellers. Comfortable hiking shoes and waterproof clothing are essential, as are sealable bags for storing clothes in your backpack. Mattresses and bedding are supplied at the three camps described opposite, and potable water is available throughout, but you will need to bring all your own food. Mandatory guides and optional porters are available at Manantenina. The best times to hike are the relatively dry months of April and May or September to December.

Washing the day's catch in Antalaha.

Helmet vanga.

The Marojejy Massif hosts an impressive variety of fauna.

the critically endangered silky sifaka, a striking all-white lemur listed among the world's 25 Most Endangered Primates, with a global population estimated at fewer than 1,000. Eleven other primate species occur in the park, among them the diurnal indri, eastern fork-marked lemur, white-fronted brown lemur, red-bellied lemur and eastern lesser bamboo lemur.

Tickets and guides for Marojejy can be arranged at the main visitor centre, which stands in the village of **Manantenina**, 65km (38 miles) southwest of Sambava along the surfaced Andapa Road. It is possible to explore the lowland forest on a day visit using on the Mantella Trail (four hours in either direction), which leads to Mantella Camp, near the base of the Cascade de Humbert, and offers a good chance of spotting the helmet vanga (they often nest in epiphytic ferns). Far better, especially if you want to stand a real chance of seeing silky sifaka and other highland forest species, would be to arrange a multiple-night trek taking in Mantella Camp (elevation 450 metres/

1,475ft), Marojejia Camp (elevation 775 metres/2,540ft) and Simpona Camp (elevation 1,250 metres/4,100ft), all of which offer accommodation in simple but well-maintained cabins.

The main town of the Sava interior is **Andapa ㉒**, which supports a population of around 30,000 at a relatively bracing altitude of 530 metres (1,730ft) about 105km (65 miles) southwest of Sambava along the same surfaced road that runs past Marojejy. On the outskirts of town, the **Parc Privé de Beradaka** (tel: 034-2583694), as its name – literally 'Big Frogs' – suggests, is home to a few dozen species of colourful frog, all free-ranging and best seen with a guide. Also worth a visit is the **Cascade d'Andapa Sud**, an impressive twin waterfall that erupts over a rock face about 2km (1.2 miles) from town and is held sacred by locals.

Andapa houses the office for the wild and little visited **Réserve Spéciale d'Anjanaharibe Sud ㉓** (http://anjana haribe.marojejy.com), which extends over 172 sq km (66 sq miles) and rises to an altitude of 2,064 metres (6,771ft) at Anjanaharibe-Anivo Peak. Anjanaharibe protects a similar montane forest habitat to Marojejy, and is also home to the critically endangered silky sifaka, as well as the northernmost (and only all-black) population of indri. Although Anjanaharibe is less well-developed for overnight hikes than Marojejy, the trails do start at a higher altitude, which means you stand a far better chance of seeing silky sifaka and indri on a day visit. The 4.3km- (2.5-mile) **Ranamofana Trail**, though fairly strenuous, is most likely to yield lemur sightings, but the shorter Takhtajania Trail – named after one the oldest flowering plants on earth, a large-leafed red-blooming shrub only known from Anjanaharibe – also comes with a chance. The entrance to the reserve is at Andasibe-Mahaverika, which lies 20km (12 miles) from Andapa on a 4x4-only road.

Leaf-tailed gecko, Parc National de Marojejy.

GIVE
MEANING
TO
TRAVEL

Contact : 01 42 66 00 00
www.airmadagascar.com 🐦 f

Air Madagascar

MADAGASCAR

TRAVEL TIPS

TRANSPORT

GETTING THERE

By air

Antananarivo's Ivato International Airport (TNR), which stands in the eponymous suburb about 15km (9 miles) north of the city centre, is the most useful port of entry to people planning extended travels around Madagascar, as it lies in the heart of the country and is the main domestic flight hub (the capital is also an important centre for domestic tour operators and terrestrial public transport). A good selection of international flights also services Fascene Airport (NOS) on the island of Nosy Be, but these cater mainly to people on package holidays to this popular beach destination. There is also a very limited international flight service to Sainte-Marie Airport (SMS) on the offshore resort of Île Sainte-Marie. Airport taxes are almost invariably included in ticket fares.

The national carrier Air Madagascar (tel: 020-2222222; www.air madagascar.com) operates flights connecting Antananarivo to Paris, Marseille, Guangzhou and various other Indian Ocean Islands. Despite

Pirogue on the Canal des Pangalanes.

its unenviable reputation for cancellations and delays (admittedly more on domestic than international flights), Air Madagascar is still worth considering, mainly because it offers its international passengers significant discounts on its overpriced domestic flights.

Other key international carriers that service Antananarivo are Air France (tel: 020-2323023; www.airfrance.com), Air Austral (tel: 020-2230331; www.air-austral.com), Air Mauritius (tel: 020-2623636; www.air mauritius.com) and Kenya Airways (tel: 020-2623636; www.kenya-airways.com). The South African Airways' subsidiary Airlink (tel: 020-2235990; www.flysaa.com or www.flyairlink.com) flies directly between Johannesburg and both Antananarivo and Nosy Be.

An exciting new development as of March 2017 is that Ethiopian Airlines (tel: 020-2230734; www.ethiopian airlines.com), Africa's oldest and best-connected airline, started operating competitively-priced four-times-weekly flights to Antananarivo, connecting to most major world cities in Europe, Africa and Asia, as well as to Los Angeles, Newark, Washington DC and Toronto, via its international flight hub in Addis Ababa.

From the UK

There are no direct flights between the UK and Madagascar. The closest thing to one is the thrice-weekly flight with Air France or Air Madagascar via Paris. Flights with Ethiopian Airlines and Air Kenya tend to be a lot cheaper, also entail just one stopover (in Addis Ababa and Nairobi respectively), and don't deviate far from the most direct flight path. A more circuitous option is South African Airways/Airlink via Johannesburg.

From Europe

Coming from Paris, there are direct flights with Air France and Air Madagascar. From other destinations in Europe, the options are much the same as from the UK. Seasonal charter flights connect Milan and Rome directly to Nosy Be.

From North America

The most direct route geographically is with Ethiopian Airlines from Los Angeles, Newark, Washington DC or Toronto visa Addis Ababa. Also worth considering are Air France via Paris, or South African Airways/Airlink via Johannesburg.

From Africa

Ethiopian Airlines, Kenya Airways and South African Airways/Airlink are all good options with an extensive range of connecting flights.

From the Indian Ocean islands

Air Mauritius, Réunion-based Austral Air and Air Madagascar all operate an extensive network of hops between the various Indian Ocean islands.

From Australia and Asia

The most established options are South African Airways/Airlink or Air Mauritius, but Ethiopian Airlines or Kenya Airways might well work out cheaper.

By sea

Several cruise ships operate itineraries connecting Madagascar and other Indian Ocean island to each other and/or Dubai, Durban or Cape Town. Mostly these only involve one or two short stops on Madagascar so are not ideal for those wanting to explore the country in any depth. Operators include Costa Cruise Lines (www.costa cruise.com), Oceania Cruises (www. oceaniacruises.com) and Crystal Cruises (www.crystalcruises.com).

By road/coach/bus

Since Madagascar is an island, it is not connected to any other country by road.

Bush taxi on the road from Antsiranana to Ankify.

GETTING AROUND

Madagascar is a challenging destination to get around. The road network is limited, distances are long, and many trunk routes one might reasonably expect to comprise smooth multi-lane asphalt ribbons are narrow, winding and either heavily potholed or totally unsurfaced. Public transport is also limited and what does exist tends to be cramped, slow and tough going even by African standards. Domestic flights are very expensive and prone to last-minute delays, schedule changes and cancelations. So while hardy backpackers with plenty of time on their hands might find themselves in their element in Madagascar, visitors with time restrictions or a low tolerance for discomfort almost invariably smooth the way ahead by making all ground arrangements with an operator who will not only provide private road transport (usually in a 4x4 with a local driver-guide) but also book and/or arrange all accommodation, meals, flights and activities as required.

To and from the airport

Although Ivato International Airport lies only 15km (9 miles) from central Antananarivo, the narrow road tends to be congested at all times, and the drive can easily take up to 90 minutes in rush hour (for which reason, visitors overnighting in the capital between flights are advised to seek a hotel close to the airport). There is no longer a general shuttle bus service between the airport and the city centre, but most hotels can arrange for you to be met at the airport, and many tour operators would do so automatically as part of the package provided. Alternatively, taxis are freely available at fixed rates, and cost around US$10–20, depending on how far away your hotel is. Another option would be to exit the airport on foot and pick up a *taxi-brousse* to your hotel, but this is recommended only to experienced backpackers who speak some French and have some local currency to hand.

By air

The best way to cover longer distances in Madagascar is to fly. The more established of the two domestic carriers is the state-owned national carrier Air Madagascar (tel: 020-2222222; www.airmadagascar. com), which operates regular scheduled flights between its hub at Antananarivo's Ivato International Airport and the following locations: Morondava (MOQ), Toliara (TLE), Fort Dauphin (FTU), Toamasina (TMM), Île Sainte-Marie (SMS), Maroantsetra (WMN), Mahajanga (MJN), Nosy Be (NOS), Diego Suarez (DIE) and Sambava (SVB). These flights are surprisingly pricey (most one-way legs cost in excess of US$250, even when one allows for the discount of around 30 percent offered to anyone who flew into the country with Air Madagascar. In addition, schedule changes and unexpected delays are so commonplace that locals have come to refer to the carrier as Air Maybe. For this reason, where possible, most operators now prefer to book with Air Madagasikara (tel: 032-0597007; www.madagasikara airways.com), a significantly cheaper and more reliable private airline that started up in 2015 and operates a fast-expanding network of flights connecting Ivato International Airport to most of the towns and islands serviced by Air Madagascar. Either way, the unpredictability of domestic flights and the airlines' penchant for delays makes it inadvisable to plan on taking two domestic flights in the same day, or to leave too tight a gap between any domestic flight and an international departure.

By boat

The opportunities to get around Madagascar by boat are limited. A popular option with adventurous travellers are river trips on the Tsiribihina or Manambolo, both of which run downstream to the west coast north of Morondava and can be arranged through the Remote River Expeditions (tel: 020-9552347; www.remoterivers.com). A more sedate option are boat trips along the Pangalanes Canal, which are normally arranged in conjunction with a local hotel such as Orania Lodge or Hôtel Palmarium. In the northwest, many travellers cross from the mainland port of Ankify

to Nosy Be by boat, a 30–45 minute trip that can be arranged on the spot. In the northeast, several motorboats ply back and forth daily between Soanierana Ivongo and Île Sainte-Marie, a 90-minutes' trip best booked ahead with the *Gasikara* (tel: 020-5398749; www.sainte-marie-tours.com) or *El Condor* (034-7043301; www.bluemarine-madagascar.com).

By rail

The only railway of interest to tourists is the colonial-era 163km (102-mile) narrow-gauge Fianarantsoa-Côte Est (FCE) line between Fianarantsoa and Manakara in the southeast. Navigating more than 100 tunnels and bridges in either direction, trains leave Fianarantsoa at 7am on Tuesday and Saturday, and Manakara at 7am on Wednesday and Sunday. For more details see page 156.

By road

Madagascar has a very limited network of surfaced road and almost all of these are single carriageway with some potholed stretches. The main surfaced roads are the RN7 southwest from Antananarivo to Toliara via Antsirabe and Fianarantsoa, the RN25/12 southeast from Fianarantsoa to Manakara via the Parc National de Ranomafana, the RN34 west from Antsirabe to Morondava, the RN2/5 northeast from

Antananarivo to Soanierana Ivongo via the Parc National Andasibe-Mantadia and Toamasina, the RN4 northwest from Antananarivo to Mahajanga via Ambondromamy, and the RN6 north from Ambondromamy to Diego Suarez via Ambanja. These roads are variable in condition, and often require some caution due to sharp bends and/or potholes, but can typically be covered at an average rate of around 50km (30 miles) per hour. Most other roads in Madagascar are unsurfaced and may be very slow-going or totally impassable during the rainy season.

Most rental companies only offer chauffeured cars, partly due to insurance regulations, and the more normal option is to arrange a car and driver as part of a package through a local tour operator. Most operators forbid their drivers from travelling after dark. The poor condition of the roads and assertive (read: reckless) local driving style mean that self-drive car rental is not very realistic in Madagascar. However, if you do arrange a self-drive vehicle, you will need an International driving license, and must be at least 23 years of age. Be aware that filling stations are few and far between, and may sometimes be dry, so keep filling up as you pass through towns. Expect to be stopped regularly at police roadblocks and to be asked for a bribe if you are speeding, cannot produce your license,

are not wearing or seatbelt, or the officer just feels like chancing it. Try to avoid covering more than around 300km (180 miles) in any given day. Be alert to the risk of dopy or drunk pedestrians, or livestock (in particular zebu cattle) sauntering unexpectedly across the road.

By coach, bus and taxi-brousse

Coach would be a misleadingly fancy term applied to even the least clapped out of the buses that service a handful of major routes in Madagascar. A more common form of public transport is the *taxi-brousse* (bush taxi), a generic term that embraces pretty much any passenger-carrying vehicle that isn't a bus and has four (or more) wheels and an engine. The most normal type of *taxi-brousse* is a 12–16 seater minibus, but some vehicles are larger, while more remote routes might be serviced by 4x4s and some good roads are covered by relatively nippy Peugeot 504/5s. *Taxis-brousses* are suited only to adventurous and flexible travellers who are not in a rush and prepared to put up with cramped and sweaty conditions. On most routes, there are no fixed departure times, vehicles only leave when they are full, and they then stop regularly to pick up and drop passengers, so travel times tend to be very slow. Breakdowns are commonplace, as are accidents, and it is highly inadvisable to travel at night. Fares are fixed and very inexpensive, but tourists are sometimes overcharged by touts or asked to pay extra for their luggage.

By taxi and other local transport

Taxis are easily located in Antananarivo and other large cities. Elsewhere, the best option for short hops is the ubiquitous *tuk-tuks* (motorised rickshaws) and *pousse-pousses* (bicycle rickshaws) that throng the streets of most larger towns, or the zebu-drawn carts that take their place in some villages. Fares are negotiable but very cheap. Motorcycles, scooters, quad bikes and bicycles can be hired inexpensively by the day or half-day in Nosy Be and a few other resort areas. These are intended to be used as local transport, for instance between your hotel and the beach or supermarket.

Getting from Morondava to Belo-sur-Mer takes 4 to 5 hours for only 96km (60 miles).

A

Accommodation

There is no shortage of accommodation in Madagascar. Truly upmarket five-star operations are admittedly thin on the ground, though there are a few isolated boutique beach and bush resorts that compare with the finest East and Southern Africa has to offer, and are also equally over-the-top on the price front. These few luxurious anomalies aside, the trend at the upper end of the market is towards medium-small non-chain lodges, hotels and beach resorts, many of which are owner-managed, or have the informal hands-on feel of somewhere that might be. Decent accommodation of this sort can be found at pretty much all major beach resorts and large towns, as well as along the borders of the more popular national parks and protected areas. Typically, a tourist-class establishment that might nudge into the three-star category internationally would charge around €100 for a double room (usually on a bed-and-breakfast basis) while more homely and low-key tourist hotels will charge around half that price, excluding breakfast. For those on a tighter budget, most towns offer the option of several pensions, guesthouses and borderline-homestays aimed mainly at backpackers and/or the local market, and rates tend to be very reasonable, typically starting at around €10.

Most tourists visit on organised tours and all accommodation is booked by the operator. For independent travellers, you can either make an email reservation directly with the hotel, bearing in mind that many receptionists are less responsive than one might hope for, or through online sites such as www.airbnb.com and www.booking.com.

Admission charges

Practically all formal tourist attractions charge an admission fee, and this almost invariably quoted and payable in the local currency (ariary). Typically, museums, cultural attractions and minor reserves charge the equivalent of €3–10 per person. National parks and other properties under Madagascar National Parks (MNP; www.parcs-madagascar.com) charge daily entrance fees equivalent to €15–20 per person, depending on the category of the individual protected area. All MNP properties and many private reserves also charge a mandatory guide fee. This varies significantly from one place to the next, and for walks of various durations, but typically it will work out at €10–30 per party per excursion. Substantial discounts are usually offered to children and to Malagasy citizens.

B

Budgeting for your trip

Most visitors to Madagascar are on pre-booked trips that include transport, accommodation, guides and some or all meals and activities, in which case the only ad hoc expenses are likely to be tips, drinks, souvenirs and the occasional meal. For independent travellers, Madagascar can be very cheap or extremely expensive, depending, among other things, on whether you get around by *taxi-brousse* (nominal fares) or air (most legs are around €250 one-way), eat at local or tourist-oriented restaurants, and sleep in local guesthouses or bona fide tourist hotels, as well as how much you opt to spend on organised activities such

as day walks in national parks, diving or snorkelling and the like.

Within Madagascar, most prices are quoted in the local currency, the ariary. However, this is prone to ongoing devaluation against harder currencies, a trend reflected in the corresponding inflation of most local goods in line with the Euro (as opposed to the US dollar or pound sterling)

Sample costs

A local beer: From under €1 per 500ml bottle in a supermarket to around €2–3 in a posh restaurant or hotel

A glass of house wine: €2–4

A main course at a budget/moderate/expensive restaurant: €2–4/€5–8/€10–15

A room in a cheap/moderate/deluxe hotel: €10–25/€30–60/€80–200

A taxi journey to and from the main airport for the destination: €10–20

C

Children

The Malagasy people generally adore children and most hotels will gladly accommodate them. Children are also offered discounts on admission fees to most places of interest. That said, away from Nosy Be and a handful of other dedicated beach resorts, the challenges of travel in Madagascar (and the unpackaged nature of its main attractions) are likely to be even more daunting with young or easily bored children in tow. Very few hotels offer formal babysitting services.

Climate

Madagascar experiences wide regional variations in climate, with

the temperate highlands of the interior generally being significantly cooler and less humid than the coast. Rainfall in highest in the east and lowest in the southwest, which means that seasonal considerations are more of a factor when visiting the east coast than the far southwest. The selected climate charts will give you a good idea of seasonal weather conditions by region, but for most visitors, the broad advice outlined below will apply countrywide.

Summer (December to March)

The weather is hot and humid countrywide, with high rainfall in most regions, but particularly the east coast, which is also frequently hit by cyclones at this time of year. The high rainfall makes it the least attractive time of year to travel in Madagascar, as many national parks become inaccessible, wildlife is difficult to locate in the dense foliage, and some lodges close for the season. On the plus side, the countryside tends to be very lush during the rainy season, and most hotels offer negotiable discounts.

Autumn/early winter (April to June)

The weather is hot and humid on the coast, with some rainfall, but cooler and drier upcountry. The countryside remains green in the aftermath of the rainy season, but most roads are passable and national parks accessible. Tourist arrival numbers are low in April but start building toward high season volumes over the course of late May into June. Overall this is an excellent time to visit Madagascar.

Midwinter (July and August)

The weather is similar to that from April to June, but drier and slightly cooler. Climatically there is no finer time to visit Madagascar, but it is also peak tourist season, since it coincides with summer school holidays in the northern hemisphere. As a result, hotels tend to charge inflated seasonal rates, and parks and other natural attractions can become unpleasantly busy with noisy tour parties and families. If peace and quiet are high on your priority list, and your travel isn't dictated by school holidays, it's best to avoid this time of year.

Late winter/spring (September to November)

The weather is similar to April to June, but tourist volumes are down

from midwinter. Overall this is also a great time of year to travel in all parts of Madagascar.

Special interests

Certain special interest groups might want to adjust their travel times around the season that offers the best conditions for their favoured pursuit. These include the following:

Birding: Most of the key birds are endemic residents that might be seen all year through. That said, ornithological tours tend to favour the late spring and early summer, when the more elusive species of the rainforest interior go into breeding mode and are thus more easily located by call. October and November are probably the optimum months, as the onset of the rains in December reduces visibility and mobility.

Frogs and reptiles: Many frogs and lizards hibernate or become inactive during the cool dry winter months. Frog activity peaks at the height of the rainy season, over January and February, when the night air of national parks such as Ranomafana and Andisibe-Mantadia resonates with their varied mating calls.

Hiking: The wettest and cusp seasonal months are to be avoided, while underfoot conditions are best from May to October.

Mammals: Lemur viewing isn't strongly seasonal but some smaller species hibernate and are more difficult to see in midwinter. Baby lemurs start to appear in November, adding greatly to the excitement of an encounter. October to November is when fossas go into breeding mode and tend to be most conspicuous.

Snorkelling and diving: Visibility tends to be best and water calmest

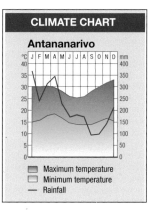

CLIMATE CHART

Antananarivo

- Maximum temperature
- Minimum temperature
- Rainfall

over August to October, when storms are few and far between, and there's less sediment is brought down by rivers.

Whale-watching: Best along the east coast during the northerly migration over July to September.

What to wear

Light summery clothes are the order of the day along the coast, but you'll need a sweater, jacket or sweatshirt for the evenings, as it often gets quite windy. Antananarivo and other highlands destinations can get unexpectedly chilly at night, so you will want long trousers and a few layers if warm clothing. Other essentials all-year-round are a good sunhat for the beach and other excursions, and decent rain gear (ideally a poncho and waterproof trousers) for rainforest walks. Open sandals or flip-flops are fine for beach destinations, but trainers are the minimum requirement for forest and other walks, and proper walking or hiking boots are preferable. Local dress codes are very informal but it is unacceptable for women to go topless on beaches, so bring a bikini.

Crime and safety

Violent crime against tourists remains a rarity in most parts of the country. The one major exception is Batterie Beach north of Toliara, which is specifically highlighted by the British Foreign and Commonwealth Office (FCO) as a place to be avoided at all costs following several violent attacks and fatalities. Parts of Antananarivo are also risky at night, and nocturnal road travel outside urban areas carries a high of bandit attacks. Elsewhere, snatch theft and pickpocketing are no more than a minor risk provided you take the usual commonsense precautions i.e. never wear ostentatious jewellery, or leave valuables lying around your hotel rooms, or walk alone on unlit alleys after dark.

Before you travel, log onto the websites run by the FCO (www.fco. gov.uk) and US state department (https://travel.state.gov) for the latest official advice and news about periodic unrest or outbreaks of disease. Make scans of all important documents, including your passport, visa, insurance documents and vaccination certificates, and carry them on

your laptop or smart phone, or email copies to a webmail address you can easily access during your trip. Also, leave a copy of everything at home, with someone you can contact if you get into difficulties.

On the road, the safest place for your passport, tickets and excess money is the hotel safe, or a well concealed money-belt. Malagasy law dictates that you carry your passport, or a certified copy thereof, on your person at all times. A certified passport copy can be obtained by taking the original and a photocopy to any police station.

Customs regulations

Visitors and residents are allowed the free import of 500 cigarettes or 25 cigars or 500 grams of tobacco, as well as 1 bottle of alcoholic beverage.

Visitors and residents can import up to 400,000 Malagasy ariary in local currency, and an unlimited amount of foreign currency, though any sum of money greater than €7,500 must be declared at customs.

Visitors and residents can export up to 400,000 Malagasy ariary in local currency and an unlimited amount of foreign cash, but a written declaration of all money exported must be made at customs.

Import of the following items is prohibited: illegal drugs, weapons, explosives and ammunition, knives and other deadly weapons, counterfeit money and goods, electronic equipment, pornographic materials, and plant, meat or other animal products.

D

Disabled travellers

Madagascar has few facilities for disabled travellers and travel conditions are generally not conducive to those with limited mobility. Most tour operators will do their best to smooth things for visitors with disabilities, but even then you may find that hotels advertising disabled rooms are guilty of overstating the case. Few storeyed hotels have lifts and bungalow accommodation is often accessed via narrow rocky paths or outside staircases.

E

Eating out

Restaurants can be found in the smallest of towns but most are quite simple establishments that serve a simple (but often very tasty) plat du jour – most likely, chicken or beef stew with rice – for a couple of euros to a predominantly Malagasy clientele. Almost all tourist hotels and a few restaurants in most larger towns and established resorts serve up a more sophisticated and varied menu of French-Malagasy grilled and stewed meat and fish dishes, along with pizzas, burgers and sandwiches, catering to western palates. Typically, mains at establishments of this sort cost up to €5. Only in Antananarivo will you find a good range of international restaurants, and although these tend to be dominated by French and to a lesser extent Italian cuisine, you will also find Indian, Chinese, Southeast Asian, Lebanese and other African cuisines represented. Mains tend to cost a bit more in Antananarivo but even her there is no need to pay a small fortune to eat well. Practically all restaurants in Madagascar are licensed (and if they aren't, someone will most likely be happy to pop out and bring you a beer from another place). Local beers and rum are inexpensive, but wine is a lot pricier and by-the-glass servings are often quite rough box wines.

Electricity

Standard voltage is 220 V and standard frequency is 50Hz. The most common power socket is the standard European plug with two round pins. Some hotels have other sockets, however, so it is worth carrying an adaptor set wherever you are coming from.

Embassies and consulates

Foreign representatives in Madagascar
Australia
represented by Australian High Commission
2nd Floor, Rogers House
5 President John Kennedy Street
Port Louis
Mauritius
Tel: +230-2020160
http://mauritius.embassy.gov.au

Canada
Ivandry Business Centre
Rue Velo Rainimangalahy,
Antananarivo
Tel: 020-2243256
http://www.canadainternational.gc.ca/southafrica-afriquedusud/contact-antananarivo-contactez.aspx
France
Rue Jean-Jaurès
Antananarivo
Tel: 020-2239850
https://mg.ambafrance.org
Ireland
c/o Embassy of Ireland
2nd Floor, Parkdev Building
Brooklyn Bridge Office Park
570 Fehrsen Street
Pretoria
South Africa
Tel: +27 (0)12 4521000
https://www.dfa.ie/embassies/irish-embassies-abroad/sub-saharan-africa/madagascar
South Africa
Rue Ravoninahitriniarivo
Antananarivo
Tel: 020-2243350
http://www.dirco.gov.za/madagascar
UK
Rue Ravoninahitriniarivo
Antananarivo 101
Tel: 020-2233053
www.gov.uk/world/organisations/british-embassy-antananarivo
USA
Lot 207 Andranoro-Antehiroka
Antananarivo
Tel: 020-2348000
https://mg.usembassy.gov

Malagasy embassies and consulates abroad
Australia
Level 9
47 York Street
Sydney, NSW 2000
Tel: +61 (0)2-92992290
Canada
03 Rue Raymond
Ottawa
Tel: +613-567 0505
http://madagascar-embassy.ca
France
4 Avenue Raphaël
Paris
Tel: +33 (0)1 45 04 62 11
www.ambassade-madagascar.com
South Africa
77 Newlands Ave
Cape Town
Tel: + 27 (0)21-6747238
www.madagascarconsulate.org.za
UK
c/o 4 Avenue Raphaël

Paris
Tel: +33 (0)1 45 04 62 11
www.ambassade-madagascar.com
USA
2374 Massachusetts Ave
Washington DC
Tel: +1 202-265 5525
www.madagascar-embassy.org

Emergencies

Police: 17 or 117 from a mobile phone.
Fire Brigade: 18 or 118 from a mobile phone.
Gendarmerie: 19 or 119 from a mobile phone.
Ambulance and medical: 17 (117 from mobile phone) or 020-2235753

Etiquette

The most important point of etiquette is to respect local *fady* (taboos), the most significant and universal of which not to point at things, but to indicate the required direction with your knuckle and index finger crooked backwards. Although Madagascar is predominantly Christian and traditional, it is conventional (as in Muslim and Hindu countries) to reserve the left hand for ablutions and the right hand for eating and passing things. Greetings are not significantly different to most Western countries: men and sometimes women usually shake hands upon greeting. If you are invited to visit Malagasy people at home, it is customary to bring a bottle of rum as a gift.

Festivals

Madagascar has a rather limited bouquet of festivals, but the following will be of interest to some visitors:
Zegny'Zo Arts Festival, Diego Suarez
Usually held over the third week of May, this street festival curated in collaboration with the Alliance Française celebrated its 10th anniversary in 2017. Attractions include dancing, puppetry, drama, street painting, music, circus acts and parades.
Donia Festival, Nosy Be
www.festival-donia.com
Held over Pentecost (May or June), this week-long festival offers a

great opportunity to see traditional and contemporary musicians from Madagascar and elsewhere in Africa and the Indian Ocean.
Carnaval de Madagascar, Antananarivo
Tel: 020-2227051
http://carnaval-madagascar.com
Held during the mid-June build up to the Fête de l'Indépendance, this three-day carnival hosts musical and other traditional artists from all over the Indian Ocean region.
Fête de l'Indépendance, countrywide
Independence Day (26 June) is still vigorously celebrated all over Madagascar six decades after the event. The biggest celebrations are in Antananarivo, where much of the city centre closes down for several days, but there's a party atmosphere, with live music and the like, in most large towns.
Madajazzcar, Antananarivo
Tel: 020-2266115
www.facebook.com/Madajazzcar-Festival-official-151933077358
Established in 1988 and still going strong more than 30 years later, this two-week festival is held in October and features a combination of home-grown jazz musicians and their counterparts from the US, Europe, Asia, mainland Africa and the nearby islands of Mauritius and Réunion.

Health and medical care

It is vital that your travel insurance policy is comprehensive and includes emergency evacuation and repatriation, as medical care in Madagascar does not conform to European and North American standards. Have a dental check-up before you go and get a spare pair of prescription glasses or contact lenses if you wear them. If you are on medication, make sure you carry enough to last you, plus a prescription and letter from your doctor.
Health advice In the UK, detailed health advice, tailored to individual needs, is available from Medical Advice for Travellers Abroad (MASTA; www.masta-travel-health.com. Traveller advice is also available on the NHS website www.fitfortravel.nhs.uk and the International Association for the Medical Assistance of Travellers

(IAMAT; www.iamat.org), which also provides members (membership is free) with health information and a list of approved doctors all over the world.
Inoculations Consult your doctor about inoculations at least two months before you leave. Yellow fever is not present in Madsgacar but a yellow fever inoculation may be required if you are travelling from or via an infected area. Diphtheria, polio and tetanus vaccinations are also a good idea. Boosters are required every 10 years after a trio of injections while young. Meningitis and typhoid inoculations are recommended, especially for longer stays.

A series of inoculations exists for hepatitis A and B. For hepatitis A, long-term protection (10 years) is available by an initial injection followed by a booster at 6–12 months. For short-term protection, an injection of gamma globulin will protect you immediately for up to six months, depending on dosage.

Rabies vaccinations are usually only given if you are likely to be in close contact with animals during your stay. A full course of three injections takes several weeks to administer.

First-aid kit
The following items should be in your first-aid kit: strong mosquito repellent; malaria prophylactics; sting-relief cream; antihistamine pills; plasters, antiseptic wipes and spray for blisters and cuts; syringes; Imodium for diarrhoea. Also, take your own condoms and tampons (if required).

Hygiene
Many areas in Madagascar are subject to occasional outbreaks of cholera and dysentery due to poor sanitation and hygiene. Be conscientious about washing your hands regularly with soap and water. Good hotels will ensure your water supply is safe. Elsewhere, use bottled, boiled or otherwise purified water for drinking and brushing your teeth. Avoid ice and take care with juices as their water sources may be suspect. You may also be better off avoiding uncooked vegetables, salads, unpeeled fruit or frozen products unless properly prepared. Wash all fresh food thoroughly in boiled or bottled water before you eat it.

Sun protection

The tropical sun is strong, so sunblock and a head covering – ideally a wide-brimmed hat – are mandatory for those coming from temperate climates. If your skin is fair, use sunscreen whenever you are going to be out in the sun. Even if you have dark skin, you are still at risk if out all day – particularly if you are going to be swimming or snorkelling. The water reflects the sun's rays, multiplying the effect, and the coolness of the water is deceptive.

Most first-time visitors experience a degree of heat exhaustion and dehydration that can be avoided by drinking lots of water and slightly increasing the amount of salt in the diet. Dehydration is more serious in children, so monitor their intake of liquids carefully.

Health risks

HIV/AIDS infection rates are low in Madagascar, at least by comparison to much of mainland Africa, but many other STDs are rife, so avoid high-risk activities such as unprotected sex.

Bilharzia Madagascar has one of the world's highest rates of bilharzia, a nasty disease transmitted by flukes that live in snails that like still well-vegetated freshwater habitats. Sea water is safe, as are swimming pools and fast-flowing streams or rivers, but all other inland freshwater bodies should be viewed as suspect. If in doubt, rub yourself dry thoroughly with a rough towel and ask for a test on returning home. There is a relatively straightforward treatment to this disease if it is caught in time.

Diarrhoea The best way to avoid tummy bugs is by being fastidious about drinking and brushing your teeth with purified or bottled water. Watch out for ice in drinks, and wash your hands with soap before you eat. If you are felled, the biggest risk is dehydration, which is most dangerous to children. Rehydration requires salt and sugar as well as liquid. Stop eating anything but dry toast or biscuits (preferably salty), but carry on drinking plenty of water and fruit juice. Coca Cola and ginger ale both help inject calories and settle the stomach, but avoid alcohol, coffee, tea and any dairy products other than yoghurt. Diarrhoea usually clears itself up within a few days. If there is no sign of improvement within 48 hours, however, it could be caused by a parasite or infection, so get to a doctor.

Malaria The most serious health risk to travellers in Madagascar, malaria is transmitted by the female anopheles mosquito, a nocturnal and crepuscular species that is usually most active at dusk and dawn. The risk of contraction is highest in the rainy season, when mosquitos are most active, and along the coast and other low-lying areas, but it could happen almost anywhere in Madagascar at any time. Seek advice about the most suitable medication for you and your family from your doctor or a tropical medicine institute at least two months before your departure.

The most common prophylactics are Larium (which can have unpleasant, and in rare cases dangerous, side effects); the antibiotic doxycycline (which can cause photosensitivity in some people); and Malarone (which has few side effects and is effective, but is unsuitable for children). None of these offers 100 percent protection, so try to avoid getting bitten in the first place. Cover up in the evening, make liberal use of insect repellent containing DEET, and sleep in screened room under a mosquito net, ideally one impregnated with permethrin.

Malaria usually manifests about 7–14 days after being bitten by an infected mosquito, but can be dormant for months. Initial symptoms of the most dangerous form are rather similar to those of common flu, for instance aching joints, headaches and a quickly rising temperature. If you start displaying these or other flu-like symptoms at any stage within six months of your return home, you should consult a doctor immediately – be sure to tell them where you have been travelling.

Automobile accidents Car crashes are a leading cause of injury among travellers to Madagascar, so walk and drive defensively, wear a seat belt and avoid travelling at night.

Bugs and beasties Madagascar has no snake or spiders that pose a significant health threat to humans (its few venomous snakes are all back-fanged biters, and could do damage only if you literally inserted a finger in their mouth). Some venomous scorpions and centipedes are present, and although their bites are more in the ballpark of unpleasant than life-threatening, you should avoid putting your hands on a rock or into a crevice without checking it first. Blood-sucking leeches are present in most forests, but although they can be a nuisance, they present no real health threat. Stick to wide clear paths when walking in the forest, tuck your trousers into your socks, and you should be fine. If a leech does take hold, don't fret. The bite is totally painless, thanks to the injection of an anaesthetic anticoagulant fluid, it isn't known to transmit disease, and if you aren't too squeamish, the leech will drop off of its own accord after 15 minutes or so.

Health care and hospitals

There are some good private clinics, hospitals and other medical practitioners in Antananarivo. Elsewhere, facilities are more basic and unreliable. In a real emergency, you might consider being flown to South Africa, which has world-class private medical facilities. The following are recommended:

Polyclinique Ilafy
RN3, 5km (3 miles) north of the city centre
Tel: 020-2242566 or 033-1107391
www.sodiatgroupe.mg/polyclinique-ilafy.php
This large 24-hour clinic is equipped with several ambulances and can handle most medical emergencies as well as everyday illnesses and dental issues.

Espace Médical Ambodivona
Tana Waterfront, RN3
Tel: 020-2262566 or 034-0200911
Email: esmed@moov.mg
Another good 24-hour clinic and hospital equipped to deal with medical emergencies.

Pharmacie Métropole
7 Rue Ratsimilaho Antaninarenina
Tel: 020-2267522 or 033-1520025
www.pharmacie-metropole.com
Well-stocked and central pharmacy open Mon–Sat 8.30am–12.30pm and 2–6.30pm

Pharmacie d'Isoraka
Avenue du Général Ramanantsoa
Tel: 020-2269412
www.facebook.com/pharmacieisoraka
Set in the old central suburb of Isoraka, this is open daily 8am–noon and 2–6pm.

I

Internet

Most hotels and many smarter restaurants and cafés in Antananarivo and other large towns and beach resorts offer free WiFi to clients. WiFi is less widely available in more remote areas such as lodges bordering national parks. Even where it is readily available, Internet tends to be very slow compared to most westernised countries, and dips in service are a regular occurrence. Internet cafés can be found in most larger towns, though they tend to be less common than a few years back due to the growth in smartphone usage. If you are likely to need regular Internet connectivity, your best bet is to buy a local SIM card and data bundle (both very inexpensive) with one of the three main mobile phone providers listed under the Telephone section, and insert it in your phone.

L

LGBTQ travellers

Madagascar is unusual in Africa insofar as same-sex sexual activity is legal, provided both parties are at least 21 years of age. However, societal discrimination against the LGBTQ community remains strong, and there are no laws prohibiting hate speech or discrimination of this sort. Same-sex marriage is not recognised and only married heterosexual couples are permitted to adopt children. Gay and lesbian travellers are unlikely to face any problems provided they avoid public displays of affection.

M

Media

There is no English-language press in Madagascar. Of the four main daily newspapers, the Madagascar Tribune (www.madagascar-tribune.com) is of greatest interest as the only one with exclusively French content, the others are all a mix of French and Malagasy. For international news, you're better off checking international news websites such as www.bbc.com online.

1000 ariary note.

The main radio broadcaster is the state-owned Radio Nationale Malagasy (RNM), which has a countrywide and dominates the airwaves in rural areas. A few private broadcasters operate in Antananarivo and other large towns. Coverage is entirely in Malagasy and French.

The main terrestrial television broadcaster Television Malagasy (TVM) tends towards the parochial and only operates in Malagasy and French. Most hotels also offer a bouquet of satellite channels either with the French-dominated Canal+ or predominantly Anglophone South African service DSTV.

Money

The local currency is the Malagasy ariary (MGA), which was also the local name for a silver dollar in pre-colonial times. It was introduced in 1961 at the equivalent of five Malagasy francs, and banknotes were denominated in both currencies until the franc was officially discontinued in 2005. Particularly in rural areas, many local people still think in franc rather than ariary terms, so if you are quoted a disproportionately high price for anything, odds are it is in francs and needs to be divided by five to get the ariary price. Bank notes are issued in denominations of MGA 100, 200, 500, 1,000, 5,000 and 10,000, which at the current exchange rate means that the largest note is equivalent to roughly €3, US$3 or £2.50!

The easiest way to access money is to draw local currency from ATMs using a credit or debit card. Visa and Mastercard are the most widely accepted cards and both can be used at ATMs attached to most major banks. The most reliable option appears to be the Banque Fampandrosoana ny Varotra-Société Générale (BFV-SG; look out for the prominent red signpost), but the Bank of Africa (BOA), Bank Negara Indonesia (BNI Madagascar) and Banque Malgache de l'Océan Indien (BMOI) are also more erratically reliable. Most ATMs limit withdrawals to MGA 300,000 or 400,000, but you can make several withdrawals in a row on one card. If you are relying primarily on cards as a source of funds, plan ahead, as ATM facilities are usually available only in larger towns. it's safer to carry some hard currency cash as a backup. The euro is the most widely recognised currency in Madagascar, but the US dollar, British pound and South African rand are also accepted by most banks and bureaux de change. Travellers' cheques are all but obsolete in Madagascar.

Tipping is a way of life in Madagascar. Most drivers, guides, porters and other locals who provide a service will expect a tip as a matter of course. A small note (up to MGA 500) should suffice in the case of a porter, but guides would expect a sum equivalent to 5–15 percent of the official park or guide fee, while up to €5 per day would be good for a driver. Tipping is not customary in small local eateries or bars, but you might want to leave any small change for the waiter or waitress. In more formal restaurants, a 5–10 percent tip is customary.

N

Nightlife

Madagascar doesn't exactly have a thumping nightlife but most towns

and tourist resorts are equipped with scattering of characterful little bars and bistros. In certain beach resorts, particularly on Nosy Be, prostitution is a conspicuous facet of many tourist-oriented bars. The minimum legal drinking age is 18.

Opening hours

Shops, museums and other such institutions typically open Monday to Friday from 8am or 9am to 5pm or 6pm, but many close for lunch for at least an hour between noon and 2pm. Many small shops stay open over the weekend but others close on Sunday. Banking hours are 8am–4pm. Banks and offices almost invariably close over weekends and on public holidays.

Postal services

The national postal service Paositra Malagasy (www.paositramalagasy.mg) has post offices in most large towns. International mail is slow and unreliable, so fine for postcards and other non-essential correspondence, but you are better off entrusting any items of important or value to a courier such as DHL (tel: 020-2242839 or 034-4217777; www.dhl.com/en/mg/country_profile.html).

Public holidays

Banks and government offices generally close on public holidays, as do some retail businesses. Where a public holiday falls over a weekend, the following Monday may be treated as a holiday. Fixed date public holidays are listed below. Variable-date holidays recognised countrywide are Easter Sunday and Monday, Ascension Thursday and Whit Sunday and Monday. The Islamic holidays Id al Fitr and Id al Adha are taken by Muslims only.

1 January: New Year's Day
8 March: Women's Day
29 March: Martyrs' Day
1 May: Labour Day
26 June: Independence Day
15 August: Assumption Day

1 November: All Saints' Day
25 December: Christmas Day

Religious services

The Malagasy Constitution provides for freedom of religion and religious tolerance is high. Catholicism, Protestantism and Islam are all widely practiced, as are traditional religions. Interested tourists will find that most towns have at least one Catholic, Anglican and/or Lutheran church that hold a service on Sunday mornings. The concept of atheism is rather unfamiliar to the Malagasy, but many people are pantheists who combine traditional and Christian beliefs.

Shopping

Madagascar offers some great opportunities for craft and souvenir shopping. Popular items with foodies include the world's finest vanilla, sold in clumps of dried beans that look like irregularly-shaped licorice sticks, and other homegrown products such as cloves, green or black pepper, and coffee. Wonderfully fragrant massage oils are made from the yellowish ylang-ylang flower and various other local products, and it's worth checking your home country's duty-free allowances to bring back a couple of bottles of local rum, which might be infused with anything from ginger or vanilla to lemons and oranges.

Local handicrafts are also popular with souvenir shoppers. These include scarves and other garments woven from traditionally-manufactured wild silk, patch-worked cloth squares known as *lamba*, and a wide variety of metalwork, basketry, woodcarving and zebu horn and leather goods. The country's finest craftsmen are probably the Zafimaniry woodworkers of Fianarantsoa, whose intricate work forms the only Madagascar inclusion on the Unesco Intangible Cultural Heritage List.

Most towns have small markets or boutique selling handicrafts, none so impressive or varied as the 100-stall-strong Marché Artisanal

de la Digue, which lies alongside the main road between Antananarivo and Ivato International Airport. In many cases, however, it is more supportive of local communities and craftsmen to buy their products – be it vanilla or woodwork – from individuals or local markets close to the source.

When purchasing wood products, ensure they are not made out of rare and endangered types of wood, such as rosewood (also known as palissandre), which is important traditionally but has been harvested at an ecologically destructive rate in recent years. The export of any product or by-product made from restricted indigenous flora or fauna is forbidden unless a suitable permit has been issued.

Tax

A Value-Added Tax (VAT) of 20 percent is levied on many items and services, but it is invariably incorporated into the asking price and thus hidden from the consumer. The same goes for duties on items such as alcoholic beverages and cigarettes.

Telephones

The international dialling code for Madagascar is +261. All local numbers contain 10 numerals. There are no area codes as such, but land lines start with '020' while mobile numbers start with '03'. In both case the leading zero is dropped when dialling from outside the country (so a local number 020-xxxxxxx is dialled as +261-20-xxxxxxx from abroad).

Madagascar has a good mobile network and it is well worth making the minor investment required to buy a local SIM card, airtime and a data bundle for internet browsing, downloading emails and using apps such as whatsapp, facebook and facetime. Three providers are available and all are very cheap by international standards. Orange Madagascar (www.orange.mg) is regarded to offer the best service within Antananarivo but the state-owned Telma (www.telma.mg) has a more extensive network in remote areas. Another option is Airtel (www.africa.airtel.com/madagascar). All three

have kiosks at the airport where you can set yourself up within a few minutes of landing.

International dialling codes out of Madagascar

Australia: +61
Canada: +1
Ireland: +353
New Zealand: +64
South Africa: +27
UK: +44
USA: +1

Time zone

Madagascar is in the Eastern Africa time zone (GMT/UST+3), which means it is three hours ahead of the UK in winter and two hours ahead in summer, and 7–9 hours ahead of the mainland USA. Because it lies so close to the tropics, the difference in the duration of summer and winter daylight is relatively minimal. But it is a lot further east than most of East Africa, which means the sun tends to rise/set rather early (daylight hours range from around 5am–5.45pm in December to 6.30am–5.20pm in June).

Toilets

Western-style flush toilets are the norm, but some bush camps might have squat or long-drop toilets. Public toilets are not readily available.

Tourist information

The official tourism body is the Office National du Tourisme de Madagascar (ONTM; tel: 020 2266115), which operates a very useful and informative website https://madagascar-tourisme.com/en. Also very useful to visitors is the website maintained by Madagascar National Parks (MNP; tel: 034-4941538; www.parcs-madagascar.com), which details more than 40 protected areas countrywide. Regional tourist offices are variable in their usefulness on-the-ground, but many operate good websites. These include the following:
Antananarivo: www.tourisme-antananarivo.com
Antsirabe: www.antsirabe-tourisme.com
Fianarantsoa: www.tourisme-fianara.com
Morondava: www.morondavatourisme.com
Fort Dauphin: www.fort-dauphin.org
Île Sainte-Marie: http://saintemarie-tourisme.mg

Mahajanga: www.majunga.org
Nosy Be: www.nosybe-tourisme.com
Diego Suarez: www.office-tourisme-diego-suarez.com

Tour operators

Most visitors to Madagascar on anything more ambitious than a straight beach holiday make all their arrangements through a local or specialist international tour operator. The following companies all contributed significantly to the research of this guidebook and can be unreservedly recommended:
Insight Guides
Insight Guides offers ready-made and customisable trips to all the best locations in Madagascar, all devised by our local experts. Browse our exciting selection on www.insight-guides.com/tour/Madagascar.
Malagasy Tours
Tel: 020-2235607
www.malagasy-tours.com
Under the same committed French-Malagasy ownership since it started up in 1994, this pioneering and hands-on operator offers a diverse range of package and bespoke itineraries and exceptional standards of guiding. It is particularly worth contacting for special interests such as birding, lemurs, orchids, river-rafting or family-friendly destinations, or hiking in the remote Makay and Andringitra massifs.
Mora Travel
Tel. 020-2202012 or 085-8772236
www.moratravel.com
Madagascar's first Travelife-certified operator on account of its commitment to sustainable tourism, this highly responsive and on-the ball Dutch-owned set-up was founded in 2000 and specialises in bespoke packages with an emphasis on allowing visitors to experience the island's wildlife and cultures with the participation of local guides and community organisations.
Rainbow Tours
Tel: +44 (0)20 7666 1250
www.rainbowtours.co.uk
The UK's leading operator to Madagascar has a team headed up by destination-expert and prolific writer Derek Schuurman, a committed conservation campaigner who has been visiting the island regularly, and operating trips there, since the early 1990s.
Za Tours
Tel: 020-2242286
www.zatours-madagascar.com

Established in 1997, this well-organised all-rounder offers a variety of wildlife and beach itineraries aimed at both the generalist and special interest visitors. Knowledgeable guides lead a selection of cultural excursion ranging from Urban Hipster outings in Antananarivo to ethnological tours exploring the different funereal and other traditions of the island's ethnic groups.

Visas and passports

All visitors must be in possession of a passport valid for at least six months after their intended departure date and with at least one page empty. Visas are required by all visitors. Single-entry tourist visas valid for up to 90 days can be bought without fuss at the two main international airports and cost the MGA equivalent of around €20/30/40 for 30/60/90 days. Multiple-entry and business or other non-tourist visas must be arranged in advance through a Madagascar embassy or consulate.

Weights and measures

Madagascar uses metric measurements.

Women travellers

Single female travellers generally have a positive experience in Madagascar and they face few risks specific to their gender. That said, as would be the case almost anywhere in the world, they can expect to attract the interest of single men, but perhaps slightly more so due to the image of promiscuity associated with films and other western media. It will help deflect attention to dress modestly, to wear a wedding ring, and to tell anybody who cares to ask that you are married and have a husband waiting somewhere. On public transport, try so sit next to another woman. It is unusual for mild flirtation or curiosity to escalate into something more threatening or persistent but in the unlikely event it does, try to enlist the support of a local woman or older man.

LANGUAGE

The official languages of Madagascar are French and Malagasy. English is also quite widely spoken by guides, hotel receptionists, restaurant staff and other working within the tourist industry, but not by the average Malagasy. French is sufficient to get around in towns and other places that regularly receive tourists, but in more rural areas it may be useful – and will win you plenty of friends – to know a few words of Malagasy.

USEFUL WORDS AND PHRASES

How much is it? C'est combien?
What is your name? Comment vous appelez-vous?
My name is... Je m'appelle...
Do you speak English? Parlez-vous anglais?
I am English/American Je suis anglais(e)/américain(e)
I don't understand Je ne comprends pas
Please speak more slowly Parlez plus lentement, s'il vous plaît
Can you help me? Pouvez-vous m'aider?
I'm looking for... Je cherche...
Where is...? Où est...?
I'm sorry Excusez-moi/Pardon
I don't know Je ne sais pas
No problem Pas de problème
Have a good day! Bonne journée!
That's it C'est ça
Here it is Voici
There it is Voilà
Let's go On y va/Allons-y
See you tomorrow A demain
See you soon A bientôt
Show me the word in the book Montrez-moi le mot dans le livre
At what time? A quelle heure?
When? Quand?
What time is it? Quelle heure est-il?
yes oui
no non
please s'il vous plaît

thank you merci
(very much) (beaucoup)
you're welcome de rien
excuse me excusez-moi
hello bonjour
hi/bye salut
OK d'accord
goodbye au revoir
good evening bonsoir
here ici
there là
left gauche
right droite
straight on tout droit
far loin
near près d'ici
opposite en face
beside à côté de
over there là-bas
today aujourd'hui
yesterday hier
tomorrow demain
now maintenant
later plus tard
right away tout de suite
this morning ce matin
this afternoon cet après-midi
this evening ce soir

On arrival

I want to get off at... Je voudrais descendre à...
What street is this? Sur quelle rue sommes-nous?
How far is...? A quelle distance se trouve...?
airport l'aéroport
railway station la gare
bus station la gare routière
bus l'autobus, le car
bus stop l'arrêt
platform le quai
ticket le billet
return ticket aller-retour
toilets les toilettes
This is the hotel address C'est l'adresse de l'hôtel
I'd like a (single/double) room... Je voudrais une chambre (pour une/deux personnes)...

...with shower avec douche
...with bath avec salle de bain
Is breakfast included? Le prix comprend-il le petit-déjeuner?
May I see the room? Puis-je voir la chambre?
washbasin le lavabo
bed le lit
key la clé
elevator l'ascenseur
air-conditioned climatisé

Emergencies

Help! Au secours!
Stop! Arrêtez!
Call a doctor Appelez un médecin
Call an ambulance Appelez une ambulance
Call the police Appelez la police
Call the fire brigade Appelez les pompiers
Where is the nearest telephone? Où est le téléphone le plus proche?
Where is the nearest hospital? Où est l'hôpital le plus proche?
I am sick Je suis malade
I have lost my passport/purse J'ai perdu mon passeport/porte-monnaie

Shopping

Where is the nearest bank (post office)? Où se trouve la banque (Poste) la plus proche?
I'd like to buy Je voudrais acheter
How much is it? C'est combien?
Do you take credit cards? Est-ce que vous acceptez les cartes de crédit?
I'm just looking Je regarde seulement
Have you got? Avez-vous...?
I'll take it Je le prends
I'll take this one/that one Je prends celui-ci/celui-là
What size is it? C'est quelle taille ?
Anything else? Avec ceci?
size (clothes) la taille
size (shoes) la pointure
cheap bon marché

expensive cher
enough assez
too much trop
a piece of un morceau de
each la pièce (eg ananas, €2 la pièce)
receipt le reçu
chemist la pharmacie
bakery la boulangerie
bookshop la librairie
library la bibliothèque
delicatessen la charcuterie/ le traiteur
fishmonger la poissonnerie
grocery l'alimentation/l'épicerie
tobacconist le tabac (also sells stamps and newspapers)
market le marché
supermarket le supermarché
junk shop la brocante

Sightseeing

town la ville
old town la vieille ville
street la rue
square la place
cathedral la cathédrale
church l'église
keep le donjon
mansion l'hôtel
hospital l'hôpital
town hall l'hôtel de ville/la mairie
nave la nef
stained glass le vitrail
staircase l'escalier
tower la tour (La Tour Eiffel)
walk le tour
museum le musée
art gallery la galerie
exhibition l'exposition
tourist information office l'office du tourisme/le syndicat d'initiative
free gratuit
open ouvert
closed fermé
every day tous les jours
all year toute l'année
all day toute la journée
swimming pool la piscine
to book réserver
town map le plan
road map la carte

Dining out

Prix fixe is a fixed-price menu. A la carte means differently priced dishes chosen from the menu.
breakfast le petit-déjeuner
lunch le déjeuner
dinner le dîner
meal le repas
first course l'entrée/les hors d'œuvre

main course le plat principal
made to order sur commande
drink included boisson comprise
wine list la carte des vins
the bill l'addition
fork la fourchette
knife le couteau
spoon la cuillère
plate l'assiette
glass le verre
napkin la serviette
ashtray le cendrier
I am a vegetarian Je suis végétarien(ne)
I am on a diet Je suis au régime
What do you recommend? Qu'est-ce que vous recommandez?
Do you have local specialities? Avez-vous des spécialités locales?
I'd like to order Je voudrais commander
That is not what I ordered Ce n'est pas ce que j'ai commandé
Is service included? Est-ce que le service est compris?
May I have more wine? Encore du vin, s'il vous plaît
Enjoy your meal Bon appétit!

In the café

les boissons drinks
café coffee
...au lait or crème ...with milk or cream
...déca/décaféiné ...decaffeinated
...espresso/noir ...black espresso
...filtre ...filtered coffee
thé tea
tisane herb infusion
chocolat chaud hot chocolate
lait milk
eau minérale mineral water
gazeux fizzy
non-gazeux non-fizzy
limonade fizzy lemonade
citron pressé fresh lemon juice served with sugar
orange pressée fresh squeezed orange juice
entier full (eg full cream milk)
frais, fraîche fresh or cold
bière beer
...en bouteille ...bottled
...à la pression ...on tap
apéritif pre-dinner drink
kir white wine with cassis, blackcurrant liqueur
kir royale kir with champagne
avec des glaçons with ice
sec neat
rouge red
blanc white
rosé rosé
brut dry

doux sweet
crémant sparkling wine
vin de maison house wine
vin de pays local wine
carafe/pichet pitcher
...d'eau/de vin ...of water/wine
demi-carafe half-litre
quart quarter-litre
panaché shandy
digestif after-dinner drink
Where is this wine from? De quelle région vient ce vin?
cheers! santé!
hangover gueule de bois

Days of the week

Days of the week, seasons and months are not capitalised in French.
Monday lundi
Tuesday mardi
Wednesday mercredi
Thursday jeudi
Friday vendredi
Saturday samedi
Sunday dimanche
Seasons
spring le printemps
summer l'été
autumn l'automne
winter l'hiver
Months
January janvier
February février
March mars
April avril
May mai
June juin
July juillet
August août
September septembre
October octobre
November novembre
December décembre
Saying the date
20 October 2016 le vingt octobre, deux mille seize
Numbers
0 zéro
1 un, une
2 deux
3 trois
4 quatre
5 cinq
6 six
7 sept
8 huit
9 neuf
10 dix
11 onze
12 douze
13 treize
14 quatorze
15 quinze

16 seize
17 dix-sept
18 dix-huit
19 dix-neuf
20 vingt
21 vingt-et-un
30 trente
40 quarante
50 cinquante
60 soixante
70 soixante-dix
80 quatre-vingts
90 quatre-vingt-dix
100 cent
200 deux cents
500 cinq cents
1000 mille
1,000,000 un million
Note that the number 1 is often written like an upside down V, and the number 7 is always crossed.

SOME MALAGASY WORDS AND PHRASES

Hello *Manao ohoana (or Salama)*
Goodbye *Veloma*
How are you? *Manao ohoana ianao?*
Fine (and you?) *Tsara (ary ianao?)*
Please/Excuse me *Asafady*
Thank you *Misaotra*
Help *Vonjeo*

Do you speak English/French? *Miteny Anglisy/Frantsay ve ianao*
I can't speak French/Malagasy *Tsy mahay miteny Frantsay/Gasy aho*
Yes *Eny*
No *Tsia*
What is your name? *Iza no anaranao*
My name is... *Ny anarako dia...*
Where are you from? *Avy aiza ianao...*
I am from... *Avy any... aho*
Do you have...? *Misy ... ve?*
Menu *Sakafo*
Where is the toilet? *Aiza ny trano fidiovana?*
(Drinking) water *Rano (fisotro)*
Tea *Dite*
Coffee *Kafe*
Salt *sira*
Sugar *siramamy*
Pepper *poavra*
Cold *hatsiaka*
Hot *mafana*
Good *tsara*
Bad *ratsy*
Spicy *masiaka*
How much does it cost? *Ohatrinona ny vidin'ity?*
Where is...? *Aiza no misy?*
Hospital *hopitaly*
Market *tsena*
Shop *fivarotana*
Bank *banky*

Hotel/restaurant *hotely*
Black *mainty*
Blue *manga*
Brown *volon-tany*
Green *maintso*
Red *mena*
White *fotsy*
Yellow *mavo*
0 *aotra*
1 *iray, iraika*
2 *roa*
3 *telo*
4 *efatra*
5 *dimy*
6 *enina*
7 *fito*
8 *valo*
9 *sivy*
10 *folo*
11 *iraika ambin'ny folo*
12 *roa ambin'ny folo*
20 *roapolo*
30 *telopolo*
40 *efapolo*
50 *dimampolo*
100 *zato*
101 *iraika amby zato*
200 *roanjato*
500 *dimanjato*
1,000 *arivo*
10,000 *iray alina*
100,000 *iray hetsy*
1,000,000 *iray tapitrisa*

FURTHER READING

English-language literature about Madagascar is rather thin on the ground. A small excellent selection of field guides covers the island's mammals, birds and to a lesser extent other wildlife, and a couple of decent histories and other general books are in print, but – incredibly – not a single Malagasy novel, written in French or Malagasy, has ever been translated into English, and there is a similar paucity of English-language books about more specialised aspects of its history and culture. The best of what actually is in print is detailed below.

TRAVELOGUE

Muddling Through in Madagascar (Dervla Murphy). Classic account of an independent journey made by the Irish writer and her 14-year-old daughter in the early 1980s.
Madagascar: The Eighth Continent: Life, Death and Discovery in a Lost World (Peter Tyson). A well-written and readable overview of Madagascar's quirky wildlife, what makes it so special, and the pressures it faces in the modern world.

HISTORY

Madagascar: A Short History (Solofo Randrianja & Stephen Ellis). The pick of a handful of one-volume English-language histories of Madagascar packs a lot of readable information and details footnotes into its 300 pages, but stops short at 2002.
A History of Madagascar (Mervyn Brown). Very solid on the island's early history, this authoritative short history make a good counterpoint to Randrianja & Ellis, but is similarly out of date when it comes to recent events.

FIELD GUIDES

Birds of the Indian Ocean Islands (Ian Sinclair & Olivier Langrand). Long-regarded to be the definitive bird field guide to Madagascar and nearby islands, this is now in its fourth edition and has excellent up-to-date plates and distribution maps.
Birds of Madagascar and the Indian Ocean Islands (Roger Safford, Adrian Skerrett & Frank Hawkins). The newest field guide to the unique avifauna of Madagascar and other nearby islands has more detailed text than its more established rival, but otherwise they follow a similar formula and this one is twice the price.

⊘ Send Us Your Thoughts

We do our best to ensure the information in our books is as accurate and up-to-date as possible. The books are updated on a regular basis using local contacts, who painstakingly add, amend and correct as required. However, some details (such as telephone numbers and opening times) are liable to change, and we are ultimately reliant on our readers to put us in the picture.

We welcome your feedback, especially your experience of using the book "on the road". Maybe you came across a great bar or new attraction we missed.

We will acknowledge all contributions, and we'll offer an Insight Guide to the best letters received.

Please write to us at:
Insight Guides
PO Box 7910
London SE1 1WE

Or email us at:
hello@insightguides.com

Lemurs of Madagascar (Russell Mittermeier, W.R. Konstant, Frank Hawkins & Edward Louis). This definitive and copiously detailed guide to the 101 lemur species of Madagascar doubles as a field guide and overview of lemur behaviour, conservation and evolution. The revised and expanded 3rd edition represents a major leap forward from its predecessors.
Wildlife of Madagascar (Ken Behrens & Keith Barnes). Perfect for dedicated wildlife enthusiasts who don't want to carry a small library of specialised field guides, this vibrantly laid-out and beautifully illustrated handbook covers all the birds and mammals you are likely to see along with some of the more common reptiles, frogs and insects.
Turtles and Tortoises of Madagascar and Adjacent Indian Ocean Islands (Thomas E. Leuteritz, Justin Gerlach, Russell A. Mittermeier & Stephen D. Nash). Excellent and budget-friendly pocket identification guide to the endangered turtles of Madagascar and other islands.
Mammals of Madagascar: A Complete Guide Paperback (Nick Garbutt). This well-organised and very detailed guide by one of the most prominent photographers and naturalists working in Madagascar suffers only from being a little dated when it comes to recently described lemur species.

OTHERS

Thank You, Madagascar: The Conservation Diaries of Alison Jolly (Alison Jolly). Compassionate, down-to-earth and wryly humorous, the posthumous memoir of the prominent and much loved lemur researcher Alison Jolly provides an unexpectedly good introduction to the contradictions of modern Madagascar.
The Aye-Aye and I (Gerald Durrell). The popular conservationist Gerald Durrell's quest to find an aye-aye in the wild is relayed with his customary good-natured humour and did much to create greater awareness of this strangest of all primates.
Voices from Madagascar (compiled by Jacques Bourgeacq & Liliane Ramarosoa). Subtitled 'An Anthology of Contemporary Francophone Literature' this collection of short stories and poems, all translated into English, gives plenty of insight into Malagasy customs and traditions.

CREDITS

PHOTO CREDITS

Alamy 1, 8T, 11B, 12/13, 14/15, 16/17, 20, 29B, 39, 45, 55, 58, 70, 85, 87, 96BR, 99, 101, 110BL, 183, 196, 204, 205, 238, 273
Anjajavy Le Lodge/Amanda Dawes 239
AWL Images 112/113
Christina Randrianarimanana 237
Constance Hotels & Resorts 252B
Dan Mirica/Picfair 164
Francesco Veronesi 272T
Getty Images 28, 29T, 30, 35, 36, 38, 41, 42R, 42L, 43, 44, 46, 47, 48, 49, 50, 51, 52, 53, 54, 56, 57, 59, 75, 84, 88L, 92, 118, 200, 212B, 214, 235B, 240/241T, 269
Granger/REX/Shutterstock 33
iStock 10T, 11TR, 11MR, 18, 23, 66, 72, 76, 80, 88R, 91, 107, 110BR, 119B, 137, 169B, 169T, 170B, 170T, 172, 173, 181T, 182, 206, 207, 240BR, 250, 253, 265T, 270, 271, 272B, 276B, 276T, 278/279, 284, 290
Mint Images/REX/Shutterstock 86
Public domain 26/27, 31, 32, 34, 37, 40
Robert Harding 111BL, 216
Shutterstock 6MR, 7TR, 7ML, 7BR, 19T, 74, 79, 111BR, 111TR, 131, 142, 156, 165, 171, 180/181B, 185B, 185T, 201T, 211, 212T, 215, 217, 218, 219, 220, 228, 236, 252T, 263, 277, 278
SuperStock 4, 9B, 89, 98, 100, 110/111T, 114/115, 116/117, 221
Ariadne Van Zandbergen 6ML, 6BL, 6MR, 7ML, 7MR, 7TL, 8B, 9T, 10B, 19B, 21, 22, 24R, 24L, 25, 60/61, 62, 63, 64R, 64L, 65, 67, 68, 69, 71, 73, 77, 78, 81, 82, 83, 90, 93, 94R, 94L, 95, 96/97T, 96BL, 97BR, 97BL, 97TR, 102, 103, 104, 105, 106, 108, 109, 119T, 124, 125, 126, 127B, 127T, 128T, 128B, 129, 130, 132, 133B, 133T, 134, 138, 139, 140B, 140T, 141, 143, 144, 145, 147B, 147T, 148, 149, 150, 151B, 151T, 152, 153, 154B, 154T, 155, 157T, 157B, 158, 159T, 159B, 160/161, 162T, 162B, 163, 167, 168, 174/175T, 174BR, 174BL, 175ML, 175BR, 175BL, 175TR, 176, 177, 179, 184, 186, 187, 189, 190, 191, 192B, 192T, 193, 194B, 194T, 195, 197, 199, 201B, 202, 203, 208, 210, 213, 222, 223, 225, 226, 227, 229, 230, 231B, 231T, 232B, 232T, 233, 234, 235T, 241ML, 241TR, 240BL, 241BR, 241BL, 242, 243, 245, 246/247, 248, 249, 251, 254, 255, 257B, 257T, 258B, 258T, 259, 260, 261, 262, 264, 265B, 266, 267, 268

COVER CREDITS

Front cover: Lemur *Shutterstock*
Back cover: Baobab trees at sunset *Ariadne Van Zandbergen*
Front flap: (from top) Frog, Boophis sp *Ariadne Van Zandbergen*; Beach on Nosy Be *Ariadne Van Zandbergen*; Boy on ox cart, Toliara *Ariadne Van Zandbergen*; Pirate ship mural *Ariadne Van Zandbergen*
Back flap: Verreaux's sifaka *Ariadne Van Zandbergen*

INSIGHT GUIDE CREDITS

Distribution
UK, Ireland and Europe
Apa Publications (UK) Ltd;
sales@insightguides.com
United States and Canada
Ingram Publisher Services;
ips@ingramcontent.com
Australia and New Zealand
Woodslane; info@woodslane.com.au
Southeast Asia
Apa Publications (SN) Pte;
singaporeoffice@insightguides.com
Worldwide
Apa Publications (UK) Ltd;
sales@insightguides.com
Special Sales, Content Licensing and CoPublishing
Insight Guides can be purchased in bulk quantities at discounted prices. We can create special editions, personalised jackets and corporate imprints tailored to your needs.
sales@insightguides.com
www.insightguides.biz

Printed in China by CTPS

All Rights Reserved
© 2018 Apa Digital (CH) AG and Apa Publications (UK) Ltd

First Edition 2018

No part of this book may be reproduced, stored in a retrieval system or transmitted in any form or means electronic, mechanical, photocopying, recording or otherwise, without prior written permission from Apa Publications.

Every effort has been made to provide accurate information in this publication, but changes are inevitable. The publisher cannot be responsible for any resulting loss, inconvenience or injury. We would appreciate it if readers would call our attention to any errors or outdated information. We also welcome your suggestions; please contact us at:
hello@insightguides.com

www.insightguides.com

Managing Editor: Carine Tracanelli
Author: Philip Briggs
Head of Production: Rebeka Davies
Picture Editor: Tom Smyth
Cartography: Carte

CONTRIBUTORS

This *Insight Guide to Madagascar* was commissioned by French-born Managing Editor **Carine Tracanelli** and written by **Philip Briggs**.

Briggs has been exploring the highways, byways and backwaters of Africa since 1986, when he spent several months backpacking on a shoestring from Nairobi to Cape Town. During the course of the 1990s, he wrote a series of pioneering guidebooks to destinations that were then practically uncharted by the travel publishing industry, among them Tanzania, Uganda, Ethiopia,

Malawi, Mozambique, Ghana and Rwanda. He first visited Madagascar in 2007 and returned in 2017 to do the ground research for this Insight Guide. He has contributed to or updated several other Insight Guides covering African destinations such as Kenya, Tanzania, The Gambia & Senegal, South Africa and Namibia.

Many of the images in this book were taken by **Ariadne Van Zandbergen**, a specialist in African wildlife and travel photography.

This book was proofread and indexed by **Penny Phenix**.

ABOUT INSIGHT GUIDES

Insight Guides have more than 45 years' experience of publishing high-quality, visual travel guides. We produce 400 full-colour titles, in both print and digital form, covering more than 200 destinations across the globe, in a variety of formats to meet your different needs.

Insight Guides are written by local authors, whose expertise is evident in the extensive historical and cultural

background features. Each destination is carefully researched by regional experts to ensure our guides provide the very latest information. All the reviews in **Insight Guides** are independent; we strive to maintain an impartial view. Our reviews are carefully selected to guide you to the best places to eat, go out and shop, so you can be confident that when we say a place is special, we really mean it.

Legend

City maps

	Freeway/Highway/Motorway
	Divided Highway
	Main Roads
	Minor Roads
	Pedestrian Roads
	Steps
	Footpath
	Railway
	Funicular Railway
	Cable Car
	Tunnel
	City Wall
	Important Building
	Built Up Area
	Other Land
	Transport Hub
	Park
	Pedestrian Area
	Bus Station
	Tourist Information
	Main Post Office
	Cathedral/Church
	Mosque
	Synagogue
	Statue/Monument
	Beach
	Airport

Regional maps

	Freeway/Highway/Motorway (with junction)
	Freeway/Highway/Motorway (under construction)
	Divided Highway
	Main Road
	Secondary Road
	Minor Road
	Track
	Footpath
	International Boundary
	State/Province Boundary
	National Park/Reserve
	Marine Park
	Ferry Route
	Marshland/Swamp
	Glacier Salt Lake
	Airport/Airfield
	Ancient Site
	Border Control
	Cable Car
	Castle/Castle Ruins
	Cave
	Chateau/Stately Home
	Church/Church Ruins
	Crater
	Lighthouse
	Mountain Peak
	Place of Interest
	Viewpoint

INDEX

MAIN REFERENCES ARE IN BOLD TYPE

INSIGHT ◉ GUIDES

OFF THE SHELF

Since 1970, INSIGHT GUIDES has provided a unique perspective on the world's best travel destinations by using specially commissioned photography and illuminating text written by local authors.

Whether you're planning a city break, a walking tour or the journey of a lifetime, our superb range of guidebooks and phrasebooks will inspire you to discover more about your chosen destination.

INSIGHT GUIDES

offer a unique combination of stunning photos, absorbing narrative and detailed maps, providing all the inspiration and information you need.

PHRASEBOOKS & DICTIONARIES

help users to feel at home, when away. Pocket-sized with a free app to download, they go where you do.

CITY GUIDES

pack hundreds of great photos into a smaller format with detailed practical information, so you can navigate the world's top cities with confidence.

EXPLORE GUIDES

feature easy-to-follow walks and itineraries in the world's most exciting destinations, with our choice of the best places to eat and drink along the way.

POCKET GUIDES

combine concise information on where to go and what to do in a handy compact format, ideal on the ground. Includes a full-colour, fold-out map.

EXPERIENCE GUIDES

feature offbeat perspectives and secret gems for experienced travellers, with a collection of over 100 ideas for a memorable stay in a city.

www.insightguides.com

⊙ Walking Eye App

YOUR FREE DESTINATION CONTENT AND EBOOK AVAILABLE THROUGH THE WALKING EYE APP

Your guide now includes a free eBook and destination content for your chosen destination, all for the same great price as before. Simply download the Walking Eye App from the App Store or Google Play to access your free eBook and destination content.

HOW THE WALKING EYE APP WORKS

Through the Walking Eye App, you can purchase a range of eBooks and destination content. However, when you buy this book, you can download the corresponding eBook and destination content for free. Just see below in the grey panels where to find your free content and then scan the QR code at the bottom of this page.

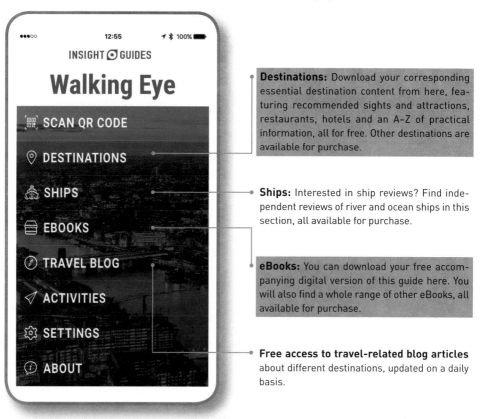

Destinations: Download your corresponding essential destination content from here, featuring recommended sights and attractions, restaurants, hotels and an A–Z of practical information, all for free. Other destinations are available for purchase.

Ships: Interested in ship reviews? Find independent reviews of river and ocean ships in this section, all available for purchase.

eBooks: You can download your free accompanying digital version of this guide here. You will also find a whole range of other eBooks, all available for purchase.

Free access to travel-related blog articles about different destinations, updated on a daily basis.

INSIGHT ⊙ GUIDES

MADAGASCAR

740007360928

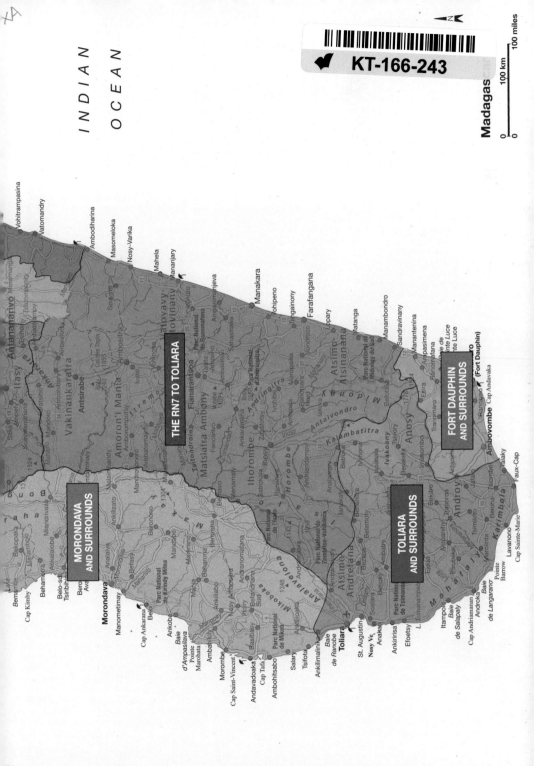

INDIAN

OCEAN

KT-166-243

Madagas

N

0   100 km
0   100 miles

MORONDAVA
AND SURROUNDS

THE RN7 TO TOLIARA

TOLIARA
AND SURROUNDS

FORT DAUPHIN
AND SURROUNDS

M o z a m